ROBERT SPAEMANN'S PHILOSOPHY OF THE HUMAN PERSON

OXFORD THEOLOGICAL MONOGRAPHS

Robert Spaemann's Philosophy of the Human Person

*Nature, Freedom, and
the Critique of Modernity*

HOLGER ZABOROWSKI

OXFORD
UNIVERSITY PRESS

OXFORD
UNIVERSITY PRESS

Great Clarendon Street, Oxford OX2 6DP

Oxford University Press is a department of the University of Oxford.
It furthers the University's objective of excellence in research, scholarship,
and education by publishing worldwide in

Oxford New York

Auckland Cape Town Dar es Salaam Hong Kong Karachi
Kuala Lumpur Madrid Melbourne Mexico City Nairobi
New Delhi Shanghai Taipei Toronto

With offices in

Argentina Austria Brazil Chile Czech Republic France Greece
Guatemala Hungary Italy Japan Poland Portugal Singapore
South Korea Switzerland Thailand Turkey Ukraine Vietnam

Oxford is a registered trade mark of Oxford University Press
in the UK and in certain other countries

Published in the United States
by Oxford University Press Inc., New York

© Holger Zaborowski 2010

British Library Cataloguing in Publication Data
Data available

Library of Congress Cataloging in Publication Data
Data available

Typeset by SPI Publisher Services, Pondicherry, India
Printed in Great Britain
on acid-free paper by
MPG Books Group, Bodmin and King's Lynn

ISBN 978–0–19–957677–7

1 3 5 7 9 10 8 6 4 2

Acknowledgements

This book is a slightly revised version of a doctoral thesis submitted to Oxford University in 2001. There are always many gifts involved in the writing of a thesis and in revising it for publication, gifts by different people who help in exploring ideas, in thinking, and in formulating one's own ideas. Among those many people, some deserve special mention: Oliver O'Donovan, who in such a memorable and important way taught me not only the art of thinking but also what it means to be a *Doktorvater*, infinitely more than a mere supervisor; John Webster and Jean-Yves Lacoste, whose valuable advice and comments on the manuscript helped me very much; John Milbank, David Ford, Douglas Hedley, and Brian Hebblethwaite, who helped greatly in the initial phase of conceiving the subject of my research; and others who were there when I needed them, with help, advice, and their company—Kathryn Bevis, Jennifer Cooper, Alfred Denker, Stephan van Erp, Bernard Green OSB, Kelly Grovier, Christina Kotte, Sandra Lipner, Joan Lockwood O'Donovan, Stephan Loos, Michael Noonan, Christoph Stumpf, Ingrid Wegerhoff, my parents, and my brother Maik. I am deeply indebted to Lesley Rice and Jane Wheare for careful readings of the text and many important remarks and corrections. I would like to dedicate this book in gratitude to my parents.

Contents

Abbreviations

Basic Moral Concepts	*Basic Moral Concepts*, trans. T. J. Armstrong (London: Routledge, 1989).
Das unsterbliche Gerücht	*Das unsterbliche Gerücht: Die Frage nach Gott und die Täuschung der Moderne* (Stuttgart: Klett-Cotta, 2007).
Die Frage 'Wozu?'	*Die Frage 'Wozu?': Geschichte und Wiederentdeckung des teleologischen Denkens*, 3rd edn. (München/Zürich: Piper, 1991) (with Reinhard Löw).
Einsprüche: Christliche Reden	*Einsprüche: Christliche Reden* (Einsiedeln: Johannes, 1977).
Essays zur Anthropologie	*Das Natürliche und das Vernünftige: Essays zur Anthropologie* (München/Zürich: Piper, 1987).
Glück und Wohlwollen	*Glück und Wohlwollen: Versuch über Ethik* (Stuttgart: Klett-Cotta, 1989).
Grenzen	*Grenzen: Zur ethischen Dimension des Handelns* (Stuttgart: Klett-Cotta, 2001).
Happiness and Benevolence	*Happiness and Benevolence*, trans. Jeremiah Alberg (Notre Dame: Notre Dame University Press, 2000).
Kritik der politischen Philosophie	*Zur Kritik der politischen Utopie: Zehn Kapitel politischer Utopie* (Stuttgart: Klett, 1977).
Moralische Grundbegriffe	*Moralische Grundbegriffe*, 5th edn. (München: Beck, 1994).
Paradigm Lost	'Laudatio: Niklas Luhmanns Herausforderung der Philosophie', in *Paradigm Lost: Über die ethische Reflexion der Moral*, 3rd edn. (Frankfurt am Main: Suhrkamp, 1996).
Personen	*Personen: Versuche über den Unterschied zwischen 'etwas' und 'jemand'* (Stuttgart: Klett-Cotta, 1996).

Persons   *Persons: The Difference between 'Someone'*
                                       and 'Something', trans. Oliver O'Donovan
                                       (Oxford: Oxford University Press, 2006).

Philosophische Essays   *Philosophische Essays: Erweiterte Ausgabe*
                                       (Stuttgart: Reclam, 1994).

Reflexion und Spontaneität   *Reflexion und Spontaneität: Studien über*
                                       Fénelon, 2nd edn. (Stuttgart: Klett-Cotta,
                                       1990).

Rousseau—Bürger ohne Vaterland   *Rousseau—Bürger ohne Vaterland: Von*
                                       der Polis zur Natur, new edn. (München/
                                       Zürich: Piper, 1992).

Der Ursprung der   *Der Ursprung der Soziologie aus dem Geist*
Soziologie aus dem   *der Restauration: Studien über L. G. A. de*
Geist der Restauration   *Bonald* (Stuttgart: Klett-Cotta, 1998).

1

Philosophy in a time of crisis

Uncertain himself about what has gone wrong, he feels in his bones that the
happy exurb stands both in danger of catastrophe and somehow in need of it.

Walker Percy

1.1 THE CRISIS OF MODERNITY

It is almost a truism to speak of the 'end of the modern world',[1] of the crisis of
modernity, or, in a less extreme way, of the critical condition of modern
rationality. Modern consciousness, as the German philosopher Robert Spaemann has often argued, 'nears its end'.[2] Because of this, he further reasons, we
can now describe it and attempt to understand and criticize it. We may also
endeavour to go beyond modernity, as have many so-called post-modern
philosophers, whose attitude toward modernity, almost by definition, is
critical and censorious. Those philosophers, most of whom are inspired by
Friedrich Nietzsche and Martin Heidegger, argue that modernity has failed
irretrievably and needs to be surpassed philosophically.[3] It is therefore time,
they think, to announce, more or less triumphantly, the end of modernity and
to enter into a new, 'post-modern' age.

While some interpret the current crisis as symptomatic of modernity as
such, others argue that it is simply a failure of modernity to realize itself.

---

[1] See Romano Guardini, *The End of the Modern World: A Search for Orientation* (Wilmington, Del.: ISI, 1998).

[2] 'Die christliche Religion und das Ende des modernen Bewußtseins: Über einige Schwierigkeiten des Christentums mit dem sogenannten modernen Menschen', *Communio*, 8 (1979), 253. (All translations of Spaemann's work in this book are my own, unless otherwise indicated.) See in this context also Peter Koslowski, *Die Prüfungen der Neuzeit: Über Postmodernität, Philosophie der Geschichte, Metaphysik, Gnosis* (Vienna: Passagen, 1989).

[3] For Nietzsche and Heidegger as 'entries into post-modernity' see Jürgen Habermas, *The Philosophical Discourse of Modernity*, trans. Frederick Lawrence (Cambridge, Mass.: MIT Press, 1987), 83–105, 131–60. Heidegger's lectures on Nietzsche play an important role for the transition towards post-modernity; see Martin Heidegger, *Nietzsche*, trans. with notes and analysis David Farrell Krell, 4 vols. (San Francisco, Calif.: Harper & Row, 1979–87).

Jürgen Habermas, for instance, who would doubtless not go so far as to associate the crisis with key presuppositions of Enlightenment rationality, characterizes modernity as a yet 'unfinished project'[4] that is in need of further attention.

Whether modernity is considered a failed or an unfinished project, it is plausible to argue that the catastrophic course of the twentieth century has demonstrated the long-disguised implications and ambiguities of many key ideas that constitute modernity, and that human beings are thus, as Romano Guardini argued, in need of a new 'search for orientation'. The current crisis of modernity also discloses, Spaemann states, that 'modernity, as a "scientific *Weltanschauung*" . . . does not have arguments; it is based on *petitiones principii*'[5] and thus relies on often well-hidden assumptions that are not sufficiently explicated and proven. It is particularly these hidden assumptions that have become questionable and problematic and may explain why modernity gives the impression of being subject to a dialectic that progressively undermines it. In the course of this crisis of modernity it has become obvious to some that the modern mind can only shape culture in a human manner as long as it is not merely modern. 'It cannot be the case that the only essential thing about modernity', Spaemann points out, 'is its being modern'.[6]

In this perceived situation of crisis accounts of the legitimacy, genesis, and development of modernity have been produced,[7] as well as numerous critical appreciations of the fundamental principles of modern reason. These latter raise the issue of why modernity has developed signs of a crisis, and what accounts for the dialectical structure of modernity, which C. S. Lewis has pointedly called the 'tragic-comedy of our situation', in which 'we continue to clamour for those very qualities we are rendering impossible'.[8]

One explanation for the crisis of modernity is that the abstract universality of modern reason is inclined to dismiss nature itself and the particular social and historical context within which reason needs to be positioned (because it

---

[4] *Die Moderne—ein unvollendetes Projekt: Philosophisch-politische Aufsätze* (Leipzig: Reclam, 1994).

[5] 'Einleitung', in *Philosophische Essays*, 8.

[6] 'Ende der Modernität?', in *Philosophische Essays*, 233.

[7] See e.g. Hans Blumenberg, *The Legitimacy of the Modern Age* (Cambridge, Mass.: MIT Press, 1983); Louis Dupré, *Passage to Modernity: An Essay in the Hermeneutics of Nature and Culture* (New Haven, Conn./London: Yale University Press, 1993); Karl Löwith, *Meaning in History: The Theological Implications of the Philosophy of History* (Chicago, Ill.: University of Chicago Press, 1957); Joachim Ritter, *Subjektivität: Sechs Aufsätze* (Frankfurt am Main: Suhrkamp, 1974); David Walsh, *The Modern Philosophical Revolution: The Luminosity of Existence* (Cambridge: Cambridge University Press, 2008).

[8] *The Abolition of Man, or Reflections on Education with Special Reference to the Teaching of English in the Upper Forms of Schools* (Glasgow: Collins, 1982), 19–20.

is *always already* positioned in this very context). The enterprise to set aside not only nature but also history and society, however, cannot but fail, for it tends to turn against itself and its own presuppositions. What does this mean? We may try an initial and rather sketchy answer at this point in our argument. Emancipation, for example, only makes sense as long as freedom is not made an absolute and strictly opposed to nature. Otherwise, freedom turns into arbitrariness and, finally, becomes mere nature and is thus annihilated. The language of rights, therefore, can, in the end, only be spoken as long as the vocabulary of the common good, characteristic of the classical political tradition, maintains some purchase.[9] Otherwise, liberalism may become a totalitarian ideology that is closed to every other view of reality, making real freedom impossible. 'Empty subjective freedom', Spaemann argues with regard to the French Revolution, thus implicitly referring to Hegel's *Phenomenology of Spirit*, 'could not but spawn terror'.[10] The idea of universal and inalienable human rights, furthermore, only makes sense as long as *every* human being—and not only some groups of human beings—is the subject of those rights, simply by being a member of the natural human species.[11] To put it more precisely, every human being needs to be understood not to *have* rights that can be attributed or not, but essentially to *be* a demand for recognition and to disclose a specific dignity, the inalienable dignity of the human person.[12]

A second cause of the crisis of modernity is that very often the natural and social sciences tend not to see the limits of their methods; that is to say, they assert that reality is *fully* explainable in scientific terms. Modern natural sciences and their technological application have undoubtedly improved the conditions of human life and helped us to understand reality to a previously

---

[9] For a critique of the language and concept of rights from a Christian point of view see Joan Lockwood O'Donovan, 'The Concept of Right in Christian Moral Discourse', in Michael Cromartie (ed.), *A Preserving Grace: Protestants, Catholics, and Natural Law* (Washington, DC: Ethics and Public Policy Center, 1997), 143–56; for a response to, and comments upon, O'Donovan's essay see pp. 57–171 of Cromartie's book.

[10] '"Politik zuerst"? Das Schicksal der Action Française', in *Wort und Wahrheit*, 8 (1953), 657. For Hegel's view of the French Revolution see G. W. F. Hegel, *Phenomenology of Spirit*, trans. A. V. Miller (Oxford: Oxford University Press, 1979), 582–95.

[11] R. M. Hare is thus wrong to say that having certain rights is a qualification for somebody's being called a person ('A Kantian Approach to Abortion', in his *Essays on Bioethics* (Oxford: Clarendon, 1993), 169; he argues in a similar vein in 'Abortion and the Golden Rule', in *Essays on Bioethics*, 151 ff.). Having certain rights is not a necessary *condition*, but a necessary *consequence* of being a person. To focus upon the having, or not-having, of certain criteria inevitably leads to a naturalist fallacy and undermines the meaning of 'person'. For Spaemann's brief critique of utilitarian ethics see also '"Fanatisch" und "Fanatismus"' in *Archiv für Begriffsgeschichte*, xv (Bonn: Bouvier/Grundmann, 1971), 274.

[12] See for the limits of freedom also Holger Zaborowski, 'Der Mensch—ein "Eigentum der Freiheit"? Zu den Herausforderungen der Freiheit', in *Spielräume der Freiheit: Zur Hermeneutik des Menschseins* (Freiburg im Breisgau/Munich: Alber, 2009), 59–97, esp. 67 ff.

unimaginable degree; so any unqualified criticism of the natural sciences and modern technology cannot but miss the point. This needs to be said against some radical critics of modern technology who speak of its failure or its demonic character where more moderate language would be much more appropriate, language as moderate (and realistic) as Heidegger's '"yes" and at the same time "no"' toward modern technology.[13]

Yet the natural sciences are based on a methodological reductionism that was initially acknowledged but is now increasingly disregarded. What originated in a deliberate *methodological* restriction came to be constructed as an epistemological and ontological statement about reality as such, so that scientific hypothesis has become the paradigm for any reality-related predication. A scientific culture of this kind is incapable of understanding not only moral and ontological absolutes or the meaning of human life, but also its own purpose, its nature, the scientist's desire for knowledge, and his personal subjective involvement in his research.[14] Moreover, science so conceived contradicts itself in not seeing the limits of a paradigm of what is, after all, only hypothetical knowledge.

Modern sciences also have a functionalistic outlook; that is, they tend to understand reality in terms of functional relations. Let us consider this a bit further. Until the rise of the modern sciences and epistemologies, the sciences and epistemology were regarded as being inseparable from ethics and ontology. The search for scientific knowledge and its understanding was thus embedded in the wider context of the search for goodness and truth. This changed notably in modernity. According to an important, perhaps the predominant, epistemological framework of the modern sciences, all reality, including goodness and truth, is understood with respect to the functional conditions of its genesis and existence. The questions pertaining to how something came about and how it functions have replaced the older, and more fundamental, question of what something essentially, or by its very nature, is and how it is related to the human pursuit of goodness and truth.

We raise no criticism against a methodological functionalism as this is a means to understanding certain dimensions of reality. There is, however,

---

[13] Martin Heidegger, *Discourse on Thinking*, Eng. trans. of *Gelassenheit*, with an introd. John M. Anderson (New York: Harper, 1969), 54. For Heidegger's interpretation of modern technology see also his 'The Question Concerning Technology', in *Basic Writings from* Being and Time *(1927)* to The Task of Thinking *(1964)*, rev. and expanded edn., ed. David Farrell Krell (San Francisco, Calif.: HarperCollins, 1993), 307–41.

[14] See in this context also Edmund Husserl's critique of the modern sciences and their claims in, for example, his *The Crisis of European Sciences and Transcendental Phenomenology: An Introduction to Phenomenological Philosophy*, trans. with an introd. David Carr (Evanston, Ill.: Northwestern University Press, 1970).

much to be said against functionalism made an absolute; for functionalism turns into a 'new dogmatism' if we do not think about those basic truths which cannot be defined from a functionalistic point of view, but in fact serve to justify functions themselves.[15] Given these tendencies of the modern sciences and the desire for objectifiable knowledge, human nature is vulnerable to being set equal to non-human objects. This conflation has huge implications. Just one may be briefly mentioned here. The intentional structure of human action and thus the difference between actions and merely natural events (such as a thunderstorm) can no longer adequately be understood.[16] Ethics is consequently clothed in quasi-scientific dress—depending on the latest fashion, it may be utilitarianism, futurology, behaviourism, other kinds of psychology, sociobiology, or evolutionary ethics.

Hence, a third element in the crisis of modernity is that reality is ultimately reduced to process. Thomas Hobbes paradigmatically maintained that 'by Philosophy, is understood the *Knowledge acquired by Reasoning, from the Manner of the Generation of any thing, to the Properties; or from the Properties, to some possible Way of Generation of the same; to the end to be able to produce, as far as matter, and humane force permit, such Effects, as humane life requireth*.'[17] Hobbes defines philosophy as genealogy; that is to say, as genetic analysis of reality. This implies that the whole is entirely explainable in terms of its parts and their coming-into-existence. Being, strictly speaking, has been made a by-product of the universal process of becoming. Hobbes, furthermore, transforms philosophy into a practical science, the results of which are supposed to be applicable 'as humane life requireth'.

Therefore, a fourth explanation of the crisis of modernity is that philosophy is treated as a practical, applied science and thus tends to be valued from an instrumentalist viewpoint. The French *philosophes*, as Spaemann points out, already defined themselves with reference to their social function within the Enlightenment context.[18] Their nature was their function; that is to say, to enlighten society. A merely theoretical contemplation of reality no longer played the fundamental role that ancient and medieval philosophers would have attributed to it.

Furthermore, not only philosophy but even God and religion have been interpreted as *merely* serving a certain function for the individual or for society—a functionalism affirmed by the French counter-revolution, for

---

[15] Robert Spaemann, 'Was ist das Neue? Vom Ende des modernen Bewußtseins', in *Die politische Meinung*, 203 (July/Aug. 1982), 25.

[16] For this problematic feature of modern thought see Spaemann, 'Einzelhandlungen', in *Grenzen*, 49 ff.

[17] *Leviathan*, ed. Richard Tuck (Cambridge: Cambridge University Press, 1999), 458.

[18] 'Laudatio: Niklas Luhmanns Herausforderung der Philosophie', in *Paradigm Lost*, 72.

instance, while being dismissed as an idle projection by nineteenth-century Marxist, Feuerbachian, and Freudian, as well as contemporary sociobiological criticisms of religion. Religion is then *entirely* understood with respect to its function and not with respect to its truth claim or its own self-understanding, which—in most, if not cases of traditional religion—does not support a merely functionalist view of religion as outlined by Richard Dawkins, for instance. Dawkins speaks of the 'god meme', which exists because of its 'great psychological appeal', for 'it proves a superficially plausible answer to deep and troubling questions about existence'.[19] However, if religion has been entirely dismissed (which is not a necessary implication of a functionalist view of religion), a 'functional equivalent' is required. Political parties or different philosophies have eagerly, and, indeed, often disastrously, taken over the role of religion.[20] What religion essentially is, namely the glorification and love of God for God's sake alone (an answer that is not only found in Christianity but common to many world religions), has been lost sight of within the functionalistic paradigm for modern reason.

While many modern thinkers still relied heavily upon their pre-modern legacy—and, more often than not, on transformations or secularizations of Christian doctrine, such as the doctrines of original sin,[21] the hypostatic union of divinity and humanity in Christ, or the coming of the kingdom of God—late modern philosophy has attempted to radicalize the thrust of modern thought against its pre-modern predecessors. Friedrich Nietzsche, as Spaemann

[19] *The Selfish Gene* (Oxford: Oxford University Press, 1989), 193. For Dawkins's view of religion see also his *The God Delusion* (Boston, Mass.: Houghton Mifflin, 2006). For a critique of Dawkins's 'theology' from a point of view close to Spaemann's see also Reinhard Löw, *Die neuen Gottesbeweise* (Augsburg: Pattloch, 1994), 120–34; Holger Zaborowski, 'Göttliche und menschliche Freiheit: Zur Möglichkeit einer Kriteriologie von Religion', in *Spielräume der Freiheit*, 99–130, esp. 123ff. For a critique of Dawkin's position see also Alister E. McGrath and Joanne Collicutt McGrath, *The Dawkins Delusion? Atheist Fundamentalism and the Denial of the Divine* (Downers Grove, Ill.: IVP, 2007).

[20] For political ideologies as forms of 'anti-religion' see also the work of Hermann Lübbe, particularly his *Religion nach der Aufklärung*, 3rd edn. (Munich: Fink, 2004), 53ff. For an account of Lübbe's philosophy of religion see my 'Kontingenzbewältigung in der Moderne: Zu Hermann Lübbes Verständnis von Aufklärung und Religion', in Hanns-Gregor Nissing (ed.), *Zur Philosophie Hermann Lübbes* (Darmstadt: Wissenschaftliche Buchgesellschaft, 2009).

[21] For the modern transformation of the doctrine of original sin see Jeremiah Alberg, *Die verlorene Einheit: Die Suche nach einer philosophischen Alternative zur Erbsündenlehre von Rousseau bis Schelling* (Frankfurt am Main: Lang, 1996); Christoph Schulte, *Radikal böse: Die Karriere des Bösen von Kant bis Nietzsche*, 2nd edn. (Munich: Fink, 1991); Robert Spaemann, 'Über einige Schwierigkeiten mit der Erbsünde', in Christoph Schönborn, Albert Görres, and Robert Spaemann (eds.), *Zur kirchlichen Erbsündenlehre: Stellungnahmen zu einer brennenden Frage*, 2nd edn. (Freiburg im Breisgau: Johannes, 1994), 37–66; Holger Zaborowski, 'Fall and Freedom: A Comparison of Fichte's and Saint Paul's Understandings of Original Sin', in Daniel Breazeale and Tom Rockmore (eds.), *After Jena: New Essays on Fichte's Later Philosophy* (Evanston, Ill.: Northwestern University Press, 2008), 162–82.

rightly points out, was aware that modernity still presupposed the Platonic and Christian notion of truth that 'God is truth and truth is divine'.[22] Hence, to become fully modern meant to overthrow this awkward pre-modern inheritance. Enlightenment rationalism, one can argue, turned into the irrationalism of a metaphysics of will, whether the will is ultimately denied in a manner reminiscent of Schopenhauer's Western Buddhism or affirmed à la Nietzsche.[23] This irrationalism may be an important element of the crisis of modernity which has not yet been overcome; it is still apparent in important strands of the 'post-modern situation'[24]—which may, after all, better be called a late modern situation.[25]

Given the crisis of late modernity, there seems to be a need for philosophers, who are, as Robert Spaemann states, 'specialists in the management of intellectual crisis'.[26] In Spaemann's interpretation, philosophy is even a very important, if not, indeed, a necessary 'condition for the public continuity of notions such as "freedom" and "human dignity"'[27] in the modern epoch of science—a milieu which has huge implications for our understanding of these notions. This is why the end of philosophy, Spaemann further argues, would be the end of free humanity.[28] The crisis of modernity is therefore not only the crisis of philosophy, but also the time when philosophy is most required. Thus, there is a need for philosophy today, and today's philosophers need to think about their own times, that is about the crisis of our time; for otherwise, Spaemann frequently argues, 'every philosophy becomes naive and thus does not fulfil what it is supposed to do'.[29]

So-called post-modern philosophy (unless it is very widely conceived) is not the only response to the shortcomings of modern reason. There is also a multifaceted trend to reconnect to a pre-modern knowledge and to bring

---

[22] Nietzsche, *Zur Genealogie der Moral*, in his *Kritische Gesamtausgabe*, ed. Giorgio Colli and Mazzino Montinari, (Berlin: de Gruyter, 1968), vi. II. 419.

[23] For Spaemann's understanding of Schopenhauer's and Nietzsche's philosophies in the context of modern philosophy see Robert Spaemann and Reinhard Löw, *Die Frage 'Wozu?'*, 187ff.; for Spaemann's reading of Schopenhauer see also his *Reflexion und Spontaneität*, 295–307.

[24] For this notion and one of the pivotal texts of the post-modernity discussion see Jean-François Lyotard, *La Condition Postmoderne: Rapport sur le Savoir* (Paris: Editions de Minuit, 1983).

[25] In this book we will normally speak of 'late modern' rather than of 'post-modern'. We only speak of 'post-modern' if we refer to a period that is truly post-modern. For comprehensive accounts of 'post-modernity' and its history see Steven Connor (ed.), *The Cambridge Companion to Postmodernism* (Cambridge: Cambridge University Press, 2004); Hans Bertens, *The Idea of the Postmodern: A History* (London/New York: Routledge, 1995); David Harvey, *The Condition of Postmodernity: An Enquiry into the Origins of Cultural Change* (Oxford: Blackwell, 1990).

[26] 'Die Herausforderung des ärzlichen Berufsethos', in *Grenzen*, 337.

[27] 'Über den Mut zur Erziehung', in *Grenzen*, 499.

[28] 'Die kontroverse Natur der Philosophie', in *Philosophische Essays*, 128.

[29] 'Philosophie zwischen Metaphysik und Geschichte: Philosophische Strömungen im heutigen Deutschland', in *Neue Zeitschrift für Systematische Theologie*, 1 (1959), 306.

back into consciousness what has been lost sight of in modernity. The representatives of this tendency are often closely related to one another. While there are some substantial differences, primarily between religiously committed and non-committed thinkers, many differences are rather differences in emphasis. All these writers converge in that they do not share basic presuppositions of modern rationality and recollect an 'older', more primordial view of reality that, as they argue, has not yet been irretrievably lost, but needs to be rediscovered. They vary, however, with respect to their specific presuppositions and with respect to the remedy that they claim to provide. Three different counter-modern tendencies are significant for our purposes.

There is, most prominently, the rediscovery of Platonic, Aristotelian, and Thomist philosophies, and the re-appreciation of natural-law theories, virtue ethics, pre-modern political philosophy, and teleological philosophies of nature. One might think of philosophers as diverse as Jacques Maritain, Etienne Gilson, Peter Geach, G. E. M. Anscombe, Alasdair MacIntyre, and John Finnis, and also of Leo Strauss, Hans Jonas, Hannah Arendt, Charles Taylor, Joachim Ritter, and their respective schools. A second group differs from this first one especially in its method. While the philosophers of the first group prefer a strictly philosophical and very often highly technical style, the second group has a greater variety of styles—very often relatively accessible ones—at its disposal. Here one might think of G. K. Chesterton, Charles Péguy, Iris Murdoch, George Grant, C. S. Lewis and many others. A third group also differs in method, but in a more substantial way. Modernity has found its theological opponents, most of whom do not consider themselves 'post-modern' (in the philosophical sense of the term) and cannot appropriately be labelled as such. Their enterprise, too, is characterized by the recollection of ideas that modern reason tends to dismiss. The borders, again, are fluid. One might think of Karl Barth and subsequent post-liberal theologians such as Hans Frei, George Lindbeck, Oliver O'Donovan, John Webster, and Colin Gunton;[30] of Radical Orthodoxy[31] and its exponents, such as John Milbank, Catherine Pickstock, and Graham Ward; and of Hans Urs von Balthasar and the increasing interest that his theology arouses.[32]

---

[30] For an overview of post-liberal theologies see John Webster and George P. Schner, *Theology after Liberalism: A Reader* (Oxford: Blackwell, 2000).

[31] For an overview of the range of theological positions proposed by Radical Orthodoxy, see John Milbank, Catherine Pickstock, and Graham Ward (eds.), *Radical Orthodoxy: A New Theology* (London: Routledge, 1999); for a good introductory account of Radical Orthodoxy see James K. A. Smith, *Introducing Radical Orthodoxy: Mapping a Post-secular Theology* (Grand Rapids, Mich.: Baker, 2004).

[32] For good discussions of Balthasar's theology see Edward T. Oakes and David Moss (eds.), *The Cambridge Companion to Hans Urs von Balthasar* (Cambridge: Cambridge University Press, 2004); Magnus Striet and Jan-Heiner Tück (eds.), *Hans Urs von Balthasar—Vermächtnis und*

This brief *tour d'horizon* cannot but fail to provide an adequate account of the wide spectrum of responses to the spirit of modernity. Yet this quick sketch, as well as the equally sketchy account of the late modern situation, offers a background against which one can read this book. For this examination of Robert Spaemann's philosophy engages in both an explicit and, more often, an implicit conversation with many of the philosophers, writers, and theologians mentioned above, as well as with the dialectical spirit of modernity itself.

1.2 ROBERT SPAEMANN'S CHRISTIANLY INFORMED CRITICISM OF MODERNITY

Robert Spaemann is a critic of modernity who comments on modernity both from a philosophical and from a Christian point of view. He does so by way of what he calls 'recollection' (*Erinnerung*). (By this, he means a recollection of what modern reason is otherwise liable either to overlook and to forget or explicitly to dismiss.) In so doing, Spaemann belongs among the outstanding interpreters and critics of modernity and late modernity and their political, religious, and ethical implications in contemporary German philosophy. The philosophical impact and the genuine originality of his writing have increasingly been acknowledged not only in Germany but also among English-speaking philosophers. In 1982 G. E. M. Anscombe wrote of Robert Spaemann that his 'is a name to note: it is my impression that in the English philosophical world Robert Spaemann is too little known'.[33] The Catholic University of America in Washington, DC, has already publicly recognized Spaemann's philosophical significance. In 1995 the university awarded Robert Spaemann an honorary doctorate '[i]n recognition of this contribution to philosophy and theology, particularly for his studies of religion and culture'.[34] Robert Spaemann's work has not yet been translated extensively into English; only three books and a few articles have appeared in English to date.[35]

Anstoß für die Theologie (Freiburg im Breisgau im Breisgau: Herder, 2005); Walter Kasper (ed.), *Im Dialog—Die Logik der Liebe Gottes* (Mainz: Grünewald, 2006).

[33] Review of Gareth B. Matthews's *Philosophy and the Young Child*, in *Philosophy and Phenomenological Research*, 43/2 (Dec. 1982), 266; see also Gareth B. Matthews, *Philosophy and the Young Child* (Cambridge, Mass./London: Harvard University Press, 1980), 94–5. Matthews refers to Spaemann's view of philosophy as 'institutionalised naïveté' (see Spaemann's 'Philosophie als institutionalisierte Naivität', in *Philosophisches Jahrbuch*, 81 (1974), 139–42).

[34] Programme of the honorary-degree ceremony at The Catholic University of America.

[35] See, for example: *Persons; Happiness and Benevolence*; 'Christianity and Modern Philosophy', in Brian J. Shanley, OP (ed.), *One Hundred Years of Philosophy* (Studies in Philosophy and the History of Philosophy, xxxvi) (Washington, DC: The Catholic University of America Press,

Needless to say, Spaemann's thought is therefore still relatively unknown to English-speaking philosophers and theologians.

Among their German-speaking counterparts single features of Spaemann's philosophy have been discussed; particularly, his ethics and moral philosophy,[36] his reappraisal of a teleological view of nature,[37] and his philosophy of the person[38]. A full-scale analysis of the outlook and the implications of his thought is still awaited. This kind of overview is particularly important because it is impossible to understand one feature of Spaemann's thought thoroughly except in the context of the whole. To criticize Spaemann's philosophy of personhood without even mentioning his reappraisal of a teleological view of nature, for instance, can only fail[39]. In a similar way, an interpretation of Spaemann's critique of consequentialism with respect to, say, Josef Fuch's moral theology that fails to take into account the whole of his thought[40] cannot do full justice

2001), 169–80; *Basic Moral Concepts*, 'Is every Human Being a Person?', trans. Richard Schenk, *Thomist*, 3/60 (1996), 463–74; 'On the Concept of Life', *Zen Buddhism Today*, 7 (Sept. 1989), 77–83; 'Remarks on the Ontology of "Right" and "Left"', *Graduate Faculty Philosophy Journal*, 10 (1984), 89–97, repr. in Reiner Schürmann (ed.), *The Public Realm: Essays on Discursive Types in Political Philosophy* (New York: State University of New York Press, 1989), 146–53; 'Remarks on the Problem of Equality', in *Ethics*, 87 (1977), 363–9.

[36] See, for instance, Pleines, Jürgen-Eckardt, 'Das Dilemma der Ethik. Positionen und Probleme der Gegenwart', in *Philosophische Rundschau*, 38, 48–82 (see 52–56 for Pleines's discussion of Spaemann's philosophy); Schenk O.P., Richard, 'The Ethics of Robert Spaemann in the Context of Recent Philosophy', in Shanley O.P., Brian J, *One Hundred Years of Philosophy* (Washington, D.C.: The Catholic University of America Press, 2001) (=Studies in Philosophy and the History of Philosophy, vol. xxxvi), 156–168.

[37] See Zwierlein, Eduard, 'Das höchste Paradigma des Seienden. Anliegen und Probleme des Teleologiekonzeptes Robert Spaemanns', *Zeitschrift für philosophische Forschung* 41 (1987), 117–29; Isak, Rainer, *Evolution ohne Ziel? Ein interdisziplinärer Forschungsbeitrag* (Freiburg im Breisgau: Herder, 1992); Hsiao-chih Sun, Johannes, *Heiligt die gute Absicht ein schlechtes Mittel? Die Kontroverse über Teleologie und Deontologie in der Moralbegründung unter besonderer Berücksichtigung von Josef Fuchs und Robert Spaemann* (St. Ottilien: EOS-Verlag, 1994); Gonzalez, Ana Marta, *Naturaleza y dignidad. Un estudio desde Robert Spaemann* (Pamplona: Ediciones Universidad de Navarra, S.A., 1996).

[38] See Jantschek, Thorsten, 'Von Personen und Menschen. Bemerkungen zu Robert Spaemann', in *Deutsche Zeitschrift für Philosophie*, 46 (1998), 465–484; Langthaler, Rudolf, 'Über "Seelen" und "Gewissen". Robert Spaemanns Aktualisierung thomistischer Motive', *Deutsche Zeitschrift für Philosophie*, 46 (1998), 485–500; Larmore, Charles, 'Person und Anerkennung', *Deutsche Zeitschrift für Philosophie*, 46 (1998), 459–64; Schick, Friedrike, 'Philosophie des Geistes und Philosophy of Mind—Bewußtsein und Subjektivität im Spiegel neuerer Theorien', *Philosophische Rundschau*, 45 (1998), 239–60, particularly 255–60; Zaborowski, Holger, 'Personen, Menschen und die Natur jenseits des Naturalismus. Eine Antwort auf kritische Einwände gegen Robert Spaemanns Philosophie des Personseins', *Philosophisches Jahrbuch*, 109 (2002), 185–95.

[39] For this kind of misconception of Spaemann's understanding of personhood, see, for instance, Jantschek, Thorsten, 'Von Personen und Menschen. Bemerkungen zu Robert Spaemann'. For a critique of Jantschek's interpretation of Spaemann, see Zaborowski, Holger, 'Personen, Menschen und die Natur jenseits des Naturalismus. Eine Antwort auf kritische Einwände gegen Robert Spaemanns Philosophie des Personseins'.

[40] See Hsiao-chih Sun, *Heiligt die gute Absicht ein schlechtes Mittel?*, 6.

to his argument. It should be said, though, that the coherence and complexity of Spaemann's thought make it a difficult challenge to provide a comprehensive and systematic account. There is always the danger of losing sight either of the overall context or of the details and subtle nuances of his philosophy.

Spaemann's thought can be compared to a hologram in which the parts resemble the whole and one another: the components of Spaemann's philosophy elucidate one another. Unlike many other philosophers, Spaemann offers many entrées to the paths of his thinking. Accordingly, his writings can be characterized in very diverse ways. One can argue plausibly that the leitmotif of Spaemann's philosophy is his critique of modernity. This critique, however, is not merely oppositional and judgemental. Spaemann claims to defend the Enlightenment against its self-interpretation by 'filling out' (*ergänzen*) the contemporary consciousness.[41] He intends to liberate philosophy and the consciousness of our time from its fragmentary and one-sided character without attempting to develop a closed system of philosophy, in the modern sense of 'philosophical system',[42] because philosophy is itself essentially an act of freedom: it is 'thinking oneself' (*Selbstdenken*).[43] So his philosophy is a philosophy of freedom, too, a philosophy that takes seriously that thinking is only thinking proper if it is pursued freely—if, in other words, it is an act of freedom. One can equally well maintain that the leitmotif of his philosophy lies in the analysis of the human person, of his dignity, and of the paradigmatic character of personal action and responsibility; or, that it consists in the rediscovery of a teleological view of nature.

In Spaemann's view, philosophy is not poiesis but praxis. It is meaningful in itself—a human activity that finds its end in itself—and not with respect to its supposed historical or political goals. Over against the modern assimilation of praxis to poiesis that no longer maintains that, as Aristotle points out, 'the reasoned state of capacity to act is different from the reasoned state of capacity to make',[44] Spaemann draws renewed attention to the fundamental differences between these two kinds of human 'action' and to their ethical implications. 'Making', or poiesis, another leitmotif of his thought, is not all that can be 'done'. Human life and its flourishing and happiness depend significantly upon 'practice', or praxis, and the recognition of the limits of instrumental and technological reason. It is in acting well, not simply in

---

[41] 'Einleitung', in *Philosophische Essays*, 14.
[42] For Spaemann's account of the history of the idea of philosophical systems see *Reflexion und Spontaneität*, 68–9.
[43] 'Die kontroverse Natur der Philosophie', in *Philosophische Essays*, 126.
[44] For this and the difference between praxis and poiesis see Aristotle, *Nicomachean Ethics*, 1140a1, in *The Complete Works of Aristotle: The Revised Oxford Translation*, ed. Jonathan Barnes, ii (Princeton, NJ: Princeton University Press, 1984), 1799–1800; see also *Happiness and Benevolence*, 174 (*Glück und Wohlwollen*, 223) for Spaemann's explicit reference to, and analysis of, this important Aristotelian distinction.

making, that human life finds its fulfilment. The very existence of a human person, Spaemann reasons, shows most prominently how and why poiesis—the making of something—is limited and how human action is dependent upon what cannot purposefully be 'made'.[45] Philosophy, he maintains, reflects this praxis-related dimension of human life, defending the ideas of freedom and human dignity in the face of a vision of a world with respect to which one may wonder 'if in the long run there will be room for human beings'.[46]

This complex web of leitmotifs reflects the complex character of reality in its unity, which, according to one of the main thrusts of Spaemann's thought, cannot and must not be subjected to reductive or ultimately dualistic interpretations, nor to philosophical and political ideologies. Reality, in its fullest sense, transcends the effort of every philosophical endeavour, of every supposedly comprehensive system of reality, and thus also of every mechanistic and naturalistic reductionism. Spaemann's philosophy is systematic in that it explores the coherence of different features and areas of reality. However, it is not systematic in the sense that it develops a closed systematization of reality subject to a priori principles of, say, subjectivity, or a specific political ideology, or the methodology of scientific reasoning.[47]

Spaemann thus does not renew the attempt systematically to reconstruct or interpret the course of history, the nature of human society, the structure of intersubjectivity, and the genesis of individual and collective self-consciousness by means of transcendental philosophy or by a scientistic account of human nature, for instance. To the contrary, Spaemann's work exhibits an anti-idealist and anti-scientistic thrust, which, as we will argue, comes perhaps closest to Schelling's self-critical philosophical objections to idealism and his emphasis on freedom, on history, and on the gift of creation.[48] Both Spaemann's criticism

---

[45] For the difference between poiesis and praxis with particular attention to the existence and qualitative identity of human beings see Spaemann's 'Die Herausforderung des ärztlichen Berufsethos', in *Grenzen*, 344; see also 'Was ist philosophische Ethik?', in *Grenzen*, 24; 'Die schlechte Lehre vom guten Zweck', in *Grenzen*, 398–9.

[46] *Die Frage 'Wozu?'*, 13.

[47] Richard Schenk makes the same point in 'The Ethics of Robert Spaemann', 162.

[48] Spaemann has rarely written about Schelling explicitly. For his explicit view of Schelling's philosophy see 'Christentum und Philosophie der Neuzeit', in Herrmann Fechtrup, Friedbert Schulze, and Thomas Sternberg (eds.), *Aufklärung durch Tradition: Symposion der Josef Pieper Stiftung zum 90 Geburtstag von Josef Pieper, Mai 1994 in Münster* (Münster: LIT, 1995), 137 ff. (repr.in *Das unsterbliche Gerücht*, 65–91); see also Spaemann and Löw's *Die Frage 'Wozu?'*, 152–61. For an account of Schelling's later philosophy see e.g. Andrew Bowie, *Schelling and Modern European Philosophy: An Introduction* (London/New York: Routledge, 1993), esp. 127 ff.; Dale Snow, *Schelling and the End of Idealism* (New York: SUNY, 1996), 181 ff.; Holger Zaborowski, 'Why There Is Something Rather Than Nothing: F. W. J. Schelling and the Metaphysics of Freedom', in John Wippel (ed.), *The Ultimate Why Question* (Studies in Philosophy and the History of Philosophy) (Washington, DC: The Catholic University of America Press, forthcoming). It is

of idealism and that of materialism presuppose a Christian view of creation and its realism. 'The idealist opinion', he reasons, 'contradicts the realism of all Christian philosophy, for which the world is not an unreal transcript of a world of ideas that have being as such, but a creation of God'.[49] His criticism of materialism follows similar lines. It is exactly because of his realism that Spaemann's philosophy cannot be adequately characterized as anti-modern, for he does not share in the irrational and anti-realist outlook of a great many anti-modern philosophers, but attempts to preserve the realistic features of modern philosophy too. In his 'overcoming of modernity' he wants to 'embed the true contents of human self-realization, for which we are indebted to modernity, in insights which come from far away'.[50]

In doing so, Spaemann endeavours to understand reality consistently and without neglecting its major spheres or dichotomizing it into an objective realm of mere nature and a subjective realm of freedom. His view of reality finds its centre in the human person. The person and his experience of self is, according to Spaemann, paradigmatic of our understanding of reality: 'Personality is the paradigm for being—not as "something in general", but as transcendence of objectivity, "being in itself"'.[51] To experience the claim that lies in the existence of the other person means fully to experience reality. The person freely relates to his nature. Or, as Robert Sokolowski has nicely summarized Spaemann's view of the person: 'As person we shepherd ourselves, and we must cultivate ourselves in accordance with the nature that we have'.[52] So nature and freedom do not provide philosophy with alternative, but with complementary, 'foundations'. They are, properly understood, intrinsically related to one another in the experience of the other and of the self as *Selbstsein*. In providing a philosophy of the person, as we will see, Spaemann overcomes many of the important shortcomings of modernity and shows that reality cannot be fully understood on entirely modern premises.

---

beyond the scope of this examination of Spaemann's philosophy to provide a detailed comparison between Spaemann's and Schelling's thought. We can only occasionally draw attention to the similarities between Spaemann's and Schelling's philosophies without further examining fundamental differences between them. For the relation between Spaemann and Schelling see also Holger Zaborowski, 'Göttliche und menschliche Freiheit', 111 ff.

[49] 'Die Zerstörung der naturrechtlichen Kriegslehre', in *Grenzen*, 316. For Spaemann's view of the Christian understanding of creation see also his ''Leibniz' Begriff der möglichen Welten', in Venanz Schubert (ed.), *Rationalität und Sentiment: Das Zeitalter Johann Sebastian Bachs und Georg Friedrich Händels* (Wissenschaft und Philosophie: Interdisziplinäre Studien, v) (St Ottilien: EOS, 1987), 13–14.

[50] 'Ende der Modernität?', in *Philosophische Essays*, 234–5.

[51] *Persons*, 67 (*Personen*, 76).

[52] 'The Christian Difference in Personal Relationships', in Sokolowski, *Christian Faith and Understanding: Studies on the Eucharist, Trinity, and the Human Person* (Washington, DC: The Catholic University of America Press, 2006), 204.

Reason, his argument goes, is related to reality. Reality, however, is always already given. It is a gift of which we have to become more fully aware. It is already there and is not the product of our imagination and making. Consequently, it is not constructed or posited by human reason and autonomy, and cannot be understood adequately by means of an aprioristic philosophy of consciousness. Subjectivity and freedom, Spaemann argues, can only fully be understood if what precedes and limits them is not overlooked. Thus, the notions of nature and substance must not be lost sight of, for otherwise the subject is in danger of being reduced to a mere instantiation of sense perception and memories, and of freedom that has become its own measure. Spaemann also takes issue with the view that the dismissal of a religious view of reality (the view of reality as a creation, for instance) does not have huge implications for our general view of reality.[53] Such a paradigmatic shift in the understanding of reality has far-reaching implications. In his philosophy he discloses those implications and argues that we have to make a decision about how to view reality. This, he shows, is not a question of strictly theoretical significance, but rather a practical question that concerns the future and self-understanding of mankind.

Spaemann thus attempts to advance considerations that are not meant to be 'up to date'.[54] This may be one of the reasons why his philosophy is in fact 'up to date' after all. Spaemann's philosophy, it will be pointed out, provides a powerful counterposition to many of the prevailing currents of modern philosophy. It is powerful in that it appeals to 'common sense' and recollects what Spaemann considers self-evident and what can only be denied at very great expense—that is, at the cost of self-contradiction and the dismissal of fundamental dimensions of human experience. For denying personal identity in a book of several hundred pages cannot but be self-contradictory. Who, it must be asked, has written this book which, one would presume, reflects a consistent argument by a writer who, however he may have changed over the course of writing the book and afterwards, is still the same person? And who is supposed to read the book and to understand its argument? In the same manner, as Spaemann shows, the ethical urgency of a great many sociobiological writings runs counter to the arguments they propose. If ethics is nothing but a mere by-product of the natural evolutionary process, and if Being and meaning are dichotomized, why should it make sense to appeal to

---

[53] For this idea see 'Über den Begriff der Menschenwürde' in *Grenzen*, 29; see also 'Religion und "Tatsachenwahrheit"', in *Das unsterbliche Gerücht*, 171 ff. See also my 'Göttliche und menschliche Freiheit' for a discussion of the significance of the concept of creation.

[54] Spaemann explicitly calls his considerations about the relation between Christianity and philosophy 'not up to date' in 'Christentum und Philosophie der Neuzeit', 123.

the reader's conscience and to promote a conduct which, say, preserves the natural conditions of the existence of humanity? If morality itself is a product of an utterly random evolutionary process, why is it not sufficient to trust that evolution will find its way with or without human beings on its side?[55]

In a period when philosophical, scientific, and technological developments disclose the unintentional implications of modernity and its analysis of reality, Spaemann does not merely criticize the history of modern philosophy and its development towards a representation of reality as process. He also provides a counter-model for understanding reality that, given the prevailing tendencies of modern and late modern reason, is highly original without claiming to be so. Its originality lies, so to speak, in its renunciation of originality, in its confessed indebtedness to the tradition of Western philoso-phy[56] and, consequently, to what is already given as well as to what is beyond the reach of autonomous human reason—nature, freedom, history, the 'other', and God. Thus, in the opening sentence of *Happiness and Benevolence* he can express the hope 'that these thoughts on ethics contain nothing fundamentally new'.[57]

In Spaemann's view, philosophy does not discover utterly new things, but brings back to mind what we have once known. It is for this reason that Spaemann's thought can be called revolutionary, in the sense in which he understands the word: Spaemann remarks in passing apropos of Rousseau that 'all great revolutions have understood themselves not as innovations, but as restoration, as recourse to an old forgotten and betrayed truth'.[58] Spae-mann's approach thus also transcends and questions the common dichoto-mization of restorative and revolutionary thought and draws attention to a deeper criterion that makes it possible to distinguish between different kinds of revolution and restoration. 'Restoration as such', he argues, 'is neither good nor bad. It is good if something good is restored; it is bad if something bad is restored'.[59] It depends, he reasons, 'upon the quality of a society whether disintegration is desirable or not'.[60]

---

[55] Spaemann refers to the selfcontradiction of a great many writers in the area of evolution-ary metaphysics and sociobiology in *Die Frage 'Wozu?'*, 259.

[56] For Spaemann's view of how we can benefit from 'classic authors' and how they teach us temporarily to suspend our own kind of questioning so that we can understand their questions and problems see *Reflexion und Spontaneität*, 32–3.

[57] *Happiness and Benevolence*, vii (*Glück und Wohlwollen*, 9).

[58] 'Von der Polis zur Natur—Die Kontroverse um Rousseaus ersten "Discours"', in *Rousseau: Bürger ohne Vaterland*, 37.

[59] 'Über den Mut zur Erziehung', in *Grenzen*, 492.

[60] 'Überzeugungen in einer hypothetischen Zivilisation', in Oskar Schatz (ed.), *Abschied von Utopia? Anspruch und Auftrag des Intellektuellen* (Graz: Styria, 1977), 311.

His philosophy, we will argue, provides us with a revolutionary example of a good restoration. Philosophy is to preserve, and to remind us of, the largely unspoken-of limits of human action and the background of specific ideas and traditions. Over against a 'grown-up view of reality', it 'naively' remembers particularly reason and freedom as 'prejudices of our childhood'[61] in order to preserve humanity from the abolition of itself. We need these prejudices (*Vorurteile*) of our childhood, Spaemann reasons, because they are 'the presupposition for our judgements (*Urteile*)'.[62] We cannot live meaningfully as human beings without them.

Spaemann characterizes philosophy explicitly as a Socratic endeavour. In this he once again finds support from Jean-Jacques Rousseau, who made much of Socrates' celebrated profession of ignorance and criticized those Enlightenment thinkers who thought they could find in Socrates a champion to oppose Christ.[63] Against the supposedly enlightened and antichristian wisdom of modernity Spaemann makes his own case for Socratic ignorance—like Socrates, he confesses 'that I do not think that I know what I do not know'[64]—and, in the manner of Rousseau's Socrates, engages in combat against sophistry, both ancient and modern. Philosophy is a conversational enterprise that, through the very fact that it is conversational and realistic, does justice to what cannot properly be understood from a relativistic point of view. To raise questions and to remind people of what they already know thus tends to be more important than attempting fully to answer such questions which, for the most part, cannot be answered even in the long run. So in Spaemann's view philosophy is essentially characterized by a 'philosophical anarchy',[65] by a non-dominion. His philosophy

[61] Spaemann, 'Philosophie als institutionalisierte Naivität', 141. This view of philosophy shows some resemblances to Fénelon's ascetic and mystical ideal of childhood, which Spaemann examines in *Reflexion und Spontaneität*, 148–69.

[62] 'Politisches Engagement und Reflexion: Rede zum 17 Juni 1964', in *Kritik der politischen Utopie*, 35. For another important defence of prejudices see Hans-Georg Gadamer, *Truth and Method*, 2nd, rev., edn, trans. and rev. Joel Weinsheimer and Donald G. Marshall (London: Continuum, 2006), 267 ff.

[63] 'Von der Polis zur Natur', in *Rousseau: Bürger ohne Vaterland*, 38. For Spaemann's identification with Socrates (or Plato) see also his 'Vorwort', in *Das unsterbliche Gerücht*, 10; 'Über die gegenwärtige Lage des Christentums', in *Das unsterbliche Gerücht*, 226. See also JeanJacques Rousseau, *Discourse on the Sciences and Arts (First Discourse)*, ed. Roger D. Masters and Christopher Kelly, trans. Judith R. Bush, Roger D. Masters, and Christopher Kelly (Hanover: University Press of New England, 1992). For Rousseau's 'Socratism' see also Mark Hulliung, *The Autocritique of Enlightenment: Rousseau and the Philosophes* (Cambridge, Mass.: Harvard University Press, 1994), 224 ff.

[64] Plato, *Apology*, 21d, in *The Collected Dialogues of Plato*, ed. Edith Hamilton and Huntington Cairns (Princeton, NJ: Princeton University Press, 1987), 6.

[65] 'Die kontroverse Natur der Philosophie', in *Philosophische Essays*, 128. See also his 'Wie praktisch ist die Ethik?', in *Grenzen*, 37: 'Philosophie kann nur im Medium der Anarchie gedeihen'.

does not challenge or contradict Christianity, therefore; indeed, we will argue that the opposite is the case. He thus strongly criticizes the absolutism and reductionism of modernity because 'the categories of modern consciousness do not seem to be suitable to depict unabbreviated and without profound corrections what Christianity is all about'.[66] If modern philosophy tends to be 'philosophy *sub specie Dei*'—as Spaemann convincingly said of nominalism and of utilitarianism[67]—this needs to be explored and criticized for what it really is: an arrogant pretension that tends to turn inhumane because it no longer upholds the difference between creator and creation, or, to put it differently, between an infinite being and finite beings, and no longer sees the proper possibilities and limits of philosophical reasoning.

In addition to the thematic consistency of Spaemann's thought, his philosophy is also characterized by consistency over time. Spaemann admits in the preface to the 1998 edition of his doctoral dissertation that he has not moved far from his original standpoint.[68] This is not to say that his thought is self-referential and repetitive. Spaemann's philosophy is rather the continuous examination of an original and self-evident insight about the very nature of reality. The history of philosophy, too, is characterized by such a continuity, according to Spaemann. He subjects philosophy and its continuity neither to the logic of progressive development nor to the anti-logic of discontinuous events, or chains of events, among which communication and mediation seem to be utterly impossible. In taking this approach he does not dismiss the history of philosophy and the particular form philosophical thought has taken, but rather affirms it as 'an integral component of philosophy'.[69] This is why Spaemann's philosophical endeavour recalls the tradition of Western thought with implied approval, while he criticizes Martin Heidegger because Heidegger, in his view, does not 'appeal to the philosophical and religious tradition of Europe'.[70] Spaemann shares many of his key ideas with Heidegger, particularly the understanding of philosophy as free philosophizing and important elements of his criticism of modernity, but he follows, as we will see, a different trajectory in that he recalls the philosophical and religious tradition in a more affirmative manner than Heidegger.

---

[66] 'Vorbemerkungen', in *Einspruch: Christliche Reden*, 7.

[67] Spaemann, 'Leibniz' Begriff der möglichen Welten', 35; for Spaemann's critique of utilitarianism as taking on God's position see also Spaemann, *Happiness and Benevolence*, 124; 129f. (*Glück und Wohlwollen*, 164; 170f.)

[68] *Der Ursprung der Soziologie aus dem Geist der Restauration* (Stuttgart: KlettCotta, 1998), 9.

[69] 'Die kontroverse Natur der Philosophie', in *Philosophische Essays*, 119.

[70] 'Philosophie zwischen Metaphysik und Geschichte', 299.

The focus of this book is particularly upon the philosophical thought of Robert Spaemann, although we will also examine his religious writings as well as some of his writings on current political events. It would be impossible to separate these other ideas from his philosophical views. Moreover, the final motif of his philosophy, particularly of his criticism of modernity, may well be a religious one. 'Only a Christianity', he points out, 'that makes explicit the opposition to the modern world on a level with modernity is capable of filling people with enthusiasm'.[71] This is why the 'apologetic' exploration and defence of Christianity—which 'as an "absolute religion" [is] alien to the modern civilization and cannot be assimilated to it',[72]—is another of the leitmotifs of this philosophy. Spaemann's criticism of modernity is therefore ultimately informed by a Christian point of view, though it can also be appreciated in purely philosophical terms. It is, however, important to point out that he would resist the tendency to confuse philosophy with theology, because it leads either to a corrupt theology or to a substandard philosophy. His philosophy appeals to human reason and may well provide Christianity with 'foundations', though it does not presuppose Christian theology in any way. It does presuppose an openness in his readers to conversion, in order to understand reality more fully. But 'to encounter reality', Spaemann argues, 'means to encounter the invisible'.[73]

1.3 ROBERT SPAEMANN—A BIOGRAPHICAL SKETCH

Robert Spaemann was born on 5 May 1927 in Berlin.[74] His father, Heinrich, himself a prolific religious writer,[75] was an architect with an interesting religious 'career'. In 1942 Heinrich Spaemann was ordained a priest in the

---

[71] 'Die Existenz des Priesters: Eine Provokation in der modernen Welt', in *Communio*, 9 (1980), 499.

[72] 'Vorbemerkungen', in *Einsprüche: Christliche Reden*, 9.

[73] 'Wirklichkeit als Anthropomorphismus', in Oswald Georg Bauer (ed.), *Was heißt 'wirklich'? Unsere Erkenntnis zwischen Wahrnehmung und Wissenschaft* (Waakirchen/Schaftlach: Oreos, 2000), 34: 'Sich auf die Wirklichkeit einlassen heißt, sich auf das Unsichtbare einlassen'.

[74] For biographical information see Rolf Schönberger, 'Robert Spaemann', in Julian Nida-Rümelin (ed.), *Philosophie der Gegenwart in Einzeldarstellungen: Von Adorno bis Wright* (Stuttgart: Kröner, 1991), 571–5; see also Spaemann's *Philosophische Essays*, 262; Robert Spaemann and Hanns-Gregor Nissing, 'Die Natur des Lebendigen und das Ende des Denkens: Entwicklungen und Entfaltungen eines philosophischen Werks. Ein Gespräch', in Nissing (ed.), *Grundvollzüge der Person: Dimensionen des Menschseins bei Robert Spaemann* (Munich: Institut zur Förderung der Glaubenslehre, 2008), 121–36.

[75] See e.g. Heinrich Spaemann, *Was macht die Kirche mit der Macht? Denkanstöße* (Freiburg im Breisgau: Herder, 1993); *Er ist dein Licht: Meditationen für jeden Tag. Jahreslesebuch*, ed. Ulrich Schütz (Freiburg im Breisgau/Basle/Vienna: Herder, 1992); *Stärker als Not, Krankheit und*

Roman Catholic Church following his conversion, with his whole family, to Catholicism in 1930 and his wife's early death in 1936. Robert Spaemann studied philosophy, theology, history, and French at the universities of Münster, Munich, Paris, and Fribourg. In 1952 he finished his doctoral studies in philosophy with a thesis on the significance of the French counter-revolutionary L. G. A. de Bonald entitled 'The Origin of Sociology in the Spirit of Restoration: Studies on L. G. A. de Bonald' (*Der Ursprung der Soziologie aus dem Geist der Restauration: Studien über L. G. A. de Bonald*). His doctoral thesis was supervised by the philosopher Joachim Ritter, a figure whose intellectual achievement is still relatively neglected despite his lasting impact on his many disciples and particularly on the so-called Ritter-Schule. Spaemann then worked as an editor for a publishing house until 1956. From 1956 to 1962 he worked as an assistant professor (*Assistent*) at Münster University. He finished his 'Habilitation', entitled 'Reflexion und Spontaneität: Studien über Fénelon', in 1962 and attained the *venia legendi*, the academic-teaching permission, for philosophy and pedagogy. He was appointed Professor of Philosophy at the *Technische Hochschule Stuttgart* in 1962. In 1969 he was appointed to a professorship at the University of Heidelberg, where he succeeded Hans-Georg Gadamer. In 1973 Spaemann was appointed professor at the distinguished Faculty of Philosophy of the University of Munich, where, among others, Dieter Henrich[76] and Werner Beierwaltes were his colleagues. Spaemann retired in 1992. He has numerous disciples, of whom the philosopher and economist Peter Koslowski,[77] the philosopher and pharmaceutical chemist Reinhard Löw,[78] and the philosophers Thomas

---

Tod: Besinnung und Zuspruch (Freiburg im Breisgau: Herder, 1991); *Das Prinzip Liebe* (Freiburg im Breisgau: Herder, 1986).

[76] For a brief account of Henrich's philosophy see Volker Rühle, 'Dieter Henrich', in Nida-Rümelin, *Philosophie der Gegenwart in Einzeldarstellungen*, 252–5.

[77] Peter Koslowski (b. 2 Oct.1952) was one of the directors of the *Forschungsinstitut für Philosophie* in Hanover. His publications include *Philosophien der Offenbarung: Antiker Gnostizismus, Franz von Baader, Schelling* (Paderborn: Schöningh, 2001); Peter Koslowski (ed.), *Sociobiology and Bioeconomics: The Theory of Evolution in Biological and Economic Theory* (Berlin: Springer, 1999); *Der Mythos der Moderne: Die dichterische Philosophie Ernst Jüngers* (Munich: Fink, 1991); *Die Prüfungen der Neuzeit; Evolution und Gesellschaft: Eine Auseinandersetzung mit der Soziobiologie*, 2nd edn. (Tübingen: Mohr, 1989); *Gesellschaft und Staat: Ein unvermeidlicher Dualismus* (Stuttgart: KlettCotta, 1982).

[78] Reinhard Löw (b. 2 Feb. 1949; d. 25 Aug. 1994) was Professor of Philosophy at the University of Munich and one of the directors of the *Forschungsinstitut für Philosophie* in Hanover. His monographs include *Philosophie des Lebendigen: Der Begriff des Organischen bei Kant, sein Grund und seine Aktualität* (Frankfurt am Main: Suhrkamp, 1980); *Nietzsche, Sophist und Erzieher: Philosophische Untersuchungen zum systematischen Ort von Friedrich Nietzsches Denken* (Weinheim: Acta Humaniora/VCH, 1984). He also edited *Islam und Christentum in Europa* (Hildesheim: Morus, 1994). Reinhard Löw and Robert Spaemann coauthored *Die Frage 'Wozu?'*.

Buchheim, Walter Schweidler, and Rolf Schönberger are among the closest and most important.[79] Spaemann is an honorary professor at Salzburg University and has been a visiting professor at, among other places, Rio de Janeiro and Salzburg Universities and the Sorbonne. Spaemann lives in Stuttgart and lectures widely on philosophical and theological questions.

1.4 AN OUTLINE OF THE ARGUMENT

Arthur Madigan wrote in his brilliant review article of Spaemann's *Philosophische Essays* that 'if Spaemann himself, or someone thoroughly familiar with his work, were to weave from his many studies a single connected narrative, its wealth of detail and persuasive power might win for Spaemann's insights and arguments the wider attention and closer scrutiny that they certainly deserve'.[80] What Madigan demanded still needs to be accomplished. A first step towards a comprehensive account of Spaemann's philosophy, its sources, the standpoints against which his thought is directed, and the implications of his *œuvre* will be taken in this book. Given the wealth of Spaemann's work and the limits of this study, comprehensiveness can only be an ideal. However, we will discuss and examine at least the main features of Spaemann's thought and provide a narrative that makes it easier to see the wealth and persuasive power of Spaemann's thinking.

Philosophy, perhaps, is the only discipline for which the reflection about its own task, its nature, its limits, and its intrinsic constraints is an essential and constitutive part of its endeavour. A philosopher cannot but raise this issue both from a historical and from a systematic point of view. Robert Spaemann, too, provides his readers with theoretical contributions to the discussion of the nature of philosophy, and these form the basis for the interpretation of his own philosophy. The second chapter of this study, 'Conversation, recollection, and the search for happiness: Spaemann's notion of philosophy', will therefore discuss Spaemann's self-understanding as a philosopher. It will be concerned with questions such as what philosophy in a late modern context essentially is, what role it plays, and how it is properly pursued.

---

[79] Robert Spaemann and Walter Schweidler coedited *Ethik: Lehr und Lesebuch: Texte, Fragen, Antworten* (Stuttgart: Klett-Cotta, 2006). Rolf Schönberger, Thomas Buchheim, and Walter Schweidler coedited *Die Normativität des Wirklichen: Über die Grenze zwischen Sein und Sollen. Robert Spaemann zum 75. Geburtstag* (Stuttgart: Klett-Cotta, 2002).

[80] 'Robert Spaemann's *Essays*', *Review of Metaphysics*, 51/1 (Sept. 1997), 132. (Madigan's review is reprinted as the afterword in *Happiness and Benevolence*, 201–29.)

In Chapter 3, 'The dialectic of Enlightenment: Spaemann's critique of modernity' we will examine Spaemann's critique of modernity and its dialectic on the basis provided in the preceding chapter. A more systematic account of how Spaemann views modernity, how it arose, and how it relates to late modernity will allow us to understand Spaemann's interpretation of modern rationality as a dialectic, following Adorno and Horkheimer. This will then lead us to an original move on Spaemann's part.

Spaemann argues that not only the Enlightenment but also the counter-Enlightenment shows a dialectical structure. This is why nineteenth-century counter-Enlightenment is, in Spaemann's eyes, largely a continuation of modernity rather than a sufficiently penetrating criticism of its fundamental principles. This irony of a deeply modern anti-modernism is particularly evident in the political theology of L. G. A. de Bonald, whose functionalistic defence of Christianity Spaemann examined in his doctoral dissertation. We will scrutinize his (published) doctoral dissertation in Chapter 4, 'Society, philosophy, and religion: Spaemann and the dialectic of anti-modernism', paying particular attention to Spaemann's interpretation of the dialectic of Bonald's counter-revolutionary writings and to the way Spaemann's criticism renders questionable or even impossible certain ways of pursuing the relation between truth and religion on the one hand and history and society on the other. We will also see that *The Origin of Sociology in the Spirit of Restoration* is based upon a modification and extension of Adorno and Horkheimer's thesis of the dialectic of Enlightenment.[81] The French counter-revolution, as Spaemann's argument goes, also turned against itself and its own presuppositions in a typically modern way. Spaemann's doctoral dissertation thus not only thematizes a particular and historically limited dialectic, but also analyses a dialectic that is characteristic of modernity and is thus still the dialectic of Enlightenment. Because of this, our reading of *The Origin of Sociology in the Spirit of Restoration* will not only focus on Bonald, but also on indirect targets of Spaemann's critique of Bonald's functionalism.

Chapter 5, 'Nature, freedom, and persons: Spaemann's philosophy of *Selbstsein*', engages in an explicit discussion of contemporary philosophy. Post-structuralist and analytical philosophy have shown an interesting convergence with respect to the notion of personal identity. While post-structuralist philosophers such as Jacques Derrida and Michel Foucault

---

[81] See Theodor W. Adorno and Max Horkheimer, *Dialektik der Aufklärung*, in Horkheimer, *Gesammelte Schriften*, ed. Alfred Schmidt and Gunzelin Schmid Noerr (Frankfurt am Main: Fischer, 1987), 11–290. (For the English translation see Theodor W. Adorno and Max Horkeimer, *Dialectic of Enlightenment* (London: Verso, 1986)). For a discussion of Adorno's and Horkheimer's interpretation of the dialectic of Enlightenment see e.g. Jürgen Habermas, *The Philosophical Discourse of Modernity*, 106–30.

speak of the 'death of the subject', more or less ironically, philosophers of the post-Humean and post-Lockean analytic tradition such as Derek Parfit deny that a person is fully identical with himself over the course of his life time, that all human beings are persons, and that 'person' is a fundamental notion in the first place. In this chapter these tendencies will be assessed in light of Spaemann's philosophy, in which he defends a person-centred view of reality and, moreover, provides philosophical arguments for the traditional and, as he argues, self-evident view not only that all human beings are persons, but also that there is such a phenomenon as personal identity and that philosophies that do not consider the fundamental and paradigmatic character of the person inevitably contradict themselves and undermine their own truth claims. This chapter will also be concerned with Spaemann's ontology, ethics, and philosophy of religion as outlined in *Persons* and in *Happiness and Benevolence*. In reassessing the fundamental character of the person, we will argue, Spaemann bridges the gap between freedom and nature. The modern dualism of, and dialectic between, spirit and nature, his argument runs, can be overcome because persons are not simply imprisoned minds or souls, nor are they mere matter. Discussing Spaemann's attempt to develop a new person-centred account of reality as opened up in the act of love, which he considers 'the disclosure of reality that is completely adequate to reality',[82] may also show how the single features of Spaemann's thought belong coherently together.

In the final chapter we will further analyse Spaemann's philosophy of religion and his understanding of Christianity. We will focus mainly upon the question of how Spaemann's philosophy provides a model for relating Christianity and philosophy in a 'post-modern' yet not anti-modern way. We will show that Spaemann's philosophy not only does not compete with or question the truth claims of Christianity and the theological nature of theology,[83] he even provides Christian theology with the means for a better self-understanding and a better appreciation of reality vis-à-vis modern criticisms, transformations, and distortions of Christianity. In doing so, we will also examine what alternative to modernity Spaemann's philosophy offers. In comparison to many late modern writers, Spaemann provides a substantial alternative to a cast of mind that seems if not wholly flawed then at

---

[82] 'Wirklichkeit als Anthropomorphismus', 26; for Spaemann's Christian view of love see also his 'Wenn die Liebe auf Widerspruch stößt', *Caritas: Zeitschrift für Caritasarbeit und Caritaswissenschaft*, 57 (1956), 278–80.

[83] See esp. for this concept John Webster, *Theological Theology: An Inaugural Lecture Delivered Before the University of Oxford on 27 October 1997* (Oxford: Clarendon, 1998). Even though Webster's argument is developed against a background different from Spaemann's, there are still many similarities in their respective positions.

least fundamentally problematic, because it ultimately does not take seriously the gift of Being as a creation and the reality of human fallenness.

The burden of this book is, therefore, to elucidate Spaemann's thought rather than to mount a detailed critique of certain features of it. So, examining the positive impulses of Spaemann's thought for contemporary thinking may be an appropriate way of concluding the enquiries into his philosophy that follow. What needs to be done, then, is the reading of Spaemann's writings, and, that is to say, also the rereading of the Western philosophical (and theological) tradition. If Spaemann's writings become more accessible, and if, apart from the biographical and historical information, some insightful remarks upon philosophy in our time of crisis are provided, the following endeavour may, however failingly, come close to what it intends to achieve.

2

Conversation, recollection, and the search for happiness: Spaemann's understanding of philosophy

God grant the philosopher insight into what lies in front of everyone's eyes.

Ludwig Wittgenstein

2.1 THE FORM OF PHILOSOPHY

Philosophy, freedom, and the move upwards

Philosophers as diverse as Johann Gottlieb Fichte, Arthur Schopenhauer, and Ludwig Wittgenstein have used the metaphor of the ladder to demonstrate what philosophy is. Fichte states that whoever has climbed up the 'science of knowledge' no longer cares about the ladder. So ultimately the science of knowledge makes itself superfluous.[1] Schopenhauer argues that for 'the man who studies to gain insight, books and studies are merely rungs of the ladder on which he climbs to the summit of knowledge'.[2] Under the influence of Schopenhauer, Wittgenstein writes that '[m]y propositions serve as elucidations in the following way: anyone who understands me eventually recognises them as nonsensical, when he has used them—as steps—to climb up beyond them. (He must, so to speak, throw away the ladder after he has climbed up it.) He must transcend these propositions, and then he will see the world aright'.[3] The metaphor of the ladder originates from the field of metaphors by which already Plato, in the

---

[1] *Wissenschaftslehre 1804*, 2nd edn., in *Johann Gottlieb Fichte—Gesamtausgabe der Bayerischen Akademie der Wissenschaften*, ed. Reinhard Lauth, Hans Jacob, and Hans Gliwitzky (Stuttgart/Bad Cannstatt: Frommann and Holzboog, 1985), II, 8, 378.

[2] *The World as Will and Representation*, ii, trans. E. F. J. Payne (New York: Dover, 1958), 80.

[3] *Tractatus Logico-Philosophicus: The German Text of Ludwig Wittgenstein's* Logisch-Philosophische Abhandlung, trans. D. F. Pears and B. F. McGuiness, introd. Bertrand Russell (London: Routledge & Kegan Paul, 1961), 151 (6. 54).

Politeia, aimed at capturing what philosophy in essence is.[4] Plato describes moving out of the cave as a movement upwards towards true vision. It is an ethically significant movement towards the sun, the idea of the good, as the ultimate ontological and epistemological source of all things. Plato thus (co-) inaugurates the Western tradition of characterizing philosophy and knowledge through metaphors not only of vision and light, but also of ascent; that is to say, as a move upwards towards a true understanding of reality.

It hardly needs to be pointed out that Fichte's, Schopenhauer's, and Wittgenstein's philosophies differ notably from one another; yet they concur as far as their understanding of philosophy itself is concerned. While Robert Spaemann's thought diverges substantially from each of their philosophies, he too at least implicitly interprets philosophy as a ladder; that is, as a means to move upwards and to achieve a kind of higher position. In one of his attempts to describe philosophy Spaemann refers to Hegel's view that philosophy is knowledge of what really is.[5] 'To comprehend what is,' as Hegel points out, 'this is the task of philosophy, because what is, is reason'.[6] The philosopher, Spaemann argues, therefore remembers reasonable and self-evident truth. A philosopher's positions are not meant to be the private opinions of a single individual. Rather, Spaemann states, it is desirable that it become 'clear to the reader that what is remembered is self-evident, that the reader forget who told him about this, and that he consider it mere chance that he has not always seen this in this way'.[7] Particular philosophies, Spaemann reasons, have an auxiliary function, comparable to Fichte's, Schopenhauer's, and Wittgenstein's ladder, and make themselves superfluous. In his particularity the philosopher needs to do justice to the universal claim of truth and reality, so he needs to be reticent about what is merely his private view and opinion.

The notion of philosophy as a ladder is linked with the idea that one needs to perform philosophy oneself, freely. One cannot ask other people to climb the

---

[4] Plato, *Politeia*, 514f.

[5] 'Einleitung', in *Philosophische Essays*, 4; Spaemann also refers to this crucial idea of Hegel's philosophy in *Die Frage 'Wozu?'*, 14. Spaemann does not provide a bibliographical reference, but he presumably refers to the passage that we quote below.

[6] See *Hegel's Philosophy of Right*, trans. T. M. Knox (Oxford: Oxford University Press, 1967), 11.

[7] 'Einleitung', in *Philosophische Essays*, 4. It needs to be said, though, that he has commented critically on Wittgenstein's use of the metaphor of the ladder: 'But these conceptions are all, to use Wittgenstein's metaphor, ladders kicked away after use. Even this famous metaphor, however, raises a difficulty: in thought there is nothing but the ladder to distinguish above from below. If one kicks the ladder away, the distinction of above from below disappears, and one finds oneself at the bottom again' (*Persons*, 145 (*Personen*, 155)). So the problem lies not in the ladder itself, but in throwing it away. That is to say, it is, according to Spaemann, necessary to remain aware of one's ladder, the concrete and particular way of one's philosophizing.

ladder in one's place. Hence Wittgenstein's statement: 'No one can think a thought for me in the way no one can don my hat for me'.[8] Fichte and Schopenhauer presuppose a similar view of the individual's deliberate involvement in philosophy. Their ideas about the nature of philosophy reflect the decisive significance of freedom for philosophy. Books and studies are but a means to gain insight, such that Wittgenstein, in a very radical move, goes so far as to call them 'non-sensical'. Philosophy, Spaemann correspondingly says, is 'thinking for oneself' (*Selberdenken*).[9] In order to understand philosophy, he suggests, one must oneself philosophize.[10] The idea that philosophy presupposes freedom means that philosophizing often implies the conversion of the philosophizing individual rather than the mere accumulation of factual knowledge toward which one could take a neutral and objectifying position. Philosophy thus conceived is, as Pierre Hadot has argued with regard to ancient philosophy, a kind of 'spiritual exercise',[11] and thus not an enterprise that could easily accommodate the principles of scientific and technological rationality.

In a well-known statement with regard to the eighteenth- and early nineteenth-century controversy between dogmatism and idealism Fichte asserted that one's philosophical taste depends upon what kind of human being one is.[12] Robert Spaemann explicitly subscribes to this idea, and calls it an 'unrealistic naivety' to think that someone does not choose the philosophy that favours his beliefs.[13] In Spaemann's view, to be a philosopher is to become personally involved—and challenged.

---

[8] Wittgenstein, Ludwig, *Culture and Value. A Selection from the Posthumous Remains*, ed. by Georg Henrik von Wright in collaboration with Heikki Nyman, revised edition of the text by Alois Pichler, trans. Peter Winch (Oxford: Blackwell Publishers, 1998), 4e. For the metaphor of the ladder see also Fritz Mauthner, *Beiträge zu einer Kritik der Sprache, i. Zur Sprache und zur Psychologie*, in his *Das philosophische Werk: Nach den Ausgaben letzter Hand herausgegeben von Ludger Lütkehaus* (Vienna/Cologne/Weimar: Böhlau, 1999), I, 1, 1–2 ('Will ich emporklimmen in der Sprachkritik, die das wichtigste Geschäft der denkenden Menschheit ist, so muß ich die Sprache hinter mir und vor mir und in mir vernichten von Schritt zu Schritt, so muß ich jede Sprosse der Leiter zertrümmern, indem ich sie betrete. Wer folgen will, der zimmere die Sprossen wieder, um sie abermals zu zertrümmern'); Sextus Empiricus, *Against the Logicians*, in *Works*, trans. R. G. Bury (Cambridge, Mass.: Harvard University Press, 1933), 489; for Wittgenstein's use of this metaphor and its history (particularly the reference to Sextus Empiricus) see Max Black, *A Companion to Wittgenstein's Tractatus* (Cambridge: Cambridge University Press, 1964), 377.

[9] 'Die kontroverse Natur der Philosophie', in *Philosophische Essays*, 117.

[10] 'Philosophie zwischen Metaphysik und Geschichte: Philosophische Strömungen im heutigen Deutschland', in *Neue Zeitschrift für Systematische Theologie*, 1 (1959), 290.

[11] *Exercices spirituels et philosophie antique* (Paris: Etudes Augustiniennes, 1981).

[12] *Versuch einer neuen Darstellung der Wissenschaftslehre*, in *Johann Gottlieb Fichte—Gesamtausgabe der Bayerischen Akademie der Wissenschaften*, ed. Lauth, Jacob, and Gliwitzky, I, 4, 195. For a brief account of the history of the (nationalistic and elitist) interpretation of this passage see Christoph Asmuth, *Das Begreifen des Unendlichen: Philosophie und Religion bei Johann Gottlieb Fichte 1800–1806* (Spekulation und Erfahrung, II, 41) (Stuttgart/Bad Cannstatt: frommann-holzboog, 1999), 175–6.

[13] 'Wovon handelt die Moraltheologie? Bemerkungen eines Philosophen', in *Einsprüche: Christliche Reden*, 68–9.

How one understands philosophy determines not only the content of one's philosophy but also its style. This is why we must briefly consider Spaemann's style, that is the 'form' of his philosophy,[14] before we proceed to provide a more extensive account of how he determines the nature of philosophy.

Spaemann's philosophy and its form

It has already been suggested that although Spaemann's philosophy is very consistent, it is not systematic in the modern sense of systematic philosophy. Spaemann does not provide his readers with a closed system of philosophy because of his conviction, shared by many late modern philosophers, that the 'great narrative' of a comprehensive intellectual system of reality is an arrogant pretension that violates the limits of human rationality. We will see, for instance, that he develops a view of the reality of *Selbstsein* that requires a recollection of natural teleology. But can we, Spaemann wonders, 'talk about teleology strictly and systematically'?[15] We cannot, he suggests, for very good reasons, so we ought not even to endeavour to philosophize in a systematic and comprehensive way. This view of the fundamental limits of philosophical reasoning is also reflected in the very style of Spaemann's philosophy.

Spaemann has a certain preference for the discursive. Even *Happiness and Benevolence* and *Persons*, his two most comprehensive books, can be read as collections of essays. This is the case primarily for two reasons. First, the order of the chapters, although meaningful and well thought out, could be changed without altering the substance and coherence of the book. Second, most chapters can easily be read and understood individually because they are relatively self-contained studies. Accordingly, the subtitle of *Personen* (*Persons*) is *Versuche über den Unterschied zwischen 'etwas' und 'jemand'* (*Investigations into the Difference between 'Something' and 'Somebody'*); *Glück und Wohlwollen* (*Happiness and Benevolence*) has the subtitle *Versuch über Ethik* (*Investigation into Ethics*).[16] Both books contain several discursive studies and have the character of 'attempts' (*Versuche*), not of a comprehensive system. Other works by Spaemann, too, have at least partly the character of collections of essays. The subtitle of Spaemann's doctoral dissertation (and subsequent

---

[14] Harald Seubert argues that not only Spaemann's argument but also the 'gesture' (*Gestus*) of his philosophy demonstrates that the personalist viewpoint is right ('Die Aktualität des Guten: Über ein neues Paradigma in der Ethik', *Ethica*, 7 (1999), 73).

[15] *Die Frage 'Wozu?'*, 11.

[16] It is unfortunate that Jeremiah Alberg, in his translation of *Happiness and Benevolence*, did not translate this subtitle. Spaemann's titles and subtitles are generally very telling with regard to his philosophy and his self-understanding as a philosopher.

book) *The Origin of Sociology in the Spirit of Restoration* (*Der Ursprung der Soziologie aus dem Geist der Restauration*) is *Investigations into L. G. A. de Bonald* (*Studien über L. G. A. de Bonald*); his 'habilitation', *Reflection and Spontaneity* (*Reflexion und Spontaneität*) is subtitled *Investigations into Fénelon* (*Studien über Fénelon*).[17] These subtitles are not only expressive of the discursive and investigative character of Spaemann's philosophy; they also reflect that Spaemann's style is conversational and lacks any motive to provide an ultimate, systematic answer to philosophical questions because, he asserts, philosophy cannot provide such answers. Philosophy, as he says, is the individual's attempt to think the universal and thus is fundamentally a matter of debate.[18] Controversies and debates thus characterize philosophy, and as long as there is philosophy, he thinks, there will be no final system of thought on which everyone could agree and, therefore, no end of philosophy.

Spaemann also prefers a style that is accessible to non-philosophers as well as to professional philosophers—not only in *Moralische Grundbegriffe* (*Basic Moral Concepts*), which was specifically written for a lay audience. Few of his writings can only be appreciated by professional philosophers, and few address issues of interest only to Spaemann's professional colleagues. Yet he does not popularize philosophy at the expense of conceptional precision and theoretical profundity. He is able to address two different audiences simultaneously. Clarity and intellectual depth, his writings make sufficiently plain, are not mutually exclusive. Professional philosophers will find a complex web of allusions, comments upon philosophical problems (both critical and affirmative), and contributions to philosophical debates that may be overlooked by the non-professional reader without his losing sight of the thrust of Spaemann's argument. Spaemann's appeal to an audience that is not limited to professional philosophers corresponds to his criticism of a culture that furnishes supposed experts with a principle role vis-à-vis particular kinds of question, even though it may be more appropriate to rely on common sense to provide an answer to those questions. His philosophy puts an emphasis upon our everyday understanding of reality—that is to say, upon how we always already would understand reality and ourselves if we did not often let our view of reality be distorted—and not upon professional expertise. Therefore he attempts to wake up the students of his writings so that they can

---

[17] The limits of this book preclude a detailed discussion of Spaemann's interpretation of Fénelon's book. I will, however, discuss other works by Spaemann to illustrate the central thesis of *Reflexion und Spontaneität: Studien über Fénelon* and occasionally refer to this book.

[18] 'Die kontroverse Natur der Philosophie', in *Philosophische Essays*, 104–29. It is obvious that Spaemann has a considerable interest in educational issues and in the 'educational dimension' of philosophers such as Rousseau and Fénelon (see *Rousseau: Bürger ohne Vaterland, passim*, and *Reflexion und Spontaneität*, esp. pp. 237–69).

participate in reality in an improved and fuller manner. In so doing, he provides what he calls an 'education into reality'.[19]

For this reason, Spaemann's philosophy engages in a conversation not only with his contemporaries but also with those attempts in the history of philosophy that Spaemann deems most momentous for our understanding of reality. Because of this, Spaemann's thought lacks the self-referential or text-focused attitude of a great deal of late modern philosophy.[20] He impetuously criticizes a theology that is mainly concerned with texts and establishes itself as a fiction-based theology '*etsi deus non daretur*'.[21] In a similar way, though implicitly, he is critical of self-referential and text-focused philosophies that lose sight of reality *etsi mundus non daretur*. In his philosophy Spaemann tends to apply an almost Nietzschean method, in that he asks for the hidden motifs behind the development of modernity.[22] We need to remember what is self-evident, Spaemann thinks, because in modernity it has been obscured by power claims and interests. He argues, for instance, that 'behind the propagation of evolutionism, there must stand an ideological motive'.[23] In this situation, in which, as he thinks, 'the constitution of the modern sciences itself has non-scientific reasons',[24] Spaemann employs historical analysis, one of the principal methods of modern philosophy, in order to challenge the central claims of modern thought. In doing so—in asking for the genesis of genealogy and also for the hidden function of functionalisms (such as evolutionism)—he turns genealogy and functionalism against themselves.[25]

Spaemann's enterprise is somewhat reminiscent of Thomas Kuhn's approach to the history of science, which traces the rise of a new paradigm

---

[19] For Spaemann's understanding of education see 'Erziehung zur Wirklichkeit: Rede zum Jubiläum eines Kinderhauses', in *Grenzen*, 503–12.

[20] For an important criticism of this self-referential tendency of contemporary culture see also George Steiner, *Real Presences* (Chicago, Ill.: University of Chicago Press, 1991).

[21] 'Das unsterbliche Gerücht', in *Das unsterbliche Gerücht*, 14.

[22] Reinhard Löw points out that 'Spaemann's critique of modernity finds itself pronounced in some points in Nietzsche' (*Nietzsche, Sophist und Erzieher: Philosophische Untersuchungen zum systematischen Ort von Friedrich Nietzsches Denken* (Weinheim: Acta humaniora, 1984), 153).

[23] 'Sein und Gewordensein: Was erklärt die Evolutionstheorie?', in *Philosophische Essays*, 203. For Spaemann's Nietzschean 'interest' in the interest behind certain kinds of modernisms see also e.g. Spaemann, *Persons*, 52 (*Personen*, 61).

[24] 'Naturteleologie und Handlung', in *Philosophische Essays*, 43.

[25] In so doing, he follows Joachim Ritter (see Robert Spaemann and Hanns-Gregor Nissing, 'Die Natur des Lebendigen und das Ende des Denkens: Entwicklungen und Entfaltungen eines philosophischen Werks. Ein Gespräch', in Nissing (ed.), *Grundvollzüge der Person: Dimensionen des Menschseins bei Robert Spaemann* (Munich: Institut zur Förderung der Glaubenslehre, 2008), 122).

back to a scientific revolution that has a twofold parallel to political revolutions. First, both political and scientific revolutions are characterized by a 'growing sense... often restricted to a narrow subdivision of the scientific community, that an existing paradigm has ceased to function adequately in the exploration of an aspect of nature to which that paradigm itself had previously led the way'.[26] Second, and more important in our context, the choice of a paradigm, be it political or scientific, implies 'a choice between incompatible modes of community life'.[27] Prior to this choice, Kuhn's theory of scientific progress runs, there is a fundamental crisis of society or of the scientific community and an escalating polarization between different camps. In order fully to understand the paradigm shifts of modernity, Spaemann makes clear, one also needs to consider the interests and motivations that are latent in those shifts, and one needs to show that interest-driven philosophies and paradigms often fail to do justice to reality as it really is and as it discloses itself to us. This is why philosophy today needs also to be a critique of modernity, its interests, and its truth claims.

Spaemann's focus on reality shows some repercussions of twentieth-century phenomenology. For this reason, we will proceed briefly to examine the relation between phenomenology and Spaemann's philosophy. Without this comparison, one might easily misconstrue what Spaemann means by calling his method a 'metaphysical realism'.[28] First, we will provide a brief account of Husserl's and Heidegger's phenomenology, its method, and its philosophical consequences. We will then discuss to what extent Spaemann's philosophy echoes phenomenology and, more specifically, Heidegger's hermeneutics of facticity.

Spaemann's philosophy and phenomenology

Edmund Husserl initiated a new philosophical method in what he considered the time of the 'crisis of European sciences'.[29] Husserl envisioned that late

---

[26] Thomas S. Kuhn, *The Structure of Scientific Revolutions* (Chicago, Ill.: University of Chicago Press, 1970), 92.

[27] Kuhn, *Structure of Scientific Revolutions*, 93–4.

[28] For Spaemann's understanding of 'metaphysical realism' see esp. *Persons*, 77 ff. (*Personen*, 87 ff.).

[29] See Edmund Husserl, *The Crisis of European Sciences and Transcendental Phenomenology: An Introduction to Phenomenological Philosophy*, trans. with an introd. David Carr (Evanston, Ill.: Northwestern University Press, 1970). Spaemann refers briefly to this book in 'Philosophie zwischen Metaphysik und Geschichte', 306–7. For Husserl's philosophical claim see also 'Philosophy as a Rigorous Science', in his *Shorter Works*, ed. Peter McCormick and Frederick A. Elliston (Notre Dame, Ind.: University of Notre Dame Press, 1981), 166–97.

nineteenth-century philosophy, above all its historicist, naturalist, and psychologist strands, would not only transform philosophy, but inevitably undermine it. Truth would, in that case, be subject to the laws of history, biology, and psychology. Over against this development of nineteenth- and early twentieth-century thought Husserl expounded phenomenology as a method which—in spite of its remaining heavily indebted to modern philosophy, predominantly to Descartes[30]—challenges several of the crucial presuppositions of modern philosophy. Phenomenology challenges, for instance, the polarization of subject and object and the idea that human beings can attain to knowledge only of things as they appear to us, as opposed to things in themselves, as Kant and the Kantian tradition argued. Husserl rehabilitated an epistemology and an ontology that take seriously and reassess how things themselves appear to us. Many decisive problems of modern epistemology, he demonstrated, are pseudo-problems caused by the way a question is formulated rather than by how things themselves really are.[31] In so doing, Husserl inaugurated one of the most influential schools of twentieth-century philosophy.

In the subsequent development of phenomenology Martin Heidegger developed a criticism of Husserl's notion of philosophy as 'rigorous science'. Heidegger, roughly speaking, increasingly rejected any notion of philosophy as a science. For him, philosophy does not need to be equated with modern natural science and its epistemological claims. Furthermore, it must not and, ultimately, cannot understand itself as a rigorous science. In his view, philosophy is a 'hermeneutics of facticity'.[32] Thus, Heidegger laid the 'foundations' of an assessment of philosophy that is at odds not only with Husserl's phenomenology, but also with analytic and positivist philosophies. In arguing that philosophy is a hermeneutics of facticity, Heidegger contends that philosophy ought to describe factual human life phenomenologically without falling prey

---

[30] For the close connection between Husserl's and Descartes's philosophies see Paul S. MacDonald, *Descartes and Husserl: The Philosophical Project of Radical Beginnings* (New York: State University of New York Press, 2000).

[31] Admittedly, this is a rough and rather simplicistic outline of Edmund Husserl's enterprise. For a comprehensive account of phenomenology see Robert Sokolowski, *Introduction to Phenomenology* (Cambridge: Cambridge University Press, 2000). For a discussion of a diverse range of issues concerning Husserlian phenomenology see also Barry Smith and David Woodruff-Smith (eds.), *The Cambridge Companion to Husserl* (Cambridge: Cambridge University Press, 1995).

[32] See esp. Martin Heidegger, *Ontologie (Hermeneutik der Faktizität)*, ed. Käte Oltmans-Bröker, 2nd edn. (Frankfurt am Main: Klostermann, 1995) (*Gesamtausgabe*, 63). For an account of the differences between Husserl's and Heidegger's notions of phenomenology see Friedrich-Wilhelm von Herrmann, *Hermeneutik und Reflexion: Der Begriff der Phänomenologie bei Heidegger und Husserl* (Frankfurt am Main: Klostermann, 2000).

to the reality-concealing presuppositions and biases of a scientific view. Hence, one can read Heidegger's early phenomenology (which found later expression in his *Being and Time* and in his later philosophy) as a reappraisal of a view of reality as it appears to us prior to any scientific or theoretical prejudice.[33]

Spaemann, however, is not a phenomenological philosopher in the sense of belonging to a specific phenomenological school, following a particular method, and raising a certain, very specific, kind of question. It is difficult to demonstrate an explicit debt of Spaemann's thought to Heidegger's philosophy. Heidegger's name surfaces only occasionally in Spaemann's writings. One reason may be that Spaemann disdains not only what he considers the anti-metaphysical implications of Heidegger's thought, but also his political involvement.[34] In one of the most polemical passages of his philosophical writings he mentions the story that Heidegger, when visiting Karl Löwith in Rome in 1936, wore the Nazi-party badge. Spaemann states that this shows the naivety as well as the lack of instinct and taste of a 'politically disoriented petty bourgeois'. He further remarks polemically that Heidegger published verses that other educated people would have left in the drawer.[35] It is furthermore striking that Spaemann makes no explicit reference to Martin Heidegger when he refers to Adorno's and Horkheimer's *Dialectic of Enlightenment*, Thomas Aquinas' *Summa Theologica*, and Joachim Ritter's thought[36] as main influences on his philosophical development (and Marx, Lenin, and Lukács as weighty, though less significant).[37]

Nonetheless, Spaemann's writings bear clear evidence of Heidegger's influence, or at least of a certain sympathy of thought.[38] Spaemann's comments on

---

[33] For an account of Heidegger's early thought and its development see Theodore Kisiel, *The Genesis of Martin Heidegger's 'Being and Time'* (Berkeley, Calif.: University of California Press, 1993).

[34] For a discussion of Heidegger's political involvement on the basis of current research see my '"Der verwüstenden Sandstürme nicht vergessen . . ."—Zur Diskussion über das Verhältnis Martin Heideggers zum Nationalsozialismus', in Bernd Martin (ed.), *'Die Wahrheit wird Euch frei machen': Historische Festschrift zur 550. Jahrfeier der Alber-Ludwigs-Universität Freiburg im Breisgau*, ii (Freiburg im Breisgau: Alber, 2007), 355–73.

[35] 'Zur Einführung: Philosophiegeschichte nach Martin Heidegger', in Thomas Buchheim (ed.), *Destruktion und Übersetzung: Zu den Aufgaben der Philosophiegeschichte nach Martin Heidegger* (Weinheim: VCH, 1989), 1. For Löwith's account see his *Mein Leben in Deutschland vor und nach 1933: Ein Bericht* (Stuttgart: Metzlersche, 1986), 57.

[36] For Spaemann's brief explicit appreciation of Joachim Ritter's thought see 'Philosophie zwischen Metaphysik und Geschichte', 312 ff.

[37] 'Einführung', in *Philosophische Essays*, 10–11; for the impact of Adorno and Horkheimer on his philosophy see also Spaemann and Nissing, 'Die Natur des Lebendigen und das Ende des Denkens', 126.

[38] For Spaemann's appreciation of Heidegger's philosophy see also 'Philosophie zwischen Metaphysik und Geschichte', 298 ff. (see p. 301 for Spaemann's critical remarks on Heidegger's poetry); for his interpretation of Heidegger's understanding of the history of philosophy see his 'Zur Einführung'.

Joachim Ritter's lectures and their focus on origin and future may well also
be an allusion to Heidegger's philosophy, because this motif echoes not only
Heidegger's renowned phrase[39] but also a crucial idea in his philosophy. Spaemann's anthropology and his criticism of modernity also show a resemblance
to Heidegger's thought and his critique of modern technology. Spaemann
implicitly refers to Heidegger, for instance, when he points out that 'we need
anxiety [*Sorge*], which arises out of the threat of extinction, in order to be able
to lead fulfilled lives [*Dasein*]'.[40] And he explicitly refers to Heidegger's critique
of modern rationality in the context of his own critical interpretation of
modernity.[41] Spaemann also argues that 'philosophical contemplation tries
to get the "things themselves" into sight'.[42] This is an allusion to the method
of phenomenology; for Heidegger (with Husserl on his side) argued that 'the
term "phenomenology" expresses a maxim which can be formulated as "To the
things themselves!"'.[43] Heidegger further concludes: 'It is opposed to all free-
floating constructions and accidental findings; it is opposed to taking over any
conceptions which only seem to have been demonstrated; it is opposed to
those pseudo-questions which parade about as "problems", often for generations at a time'.[44] Phenomenology, in other words, rehabilitates a self-evident,
yet often disguised, knowledge, and this is why there are significant parallels
between phenomenology and Spaemann's philosophy. Spaemann also shares
Heidegger's idea that philosophy is not a science and must not be subject to the
methods that are employed by scientific reasoning. While there are significant
differences between Heidegger's thought and his own, especially with respect
to ethics, Spaemann offers a similarly trenchant criticism of modern philosophy and its ontological and epistemological claims. Like Heidegger, Spaemann
rediscovers a dimension of human life that has been overlooked by modern
philosophy as well as by the social and natural sciences. In developing a kind of
phenomenological view of reality, at least partly inspired by Heidegger (and

---

[39] See Martin Heidegger, 'Aus einem Gespräch von der Sprache', in *Unterwegs zur Sprache*
(Pfullingen: Neske, 1959), 96: 'Herkunft aber bleibt stets Zukunft'.

[40] *Basic Moral Concepts*, 20 (*Moralische Grundbegriffe*, 32: 'Ohne Sorge um das vom Ende
bedrohte Leben gibt es kein erfülltes Dasein'). The translator of *Moralische Grundbegriffe* did not
seem to be aware of the allusions to *Being and Time*, in which Heidegger defines care as 'the
Being of Dasein' (*Being and Time*, trans. John MacQuarrie and Edward Robinson (Oxford:
Blackwell, 1983), 225 ff.).

[41] See *Persons*, 90 (*Personen*, 100), where he refers to Martin Heidegger, 'Die Zeit des
Weltbildes', in *Holzwege*, ed. Friedrich-Wilhelm von Herrmann (*Gesamtausgabe*, 5) (Frankfurt
am Main: Klostermann, 1977), 75–113.

[42] 'Das Vertrauen als sittlicher Wert', in *Die Kirche in der Welt*, 1 (1947/8), 351.

[43] *Being and Time*, 50 (see also 58), and Edmund Husserl, *Logical Investigations*, trans.
J. N. Findlay (New York: Humanity, 2000), 252.

[44] *Being and Time*, 50.

also by Max Scheler's 'phenomenology of love'), Spaemann (like Heidegger) sees himself in the tradition of Aristotle and his 'orientation toward our everyday talk about nature, along with his unbiased eye for natural phenomena'.[45]

This feature is closely related to another dimension of Spaemann's philosophy. Like Husserl and Heidegger, he questions the polarization of subject and object and its ontological and epistemological presuppositions and implications. That is to say, he challenges one of the most fundamental presuppositions of much modern thought. Husserl made clear that there is no such thing as mere perception, or consciousness, independent of its 'object'. Perception is always perception *of something*. There is no pure act of seeing, for instance. Following the implication of Husserl's thought, subject and object are not radically opposed to one another. Human consciousness is characterized by intentionality, as Husserl shows—and therefore intentionally related to its 'object'. Spaemann, it will become clear, also challenges the polarization of subject and object, in a slightly different way from Husserl. He argues that 'the talk of subjects and objects as two always-opposed areas of Being passes reality by . . . this view makes something like reality disappear altogether'.[46] In reality, 'subjects' are always already related to 'objects'—and, as Spaemann would argue, to other 'subjects'. There is, therefore, no isolated solipsistic subject that could serve as the foundation of philosophical knowledge, as some modern philosophers have suggested. Spaemann further argues that, strictly speaking, no entirely objective knowledge is possible. Knowledge through the lens of human perception is, in Spaemann's view, not the opponent of knowledge proper; it is, as we will see, its very *conditio sine qua non*.[47] Thus, modern epistemology falls prey to a significant error if it idealizes a supposed objectivity and neutrality and dismisses subjective language as anthropomorphic. In contrast to this positivistic epistemology, Spaemann, as we will see, favours an epistemology that takes the fundamental and paradigmatic character of human self-experience as *Selbstsein* seriously.

---

[45] *Die Frage 'Wozu?'*, 79. For the influence of Aristotle on Heidegger see Alfred Denker et al. (eds.), *Heidegger und Aristoteles* (*Heidegger-Jahrbuch*, 3) (Freiburg im Breisgau/Munich: Alber, 2006).

[46] 'Wirklichkeit als Anthropomorphismus', in Oswald Georg Bauer (ed.), *Was heißt 'wirklich'? Unsere Erkenntnis zwischen Wahrnehmung und Wissenschaft* (Waakirchen/Schaftlach: Oreos, 2000), 18.

[47] For this non-objectivist and non-scientific epistemology see also Reinhard Löw, 'Natur und Zweck: Einige neuere Aspekte zum Problem der Naturteleologie', in *Scheidewege: Jahresschrift für skeptisches Denken*, 14 (1984/5), 342–58, esp. 354–5.

He thus develops a phenomenology, as it were, that helps to examine the (always already given) gift of *Selbstsein*.[48]

2.2 THE NATURE OF PHILOSOPHY

In this section we will examine what it means to define philosophy, as Spaemann does, as a recollection and as a 'continuous conversation about ultimate questions'.[49] We pursue this with the intention of then discussing, among other issues, Spaemann's understanding of history and the complementary relation between nature and freedom, and his consequent criticism of modern philosophy. For modernity is, in Spaemann's view, largely characterized by a misconception of the notions of, and the relation between, nature, freedom, and history. While modern philosophy tends to oppose history and freedom to nature, freedom, history, and nature are not incommensurable, according to Spaemann, but rather intrinsically related to one another.

Philosophy is thus, as we will disuss further in Chapter 3, conceived of by Spaemann as a theory and critique of modernity. The philosopher, therefore, does not need to accept modernity as self-evidently and unquestionably given. Philosophy can question itself in its modern form[50] and recollect alternative views of how philosophy can be pursued. The philosophical tradition and those ideas that Spaemann aims to recollect, without altogether dismissing modernity and its positive aspects, contribute in his eyes to an answer to the crisis of modernity and its philosophy. His understanding of philosophy is therefore closely related to what he calls the 'end of modernity': the 'retrieval of the human content of modernity through a different

---

[48] It may be that the phenomenological character of Spaemann's philosophy (his attempt to go back to the 'things themselves') allows him to bridge the gap between ancient and modern philosophy. For the possibility that the 'resources provided by phenomenology allow us . . . to transcend the difference between ancients and moderns' see also Robert Sokolowski, *Phenomenology of the Human Person* (Cambridge: Cambridge University Press, 2008), 273 ff.

[49] For an examination of the self-understanding of contemporary German philosophy, including the philosophy of Robert Spaemann, see Hans-Ludwig Ollig, 'Umstrittene Philosophie: Zur neueren Selbstverständnisdiskussion in der deutschen Gegenwartsphilosophie', in *Theologie und Philosophie*, 56 (1981), 161–203; 'Philosophie und Zeitdiagnose: Aspekte deutscher Gegenwartsphilosophie', in *Theologie und Philosophie*, 57 (1982), 348–88, esp. 363–6; 'Die Aktualität der Metaphysik: Perspektiven der deutschen Gegenwartsphilosophie', in *Theologie und Philosophie*, 68 (1993), 52–81, esp. 59–65.

[50] *Paradigm Lost*, 73.

self-understanding, recollection of the natural and historical contents by which modernity lives without having set them'.[51]

Before we go on to discuss further Spaemann's understanding of philosophy, it may be useful to remind ourselves of a paradigmatically modern way of defining philosophy. David Hume stated that in his enterprise to 'explain the principles of human nature, we in effect propose a compleat system of the sciences, built on a foundation almost entirely new, and the only one upon which they can stand with any security'.[52] In this quotation we can find four key principles of modern philosophy in a nutshell: first, its systematic and comprehensive character; second, its scientific nature; third, its claim to newness and originality; and fourth, its claim to establish knowledge on a secure basis. Spaemann defines philosophy in a way that is strictly opposed to the Humean notion of philosophy. His philosophy makes no attempt to be systematic (in the modern sense) or comprehensive. It is not scientific, but challenges the hypotheses of scientific reasoning and the different claims that are based upon them. It is neither new nor original. It is not foundational and does not aim to provide a basis for ultimate certainty.

In Spaemann's view, philosophy assists in the recollection of what is self-evident by way of continuing the conversation that began some 2,500 years ago in Greece. It is because of his view of this twofold character of philosophy—recollection and attention to the self-evident—that Spaemann's thought is essentially a critique of modernity and its underlying historicism, subjectivism, functionalism, and utilitarianism, which tend to forget the self-evident and to disconnect themselves from the tradition of philosophical conversation. As far as the critical character of his philosophy is concerned, Spaemann's thinking bears a resemblance to Leo Strauss's thought. However, unlike the philosophy of Strauss, who, as one can plausibly argue, failed to provide any positive material account of how an ethics beyond the modern preoccupation with passions and interests might look,[53] Spaemann's thought is not primarily judgemental or critical in so far as it recollects the apperception of Being which, as he holds, 'makes the human human'.[54]

---

[51] 'Einleitung', in *Philosophische Essays*, 17.

[52] *A Treatise of Human Nature*, ed. David Fate Norton and Mary J. Norton (Oxford: Oxford University Press, 2000), 4.

[53] For a critique of Strauss's thought see Charles Larmore, *The Morals of Modernity* (Cambridge: Cambridge Univesity Press, 1997), 65–76.

[54] *Happiness and Benevolence*, ix (*Glück und Wohlwollen*, 11).

Spaemann's philosophy as a 'metaphysical realism'

An initial way of understanding a philosopher's thought is to examine how he himself delineates it. In *Persons* Spaemann argues that a 'metaphysical realism' characterizes our relation to other persons.[55] It is evident that his philosophy, which, after all, is a philosophy of the person, can consequently be called metaphysical realism. This characterization has implications that are directed against prevailing tendencies in modern and late modern philosophy.

Spaemann is dismissive of modernity's self-contradictory abolition of metaphysics and ontology. In his view metaphysics as such (as well as ontology) cannot be transformed into, or replaced by, a philosophy of the subject. Spaemann also takes issue with the Nietzschean criticism that *all* metaphysics is but an expression of the will to power and therefore has no right to truth claims and needs to be questioned.[56] This is not to say that Spaemann is uncritical of those shortcomings of metaphysics that have led to the current crisis of metaphysical thought. Nor does Spaemann dismiss the achievements of modern philosophy. He subscribes to modern philosophy's turn towards the (human) subject as well as towards hermeneutics and an analysis of language. What he attempts to defend, though, is a philosophical position that does justice to *both* subjects *and* substances, *both* freedom *and* nature. Substance, he emphasizes, cannot be understood adequately as derivative from subjectivity, nor vice versa. This shows the ontological dimension of his understanding of metaphysics, which entails, unlike most hermeneutical philosophies, a detailed philosophy of nature and a philosophy of the absolute, which alone, in his view, can provide a theoretical warrant for the inalienable dignity of the human person.[57]

For Spaemann, metaphysics also has an ethical dimension, for 'there is no ethics without metaphysics'[58]—and vice versa.[59] His defence of metaphysics is thus also an attempt to reconceptualize the unity of ontology and ethics without denying their difference. How Spaemann interprets the connection between ontology and ethics also leads us to understand more deeply why Spaemann insists on calling his metaphysics 'realistic'. Furthermore, it will become clear why the characterization of Spaemann's philosophy as a

---

[55] *Persons*, 78–9. (*Personen*, 88–9.).
[56] See for Nietzsche's critique of philosophy e.g. his *Beyond Good and Evil: Prelude to a Philosophy of the Future*, ed. Rolf-Peter Horstmann and Judith Norman, trans. Judith Norman (Cambridge: Cambridge University Press, 20), esp. pt. I: 'On the Prejudices of Philosophers'.
[57] 'Über den Begriff der Menschenwürde', in *Grenzen*, 122.
[58] *Happiness and Benevolence*, ix, 113 (*Glück und Wohlwollen*, 11, 150).
[59] For this see also Holger Zaborowski, 'Ethik, Metaphysik und die Frage nach Gott', *Jahrbuch für Religionsphilosophie*, 1 (2002), 120–37.

'phenomenology' of the person is not a negligible addition to its realistic nature, but one of its most important aspects. For personal being, according to Spaemann, fully discloses reality: 'But if we think of Being not as the most abstract being, as "something in general", but as "absolut posit" (Kant again), the *actus essendi* preceding every possible objective attribute, then "Being" means precisely the same as Levinas's "beyond Being"'.[60] The method, then, which Spaemann employs to describe reality is to examine phenomenologically how persons lead their lives; that is, how they literally 'have' their nature (*ihre Natur haben*), and encounter and recognize other persons. This description shows, as we will discuss further in Chapter 5, that ethics and ontology are finally grounded in the most fundamental experience of reality; that is, in the experience and the free and benevolent[61] recognition of *Selbstsein* and its given reality: 'Ontology and ethics must not be separated. Love and justice are not possible under the presupposition of solipsism; that is to say, under the presupposition that the other human beings and the other creatures are only my dreams'.[62] The person, Spaemann further argues, is an 'unambiguous reality'.[63] Hence the 'necessity of viewing the other as real, as a "thing-in-itself"'.[64]

It is important to note that Spaemann thus argues that the decision as to which kind of philosophy one should pursue cannot be made irrespective of our experience of reality. To favour metaphysical realism is not the result of an arbitrary or merely theoretical decision to which reality then needs to correspond (or needs to be made to correspond). It is the result of our practical experience of personal reality, and this experience is the most fundamental and paradigmatic way of experiencing reality—which, he maintains, is the presupposition of true happiness. Reality, Spaemann consequently argues, must not be avoided. In truth, we do not even want to substitute pure pleasure for reality. Aristotle argues that although 'possession of excellence seems actually compatible with being asleep, or with lifelong inactivity . . . a man who was living so no one would call happy, unless he were maintaining a thesis at all costs'.[65] In a similar way, Spaemann raises the following question:

Let us imagine a man strapped to a table in an operating theatre. He is under anaesthesia and there are electrodes attached to his scalp. Precisely measured electrical

---

[60] *Persons*, 126–7 (*Personen*, 136).

[61] For Spaemann's understanding of benevolence see *Happiness and Benevolence*, 92 ff. (*Glück und Wohlwollen*, 123 ff.).

[62] Spaemann, 'Wirklichkeit als Anthropomorphismus', 21.

[63] *Happiness and Benevolence*, 103 (*Glück und Wohlwollen*, 137).

[64] Ibid. 113 (150).

[65] *Nicomachean Ethics*, 1095b, in *The Complete Works of Aristotle: The Revised Oxford Translation*, ed. J. Barnes (1984).

impulses are transmitted through these wires to certain brain centres which induce a permanent state of euphoria. The person's beatific expression reflects his state. The doctor who is carrying out the experiment explains to us that the man will remain in this condition for at least another ten years. When at last it is no longer possible to prolong it, the machine will be switched off and he will immediately die without feeling any pain. The doctor offers the same to us. The question is, who among us would be prepared to allow him- or her-self to be transported into this kind of bliss?[66]

This is, of course, a rhetorical question. We would not be prepared 'to be transported into this kind of bliss' because reality can never be opposed to happiness, but is always presupposed by it. The happy life that turns out well, Spaemann points out, 'in its essence has to do with truth, with reality'.[67] 'In that it discloses reality,' he therefore points out, 'happiness is different from the subjective feeling of delight'.[68] In its thinking about happiness philosophy is, in Spaemann's view, characterized by the task of waking people up to reality and ridding them of their dreams and illusions. The experience of the gift of reality discloses Being, Spaemann argues, as ultimately friendly.[69] In his view, the foundations of this experience of reality are laid in early childhood: 'The task of anyone entrusted with the care of a child is to help the child come to terms with reality, both the self-sufficiency of reality and its tendency to stand in opposition to us. In general the mother is the first self-sufficient reality a child comes across'. The result of her 'look of love'[70] is that 'the child initially experiences reality as something kind and helpful'.[71] It is not a merely theoretical or intellectual but an always already emotional experience of reality.[72]

---

[66] *Basic Moral Concepts*, 19 (*Moralische Grundbegriffe*, 30–1). See also *Persons*, 75 (*Personen*, 85): 'None of us would want to spend the whole of life in bed, maintained in a state of artificial euphoria'. For a similar thought-experiment, see Robert Nozick, *Anarchy, State, and Utopia* (New York: Basic, 1974), 42–5; see also John Finnis, *Natural Law and Natural Rights* (Oxford: Oxford University Press, 1980), 95–7.

[67] *Happiness and Benevolence*, 56 (*Glück und Wohlwollen*, 79).

[68] 'Philosophie als Lehre vom glücklichen Leben', in *Philosophische Essays*, 90.

[69] *Happiness and Benevolence*, 104 (*Glück und Wohlwollen*, 138).

[70] 'Über den Begriff einer Natur des Menschen', in *Essays zur Anthropologie*, 19.

[71] *Basic Moral Concepts*, 23 (*Moralische Grundbegriffe*, 35). For Spaemann's understanding of education see the following essays in his *Grenzen*: 'Emanzipation—ein Bildungsziel?'; 'Über den Mut zur Erziehung'; and 'Erziehung zur Wirklichkeit: Rede zum Jubiläum eines Kinderhauses'. For his critique of modern theories of education see also 'Was ist das Neue? Vom Ende des modernen Bewusstseins', in *Die politische Meinung*, 203 (July/Aug. 1982), 15ff.

[72] For the emotional dimension of our experience of reality see the interesting essay by Hinderk M. Emrich, 'Das Gefühlhafte der Wirklichkeitserfahrung', in Thomas Buchheim, Rolf Schönberger, and Walter Schweidler (eds.), *Die Normativität des Wirklichen: Über die Grenze zwischen Sein und Sollen* (Stuttgart: Klett-Cotta, 2002), 173–89.

Spaemann's reappraisal of metaphysical realism thus has a certain thrust that is directed against distinct features of modern thinking. Spaemann holds that there are substances that are the very presuppositions for human consciousness, freedom, love, and justice. Reality is for him not ultimately 'grounded' in an unsubstantial flux of becoming and ceasing to be. Nietzsche's analysis of the highest will to power as 'stamping the character of Being with becoming'[73] reflects both the spirit of modernity and modernity's failure and self-contradictory character, Spaemann thinks—to which he opposes his metaphysical realism. He therefore develops his 'substantialist' point of view over against the 'de-substantializing' enterprise of modern idealist and post-idealist philosophy and also against the tendency of evolutionary metaphysics to make becoming an absolute. It is in Spaemann's view therefore infeasible to provide a comprehensive genealogical account of reality as attempted, for instance, by Fichte, who, on Spaemann's analysis, aimed to provide a genealogical account of all natural evidence, or by Niklas Luhmann, who intended, in Spaemann's view, to integrate all of reality into the framework of functional processes.[74]

Utilitarian ethics in particular is intimately tied up with a functionalistic and genealogical ontology. Within a utilitarian framework the notions 'good' and 'evil', and even ethics as such, are defined in terms of functional relations. Thus, the idea of actions that are *intrinsice malum*—and not merely evil with respect to an end to which one may or may not subscribe—is no longer comprehensible. Ethics is thus ultimately transformed into a calculating technology, Spaemann maintains, much as ontology is transformed in modernity into a subjectivist idealism, into a subjectless nihilism, or into a sociological functionalism. While not overlooking the differences between each of these streams of modern and late modern thought, Spaemann discovers the same self-contradictory and nihilistic tendency at work in each. Idealist subjectivism, sociological functionalism, evolutionary metaphysics, the technological exploitation and manipulation of nature, and utilitarian ethics are ultimately rooted, according to Spaemann's argument, in a refusal of metaphysical realism. Therefore they also tend to turn against the self-experience of the human person, which, as has already been argued and will further be explained, presupposes such a metaphysical realism.

It would appear that Spaemann's critique of modern philosophy anticipates the approach of F. W. J. Schelling's later philosophy. Schelling argued, against what he called the negative philosophy of modernity, particularly Hegel's

---

[73] *Die Frage 'Wozu?'*, 204.

[74] Spaemann compares Luhmann's sociological functionalism and Fichte's idealist attempt to provide a genealogical account of all natural evidence in *Paradigm Lost*, 59.

idealist philosophy, that the historical gift of Being cannot be derived from mere operations of consciousness.[75] The actual gift of Being, as opposed to its mere logical possibility and necessity, can only be based upon the experience of it as given prior to any act of consciousness. Spaemann's philosophy is close to Schelling's thought; with implicit reference to Schelling's self-understanding as a 'higher empiricist', Spaemann calls Schelling's philosophy 'a kind of speculative empiricism'.[76] It is a 'higher' form of empiricism that does not presuppose a narrow notion of *empeiria* but a broad one that is reflective of a phenomenological notion of experience and of the endeavour to take into consideration not only the gift of Being as such, but, in so doing, also the contingent and the historical.

The modern universalism of reason, Spaemann consequently argues, 'will only survive if it understands itself as the opening of a field for the particular, for the historical'.[77] Spaemann thus describes phenomenologically and speculatively, as it were, what is already there—a given reality in its historical character. In doing so, he reconceptualizes the link between the 'objectivity' of Being and the 'subjectivity' of freedom over against one of the key presuppositions of modern philosophy: the distinction unto separation between the objective and the subjective. He thus remembers a much deeper and richer concept of 'objectivity' than the modern concept of it as entirely non-subjective. This is why, for Spaemann, 'immoral decisions' are not simply subjectively wrong, they are objectively wrong. They are, as he argues, 'tantamount to non-objective decisions, decisions which are not in accordance with the thing in question'.[78]

One of the main features of his philosophy is, therefore, not invention, not even discovery of *how* reality works, but remembering, recollection, or rediscovery of *what* reality essentially is. It is a kind of humble exercise in anamnesis, fighting, as Spaemann would hold, against the disturbance of memory characteristic of important strands of modernity and late modernity. This feature, however, does not limit one's freedom. On the contrary, it presupposes freedom: 'It is a free decision to treat the other as a real self, not a simulation'.[79] A deeper appreciation of reality, however, does not necessarily conform to the scientific ideal of ever-increasing understanding; but, Spaemann wonders, 'is not the intrinsic distinguishing mark of reason

---

[75] See e.g. *System der Weltalter: Münchener Vorlesung 1827/28 in einer Nachschrift von Ernst von Lasaulx*, ed. and introd. Siegbert Peetz, 2nd edn. (Frankfurt am Main: Klostermann, 1998), esp. 9 ff.

[76] 'Christentum und Philosophie der Neuzeit', in *Das unsterbliche Gerücht*, 86.

[77] 'Was ist das Neue?', 27.

[78] 'Die Herausforderung des ärztlichen Berufsethos', in *Grenzen*, 339.

[79] *Persons*, 77 (*Personen*, 87).

not to understand? The sleeping, dreaming, the fallen *Dasein* understands everything, but wrongly'.[80] The more fully one awakes towards reality, the more one realizes that reality is ultimately a mystery that cannot be fully be grasped.

Spaemann's defence of a counter-model for understanding reality therefore follows two paths: first, the path of the destruction, as it were, of the representation of Being as process, not only by means of a close historical analysis of how this representation of Being developed but also by shedding light on its implications, which are counter-intuitive in so far as they contradict the way human beings always already understand themselves; second, the path of the reconstruction of a realistic understanding of Being by means of a recollection of what Spaemann considers self-evident—that is, the experience that reality is ultimately not an endless stream of becoming, but a *mixtum compositum* of substantial Being and becoming. It is a reality of substances *and* subjects and, in its highest form, the reality of persons who freely 'have' their nature.

Persons are thus part of nature, they are *natural beings*, without being understandable from a merely naturalistic point of view. Naturalism, Spaemann makes compellingly clear, fails to understand reality adequately because it favours a dualistic, if not ultimately monistic, understanding of the relation between nature and freedom. Nature and freedom, however, are *related* to one another in a more complex way. There is neither an unbridgeable gap between nature and freedom, nor is one simply the function of the other.

An example may illustrate this. The person's free relation to his nature and to his natural drives may entail even overcoming his self-love and sacrificing the natural basis of his life in order to preserve his moral integrity. This cannot fully be explained on the basis of a materialistic monism (for it contradicts its presupposition that matter, its transformations, and its desire to preserve itself are all that is) or a mind-body dualism (for it contradicts the idea of a radical separation of mind and body). Self-sacrifice is an idea, Spaemann argues, that presupposes a metaphysical realism of the person as freely having his nature, if not even a Christian understanding of reality, which, he holds, puts the reality of sacrifice at the centre of its view of reality. In Spaemann's Christianly informed view, the world does not exist because of 'the survival of the survivors at the level of pure, digital code', as Richard Dawkins has argued.[81] It exists, on the contrary, 'because there is

---

[80] 'Zur Einführung: Philosophiegeschichte nach Heidegger', 5.
[81] Dawkins, Richard, *River out of Eden. A Darwinian View of Life* (London: Weidenfeld & Nicolson, 1995), 22.

the strange and forgotten sacrifice, of which and in which we all live'.[82] There is, Spaemann consequently underscores, 'nowhere a life without sacrifice'[83]: reality has a sacrificial structure. And it is a realist metaphysics that makes acts of self-transcendence conceivable. Furthermore, it is, according to Spaemann, Christianity that understands the 'self-sacrifice of the subject' as 'simultaneously the highest form of the realization of subjectivity'.[84]

Philosophy and recollection

Spaemann argues that it is 'the greatness of classical philosophy to realize a rationality which is not addicted to irrationality, a forgetfulness of its own natural and historical, that is non-rational, presuppositions'.[85] He reconnects himself to this tradition, such that his works can be read as extended 'essays in retrieval'. They thus echo Charles Taylor's philosophy,[86] alongside a great many other contemporary philosophers who challenge the modern tendency to make autonomous reason an absolute. In a constructive mode, philosophers such as Alasdair MacIntyre have expressed their interest in reasserting traditions of metaphysics and moral philosophy that have become questionable to many iconoclastic pioneers and fellow passengers of modernity. These traditions, MacIntyre and others argue, may well provide alternatives to the apparent shortcomings and failures of the modern understanding of reality and of the modern approach to moral reasoning. Spaemann shares MacIntyre's historical hypothesis about modernity and its ethics, as outlined in *After Virtue*; namely, that 'moral judgments are linguistic survivals from the practices of classical theism which have lost the context provided by these practices'.[87] MacIntyre has consequently stated that

---

[82] 'Vorbemerkungen', in *Einsprüche: Christliche Reden*, 12.

[83] 'Die Existenz des Priesters: Eine Provokation in der modernen Welt', in *Communio*, 9 (1980), 489.

[84] *Die Frage 'Wozu?'*, 109. Spaemann does not provide a systematic account of his philosophy, or of his theology, of sacrifice and its both ethical and ontological significance. See Gene Outka, *Agape: An Ethical Analysis* (New Haven, Conn./London: Yale University Press, 1972), 278–9 for a different ethical view that sees self-sacrifice as 'always . . . purposeful in promoting the welfare of others and never simply expressive of something resident in the agent. It is simply one possible exemplification and by-product of devotion to others for their own sake'. For a view similar to Spaemann's see John Paul II, *On the Relationship between Faith and Reason* (*Fides et Ratio*) (Washington, DC: United States Catholic Conference, 1998), 48, where the martyrs are called the 'most authentic witnesses to the truth about existence'.

[85] 'Die zwei Grundbegriffe der Moral', in *Grenzen*, 73.

[86] See Taylor, *Sources of the Self: The Making of the Modern Identity* (Cambridge: Cambridge University Press, 1998), 10.

[87] Alasdair MacIntryre, *After Virtue: A Study in Moral Theory* (London: Duckworth, 1985), 57.

modern utterance and practice can only be understood as a series of fragmented survivals from an older past and . . . the insoluble problems which they have generated for modern moral theorists will remain insoluble until this is well understood. If the deontological character of moral judgements is the ghost of conceptions of divine law which are quite alien to the metaphysics of modernity and if the teleological character is similarly the ghost of conceptions of human nature and activity which are equally not at home in the modern world, we should expect the problem of understanding and of assigning an intelligible status to moral judgements both continually to arise and as continually to prove inhospitable to philosophical solutions.[88]

In a similar way, Spaemann points out that many categorical prohibitions have already been forgotten and dismissed or are to be interpreted as what MacIntyre calls 'fragmented survivals from an older past'. MacIntyre has supposed that a justification of traditional categorical prohibitions might become impossible if a culture can no longer sufficiently reinterpret it.[89] Spaemann would agree and has set himself the task of reinterpreting and reasserting a traditional and, in his eyes, self-evident view of reality which philosophy ought to recollect and to keep alive, rather than fashioning new moralities which tend to involve philosophy in self-contradictions and insoluble problems.

What, then, does Spaemann mean by calling philosophy a 'recollection', and what are the implications of this definition? First, in this definition Spaemann reassesses the continuity of philosophy and its tradition. This is why Spaemann engages in a conversation with the classical philosophical tradition and re-evaluates its philosophical positions. The views of earlier philosophers are not negligible steps towards philosophy's current state. Philosophy, he argues, cannot understand its history by analogy with scientific paradigm shifts.[90] Philosophy is not a progressive accumulation of knowledge, it is 'immediately practical for the philosopher because philosophy is a *bios*, a *way of life*'.[91] And it is, Spaemann thinks, a way of life that has not changed as considerably since the beginning of Western philosophy as some modern and late modern philosophers have suggested. Hence, philosophy, practised properly, in Spaemann's view, evades the modern logic of historical development and progress, for it recalls a 'past knowledge'. It is 'essentially retrospective, if it does not want to become an ideology through pretending to show ways into the future'.[92] Arguing that philosophy is

---

[88] Ibid. 104–5.
[89] Ibid. 106.
[90] 'Die kontroverse Natur der Philosophie', in *Philosophische Essays*, 113.
[91] 'Wie praktisch ist die Ethik?', in *Grenzen*, 31.
[92] 'Die zwei Grundbegriffe der Moral', in *Grenzen*, 79.

essentially a recollection is not a naive restorative traditionalism pursued for its own sake. Rather, such an argument takes seriously that philosophy properly understood challenges our common modern notion of progress, history, and tradition. Recollection, moreover, makes progress possible in the first place, 'for progress depends essentially on our not forgetting what we have once already known'.[93]

Second, this definition also reassesses human culture and its continuity. At the beginning of *Happiness and Benevolence* Spaemann, as we have already pointed out, expresses his hope 'that these thoughts on ethics contain nothing fundamentally new'. He defends this lack of innovation with reference to human culture. 'The challenge which ethical reflection presents remains fundamentally unchanged since the fifth century BC. This gives us grounds for speaking of an anthropological constant, at least a constant in all developed cultures.'[94] So the challenges to which philosophy has to respond are characterized by continuity over time. However, it is not only the challenges with which human beings have to deal that remain essentially the same. The basic answers also remain the same. Descartes's standpoint 'that it was necessary, once in the course of my life, to demolish everything completely and start again right from the foundations if I wanted to establish anything at all in the sciences that was stable and likely to last'[95] is highly questionable, in Spaemann's eyes. It disregards the fundamental continuity of philosophy, human culture, and human nature.

This brings us to the third dimension of Spaemann's definition of philosophy as recollection. His conception of philosophy retrieves human nature, its continuity, and its teleology, and therefore also the concept of natural law. Spaemann often defines the self-evident as a past knowledge that we have forgotten; philosophy, therefore, has 'to remind us of something we already knew'.[96] The self-evident is internal knowledge that we have already had and that we may, or may not, remember, depending upon our cultural, historical, and social standpoint. What does this mean?

---

[93] 'Emanzipation—ein Bildungsziel', in *Grenzen*, 489.

[94] *Happiness and Benevolence*, vii (*Glück und Wohlwollen*, 9). For this claim and for Spaemann's understanding of philosophy see also Richard Schenk, OP, 'The Ethics of Robert Spaemann in the Context of Recent Philosophy', in Brian J. Shanley, OP (ed.), *One Years of Philosophy* (Studies in Philosophy and the History of Philosophy, xxxvi) (Washington, DC: The Catholic University of America Press, 2001), 156–7.

[95] René Descartes, *Meditations on First Philosophy*, in *The Philosophical Writings of Descartes*, trans. John Cottingham, Robert Stoothoff, and Dugald Murdoch, II (Cambridge: Cambridge University Press, 1984), 12.

[96] *Basic Moral Concepts*, 13 (*Moralische Grundbegriffe*, 24).

To define philosophy as recollection also means to take into serious consideration what C. S. Lewis calls the 'old "natural" *Tao*.'[97] This 'Tao' is not the product of humanity's design and making. It implies a teleological, that is to say normative, notion of nature that limits human autonomy because it is the 'natural presupposition of human existence'.[98] Gilbert Meilaender has described well what Lewis means by 'Tao':

> The Tao contains principles which must inevitably enter into any moral argument. Such principles are (1) the law of general beneficence (i.e., that we try to avoid harming others and seek to help them); (2) the law of special beneficence (i.e., special concern for those who have claims of kinship upon us); (3) duties to parents, elders, and ancestors; (4) duties to children and posterity; (5) the law of justice; (6) the law of good faith and veracity; (7) the law of mercy; (8) the law of magnanimity (i.e., willingness to expend oneself in service of the good).[99]

The Tao is, according to Lewis, within human beings even though it is often covered up by 'artificial' Taos. In the preface to the *Philosophische Essays* Spaemann explicitly mentions the Tao as 'the *nomos* of human beings' and thus implicitly refers to Lewis's idea of the Tao as a natural principle, or law, according to which human actions need to be evaluated.[100]

Spaemann points out that during the Nazi period some doctors did not accept the societal consensus as the criterion of their action, but rather held themselves to precepts, or laws, 'which are established in the "unpreconceivable" [*unvordenklich*]'.[101] This 'unpreconceivable' natural law, as Spaemann's use of the Schellingian notion *unvordenklich* implies, cannot be preconceived, that is to say derived in an a priori way, by means of a philosophy of mere consciousness. It is always presupposed in the exercise both of our freedom and of our consciousness and needs to be recollected freely. We cannot 'get behind' it or imagine the world without it.

Spaemann's recollection of natural law as an immediate measure of human action shows clearly how philosophy as recollection is a counter-model to the modern understanding of philosophy as genealogical critique of given norms and as autonomous invention of new ones. His philosophy, therefore, is a defence of immediacy over against the preoccupation with mediated knowledge as well as with the mediation of knowledge. Philosophy, as he understands

---

[97] *The Abolition of Man, or Reflections on Education with Special Reference to the Teaching of English in the Upper Forms of Schools* (Glasgow: Collins, 1982), 38.

[98] Spaemann, 'Natur', in *Philosophische Essays*, 37.

[99] *The Taste for the Other: The Social and Ethical Thought of C. S. Lewis* (Grand Rapids, Mich.: Eerdmans, 1998), 189 ff.

[100] 'Einleitung', in *Philosophische Essays*, 6.

[101] 'Die Herausforderung des ärztlichen Berufsethos', in *Grenzen*, 337.

it, 'insists indeed on a kind of immediacy, which is an anachronism in the modern world'.[102] Philosophy is, as Spaemann accordingly argues, an 'after-thought'; it is *Nach-denken*.[103] Like his teacher Joachim Ritter and his fellow disciples Hermann Lübbe and Odo Marquard, Spaemann rejects the ideological transformation of philosophy into quasi-scientific futurology, into prophetical Utopianisms, or into a social technique of first conceptualizing and then realizing an ideal future society. In Spaemann's view, philosophers mainly think about what is intuitive and immediate knowledge. They must not, and cannot, prophesy about the future, but should limit themselves to exploring the conditions of true humanity. Like Plato and Aristotle, and their followers over the ages, Spaemann aims at 'rescuing the phenomena'. Those 'phenomena', however, are already immediately there; they need not, and cannot, be made up. Philosophy, he states, 'tries to say what is'.[104] As such, it is mainly concerned with praxis, not with poiesis. For it is a praxis itself that needs to be distinguished from politics, technology, and the sciences. These remarks upon the 'non-political' and non-Utopian character[105] of philosophy lead us to consider another important implication of Spaemann's definition of philosophy as recollection. This definition is distinctly anti-historicist.

Recollection versus historicism

We have seen that Spaemann's idea that philosophy is a recollection of what is self-evident entails continuity in three different yet closely related senses: first, the continuity of philosophy and its tradition; second, the continuity of the challenges to which human beings need to react and of the answers that have been, and can be, provided; and third, therefore, the continuity of human nature and the natural law. This is why Spaemann specifies, as we will see as our argument progresses, that recollection essentially means to remember nature freely and to perceive it and its teleological structure sympathetically, as he puts it. Human beings need to remember freely what is not the 'product'

---

[102] 'Philosophie als institutionalisierte Naivität', in *Philosophisches Jahrbuch*, 81 (1974), 141. Spaemann's defence of immediacy is reminiscent of Fénelon's defence of spontaneity and his critique of reflection; for this and the connection between reflection and the fall, see esp. *Reflexion und Spontaneität*, 125 ff.

[103] For the difference between philosophy and the arts see *Persons*, 89–90 (*Personen*, 99); see also 'Was ist das Neue?', 11.

[104] 'Einleitung', in *Kritik der politischen Utopie*, xii.

[105] See Hans Jonas, *The Imperative of Responsibility: In Search of an Ethics for the Technological Age*, trans. Jonas with David Ferr (Chicago, Ill.: University of Chicago Press, 1984), for another important examination of the non-Utopian character of philosophy that shows important parallels to Spaemann's philosophy.

of their freedom—the natural conditions of freedom. Otherwise, Spaemann argues, freedom turns into mere nature: 'Only if we remember nature as it is will we go beyond nature'.[106] The recollection of this teleological view of nature also has implications for our conception of history and its development and continuity, as did modernity's transformation of the understanding of nature.

The dismissal of a teleological view of nature is closely related to what Oliver O'Donovan has called the 'turn of modern thought towards what is usually called "historicism"'.[107] He describes the 'heart of historicism . . . in the thesis that all teleology is historical teleology. The concept of an "end", it is held, is essentially a concept of development in time. Nothing can have a "point," unless it is a historical point; there is no point in the regularities of nature as such'.[108] George Grant has also shown why the dismissal of natural teleology is closely related to the rise of modern historicism. Because of the morally indifferent character of a non-teleological notion of nature, it is thought that

[o]ur will alone is able, through doing, to actualise moral good in the indifferent world. It is here that history as a dimension of reality, distinguished from nature, comes to be thought. History [for modernity] is that dimension in which men in their freedom have tried to 'create' greater and greater goodness in the morally indifferent world they inhabit.[109]

So historicism, that is to say the idea of history as opposed to nature and as an absolute progress, and the interpretation of nature as mere and directionless, that is to say non-teleological matter, are linked with one another. Historicism, or what Spaemann calls 'spiritualism', and naturalism, one can argue, are the extensions of the Cartesian dualism of *res cogitans* and *res extensa*, of history-determining subjectivity and mere matter-of-fact objectivity.[110] Yet history and nature are, in Spaemann's view, *not* incommensurable and must not be polarized in a dualistic way. History, particularly the history of philosophy, can, Spaemann therefore argues, be substituted neither for morality nor for nature as the teleological norm of human action and human perfection. Spaemann's philosophy thus has an anti-historicist thrust and is directed against any view of history as substantial progress towards the

---

[106] 'Natur', in *Philosophische Essays*, 36.
[107] *Resurrection and Moral Order: An Outline for Evangelical Ethics* (Grand Rapids, Mich.: Eerdmans, 1986), 58.
[108] Ibid.
[109] *Time as History* (Toronto: Canadian Broadcasting Corporation, 1969), 17.
[110] For Spaemann's interpretation of modernity as being subject to the dialectic of 'spiritualism' and naturalism see also *Happiness and Benevolence*, 161–2 (*Glück und Wohlwollen*, 209).

perfection of humanity, such as is expressed, for instance, by Richard Dawkins when he argues that '[w]e have so far scarcely taken the first step outward. We have been to the moon but, magnificent as this achievement is, the moon, though no calabash, is so local as scarcely to count as travelling, from the point of view of the aliens with whom we might eventually communicate'.[111] Spaemann criticizes the historicist idea that history develops progressively and is an emancipation *from* nature (rather than a finding home *in* nature as the friendly place where we always already live) so that earlier stages are, at best, 'sublated' (*aufgehoben*), and integrated into subsequent phases. He would share C. S. Lewis's view that '[i]n reality we have not advanced one step';[112] that is, there has been no absolute substantial progress, but only progress in certain areas.

Modern historicism, however, focuses upon the development and absolute progress of history. Hegel, one of the most prominent and yet most ambiguous exponents of this view, argued that the 'substance of the individual, the World-Spirit itself, has had the patience to pass through these shapes over the long passage of time, and to take upon itself the enormous labour of world-history'.[113] From this point of view, history is construed with respect to the anticipated conclusion of the history of philosophy that ultimately implies the end of history.[114] Yet in developing this view of history historicism ironically tends to eradicate history. That is, it fails to understand that the historical is contingent: neither predetermined by the laws of progress nor utterly random. Over against this flawed understanding of history, Spaemann recalls that humanity is not entirely subject to historical development, however this is conceived. This is why over the course of history, he thinks, simultaneity and understanding between people from different historical epochs is possible. Otherwise, he convincingly makes clear, there would not be a measure according to which one could speak of development. For, in Spaemann's view, an absolute notion of development or progress leaves nothing behind that could develop. Spaemann thus reacts against Hegelian teleological historicism, but also against the post-Nietzschean radical historicization of reality and the dismissal of a normative notion of nature. Over against these tendencies, he recollects a view of nature within which history and freedom as

---

[111] *River out of Eden*, 186.

[112] *The Abolition of Man*, 24.

[113] *Phenomenology of Spirit*, trans. A. V. Miller (Oxford: Oxford University Press, 1979), 17. For Hegel's understanding of history see also J. C. Flay, 'The History of Philosophy and the Phenomenology of Spirit', in *Hegel and the History of Philosophy*, ed. Joseph J. O'Malley, Keith W. Algozin, and Frederick G. Weiss (The Hague: Nijhoff, 1974), 47–61.

[114] For a contemporary revival of this idea see Francis Fukuyama, *The End of History and the Last Man* (New York: Maxwell Macmillan, 1992).

well as what he calls 'accidental progress'—that is, relative progress in certain areas such as the sciences or medicine—can adequately be conceived. Therefore Spaemann's anti-historicist recollection does not revive past ideas at the cost of present and future, nor is progress made utterly impossible or inconceivable. The opposite is the case, because for Spaemann, as we have already seen, progress depends essentially upon the fact that we do not simply forget what we have already known.[115] Recollection therefore makes innovation and progress viable and prevents it from becoming sterile and, in the end, from establishing a totalitarian reign of terror. 'Moral reason only exists as recollected nature. It sets limits to the nature-grown [*naturwüchsig*] making'.[116]

While Martin Heidegger, in Spaemann's view, dissolved the difference between historical and systematic philosophy by radically historicizing philosophy in his being-historical thinking,[117] Spaemann maintains this difference in that he engages in a Socratic conversation with main figures, that is main stages, of the history of philosophy as if they were contemporaries, without denying the historical gap and the discontinuities that separate him from earlier stages in the history of philosophy.

It is unsurprising that Spaemann's anti-historicist view also contradicts the 'pseudo-teleology' of Pierre Teilhard de Chardin's Christian appropriation of modern Enlightenment historicism,[118] which subjects nature to the philosophy and theology of history. In contrast to this, Spaemann aims at outlining a philosophy that does justice to nature in its own right and recalls the view of a non-reductionistic and non-dualistic, that is a complementary, relation between freedom and nature. For neither historicism nor naturalism (and also not the theologization of nature and history) proves capable of doing justice to what history and nature essentially are.

It is important to emphasize once again that Spaemann does not see a way of leaving behind what has already happened. The past necessarily provides

[115] 'Emanzipation—ein Bildungsziel?', in *Grenzen*, 489.

[116] 'Vorwort', in *Grenzen*, 11.

[117] For Spaemann's view of Heidegger's phenomenological understanding of historical and systematic knowledge see 'Zur Einführung: Philosophiegeschichte nach Martin Heidegger', esp. 2 ff.

[118] For Spaemann's brief critique of Teilhard de Chardin see 'Sein und Gewordensein: Was erklärt die Evolutionstheorie?', in *Philosophische Essays*, 202. Spaemann mainly criticizes Carsten Bresch, who adopted Teilhard's thought most prominently in *Zwischenstufe Leben: Evolution ohne Ziel?* (Frankfurt am Main: Fischer, 1979). For a discussion of Spaemann's, Löw's, and Bresch's natural philosophies see Rainer Isak, *Evolution ohne Ziel? Ein interdisziplinärer Forschungsbeitrag* (Freiburg im Breisgau: Herder, 1992). For a critical engagement with Teilhard de Chardin from a point of view similar to Robert Spaemann's see also Jacques Maritain, *The Peasant of the Garonne: An Old Layman Questions Himself about the Present Time* (London/Dublin: Chapman, 1968), 116–26.

the basis of what is yet to happen. This view of history indicates particularly the modernity of Spaemann's thought, since Spaemann acknowledges that modernity must be understood as the epoch that necessarily informs our own standpoint and the means of formulating an answer to the problems before us, even the problems that modernity itself has provoked. Because modernity is, in Spaemann's view, a historically unique and irreversible event,[119] a Romantic retrieval of times past is out of the question. We cannot, for instance, go back to what Spaemann considers the 'oldest European notion of freedom . . . to live in a familiar way';[120] nor, as we will see, can we go back to a political theology that does not maintain the difference between the private and the public.

How then is the rise of modernity to be understood adequately? Much like Louis Dupré, Robert Spaemann attributes the rise of modernity to important paradigm shifts in late medieval nominalist philosophy, and considers the impact of modern cultural changes to be definitive and irreversible. This is the very reason why going behind modernity in order to re-establish what one might call an ancient or medieval point of view seems to Spaemann as well as to Dupré an impossible and self-deceptive Romanticism. Nonetheless, Spaemann does not subscribe to Dupré's epochalization and temporalization of Being in the wake of Heidegger's later philosophy. He would not go so far as Dupré, who argued that '[c]ultural changes, such as the one that gave birth to the modern age, have a definitive and irreversible impact that transforms the very essence of reality'.[121]

Spaemann would modify Dupré's interpretation of modernity as an event 'that has transformed the relation between the cosmos, its transcendent source, and its human interpreter'.[122] Spaemann takes history and the history-bound disclosure of Being seriously. And yet he resists subjecting Being to history by means of a relativizing radicalization of modern historicism. Dupré, one may argue from a Spaemannian point of view, is still a transitional figure and hesitates to draw out the implications of his account of the rise of modernity. What is self-evident, according to Spaemann's fundamental argument against any kind of historicism, is not subject to historical development. The presence of the Tao calls into question the modern preoccupation with history either as progressive development, as a random chain of events, or as a

---

[119] 'Ende der Modernität?', in *Philosophische Essays*, 237.

[120] 'Emanzipation—ein Bildungsziel?', in *Grenzen*, 480–1.

[121] *Passage to Modernity: An Essay in the Hermeneutics of Nature and Culture* (New Haven, Conn./London: Yale University Press, 1993), 6.

[122] Ibid. 249.

chain of historical paradigms of Being, because the Tao underlies the whole of history and makes history, properly understood, possible.

At this point we need to scrutinize more closely what, according to Spaemann, the self-evident is. Does he leave his readers with a kind of empty formula or does he indicate concretely what he means by 'self-evident'? We will, therefore, now briefly discuss an example of self-evident knowledge. We will then introduce Spaemann's idea that philosophy is primarily the recollection of nature, and examine Spaemann's critique of the predominant role played by experts in a utilitarian and scientific culture, before we go on to consider what he means by calling philosophy a continuous conversation about ultimate questions.

Philosophy and the 'self-evident'

What is self-evident ultimately cannot be proved. The self-evident is the foundation because of which proofs make any sense at all. As C. S. Lewis neatly put it, self-evident principles are unprovable not 'because they are irrational but because they are self-evident and all proofs depend on them. Their intrinsic reasonableness shines by its own light'.[123] The recollection of the self-evident as something that cannot be proved thus has its own difficulties. Spaemann argues that 'the reflection upon the necessity of the self-evident, the reflecting restoration of immediacy, is itself not self-evident, but a controversial position'.[124] Once we start to reflect upon immediate self-evident knowledge, our knowledge is no longer self-evident, but subject to controversial discussion and criticism. This problem, however, does not absolve us from considering, and reflecting upon, our self-evident knowledge.

The eclipse of what is self-evident is, in Spaemann's view, the main problem that philosophy has to face in a culture that can well be described as amnestic. Spaemann's defence of the notion 'person' and of the inalienable dignity of all human beings as self-evident, for instance, is a response to the forgetfulness of self-evident truths in, for instance, analytical and utilitarian accounts of

---

[123] *Miracles: A Preliminary Study* (New York: Macmillan, 1947), 44. For a similar justification of his argument (and a dismissal of any claim to be original that is reminiscent of Spaemann's philosophical self-understanding) see Finnis, *Natural Law and Natural Rights*, vi: 'My arguments, then, stand or fall by their own reasonableness or otherwise. But that is not to say there is much that is original in them'.

[124] 'Die kontroverse Natur der Philosophie', in *Philosophische Essays*, 116. For Spaemann's understanding of the controversial nature of philosophy see also 'Der Streit der Philosophen', in Hermann Lübbe (ed.), *Wozu Philosophie? Stellungnahmen eines Arbeitskreises* (Berlin/New York: de Gruyter, 1978), 91–106. For a discussion of this volume and of Spaemann's essay see Lewis E. Hahn's book review in *Contemporary German Philosophy*, 4 (1980), 320–6, esp. 322–3.

personhood such as Derek Parfit's *Reasons and Persons*[125] and Peter Singer's *Practical Ethics*.[126] At this point in our argument it is helpful to contrast Spaemann's notion of philosophy as a recollecting of the self-evidence of the dignity of the human person with the innovative style of Parfit's and Singer's thought. We will not yet engage in a detailed discussion of their philosophies, but will only examine how they interpret philosophy and its impetus and thus come to a more detailed understanding of the self-evident and of its recollection.

According to Peter Singer's optimistic view of an entirely secular future, 'the development of non-religious ethical thinking is still in its infancy. We are only now breaking with a past in which religion and ethics have been closely identified'.[127] This position leads Derek Parfit to the conclusion that 'since we cannot know how Ethics will develop, it is not irrational to have high hopes'.[128] Whatever the validity of his claim that religion and ethics have been too closely identified, Singer's suggestion to break with the past is revealing. Singer disconnects from the tradition, interrupts the continuous conversation of philosophy, and inaugurates a new scientific philosophy that refrains, as Spaemann's thought shows, from thinking what we have once known. Because he thus dismisses a common ethos, he is one of those 'mere philosophers' who, as Spaemann argues, 'can, as elevated intellectuals, be extremely dangerous'.[129] This danger is particularly evident in Singer's enterprise to adopt what is in fact a fictitious point of view, that is to say an abstract view of the universe, in order to 'make the world a better place'.[130] It is important to note how philosophy is inevitably transformed in this enterprise: it becomes an instrument of autonomously fabricated ideas (such as political ideas); it loses its connection to its own tradition; and it no longer relies on the self-evidence of, for instance, the sanctity of life as the 'presupposition of humanity'.[131]

It is apparent that Spaemann's view of philosophy as a recollection of self-evident knowledge is strongly at odds with Parfit's and Singer's notions of

---

[125] Parfit, *Reasons and Persons*, 2nd edn. (Oxford: Clarendon, 1987).

[126] Singer, *Practical Ethics* (Cambridge: Cambridge University Press, 1993). Spaemann explicitly refers to Parfit and Singer in the introduction to *Persons* (2–3; *Personen*, 10–11); for his critique of 'applied' or 'practical' ethics see his 'Wie praktisch ist die Ethik?', in *Grenzen*, 33.

[127] *How Are We to Live? Ethics in an Age of Self-interest* (Oxford: Oxford University Press, 1997), 15.

[128] *Reasons and Persons*, 454.

[129] 'Wie praktisch ist die Ethik?', in *Grenzen*, 35.

[130] Singer, *How Are We to Live?*, 235.

[131] Spaemann, 'Geleitwort', in Till Bastian (ed.), *Denken—schreiben—töten: Zur neuen 'Euthanasie'-Diskussion und zur Philosophie Peter Singers* (Stuttgart: Wissenschaftliche Verlagsgesellschaft, 1990), 8.

philosophy and its future. In his brief sketch of L. G. A. de Bonald's life Spaemann states almost in passing that Bonald 'took responsibility for a limited area within the framework of a firm—or seemingly firm—order'.[132] This statement about Bonald is an important key to understanding Spaemann's criticism of utilitarian ethics (such as Singer's) and of its disrespect for self-evident morality and moral limits. It shows Spaemann's alternative to an abstractly universalized and thus inevitably hypothesized notion of responsibility. It is the model of a firmly rooted, limited, and contextual responsibility that is not concerned with the idealized future of humanity as such or the overall maximization of happiness, but simply explicates a normative and self-evident order by which human beings have always lived. Bonald, Spaemann points out, only became involved in philosophy when he realized that, because of the political and historical circumstances of his time, he would no longer be able to live his life according to the meaning he wished to affirm. According to Spaemann, philosophy properly serves to recall an immediate and self-evident knowledge whenever social practice ceases to be aware of it, and it also ought to serve to resist the invention of utterly new norms and the utilitarian universalization of responsibility that no longer takes account of the (self-evident) *ordo amoris*—the order of particular responsibilities, for instance.[133] Ethics thus recalls, and justifies, a moral order that has been and still is accepted but no longer makes sense to major currents in our modern culture. Ethics, like philosophy, is, as we have already pointed out, properly an afterthought (*Nach-denken*). It is a 'return to normality, that is to the *conditio humana*',[134] as it freely remembers, Spaemann argues, the given but not fashioned self-evident and acknowledges its reliance upon what is already there and cannot be derived autonomously.

The limitation of the autonomy of consciousness, and the recollection of what is always already there—not only nature, but also history, the other human being, and the absolute as the self-evident horizon of human life—is one of the fundamental features of Spaemann's thought. In its emphasis upon the self-evident, Spaemann's philosophy is particularly directed against the logicization of reality in the wake of Hegel's comprehensive, though inevitably

[132] *Der Ursprung der Soziologie aus dem Geist der Restauration*, 15.
[133] For the idea of an *ordo amoris* and its personalist dimension see also Max Scheler, 'Ordo Amoris', in *Schriften aus dem Nachlass, i. Zur Ethik und Erkenntnislehre* (Bern: Francke, 1957), 345–76; Dietrich von Hildebrand, *Das Wesen der Liebe* (*Gesammelte Werke*, iii, ed. the Dietrich von Hildebrand Legacy Project) (Regensburg: Habbel, 1971), 457–85; Spaemann, *Happiness and Benevolence*, 106–18 (*Glück und Wohlwollen*, 141–56); for the impact of modern civilization on the understanding of the *ordo amoris* see Spaemann, *Happiness and Benevolence*, 123 (*Glück und Wohlwollen*, 162–3).
[134] 'Vorwort', in *Grenzen*, 10.

merely logical, system of reality.[135] It is important to note at this point that utilitarian scientism currently continues the spirit of the Hegelian endeavour most prominently. Singer and Parfit continue the project of the counter-intuitive 'derealization' of reality for two main reasons that we mention here without going into any detail. First, they fail fully to understand that persons are always already there as actual persons because there is no transition from potential to actual persons.[136] Philosophy does not, and cannot, declare human beings to be persons. It has to recognize them because they are already persons.[137] This is why the fact that a person is a person does not depend upon the philosopher's insight and argumentation: personhood is an 'unpreconceivably' given reality. The status of a person, he argues, is 'the only status, indeed, that we do not confer, but acquire naturally [*natürlicherweise*]'.[138] This is why the person *always already* has a particular dignity in Spaemann's view. But what is meant when we speak of dignity? For Spaemann, dignity manifests itself in the possibility of acts of self-transcendence (that is to say, actual dignity is not dependent on such acts): 'the capacity to see oneself from outside, to relativize one's own position with respect to a position which transcends oneself... this is what we call human dignity'.[139] However, Singer's and Parfit's refusal to subscribe to the idea that 'it is crucially important that subjects are thought of as substances'[140] and their denial of personal identity and of the dignity of all human beings are rooted in the attempt to render becoming, as opposed to Being, an absolute. But once becoming has been made the paradigm for our understanding of reality, self-transcendence (and thus the idea that all human beings have the same human dignity) becomes impossible, strictly speaking, for there is only 'self-development' and 'self-change'. This 'unrealistic' understanding of reality as absolute process, however, contradicts, as we will see, what is self-evident and what is also always already presupposed by this (mis-)understanding of reality.

Second, Parfit's and Singer's philosophies of personhood, as we have already pointed out, are embedded in a historicist conception of the development of humanity and particularly of ethics. Their account of the future does

---

[135] For Spaemann's critique of Hegel's logicization of reality see 'Christentum und Philosophie der Neuzeit', 134–5.

[136] *Persons*, 255–6 (*Personen*, 261–2).

[137] For the recognition of the person see also Charles Larmore, 'Person und Anerkennung', *Deutsche Zeitschrift für Philosophie*, 46 (1998), 459–64.

[138] *Persons*, 17 (*Personen*, 26).

[139] 'Tierschutz und Menschenwürde', in *Grenzen*, 471. For an examination of human dignity in the context of modernity see also Robert P. Kraynok and Glenn Tinder (eds.), *In Defense of Human Dignity: Essays for our Times* (Notre Dame, Ind.: University of Notre Dame Press, 2003).

[140] Spaemann, 'Sein und Gewordensein', in *Philosophische Essays*, 207.

not depend upon verifiable results, but upon mere speculations based on specific ideological presuppositions such as, first, a utilitarian underpinning of ethics and social sciences; second, a reinterpretation of philosophy and ethics as scientific and technical endeavour; and, third, the future- and poiesis-oriented focus of their thought. These presuppositions disregard and conceal, but do not abolish, the self-evident.

Parfit and Singer might rejoin that Spaemann's position that all human beings are persons simply because they are human beings—and not because they have certain characteristic traits such as memory and self-consciousness—betrays an illegitimate biologism. They might state that what Spaemann considers self-evident is far from being self-evident, and that Spaemann's focus upon the self-evident, like 'belief in God, or many gods, prevent[s] the free development of moral reasoning'.[141] This, however, is not the case.[142] As we will see, Spaemann himself challenges the notion of biologism and resists the accusation of a naturalistic fallacy because he remembers a teleological view of nature that questions the dichotomization of descriptive and evaluative language. The self-evident is, according to Spaemann, what is 'in the way of nature'. This, however, does not refer to mere nature as understood by the modern natural sciences. 'Nature as such', Spaemann agrees, 'has no normative significance for human beings'.[143] This is why philosophy remembers nature as the teleological norm and condition of the exercise of freedom, not nature as understood reductively by the sciences—that is, 'the natural as such'. This view of reality cannot ultimately be proved. However, as immediate knowledge it can hermeneutically be understood and thus requires a hermeneutics of nature that appeals to the interpreter's freedom and insight. And it is on the basis of such a hermeneutics that it becomes possible to show that not to understand nature teleologically leads to a reductive naturalization of reality and, therefore, to the 'abolition of man'—and of human freedom, dignity, happiness, and, ultimately, reality itself.

Philosophy as remembering nature

The complementary relation between nature and freedom

As we have seen, philosophy is, according to Spaemann, a reassertion of ideas that have already been thought. Wittgenstein, as Spaemann recalls, defined

---

[141] Parfit, *Reasons and Persons*, 454.

[142] For Spaemann's rejection of the accusation of biologism see also *Happiness and Benevolence*, 170 (*Glück und Wohlwollen*, 219–20).

[143] *Persons*, 96 (*Personen*, 105).

philosophy as 'the bringing together of memories for a certain purpose'.[144] At this point in our argument we have to ask once again and in a more specific way what exactly philosophy remembers. What is in an eminent sense the self-evident that we did once know and, strictly speaking, always already know though very often without being aware of it? Philosophy is, in Spaemann's view, primarily the free recollection of nature. Freedom and nature, he believes, are related to one another in such a way that freedom acknowledges as its own what is naturally right and self-evident. This is not a dialectical but a complementary relation. The free recollection of the self-evident is thus anti-dialectical and, in its focus upon freedom and nature in their concreteness, an implicit turn against key presumptions of modernity in so far as dialectic, in Spaemann's view (we will discuss this further in Ch. 3), characterizes a great deal of modern thinking, its abstractions, and its intrinsic shortcomings. This, he argues, has become evident in late modernity. Our time, he holds, 'makes the dialectic of modern abstractions visible, how they switch completely into their opposite without orientation'.[145]

Remembering nature, that is reading nature hermeneutically, as it were, does not mean discovering, or entail inventing, a purely external feature of human existence, for remembering nature means becoming aware of a presupposition of human life and and freedom beyond which we cannot go and without which reasonableness and freedom would inevitably become sterile or turn into mere nature. We can read and remember nature in such a way, Spaemann thinks, because nature has always already turned to us in a readable, that is understandable, way. In so doing, we fully exercise our reason. Spaemann goes so far as to argue that reasonability 'would be an empty word if nature did not turn towards us a readable face'.[146]

'Nature', of course, has been one of the most controversial philosophical notions since Western philosophy's origins in the pre-Socratic speculations about the true character of nature.[147] In modernity these controversies about 'nature' were even more dominant, for the modern emphasis upon instrumental reason and its world-dominating powers has tended to reduce nature to the raw material of scientific exploration and technological manipulation. Doubt has been cast on the idea of a teleologically ordered nature because an explanation of reality that does not proceed in terms of efficient causality

---

[144] 'Die kontroverse Natur der Philosophie', in *Philosophische Essays*, 108.

[145] 'Einleitung', in *Philosophische Essays*, 13.

[146] 'Vorwort', in *Essays zur Anthropologie*, 9; for nature as 'a book who runs may read' see also Spaemann, *Persons*, 98 (*Personen*, 107).

[147] For Spaemann's view of the notion 'nature' and its history see esp. 'Natur', in *Philosophische Essays*; 'Zur Vorgeschichte von Rousseaus Naturbegriff', in *Rousseau: Bürger ohne Vaterland*, esp. 57 ff.

alone does not support the possibility of unlimited manipulative interference with reality. With respect to this development of modern thinking Spaemann speaks of an 'inversion of teleology' in modernity.[148] By this he wants to imply that in modernity teleology has not simply been dismissed (as some scholars argue) but has rather been transformed. In summary terms, Spaemann interprets the modern preoccupation with either an abstract notion of self-preservation, as opposed to self-transcendence, or an abstract notion of self-transcendence, as opposed to self-preservation, as the result of an inversion process during which the unity of teleological drive and the underlying substance of this drive disintegrated.[149]

Naturalism is one of the key results of the 'inversion of teleology'. It approaches nature from an external and objectifying point of view and does not remember, but aims at finding, at discovering, and at inventing what is new and external to human reason. A naturalistic epistemology becomes, in Spaemann's eyes, problematic as soon as it is conceived of ideologically as the universally valid way of attaining reality. It tends to be conceived of this way, however, because the non-teleological account of nature, in Spaemann's view, has a 'latent function' which has become most evident in the rise of the interpretation of evolutionary theory as a new metaphysics. In his philosophy of nature Spaemann discloses these hidden functions and the implications of evolutionary metaphysics,[150] for instance, and recalls an alternative view of

---

[148] Spaemann first develops his theory of the 'inversion of teleology' in modernity in *Reflexion und Spontaneität*. In this book he examines Fénelon's thought in the context of the seventeenth-century controversy between Fénelon and Bossuet about whether all forms of love can be understood as functions of self-love. While Bossuet developed a view of love that is indebted to the modern retrieval of interest-focused eudaimonism (p. 103), Fénelon emphasized the significance of 'pure', that is to say disinterested, mystical, or selfless, love. Spaemann interprets this controversy as indicative of an 'inversion' of natural teleology that leads to the modern dialectic between the paradigm of self-preservation (Bossuet) and the paradigm of self-transcendence (Fénelon). Even though his reading of Fénelon is not without sympathy (he thinks, for instance, that Fénelon's theory is closer to Thomas Aquinas' genuine teleological understanding of love than the view of most modern theories (102–3)), Spaemann clearly distances himself from his position and reveals its problematic implications. Both French bishops, he shows, are Cartesians (107, 223) and argue on the basis of a non-teleological 'bourgeois ontology' (40–1, 124–5, and *passim*) that Spaemann criticized from his first emphasis on its implications onwards. His rehabilitation of benevolence, in *Happiness and Benevolence* for instance, is therefore also, as we will see further below, an attempt to retrieve an understanding of (benevolent) love that is not subject to the one-sidedness of both Fénelon's and Bossuet's positions and integrates reflection and spontaneity, mediation and immediacy. For a critique of Spaemann's view see esp. Hans Ebeling (ed.), *Subjektivität und Selbsterhaltung: Beiträge zur Diagnose der Moderne* (Frankfurt am Main: Suhrkamp, 1976).

[149] See esp. Spaemann's 'Naturteleologie und Handlung', in *Philosophische Essays*, 55 ff.; 'Zur Ontologie der Begriffe "rechts" und "links"', in *Grenzen*.

[150] For Spaemann's explicit critique of evolutionary epistemology see esp. 'Eine materialistische Erklärung des Gegensatzes von Idealismus und Materialismus? Kritik an der Selektion/

nature that does not dismiss evolutionary theory as a scientific theory, but only as a basis for a new metaphysics.

In reaction to the reductionistic understanding of nature fostered by modern evolutionary naturalism he has reconstructed the history of the dismissal of teleology, a history that provides the background for his defence of natural teleology[151] and for his understanding of reality. Over against the objectivism of modernity Spaemann proposes a person-centred view of reality according to which the particular can represent the universal and the subjective can help to understand the objective.

It is manifest to Spaemann that the crisis of modernity is the crisis of man's own self-understanding.[152] If, as Spaemann suggests, philosophy is 'the self-understanding of humanity within the whole of reality',[153] then the crisis of modernity is also quintessentially a crisis of philosophy[154] in the modern scientific age. And it is this crisis that Spaemann analyses and tries to overcome by reminding his readers of an older, yet not thereby less valid, view of what philosophy essentially is: a hermeneutics of nature as being analogous to ourselves and a hermeneutics of how we always already understand ourselves. Spaemann therefore argues that we can only fully understand nature by analogy to our own personal self-experience.[155] This is why he proposes a 'sympathetic perception of nature, the attempt somehow to understand nature as our equal'.[156] Nevertheless, this view of nature, as he concedes, 'has so far met predominantly with polite scepticism'.[157]

Die Leistungsgrenzen der evolutionären Erkenntnistheorie/Literatur', in Rupert Riedl and Franz M. Wuketits (eds.), *Die Evolutionäre Erkenntnistheorie: Bedingungen—Lösungen—Kontroversen* (Berlin/Hamburg: Parey, 1987), 178–83, esp. 181 ff.—a response to Robert Kaspar's essay 'Materialismus, Idealismus und Evolutionäre Erkenntnistheorie' published in the same volume (pp. 167–77).

[151] For an analysis of Spaemann's notion of teleology see Eduard Zwierlein, 'Das höchste Paradigma des Seienden: Anliegen und Probleme des Teleologiekonzeptes Robert Spaemanns', in *Zeitschrift für philosophische Forschung*, 41 (1987), 117–29; Ana Marta González, *Naturaleza y dignidad: Un estudio desde Robert Spaemann* (Colección filosifica, cv) (Pamplona: EUNSA, 1996), 85 ff.

[152] For, as Walker Percy asserts, man 'could not understand himself by the spirit of the age, which was informed by the spirit of abstraction' ('The Delta Factor', in *The Message in the Bottle: How Queer Man Is, How Queer Language Is, and What One Has to Do with the Other* (New York: Farrar, Strauss and Giroux, 1986), 26; for the 'spirit of abstraction' see also Lewis, *The Abolition of Man*, 45).

[153] *Die Frage 'Wozu?'*, 23.

[154] For Spaemann's understanding of the crisis of philosophy see also 'Philosophie zwischen Metaphysik und Geschichte'.

[155] 'Natur', in *Philosophische Essays*, 23; for the analogical understanding of being see also Spaemann, *Persons*, 67 ff. (*Personen*, 76 ff.).

[156] 'Naturteleologie und Handlung', in *Philosophische Essays*, 44.

[157] *Reflexion und Spontaneität*, 14.

Yet reductionistic methodologies, Spaemann argues, cannot but fail properly to understand freedom and nature (and their complementary relation)
precisely because they do not consider the paradigmatic character of personal
self-experience and of human action for the understanding of nature. They
make a 'sympathetic cognition of nature which represents the tendencies
which lie in nature itself'[158] impossible. They also have important implications that can now be fully disclosed. Let us briefly look at one of these
implications. To the extent that evolutionary metaphysics renders 'mere
nature' an absolute and not freedom's other, for example, nature is ultimately
transformed into an absolute process the 'natural substance' of which can no
longer be conceived of. Ultimately, there are no longer thinking subjects, but
only events of thinking. With respect to this transformation, Spaemann
argues that 'every speculative notion—if it loses the context in which it has
its natural place, if it loses the relation to its opposite notion—turns dialectical in itself'.[159] This is particularly true of the decontextualization, as it were,
of nature.

This dialectic of the abstract notion of nature (and also freedom) is typical
of modernity because the modern shift of the understanding of nature, as we
will see later in our argument, goes along with a misconception about, if not
even a dismissal of, the notion 'life'.[160] Modern post-Cartesian philosophy,
Spaemann holds, has shown itself incapable of conceptualizing the notion of
life as mediating between *res extensa* and *res cogitans*.[161] This led to the
modern dialectic of mind and matter that has significantly influenced the
trajectory of modern thought and its underlying dualisms. Nature and freedom, body and mind, subjectivity and objectivity, consciousness and matter,
theoretical and practical reason, ethics and ontology were subsequently radically opposed or subjected to one another, depending, of course, on one's
standpoint.

Spaemann's interpretation of modernity correspondingly analyses modern
philosophy as oscillating between freedom, or spirit, and nature. He draws
attention to the self-contradictory character of the modern dichotomy of
nature and freedom and shows why an absolute notion of freedom ultimately
turns against itself and makes freedom impossible, as does an absolute notion
of nature. If freedom does not recollect nature, freedom turns into something
merely natural. The difference between nature and freedom can no longer be

---

[158] 'Die Aktualität des Naturrechts', in *Philosophische Essays*, 67.

[159] 'Natur', in *Philosophische Essays*, 29.

[160] For Spaemann's interpretation of the modern dismissal of the notion 'life' see Ch. 5.

[161] For 'life' as mediation between the world of objects and human action see 'Naturteleologie und Handlung', in *Philosophische Essays*, 51.

grasped. Yet it is in the very limitation of freedom that, in Spaemann's view, the 'fundamental act of freedom . . . the act of "letting be", comes to be,[162] because, he holds, freedom is only possible as 'recollected nature'.[163] Nature and culture are therefore not opposed to one another (nor identical); 'culture is nature humanized, not abrogated'.[164] This understanding has considerable implications for our understanding of history, too. If history is not opposed to nature, but related to it as to the measure and norm of human action, then the state of nature does not need to be left behind, nor do we need to retrieve a supposedly lost state of nature, because we always already live in the state of nature, and this is what makes human life human.

We have already pointed out that Spaemann does not intend naively to restore a pre-modern point of view which condemns modernity altogether. He maintains that we cannot abolish the modern notion of the subject and the modern 'discovery' of freedom. This is why nature cannot, in his view, be the immediate measure for a positive definition of human happiness, for this would be the abolition of the modern connection between happiness and freedom.[165] It is important to see that Spaemann's philosophy of nature also stands in the tradition of modern transcendental philosophy in that he asks for the conditions of the possibility of freedom and of consciousness in a way that is, once again, reminiscent of Schelling.[166] Spaemann realizes, however, that the transcendental analysis of the conditions of the possibility of knowledge and freedom must not be limited to the analysis of the mere structures of consciousness. Consciousness, his argument goes, presupposes Being. Philosophy cannot but fail if it does not take nature into account as the precondition of freedom and consciousness.

What seems necessary to Spaemann is to rebind, though not to synthesize dialectically, the *disjecta membra* of nature and freedom. Human beings do not construct their nature. They 'have', as it were, their nature, and what they already have does not need to be made up nor can it be designed, but rather it

---

[162] 'Natur', in *Philosophische Essays*, 37.
[163] 'Die Aktualität des Naturrechts', in *Philosophische Essays*, 75.
[164] *Happiness and Benevolence*, 167 (*Glück und Wohlwollen*, 215).
[165] For this idea see 'Die Aktualität des Naturrechts', in *Philosophische Essays*, 73.
[166] For a treatment of Schelling's philosophy of nature and his transformation of transcendental philosophy see *Die Frage 'Wozu?'*, 152–61. There is also an interesting connection between Spaemann's, Hans Jonas's, and Alfred North Whitehead's respective understandings of nature. Unfortunately, the limits of this study preclude its further examination. For an important observation about the difference between Spaemann's and Jonas's philosophies see Schenk, 'The Ethics of Robert Spaemann in the Context of Recent Philosophy', 164. Spaemann, Schenk argues, can 'associate human beings with an even greater dignity' than Jonas, because he 'interprets the evolving cosmos from the analogy to the human, not the other way around', as does Jonas, on Schenk's account.

needs to be remembered. If they do not freely remember nature, human beings will, in Spaemann's view, inevitably fall back into mere nature.[167] Given this teleological and normative view of nature, it is not too difficult to understand why Spaemann also attempts to recollect the concept of natural law, once again in a way that tries to revitalize a 'past knowledge' without overlooking the challenges of modern thinking and its emphasis on freedom.

Spaemann's view of natural law

A distinct feature of the paradigmatic shift of modernity and its dismissal of a normative dimension of nature is the transformation of classical natural-law theories.[168] In modernity, Spaemann points out, 'the old natural-law doctrine which was based upon the notion of the *bonum commune* was edged out by a new, rationalistic, individualistic, and entirely non-historical natural law'.[169] Nature was objectified, but human beings increasingly ceased to regard nature as the normative presupposition of freedom, history, the communal life, and an open and 'old' rationality. Consequently, nature and law, and also descriptive scientific and evaluative moral language, were opposed to one another. At least initially, the material content of natural law, Spaemann forcefully argues, was not dismissed because it was interpreted as the 'law of reason'. Hence, according to Spaemann, natural law was dichotomized in modernity into the 'right of freedom' and 'natural law *in sensu stricto*'.[170] Within the subjectivist paradigm of modern philosophy of consciousness, he maintains, natural law could survive until the remains of pre-modern natural law were completely abolished and human subjectivity was integrated into a materialist theory, for instance. So in modernity natural ends were assimilated to man-made purposes.[171] Spaemann traces this development back to what he calls the

---

[167] 'Die Aktualität des Naturrechts', in *Philosophische Essays*, 75.

[168] For the contemporary discussion about natural law see Robert P. George, *Natural Law Theory: Contemporary Essays* (Oxford: Clarendon, 1992); Holger Zaborowski (ed.), *Natural Law in Contemporary Society* (Studies in Philosophy and the History of Philosophy) (Washington: Catholic University of America Press, 2010).

[169] '"Politik zuerst"? Das Schicksal der Action Française', in *Wort und Wahrheit*, 8 (1953), 657.

[170] 'Die Aktualität des Naturrechts', in *Philosophische Essays*, 75.

[171] For a brilliant critique of this tendency see also Francis Slade, 'Ends and Purposes', in Richard Hassing (ed.), *Final Causality in Nature and Human Affairs* (Studies in Philosophy and the History of Philosophy, xxx) (Washington, DC: The Catholic University of America Press, 2000), 83–5; 'On the Ontological Priority of Ends and its Relevance to the Narrative Arts', in Alice Ramos (ed.), *Beauty, Art, and the Polis* (Washington, DC: American Maritain Association, 2000), 58–69; see also Robert Sokolowski, 'What is Natural Law? Human Purposes and Natural Ends', in *Christian Faith and Understanding: Studies on the Eucharist, Trinity, and the Human Person* (Washington, DC: The Catholic University of America Press, 2006), 214–33. See in this

'bourgeois ethics' of the Stoics and their transformation of Aristotelian natural-law theories due to the 'loss of a concrete, historical, and political ethos'[172] that still characterized Aristotle's philosophy.

However, in defining natural law as the law of reason, modern philosophers succumbed to tautologies, as Spaemann points out, subjectifying the objective content of the old natural-law theories. Thus, the normative dimension of nature—that is to say, some knowable basic goods, that Spaemann finds not only in a 'natural right' (*von Natur Rechtes*)[173] but also, more specifically, in the 'pre-established harmony between the end of an action' such as eating and sexual intercourse and its objective 'systematic function'[174]—was increasingly lost sight of.[175] This, he argues, had very problematic implications.

In our time of crisis, Spaemann's argument consequently runs, natural law as the 'unpreconceivable' measure of human action needs to be recollected, unless we accept the reduction of the human being to the level of merely objective nature (which, of course, we cannot do unless we are willing seriously to misunderstand who we always already are). Spaemann concedes (in a way familiar to us by now) that any natural-law theory needs to take seriously the irreversible development of modern philosophy—in particular, its 'discovery' of freedom and subjectivity. Contemporary philosophy cannot so easily go back to an Aristotelian notion of natural law, as Joachim Ritter has suggested,[176] and ignore what happened in between. We can, however, still learn from Aristotle, and in order to learn from him, Spaemann argues, we have to acknowledge the differences between Aristotle's time and our own. These differences concern not only the modern inversion of teleology (which Spaemann thinks can and must be undone) but also the differentiation between public and private, which is, in his view, a necessary (and thus unrevisable) implication of Christianity (whereas the paradigm shift of modern ontology is, according to him, not).

context also the interesting considerations of Michael J. Sandel, *The Case against Perfection: Ethics in the Age of Genetic Engineering* (Cambridge, Mass.: Harvard University Press, 2007).

[172] 'Christliche Religion und Ethik', in *Einsprüche: Christliche Reden*, 55; see also 'Die Aktualität des Naturrechts', in *Philosophische Essays*, 69 ff.

[173] 'Die Aktualität des Naturrechts', in *Philosophische Essays*, 60–1.

[174] 'Funktionale Religionsbegründung und Religion', in *Philosophische Essays*, 210–11.

[175] For an interesting Protestant examination of this (Catholic) view of eating and human sexuality see Gilbert Meilaender, 'Sweet Necessities: Food, Sex, and Saint Augustine', in *Journal of Religious Ethics*, 29 (2001), 3–18.

[176] See esp. Joachim Ritter, 'Naturrecht bei Aristoteles', in *Metaphysik und Politik: Studien zu Aristoteles und Hegel* (Frankfurt am Main: Suhrkamp, 1969), 133–79, esp. 177 ff.

So, what does Spaemann mean by 'natural law'? Natural law, in his view, is not a mere 'occidental order of values', a 'system of values that underlies our constitution',[177] and a 'catalogue of norms, a kind of meta-constitution'.[178] It is, he argues, 'a way of thinking which critically reviews all legal legitimizations of action'.[179] The basis for this review is that 'freedom posits itself with respect to its natural conditions into an explicit relation that respects and controls nature'.[180] Natural law is therefore not only the Tao; that is, a concrete natural set of basic moral principles or goods that one needs to respect freely. It is also, as John Finnis has put it in a way that captures Spaemann's intention well, 'a set of basic methodological requirements of practical reasonableness (itself one of the forms of human flourishing) which distinguish sound from unsound practical thinking and which ... provide the criteria for distinguishing between acts that ... are reasonable-all-things-considered ... and acts that are unreasonable-all-things-considered'.[181]

Because he acknowledges natural teleology, Spaemann questions the post-Humean idea that there is no transition at all from 'is' to 'ought'. This marks one of the most significant differences between Spaemann's and Finnis's view of natural law.[182] There are, Spaemann maintains, not only man-made purposes, but also *natural* ends, and, therefore, a transition from 'is' to 'ought' is indeed not only possible but even mandatory. Yet it is modern reasoning that increasingly tended to overlook this, however counter-intuitive this may be.[183] In the following section we will therefore further examine the rise of the modern transformation of natural teleology.

---

[177] 'Die Aktualität des Naturrechts', in *Philosophische Essays*, 63.
[178] Ibid. 78.
[179] Ibid.
[180] Ibid. 75.
[181] *Natural Law and Natural Rights*, 23. Unfortunately, Spaemann does not provide a very detailed account of what he means by natural law. His notion of natural law, however, largely corresponds to the list provided by Finnis in *Natural Law and Natural Rights* (natural law as (i) a set of basic practical principles; (ii) a set of basic methodological requirements; (iii) a set of general moral standards (p. 23)).
[182] For a critique of Finnis's and Germain Grisez's natural-law theory see Ralph McInerny, *Ethica Thomistica: The Moral Philosophy of Thomas Aquinas* (Washington, DC: The Catholic University of America Press, 1982), 54–9. McInerny goes so far as to speak of 'the Humean view Grisez and Finnis seem to espouse' (p. 55). For a defence of Grisez's and Finnis's view (though an unconvincing one) see Robert P. George, 'Natural Law and Human Nature', in George (ed.), *Natural Law Theory*, 31–41 (repr. in Robert P. George, *In Defense of Natural Law* (Oxford: Oxford University Press, 2004), in which George develops his defence of his view of natural law).
[183] For an important discussion of the 'pre-history' of this distinction see Rémi Brague, 'Zur Vorgeschichte der Unterscheidung von "Sein" und "Sollen"', in Buchheim, Schönberger, and Schweidler (eds.), *Die Normativität des Wirklichen*, 21–34.

The inversion of teleology

In the modern scientific view, as Francis Bacon has famously said, natural teleology is 'sterile': 'like a virgin who is devoted to God, it does not give birth to anything'.[184] Natural teleology is not efficacious, as it were; it does not facilitate man's dominion over nature. Spaemann reasons that the modern abolition of natural teleology is therefore due to modernity's interest in unlimited domination over nature:[185] doing away with teleology allows a 'uniform method for the explanation of natural events'.[186] The adoption of a mechanistic view of nature entails a reduction of the complexity of causality: accounts of natural events come to rely on efficient causality, to the exclusion of final causality. This has, indeed, led to an 'unprecedented efficiency in the domination of nature'.[187]

Yet 'nature', Spaemann argues, is a notion that genuinely belongs to the context of human praxis[188] and needs to be understood with reference to our own self-understanding as persons. To speak of nature in terms of natural teleology makes reality 'familiar and friendly'.[189] Particularly because the modern 'abandonment of teleology'[190] seems to reduce the familiarity and friendliness of reality, we have to ask in a more specific way why and how Spaemann thinks that the idea of natural teleology has been transformed in modernity, so as to be better able to understand and criticize this key process in the history of modern ideas.[191]

Spaemann credits Christianity in particular with significantly transforming the teleological understanding of nature because nature was no longer understood as the ultimate context of human life, but as a creation; that is,

---

[184] *De Dignitate et Augmentis Scientiarum*, iii. v, in *The Works of Lord Bacon*, II (London 1841), 340 ('nam causarum finalium inquisitio sterilis est, et, tanquam virgo Deo consecrata, nihil parit'), quoted in Spaemann, 'Naturteleologie und Handlung', in *Philosophische Essays*, 44; *Die Frage 'Wozu?'*, 13; 'Natur', in *Philosophische Essays*, 22; *Reflexion und Spontaneität*, 61.

[185] 'Natur', in *Philosophische Essays*, 22; 'Die Aktualität des Naturrechts', in *Philosophische Essays*, 67; *Die Frage 'Wozu?'*, 284 ff.

[186] *Reflexion und Spontaneität*, 67.

[187] 'Kommentar', in *Die Unantastbarkeit des menschlichen Lebens: Zu ethischen Fragen der Biomedizin*, Instruktion der Kongregation für die Glaubenslehre (Freiburg im Breisgau: Herder, 1987), 70. For a discussion of natural teleology, both from a historical and from a systematic perspective, see also Richard Hassing (ed.), *Final Causality in Nature and Human Affairs* (Studies in Philosophy and the History of Philosophy, xxx) (Washington, DC: The Catholic University of America Press, 1997).

[188] 'Natur', in *Philosophische Essays*, 19.

[189] *Die Frage 'Wozu?'*, 22.

[190] For Spaemann's interpretation of this phenomenon see e.g. *Die Frage 'Wozu?'*, 97 ff.; 'Natur', in *Philosophische Essays*, 23 ff.

[191] See for Spaemann's assessment of natural teleology also Eduard Zwierlein, 'Das höchste Paradigma des Seienden'.

as a penultimate context of human life. Teleology, then, was applied to the divine mind in order to defend the divine creation, and consequently was understood as divine conscious anticipation. According to this perspective, natural ends were essentially divine ideas or intentions. Nature was then increasingly understood from a mechanistic standpoint. Spaemann refers to Sturmius' view that a mechanistic, that is an anti-teleological, view of nature is a '*vindicatio gloriae supremae numinis*'.[192] Spaemann points out that post-fifteenth-century Christianity thus prepared the way for the modern decon-struction of 'life' and 'natural teleology'. Teleological structures became the basis for proofs of the existence of God because God, as *causa efficiens*, was defined as the source of the teleological structure inherent in any living being. On the basis of this, the universe could be conceived of as a 'machine' that had been arranged and ordered by God. The idea that living beings have a natural *telos* in themselves, Spaemann argues, was a superstitious idolatry from the fifteenth century onwards. Life as *Selbstsein*, that is as analogous to human self-experience, could no longer be adequately understood.[193]

In *Die Frage 'Wozu'* Spaemann and Reinhard Löw reconstruct the history of the inversion of natural teleology in a detailed analysis that discloses the theological motifs entailed in the propagation of a non-teleological view of nature.[194] Unlike Thomas Aquinas, they point out, Averroes did not interpret the *finis quo* (such as a house as the *finis quo* of building a house) as a final cause; rather, he considered the *finis cuius*, that is the intention to build a house, as *causa efficiens* of the building, because only a real house and not the mere idea of it could be a real *cause*. Hence, the intention to build a house can only be the (eventually efficient) reason to build it. The final cause in its two dimensions of *finis cuius* and *finis quo* is thus dismissed. The *finis cuius* is assimilated to the *causa efficiens* while the *finis quo* seems not to have any impact on what is happening at all. The crisis of teleology arises, in Spae-mann's and Löw's account, as soon as intentions (particularly divine inten-tions) are then interpreted as *causae efficientes* and the result of a movement is no longer understood to be the *causa finalis* of this movement.[195] This, they argue, happened as early as in fourteenth-century scholasticism.

The next stage in the modern transformation of the idea of natural teleol-ogy lies in a theology of nature and divine action that is based upon Averroes's transformation of the notion of final causality. Johannes Buridanus, as

[192] See e.g. Spaemann, 'Natur', in *Philosophische Essays*, 23.
[193] *Persons*, 136 (*Personen*, 146).
[194] *Die Frage 'Wozu?'*, 97 ff. For a short version of this account see *Persons*, 136–7 (*Personen*, 146–7).
[195] *Die Frage 'Wozu?'*, 97–8.

Spaemann and Löw point out, interprets the *inclinatio naturalis* as efficient causality that is brought about by God's consciousness.[196] If there were a teleological *inclinatio naturalis*, they point out, God would have to be understood as *causa efficiens* of finite reality; that is to say, he would make finite reality an object of his intentions. In Buridanus' view this cannot be reconciled with the notion of God's perfection; so teleology, be it in nature or in God, is understood as an anthropomorphism that needs to be overcome for theological reasons. Furthermore, '[i]f there were ends within nature, they would have to lie in God and would then be unrecognizable to us'.[197] They would then also be external to nature. This did not seem to be possible. Nature, Spaemann and Löw state, then becomes a mere 'machine' without any teleological dimension of its own.[198]

Another important reason for the rise of a decidedly non-teleological and even anti-teleological point of view is, in Spaemann's and Löw's view, the nominalist transformation of the understanding of general concepts. In the nominalist view, general concepts do not have a meaning independent of their concrete usage. They schematize reality and allow us to combine things in classes. Given this understanding of general notions, nothing exists that does not exist as a concrete thing. The notion of final cause—that is, of a natural end—thus cannot denote any kind of cause. For there is nothing in reality as disclosed to humans to which we could refer by using it.

According to Spaemann and Löw's account, nominalist philosophy also significantly transformed the idea of what philosophy is. After the anti-Platonic dismissal of the full cognitive claim of general concepts, philosophical *theoria* is no longer an end in itself. It becomes progressively a means of domination over nature and is therefore increasingly subject to human interests.[199] This shift implies (and reinforces) the dismissal of teleology in favour of efficient causality, because a teleological point of view—that is, as Spaemann maintains, a hermeneutical understanding of nature by analogy to the human person—is at odds with the intention to dominate and to manipulate reality. The dismissal of teleology effects a strict opposition between nature and freedom, subjectivity and its natural basis. The dialectic of freedom and naturalism thus arises.

It is important to see that the dismissal of natural teleology and the rise of the modern natural sciences are closely tied up with the development of

---

[196] Die Frage 'Wozu?', 98.
[197] *Die Frage 'Wozu?'*, 98.
[198] Ibid. 98–9.
[199] Ibid. 103–4.

utilitarianism, which corresponds to, and presupposes, a purely mechanistic philosophy of nature. Charles Taylor has accordingly argued that 'utilitarianism doesn't come from nowhere . . . Utilitarianism was partly motivated by the aspiration to build an ethic that would be compatible with this [modern] scientific vision'.[200] Utilitarianism is, furthermore, an ethics of experts; it questions common-sense morality (the morality of the self-evident) and replaces it with scientific considerations about the goods to be pursued and about the maximization of happiness. In a similar way, modern scientific naturalism is an ontology of experts in that it is at odds with the most fundamental way in which human beings experience themselves and reality. It is therefore unsurprising that Spaemann's philosophy of the 'common-sense' view of reality is also characterized by an in-depth criticism of the modern expert-centred culture and its dismissal of the self-evident understanding of reality.

The self-evident and the knowledge of experts

In Spaemann's view, philosophy is not a professional discipline that can only be pursued by experts. The focus upon expertise may even undermine what philosophy essentially is. This is the reason why utilitarianism, Spaemann points out, fails as an ethical theory. It not only dismisses moral absolutes, but also turns moral norms into technical norms by basing moral judgements on the experts' predictions of future consequences of one's actions *sub specie Dei*.[201] Spaemann argues that the advice that experts can give is limited because of the largely hypothetical character of their knowledge; only 'non-hypothetical philosophy could be practical for non-philosophers as guidance'.[202] In Spaemann's view, the effort of modernity to emancipate itself from given traditions, norms, and obligations is strangely constrained and impeded by the tendency of the same culture to rely upon experts and their technical advice.[203] Modern culture tends to rely upon consequentialist considerations by experts about the entirety of the consequences of our actions, rather than on the simple insights of one's conscience into what is

---

[200] 'Explanation and Practical Reason', in *Philosophical Papers* (Cambridge: Cambridge University Press, 1985), 38.

[201] See *Basic Moral Concepts*, 52 (*Moralische Grundbegriffe*, 68); *Happiness and Benevolence*, 123 ff. (*Glück und Wohlwollen*, 162 ff.). For a counter-critique of Spaemann's critique of utilitarianism see Jean-Claude Wolf, 'Utilitaristische Ethik als Antwort auf die ökologische Krise', in *Zeitschrift für Philosophische Forschung*, 44 (1990), 619–34.

[202] 'Wie praktisch ist die Ethik?', in *Grenzen*, 31.

[203] For Spaemann's critique of institutionalized medical ethics see 'Tierschutz und Menschenwürde', in *Grenzen*, 475.

the self-evident natural norm of human action.[204] Yet neither the focus upon supposed experts in ethical questions nor the effort to 'determine our actions by consideration of the sum total of the consequences', Spaemann argues, leads to real freedom; rather, each of these approaches 'disorientates people and makes them open to all sorts of temptations and possibilities of manipulations'.[205]

In Spaemann's view, the 'simple insight' into fundamental goods and norms is obscured by oversophisticated reflection.[206] The epistemological status of this kind of simple, elementary, and immediate knowledge differs significantly from philosophical, scientific, and technological knowledge. It is a 'certainty we all sense, so long as we do not start specifically to reflect on it'.[207] Because of the immediate character of inner knowledge, he further reasons, moral rules generally seem self-evident to us.[208] In Spaemann's view, reflection suspends the context in which moral norms naturally make sense. This is why we cannot infinitely reflect—not only because we have to act, but also because reflection as such is limited and can fail to disclose what we are looking for. What is often needed, then, is a hermeneutics of the self-evident rather than a reflection upon our moral persuasions and their validity. Ethics, Spaemann therefore holds, is ultimately not an a priori or a technological and reflection-focused science, but, as in Aristotle's view, a hermeneutics of the 'moral consciousness of the *polis*'.[209] To question the claim of experts thus means to put on trial the claim of modern sciences (broadly understood) to 'be heir of philosophy and fundamentally to exhaust the realm of what can be known'.[210]

In contrast to utilitarianism, which often openly subjects philosophy to practical considerations, Spaemann recalls a notion of philosophy as *theoria* that primarily cannot, and must not, be subject to ends other than itself. *Theoria*, Spaemann reminds us, is an end in itself and not a means to an end

---

[204] For Spaemann's analysis and critique of the notion 'conscience' see *Persons*, 164–79 (*Personen*, 175–90); *Basic Moral Concepts*, 57–67 (*Moralische Grundbegriffe*, 73–84). For a discussion of his view of conscience and its Thomistic dimensions see Rudolf Langthaler, 'Über "Seelen" und "Gewissen": Robert Spaemanns Aktualisierung thomistischer Motive', *Deutsche Zeitschrift für Philosophie*, 46 (1998), 485–500.

[205] *Basic Moral Concepts*, 53 (*Moralische Grundbegriffe*, 68); see also *Happiness and Benevolence*, 127 (*Glück und Wohlwollen*, 169).

[206] Spaemann employs the notion 'simple insights' with regard to conscientious insight into fundamental moral rules in *Basic Moral Concepts*, 52 (*Moralische Grundbegriffe*, 68).

[207] Ibid. 4 (15).

[208] Ibid. 4–5 (14–15).

[209] 'Die zwei Grundbegriffe der Moral', in *Kritik der politischen Utopie*, 7–8. Spaemann adopts Joachim Ritter's reading of Aristotle (see Ritter, 'Naturrecht bei Aristoteles').

[210] 'Philosophie zwischen Metaphysik und Geschichte', 291.

external to it. 'And this activity alone', as Aristotle points out, 'would seem to be loved for its own sake; for nothing arises from it apart from the contemplating, while from practical activities we gain more or less apart from the action'.[211] Furthermore, philosophy as *theoria* does not presuppose expertise, but simple openness towards reality.

Recollection and conversation

According to Spaemann, insight into what is self-evident does not depend upon whether one has achieved the status of an expert in self-evident phenomena, but upon whether one is able to wake up to reality or not. There is, consequently, no strictly 'scientific' way of proving the compelling character of the self-evident. Edmund Husserl and Martin Heidegger were in a similar situation. Their enterprise to challenge the absolute claim of a reductionistic understanding of reality could not be proved in a manner that would have met the standards of the scientific (and philosophical) reasoning of their time (although at least Husserl claimed that such a proof was possible). Because of this, they had to acknowledge the specific epistemological status of phenomenological knowledge. Whoever sees more, according to the phenomenological maxim, is right.

The epistemological maxim of phenomenology can also be utilized to describe the epistemological status of what is self-evident. Spaemann's claim is that whoever is able to see the self-evident is able to see more than is accounted for by scientific methodology, for instance. This ability is, in a strict sense, a *natural* ability to be aware of what is evident. This epistemology questions the modern focus upon hypotheses, because

a value judgment [*Werteinsicht*] is not a hypothesis but a prerequisite without which a hypothesis cannot be formed. There is no conceivable higher authority by means of which our insights about such values could come to be corrected and replaced by new insights. There is only one source of authority, but we only discover what that is when the process of re-evaluation has already been brought about. This source of authority is our newer and deeper insight into values. This happens spontaneously, not in the form of a hypothesis but as something which is self-evident.[212]

There is, therefore, as we have already pointed out, no ultimate proof of the self-evident that fully conforms to the standards of scientific reasoning.

---

[211] *Nicomachean Ethics*, 1177b, in *The Complete Works of Aristotle: The Revised Oxford Translation* (1984).

[212] *Basic Moral Concepts*, 34 (*Moralische Grundbegriffe*, 47).

According to an old rule of disputations, Spaemann points out, 'it is not meaningful to intend to prove something that is self-evident to everyone'.[213]

The claim to see the self-evident and thereby to see more than others—and therefore the discussion about the self-evident—however, is controversial and anarchic, Spaemann argues, because 'in the moment that I make the self-evident which is presupposed in any conversation the object of my conversation, I relocate the horizon. The new object ceases to be self-evident and becomes a possible object of controversies'.[214] This anarchy is intrinsic to philosophy and must not be dismissed, for 'the elimination of this anarchy would be tantamount to the abdication of humanity in favour of its products'.[215] The fact that philosophy is anarchic, however, does not mean that the self-evident cannot be justified at all; it means that the consideration of it by the individual philosopher causes controversies and entails conversations about it. We can now see more clearly why Spaemann's definition of philosophy as conversation does not contradict, nor relativize, what he says about philosophy as a recollection of the self-evident. While the idea that philosophy is a recollection of the self-evident *and* a continuous conversation about ultimate questions at first may seem contradictory, it corresponds to the dialectic of the universal and the particular that is characteristic of philosophy: philosophers make universal claims, but they can only do this in their own individual way.

In Spaemann's view, one needs to distinguish between theory and practice; they are incommensurable.[216] The brevity of life, therefore, does not allow for an endless and merely theoretical discussion about questions of ultimately practical significance. So Spaemann is not in favour of philosophy as an endless conversation that resists giving advice on how to act. 'Philosophy needs to arrive somewhere if it is to make sense at all.'[217] Hence, philosophy does not constitute a random conversation about virtually anything. In outlining philosophy in this way, Spaemann avoids two imminent dangers: first, the danger of philosophical 'fanaticism', that is, of providing an ultimate answer to questions that philosophy cannot ultimately answer;[218] second, the danger of reducing philosophy to mere endless conversation, an intellectual pastime that fails to do justice to the seriousness and brevity of life and to

---

[213] 'Tierschutz und Menschenwürde', in *Grenzen*, 467.
[214] 'Die kontroverse Natur der Philosophie', in *Philosophische Essays*, 115.
[215] Ibid. 129.
[216] For this view see e.g. 'Wie praktisch ist die Ethik?', in *Grenzen*, 28.
[217] 'Philosophie als institutionalisierte Naivität', 140.
[218] It can be mentioned at this point that Spaemann provides detailed analysis of the history of the notion 'fanaticism' in '"Fanatisch" und " Fanatismus"', in *Archiv für Begriffsgeschichte*, xv (Bonn: Bouvier Grundmann, 1971) and in *Reflexion und Spontaneität*, 170–209.

the fact that not even philosophers can infinitely converse about anything. Because there is a teleological nature of humanity that is not, and cannot be, dependent on human discourse and conversation, but is already given, the conversation does not find its measure in itself or in mere freedom. Because there is a self-evident measure of human action that *needs* to be recollected (because we have to act and cannot always be 'on our way'), the conversation about ultimate questions is therefore neither directionless nor utterly discourse-centred. It is from this point of view that his definition of philosophy as a continuous conversation about ultimate questions needs to be understood.

Philosophy as continuous conversation about ultimate questions

Spaemann provides his reader with a definition of philosophy which, he admits, is not a philosophical definition[219] but an assessment of philosophy from outside. Philosophy, he seems to imply, does not present us with the ultimate frame of reality within which all questions need to be, or can be, solved. One can speak meaningfully about, and even define, philosophy from a non-philosophical point of view. There is a wider context (particularly wider than the context of philosophical experts) within which philosophy needs to be positioned (without being functionalized!): 'Philosophy, too, can once more be viewed from outside. And then it does not always look good'.[220] This context is the context of everyday life, the context of our 'life-world', to use a Husserlian concept. Philosophy is part of the everyday life of human beings and their capacity radically to transcend any given context, so it must not develop a totalitarian system that integrates everything into itself by subjecting all of reality to its principles.[221]

According to Spaemann's definition, philosophy is 'a continuous conversation about ultimate questions'.[222] There are three features of this definition that need to be further investigated: First, we need to ask what are the ultimate questions that Spaemann defines as the 'objects' of philosophical conversation?

---

[219] 'Die kontroverse Natur der Philosophie', in *Philosophische Essays*, 106.

[220] 'Zur Einführung: Philosophiegeschichte nach Heidegger', 1.

[221] For Spaemann's definition of 'totalitarian thinking' see Spaemann, *Happiness and Benevolence*, 154 (*Glück und Wohlwollen*, 200–1): 'One can best characterize totalitarian thinking as defining all action, without consideration of the intention of the agent, in terms of the function it possesses in reference to a a certain system-framework of boundaries, regardless of whether the function is to stabilize or destroy the system'.

[222] 'Die kontroverse Natur der Philosophie', in *Philosophische Essays*, 106.

Second, we have to examine why and how philosophy is conversational. Third, we have to raise the issue of how the continuity of the conversation may be adequately understood. In our examination of this definition we will bring together, and show the systematic consistence of, many of the elements of his understanding of philosophy that we have already discussed in this chapter.

The nature of ultimate questions

Ultimate questions are, in Spaemann's view, questions that inevitably remain open and without any ultimate answer even after ordinary everyday or scientific discourses have come to a solution. Furthermore, these questions need to remain open. In general, ultimate questions do not always need to be raised, for the 'consensual stability of our normal, personal, social, and scientific practice of life' depends upon their remaining implicit.[223] Simply in order to live, Spaemann's argument runs, we need to refrain from constantly raising those fundamental ultimate questions. In this context Spaemann speaks of the 'incommensurability of theory and practice',[224] and frequently quotes the ancient proverb *vita brevis, ars longa*.[225] Ultimate questions are dealt with by *theoria*. They do not always need to be raised and answered, because raising those questions is not per se practice-oriented. This is not to say that philosophy ought not to deal with concrete practical questions. 'Up to the time of Kant', Spaemann states, 'philosophers and theologians did not consider it beneath their dignity to discuss questions like these. If, in studying moral philosophy, we could not get beyond empty formulae and could learn nothing about how we should live, it would not be an interesting enough subject to be worth tackling'.[226] This is why Spaemann does not restrict himself to the considerations of philosophical theory. He frequently applies the principles of his philosophy by presenting his opinion on issues in contemporary political and ethical debate, such as the relation between moral norms and the legal order.[227] So he has commented upon the

[223] 'Die kontroverse Natur der Philosophie', in *Philosophische Essays*, 106.
[224] Spaemann, 'Wie praktisch ist die Ethik?', in *Grenzen*, 28; see also 'Über die gegenwärtige Lage des Christentums', in *Das unsterbliche Gerücht*, 228.
[225] See Hippocrates, *Aphorisms*, 1. 1; Seneca, *De Brevitate Vitae*, 1. 1. Spaemann implicitly refers to this proverb in *Basic Moral Concepts*, 60 (*Moralische Grundbegriffe*, 76–7).
[226] *Basic Moral Concepts*, viii (*Moralische Grundbegriffe*, 8).
[227] For the relation between moral norms and law see 'Sittliche Normen und Rechtsordnung', in Heiner Marré, Dieter Schümmelfeder, and Burkhard Kämper (eds.), *Das christliche Freiheitsverständnis in seiner Bedeutung für die staatliche Rechtsordnung* (*Essener Gespräche zum Thema Staat und Kirche*, 30) (Münster: Aschendorff, 1996), 5–17; see pp. 18–37 for a discussion of Spaemann's essay.

issue of abortion[228] and euthanasia,[229] upon the 'Utopian semantics' which he associated with the justification of the war in the former Yugoslavia,[230] and upon the so-called Sloterdijk debate about the possibilities and limits of genetic engineering and the future of humanism.[231] Spaemann, here as *philosophe-écrivain*, shows a political commitment without having entered politics actively. The philosopher, Spaemann wants to make clear, is not meant to abolish the difference between philosophy and politics by applying his ideas directly; his is a *potestas indirecta*.

There is time for conversations about ultimate questions, yet decisions also need to be made—without ultimate certainty about the consequences, but nonetheless with the seriousness that ought to characterize ethical decision-making. In Spaemann's view, mockery,[232] irony, and playfulness, familiar attitudes of the late-modern *Zeitgeist*, cannot be main features of philosophy. Spaemann would presumably agree with Nietzsche's interesting statement that

[a]ll ironical writers depend on the foolish species of men who together with the author would like to feel themselves superior to all others and who regard the author as the mouthpiece of their presumption.—Habituation to irony, moreover, like habituation to sarcasm, spoils the character, to which it gradually lends the quality

---

[228] 'Am Ende der Debatte um § 218 StGB'; 'Haben Ungeborene ein Recht auf Leben?'; 'Verantwortung für die Ungeborenen'; 'Das Entscheidungsrecht der Frau entlastet den Mann und die Mitwelt: Die Erlaubnis zu töten kommt einer Unzurechnungsfähigkeitserklärung gleich'; 'Die schlechte Lehre vom guten Zweck: Der korrumpierende Kalkül hinter der Schein-Debatte'; 'Ist die Ausstellung des Beratungsscheins eine "formelle Mitwirkung" bei der Abtreibung?'—all reprinted in *Grenzen*.

[229] See e.g. 'Wir dürfen das Euthanasie-Tabu nicht aufgeben', in *Grenzen*. For a critique of Spaemann's position in the controversy about the ethical dimension of euthanasia see Günther Patzig, 'Gibt es Grenzen der Redefreiheit?', in *Zeitschrift für Philosophische Forschung*, 54 (2000), 581–92.

[230] 'Werte gegen Menschen: Wie der Krieg die Begriffe verwirrt', in *Grenzen*.

[231] 'Wozu der Aufwand? Sloterdijk fehlt das Rüstzeug', in *Grenzen*, 406–10. In this text Spaemann develops a critique of a lecture by Sloterdijk which was published as *Regeln für den Menschenpark: Ein Antwortschreiben zu Heideggers Brief über den Humanismus* (Frankfurt am Main: Suhrkamp, 1999). This lecture and the book were discussed by many important contemporary German thinkers. See e.g. Thomas Assheuer, 'Das Zarathustra-Projekt: Der Philosoph Peter Sloterdijk fordert eine gentechnische Revision der Menschheit', in *Die Zeit*, 36 (1999); Peter Sloterdijk, 'Die Kritische Theorie ist tot: Peter Sloterdijk schreibt an Assheuer und Habermas', in *Die Zeit*, 37 (1999); Ernst Tugendhat, 'Es gibt keine Gene für die Moral: Sloterdijk stellt das Verhältnis von Ethik und Gentechnik schlicht auf den Kopf', in *Die Zeit*, 39 (1999); Walther Ch. Zimmerli, 'Die Evolution in eigener Regie. In einem Punkt hat Sloterdijk Recht: Über die Normn für gentechnische Eingriffe muss öffentlich debattiert werden', in *Die Zeit*, 40 (1999); Manfred Frank, 'Geschweife und Geschwefel: Die düster-prophetische Rede über den "Menschenpark" beunruhigt, und die Art, wie Sloterdijk mit Kritikern umspringt, ist empörend. Auch sein Angriff auf die Kritische Theorie geht fehl. Ein offener Brief', in *Die Zeit*, 39 (1999); Magnus Striet, *Der neue Mensch? Unzeitgemäße Betrachtungen zu Sloterdijk und Nietzsche* (Frankfurt am Main: Knecht, 2000).

[232] For Spaemann's interpretation and critique of the 'mocker' and his nihilistic attitude see 'Spötter', in *Frankfurter Hefte: Zeitschrift für Kultur und Politik*, 7/3 (1948), 640–4.

of a malicious and jeering superiority: in the end it comes to resemble a snapping dog which has learned how to laugh but forgotten how to bite.[233]

Yet laughter—and, as Joachim Ritter has put it, 'humour as philosophy and as existential attitude'[234] which shows the limits of human reason—may well be features of philosophy, particularly vis-à-vis the totalitarian claim of modern reason.

What, then, is characteristic of ultimate questions? Ultimate questions, Spaemann argues, concern the fundamental issues of the human relation to reality. Any kind of practical or theoretical commitment to reality presupposes a certain at least implicit answer to questions such as that of 'what we mean when we speak of "reality" or when we call something "good", or the question how we can know that we know something'.[235] Those are questions that cannot be answered by the scientific discourse nor by concrete practical reasoning, for both scientific discourse and moral reflection and actions are based upon at least implicit answers to those ultimate questions.[236] Nor is it possible to formulate an exhaustive and ultimate answer to them. Philosophy, then, considers what is not, and cannot be, thought of in the sciences, because it transcends any given horizon of the sciences and, in so doing, provides the sciences with foundations. It is, as Spaemann says, 'the self-understanding of humanity in the whole of reality'[237] and hence 'absolute reflection'.[238]

Spaemann concedes that not only philosophy is concerned with ultimate questions; so too are political leaders, religious teachers, and prophets.[239] In contrast to those who also provide answers to ultimate questions, but in an authoritative rather than discursive way, philosophy is a conversation both among contemporaries and among philosophers of different epochs, as it were. While the ultimate questions with which philosophy is concerned have not been identical throughout the history of philosophy, he points out, they have been similar.[240] This is why philosophy is not characterized by a teaching

---

[233] *Human, All Too Human*, trans. R. J. Hollingdale, introd. Richard Schacht (Cambridge: Cambridge University Press, 1996), 146–7.
[234] 'Über das Lachen', in *Subjektivität: Sechs Aufsätze* (Frankfurt am Main: Suhrkamp, 1974), 62–92, esp. 90–1.
[235] 'Die kontroverse Natur der Philosophie', in *Philosophische Essays*, 106.
[236] For the presuppositions of discourse, or discursive reasoning, see also Spaemann, *Happiness and Benevolence*, 133 ff. (*Glück und Wohlwollen*, 175 ff.).
[237] *Die Frage 'Wozu?'*, 23.
[238] 'Philosophie als institutionalisierte Naivität', 139.
[239] 'Die kontroverse Natur der Philosophie', in *Philosophische Essays*, 106.
[240] Ibid. 107.

that completes a comprehensive system, but by a teaching that has the nature of Socratic conversation.

The conversational character of philosophy

In order to spell out what Spaemann means by arguing that philosophy ought to be conversational it may be best initially to explain what he does not mean. Spaemann does not aspire to carry on the dialogical philosophy initiated by Ferdinand Ebner, Martin Buber, and Franz Rosenzweig, even though his ethical writings reach conclusions that are close to their thoughts.[241] Nor does he endeavour to continue the linguistic transformation of Kantian transcendental philosophy as instigated by Karl-Otto Apel and Jürgen Habermas.[242] Spaemann's emphasis on the intuitive character of the knowledge of the self-evident, on the inevitability of decisions and the need to act even without absolute certainty that one's course of action can ultimately be justified, has even a specific target in the overemphasis upon discourse in modern culture and, especially, in its most philosophically advanced form, in Apel's and Habermas's theories of communicative reason.[243] In Spaemann's view, communicative rationality is limited, for 'justice does not originate from discourse, but discourse presupposes ideas of justice that one has already brought to the conversation'.[244] Discursive reason cannot be conceived of without respect to what provides it with a normative horizon within which communication makes sense in the first place.

Spaemann's criticism of discourse ethics is reminiscent of Carl Schmitt's critique of the Romantic ideal of endless conversation as most intriguingly developed in his *Politische Romantik*.[245] Yet there is a significant difference between Carl Schmitt's and Robert Spaemann's philosophies, which leads us to see how Spaemann understands the continuity and the conversational

---

[241] For a discussion of dialogical thought see Michael Theunissen, *The Other: Studies in the Social Ontology of Husserl, Heidegger, Sartre, and Buber* (Cambridge, Mass.: MIT Press, 1984); Bernhard Casper, *Das dialogische Denken: Eine Untersuchung der religionsphilosophischen Bedeutung Franz Rosenzweigs, Ferdinand Ebners und Martin Bubers* (Freiburg im Breisgau: Herder, 1967).

[242] See for Apel's and Habermas's 'discourse ethics' Apel, *Towards a Transformation of Philosophy*, trans. Glyn Adey and David Fisby, foreword Pol Vandevelde (Marquette Studies in Philosophy, 20) (Milwaukee, Wis.: Marquette University Press, 1998); Habermas, *The Theory of Communicative Action*, trans. Thomas McCarthy, 2 vols. (Boston: Beacon, 1984/1987).

[243] See esp. Spaemann, 'Die Utopie der Herrschaftsfreiheit', in *Kritik der politischen Utopie*, 116–25; 'Die Utopie des guten Herrschers', in *Kritik der politischen Utopie*, 127–41.

[244] 'Was ist philosophische Ethik?', in *Grenzen*, 25.

[245] Carl Schmitt, *Politische Romantik*, 3rd edn. (Berlin: Duncker & Humblot, 1968) (Carl Schmitt, *Political Romanticism*, trans. Guy Oakes (Cambridge, Mass: MIT Press, 1986)).

character of philosophy. While Schmitt's political theology makes a strong case for a decisionist overcoming of the Romantic lack of decisiveness, Spaemann refers to the argumentative force of given traditions, to the universality of reason, to the rationality of the *bonum commune*, and to the congruence and interrelatedness of nature and freedom. 'On the one hand,' Spaemann argues, 'philosophical peripeties are more radical than scientific paradigm shifts; on the other, the philosophical ideal of rationality is universalistic and anti-decisionistic'.[246]

In contrast to discourse ethics, dialogical thinking, and Schmittian decisionism, Spaemann evokes a view of conversational philosophy that is indebted to the classical tradition of Socratic and Platonic philosophy. In Spaemann's view, the Socratic dialogue and the Platonic 'frequent and informal discussion'[247] exemplify the style in which philosophy ought to be pursued. It is also important to note that his recollection of a Socratic view of philosophy has a religious dimension. For, Spaemann argues that 'as long as Socrates is the example of philosophy, philosophy does not conceal the view of Christ'.[248]

The decision 'to get close to the "frequent and informal" discussions which Plato talks about'[249] also has epistemological and educational implications, for '[t]he effect which he hoped for can only be produced indirectly, not intentionally'.[250] As a philosopher, Spaemann appeals to the freedom of the people with whom he engages in conversation by means of a kind of 'indirect communication'. They may be persuaded but they cannot be forced to subscribe to the ideas which Spaemann unfolds. Philosophy is based upon a free initiative. It is *Selbstdenken*,[251] thinking by and for oneself, and concerns knowledge that summons our freedom. Education, for instance, is thus not a manipulation, but a 'by-product which happens while one is doing many other things'.[252]

---

[246] 'Die kontroverse Natur der Philosophie', in *Philosophische Essays*, 113.

[247] *Basic Moral Concepts*, vii–viii (*Moralische Grundbegriffe*, 7–8). This is an explicit reference to Plato's seventh letter, in which Plato says of his teaching that '[t]here neither is nor ever will be a treatise of mine on the subject. For it does not admit of exposition like other branches of knowledge; but after much converse about the matter itself and a life lived together, suddenly a light, as it were, is kindled in one soul by a flame that leaps to it from another, and thereafter sustains itself' (*The Platonic Epistles*, trans. J. Harward (Cambridge: Cambridge University Press, 1932), 341–2. For the difference between frequent and informal discussion and scientific discourse see also Spaemann's 'Über den Mut zur Erziehung', in *Grenzen*, 502.

[248] 'Christentum und Philosophie der Neuzeit', 138.

[249] Spaemann, *Basic Moral Concepts*, viii (*Moralische Grundbegriffe*, 8–9).

[250] Ibid. viii (9).

[251] 'Die kontroverse Natur der Philosophie', in *Philosophische Essays*, 117.

[252] 'Erziehung zur Wirklichkeit: Rede zum Jubiläum eines Kinderhauses', in *Grenzen*, 503.

The continuity of philosophy and the recollection
of the self-evident

The continuity of philosophy is not only temporal. It is also constituted by
the continuity—the 'family resemblances',[253] as Spaemann says with implicit
reference to Wittgenstein[254]—of the fundamental questions and challenges
that human beings have to face, and of the self-evident answers that are
provided to these questions. In characterizing the conversation about ultimate questions as 'continuous', Spaemann also embraces the idea of philosophy as recollection. Recollection and conversation, as we have already
shown, are not mutually exclusive. We have already seen that the complementary relation between recollection and conversation is reflective of the
dialectic between the particular and the universal that is characteristic of
philosophical reasoning:

> Philosophy is concerned about true universality, about a whole insight, about 'totali-
> ty', about absolute truth . . . To think the whole, however, can always only be a matter
> of an individual attempt . . . and the attempt to think about the absolute, more than
> any other endeavour of thought, is marked by a contingent way of thinking at one's
> own risk, even by a fate of thinking.[255]

This implies, Spaemann states, that not only the particular content but also
the philosopher's own identity is at stake in a philosophical conversation.
Therefore, he points out, philosophy is characterized by a 'naivety' because
philosophers resist, or are incapable of, 'distinguishing the form and content
of the thought from the thinking person'.[256]

Philosophy beyond 'left' and 'right'

As noted earlier, philosophy rediscovers what has already been known and
remembers measures 'which are based in the "unpreconceivable"'.[257] In
philosophy, Spaemann argues, one needs to be sceptical about things that
are utterly new. Because of this conception of philosophy, one may be
tempted to call Spaemann's thought 'conservative', and, indeed, he has the
reputation of being a conservative philosopher. Spaemann himself calls his

---

[253] 'Die kontroverse Natur der Philosophie', *Philosophische Essays*, 107.
[254] For this notion see Ludwig Wittgenstein, *Philosophical Investigations*, trans. G. E. M.
Anscombe (New York: Macmillan, 1958), 21.
[255] 'Einleitung', in *Philosophische Essays*, 5–6.
[256] 'Philosophie als institutionalisierte Naivität', 141.
[257] 'Die Herausforderung des ärztlichen Berufsethos', in *Grenzen*, 337.

own habit of thought 'sceptical',[258] and points out that 'the sceptical person tends towards conservatism. The energy of the will to change things presupposes the decided conviction that it will be better otherwise'.[259] Thus, Spaemann thinks against the current of what is novel: 'all of what is human in the world, all structure, all right is wrested from the current'.[260]

Jürgen Habermas, for instance, counts Spaemann among what he calls the 'old conservatives'. They

> do not allow themselves to be contaminated by cultural modernity in the first place. They observe with mistrust the collapse of substantive reason, the progressive differentiation of science, morality, and art, the modern understanding of the world and its purely procedural canons of rationality, and recommend instead a return to positions *prior* to modernity . . . Here it is principally contemporary neo-Aristotelianism which has enjoyed some success, encouraged by the ecological question to renew the idea of a cosmological ethic. This tradition, which begins with Leo Strauss, has produced the interesting work of Hans Jonas and Robert Spaemann.[261]

The account of Spaemann as an 'old conservative', however, needs to be examined carefully.

Spaemann is certainly sceptical of commonly held versions of conservatism. Already Spaemann's 1951 interpretation of the implications of the counter-revolutionary thought of L. G. A. de Bonald shows the failure of a traditionalist conservatism that wants to preserve times past at almost any cost, without reflecting upon how it unconsciously changes what it consciously aims at preserving. In Bonald's hands, he observes, 'religion and metaphysics turn into a mere tautology of sociology'.[262] The intent of Bonald's thought to restore orthodox Catholicism has thus undermined itself. For, Bonald strives to defend an order which is 'abstract in the sense that real existence can no longer be performed within it'.[263] His focus upon an abstract order, Spaemann shows (as we will see in Chapter 4), turns into nihilism.

Spaemann is aware of the dialectic to which counter-revolutionary and, in this sense, conservative thought is likely to be subject. Progressive and conservative attitudes are, in Spaemann's view, merely another result of the

---

[258] 'Fragebogen: Robert Spaemann', in *Magazin der Frankfurter Allgemeine Zeitung* (July 1985). See here also Spaemann and Nissing, 'Die Natur des Lebendigen und das Ende des Denkens', 133: 'Meine Natur ist wohl eher kritisch, skeptisch'.

[259] 'Über den Mut zur Erziehung', in *Grenzen*, 493.

[260] 'Der Anschlag auf den Sonntag', in *Grenzen*, 274.

[261] 'Modernity: An Unfinished Project', in Maurizio Passerin d'Entrèves and Seyla Benhabib (eds.), *Habermas and the Unfinished Project of Modernity: Critical Essays on 'The Philosophical Discourse of Modernity'* (Cambridge, Mass.: MIT Press, 1997), 53.

[262] *Der Ursprung der Soziologie aus dem Geist der Restauration*, 202.

[263] Ibid. 173.

modern inversion of natural teleology that has dichotomized the mere
preservation of life, on the one hand, and the desire for the good life as
the *telos* of human action, on the other. This inversion of natural teleology is
the ontological presupposition for the dichotomy of 'conservative' and
'progressive', of the right-wing focus upon mere self-preservation often at
the expense of the good life, and the left-wing focus upon self-transcendence
towards the good life, often without regard for life as such. This inversion,
then, as we have already pointed out, shows the modern 'lack of the idea of a
natural finality of humanity and of society. The notion *telos* has been split,
but the *disjecta membra* develop energies like a nuclear fission'.[264] This
problem cannot, in Spaemann's view, be remedied by technocratic endeavours, whether of right- or of left-wing origin, but only by a reappraisal of
natural teleology, according to which 'the principle of perfection and the
principle of preservation are in the end the same: the good'.[265] This means
freely to remember nature and its *telos* and hence to let it be what it is, for us
and as such. Particularly vis-à-vis the problems of the 'technological destruction of the world'[266] and the ecological crisis with respect to which the
categories of "right" and "left" become obsolete',[267] Spaemann aims to go
beyond the distinction of 'conservative' and 'progressive' and preserves what
he considers worth preserving without losing sight of the insufficiency of
mere preservation. For he is aware that it may be fatal in our situation 'to let
things remain as they are'.[268]

Spaemann thus brings into consciousness that progressive and conservative
attitudes are as such morally neutral because their moral dimension depends
entirely upon the moral quality of their contents. Self-preservation and self-
transcendence towards the good must therefore not be dichotomized, although
'mere life' has a factual priority over what are yet merely ideas of possible
'good lives'. Spaemann correspondingly argues that 'whoever wants to
change something about an existing state of affairs needs to justify that
this can pass for a reasonable basic rule'.[269] If there are reasons for change,
Spaemann would not insist on preservation for the sake of mere preservation, but he demands a critical examination of reasons for change. This is
a risky endeavour that does not necessarily find a lot of support. As

---

[264] 'Zur Ontologie der Begriffe "rechts" und "links"', in *Grenzen*, 262; see for this dialectic
also Spaemann, *Happiness and Benevolence*, 45–6 (*Glück und Wohlwollen*, 67).

[265] 'Zur Ontologie der Begriffe "rechts" und "links"', in *Grenzen*, 261.

[266] Spaemann, 'Die christliche Religion und das Ende des modernen Bewusstseins', 255.

[267] 'Zur Ontologie der Begriffe "rechts" und "links"', in *Grenzen*, 266 ff. See here also
Spaemann and Nissing, 'Die Natur des Lebendigen und das Ende des Denkens', 129.

[268] 'Emanzipation—ein Bildungsziel', in *Grenzen*, 488.

[269] 'Todesstrafe', in *Grenzen*, 441.

Spaemann rightly points out, 'in a free society apology for what already exists requires courage'.[270]

2.3 RECOLLECTION, PRESERVATION, AND THE CHALLENGE OF THE FUTURE

Spaemann, as we have seen, presupposes that human nature is by and large continuous. Yet philosophy amounts to more than a mere repetition of what has already been said, in so far as it 'thematizes the particularity of its perspective and is a continuous attempt to overcome it'.[271] There is therefore always a need for philosophy because, Spaemann maintains, what has always been known needs sometimes to be rethought in so far as the real conditions of life and the notions that are at hand for our self-understanding change.[272] Spaemann thus presupposes *both* that human nature has essentially been the same *and* that the way human nature has been conceived has undergone considerable changes over the centuries. Given this, the question of the good life always needs to be raised again without undermining the conditions of life as such. That is to say, philosophy constantly and particularly in times of crisis needs to bring the complementary relation between nature and freedom into consciousness.

Philosophy is, as we have already pointed out, an education into reality, such that 'the educated person begins to perceive reality as it is'.[273] The educator, Spaemann points out, 'needs to know that whatever he can teach young people is recollection, past'.[274] Philosophy does not make up its results. It rediscovers self-evident knowledge and nature as the 'unpreconceivable' past of human freedom. Precisely because Spaemann's philosophy reminds his readers of what is self-evident, he takes the historical eclipses of philosophy and the intrinsic limits, and conditions, of philosophy very seriously. Thoughout history what is self-evident is expressed against the background of a personal, cultural, social, and biographical context, such as the context of modernity. Spaemann's philosophy is characterized by awareness of these limits of philosophy and, more specifically, of the shortcomings of modernity.

---

[270] 'Überzeugungen in einer hypothetischen Zivilisation', in Oskar Schatz (ed.), *Abschied von Utopia? Anspruch und Auftrag des Intellektuellen* (Graz: Styria, 1977), 311.

[271] 'Die kontroverse Natur der Philosophie', in *Philosophische Essays*, 124.

[272] *Happiness and Benevolence*, vii (*Glück und Wohlwollen*, 9).

[273] 'Wer ist ein gebildeter Mensch? Aus einer Promotionsrede', in *Grenzen*, 513.

[274] 'Über den Mut zur Erziehung', in *Grenzen*, 495.

However, he also knows that there are fundamentally positive features of modernity, such as the idea of human dignity, which must not be given up—particularly in light of the universality of modernity and its technocratic implications. Given the technological civilization of modernity, Spaemann argues, 'Europe ... must not abstain from exporting in a missionary manner the idea of human dignity which necessarily belongs to this civilization'.[275]

Spaemann's 'recollection' of nature may at first seem to be a mere limitation of history and freedom. Yet 'the integrity of nature, within the ecological niche of which life and freedom themselves find their domicile',[276] is, more closely scrutinized, the very condition of freedom, history, and 'progress'. Spaemann's understanding of philosophy therefore illustrates how the Scylla of historicism and the Charybdis of timeless and even time-neglecting naturalism can be avoided. It also shows how philosophy can bridge the gulf between the particular and the universal, between the historically contingent and the history-transcending self-evident.

The history of philosophy as a continuous conversation is thus characterized by *accidental* progress—for there is, in Spaemann's view, no *substantial* progress[277]—as well as by an arriving at where one already is and has always been. Philosophy is thus an open and anarchic endeavour and challenges any scientistic systematization and objectification of reality. 'There will be philosophy', Spaemann consequently argues, 'as long as we want a limit to our own objectification'.[278] By being 'absolute reflection' and recollection of the self-evident, philosophy can question any kind of totalitarianism, whether non-philosophical or philosophical, because it calls the normative character of nature as well as the limits of merely human freedom into consciousness. Philosophy questions the political totalitarianism of regimes that sacrifice human beings either for the sake of the self-preservation of an imagined national or racial identity, or for the sake of a paradisiacal and supposedly truly human future. It also calls into question ideological philosophies that claim to have successfully integrated the whole of reality into their reductionistic systems, even at the cost of denying the very existence of whatever is at odds with the claim of the system.

---

[275] 'Rationalität als "Kulturelles Erbe"', in *Scheidewege: Jahresschrift für skeptisches Denken*, 14 (1984/5), 311. See in this context also the interesting comparable reflections of Joachim Ritter, 'Europäisierung als europäisches Problem', in his *Metaphysik und Politik*, 321–40.

[276] 'Technische Eingriffe in die Natur als Problem der politischen Ethik', in *Grenzen*, 466.

[277] For this idea and for the difference between substantial and accidental progress see 'Unter welchen Umständen kann man noch von Fortschritt sprechen?', in *Philosophische Essays*, 130ff., esp. 144.

[278] 'Philosophie als institutionalisierte Naivität', 142.

It is because of his Socratic understanding of philosophy that Spaemann can nonetheless ask Niklas Luhmann, for example, to join the conversation with him in spite of the all-encompassing and all-integrating claim of Luhmann's sociological system. Philosophy, he argues, has to converse with Luhmann's thought as the most reflected and most modern form of non-philosophy.[279] This invitation shows that Spaemann is critical of 'the deliberate secession of philosophy from the modern world as conceived by the sciences', which he sees at work in what he considers Heidegger's mystification of philosophy.[280] For, Heidegger's model, Spaemann argues, could lead to the victory of non-philosophical positivism rather than to its defeat. Spaemann's own understanding of philosophy allows him to invite thinkers like Luhmann to a conversation, and to prove the failure of his functionalistic positivism as well as the superiority of philosophy, properly understood, over any kind of totalizing scientific analysis. 'Philosophy', Spaemann has argued, with respect to psychological explanations of philosophy, 'lives off the resistance to the destruction of its naivety through psychological reflection'.[281] And it also lives, one might add, off the resistance to its destruction through sociological reflection.

The 'logic' of conversation that aims at substituting reasonable insight and genuine knowledge for mere opinions[282] is opposed to the logic of de(con)struction and reconstruction that characterizes a great deal of late modern philosophy and modern science. The logic of conversation is the logic of controversies and philosophical anarchy. It is also the logic of understanding, of the 'fusion of horizons'[283] and of a simultaneity throughout the centuries. It is the 'logic' of nature *and* freedom, of the self-evident *and* the contingent, of the universal *and* the particular, of continuity *and* of a plurality of conversations and theories, of consistency and ontological realism *and* of an open view of the world that rejects any ultimate systematization and closure. Philosophy as a conversation establishes a community that challenges the individualism and scientism of modernity as well as the cultural relativism of late modernity.

In one of the most famous passages of *After Virtue* Alasdair MacIntyre expressed his hope for the 'construction of new forms of community within which the moral life could be sustained so that both morality and civility might survive the coming ages of barbarism and darkness ... We are waiting

[279] *Paradigm Lost*, 73. See here also Spaemann and Nissing, 'Die Natur des Lebendigen und das Ende des Denkens' 135.
[280] 'Philosophie zwischen Metaphysik und Geschichte', 301.
[281] 'Philosophie als institutionalisierte Naivität', 140.
[282] 'Die kontroverse Natur der Philosophie', in *Philosophische Essays*, 109.
[283] For this notion see Hans-Georg Gadamer, *Truth and Method*, 2nd, rev., edn., trans. and rev. Joel Weinsheimer and Donald G. Marshall (London: Continuum, 2006), esp. 301–7.

not for a Godot, but for another—doubtless very different—St Benedict'.[284] MacIntyre develops a very pessimistic view of the future of humanity in which new models for a truly 'post-modern' communal and civic life are yet to be found. Walker Percy has made a similarly sceptical statement that recommends the virtue of waiting—letting be—as crucial in what is, at best, a transitional age. He has spoken of the sadness of modern man, who 'finds himself living after an age has ended and he can no longer understand himself because the theories of man of the former age no longer work and the theories of the new age are not yet known'.[285] Spaemann, too, does not come up with a fully-fleshed-out vision of what truly post-modern philosophy might look like. He thinks that many modern ideas need to be preserved, to be sure, but also that it is still too early properly to overcome modernity and to develop a truly post-modern philosophy that remedies the failures of modernity while at the same time preserving its important insights, such as its universal claim.[286] There are two main reasons for this. First of all, Spaemann, like Percy, reasons that we are living in a transitional period and that modernity is about to expire.[287] This means we still participate in modernity and, in consequence, it would be too early to provide an outline of post-modern philosophy, although a philosophical analysis of the modern age has become possible, if not even mandatory. Second, Spaemann criticizes modern philosophies and the inversion of the long-established relation between theory and practice, an important stage of which he finds in Descartes's philosophy and thus in a typically modern philosophy.[288] He re-establishes a notion of philosophy that highlights the dominant position of contemplative, theoretical reason that must not be subordinated to practical purposes though it may and should inform them. Hence, philosophy cannot but fail and become immoral if it attempts to foresee and design future developments as if it could take God's position. '[A] philosophy of history such as Hegel's is amoral', Spaemann writes, 'but not immoral, so long as it confines itself to retrospect and never slides into deliberation.'[289]

---

[284] *After Virtue*, 109.

[285] 'The Delta Factor', in *The Message in the Bottle*, 7.

[286] See in this context Spaemann's critique of communitarianism and of its disrespect for a universal perspective that does justice to the common nature of man in 'Zur Ontologie der Begriffe "rechts" und "links"', in *Grenzen*, 267–8.

[287] Spaemann, 'Die christliche Religion und das Ende des modernen Bewußtseins', 253.

[288] 'Praktische Gewißheit: Descartes provisorische Moral', in *Kritik der politischen Utopie*, 41.

[289] *Persons*, 132 (*Personen*, 142). For an account of Hegel's early philosophy of history see my 'Reason, Truth, and History: The Early Hegel's Philosophy of History', in Alfred Denker and Michael Vater (eds.), *Hegel's Phenomenology of Spirit: New Critical Essays* (Amherst, NY: Prometheus, 2003), 21–58.

The crisis of modernity is more than just a crisis of the spirit of modernity. Hans-Georg Gadamer said that he is

convinced that the development of modern science and technology, and so, too, of the world economy, possesses irreversible consequences for the fate of humankind on this planet. It is far from my intention to suggest that the path along which we have travelled from Greek antiquity through to Christianity will extend, in some mysterious way, into a broad and promising future.[290]

Spaemann shares this sceptical point of view towards the future of humanity. In this situation he recommends, as we have seen, 'letting be', the 'the fundamental act of freedom';[291] that is, in other words, 'the ability to let things be, disinterestedly[292] ['*uninteressiertes' Seinlassenkönnen*]'. This is the crucial virtue of a time in which, as the ecological crisis has shown, the idea of substantial progress becomes questionable and human possibilities both are limited and ought to be limited. In response to the crisis of the project of modernity Spaemann reminds us of an older understanding of philosophy. As long as we are still waiting for a fully post-modern age (which will come, as Spaemann thinks, without being explicitly intended), Spaemann's thought thus provides at least a preliminary remark to a retrieved *regula Benedicti*.[293] And in so doing, he may well be one of the '"reactionaries" who were ahead of their time without knowing it'.[294]

---

[290] 'Dialogues in Capri', in *Religion*, ed. Jacques Derrida and Gianni Vattimo (Stanford, Calif.: Stanford University Press, 1998), 204.

[291] 'Natur', in *Philosophische Essays*, 37; see also *Persons*, 77 (*Personen*, 87): 'Letting-be is the act of transcendence, the distinctive hallmark of personality'.

[292] *Reflexion und Spontaneität*, 87.

[293] For Spaemann's view of the Benedictines (and their non-modern way of life) see 'Die Benediktiner', in *Kirche und Leben*, 28 (10 July 1949). For Spaemann's understanding of the religious existence see 'Wer es fassen kann . . . Warum es den Ordensstand gibt', in *Kirche und Leben*, 27 (3 July 1949).

[294] 'Sein und Gewordensein', in *Philosophische Essays*, 187. Spaemann is referring here to those who resisted Galileo Galilei.

3

The dialectic of Enlightenment:
Spaemann's critique of modernity
and its dialectic

The danger of Enlightenment.—All the half-insane, theatrical, bestially cruel, licentious, and especially sentimental and self-intoxicating elements which go to form the true revolutionary spirit, before the revolution, in Rousseau—all this composite being, with factitious enthusiasm, finally set even 'enlightenment' upon its fanatical head, which thereby began itself to shine as in an illuminating halo. Yet, enlightenment is essentially foreign to that phenomenon, and, left to itself, would have pierced silently through the clouds like a shaft of light, long content to transfigure individuals alone, and thus only slowly transfiguring national customs and institutions as well. But now, bound hand and foot to a violent and abrupt monster, enlightenment itself became violent and abrupt. Its danger has therefore become almost greater than its useful quality of liberation and illumination, which it introduced into the great revolutionary movement. Whoever grasps this will also know from what confusion it has to be extricated, from what impurities to be cleansed, in order that it may then by itself continue the work of enlightenment and also nip the revolution in the bud and nullify its effects.

Friedrich Nietzsche

3.1 PHILOSOPHY AS A THEORY AND CRITIQUE
OF MODERNITY AND ITS DIALECTIC

Robert Spaemann, as we have already shown, defines philosophy as a 'recollection' and as a continuous conversation about ultimate questions. This is a kind of restorationist endeavour, for he proposes a 'return to normality'.[1] Philosophy, he argues, 'can be defined as "restoration" of what we all know and what is shaken through sophistic reflection'.[2] It is, he points out, a 'second

---

[1] 'Vorwort', in *Grenzen*, 10.
[2] 'Philosophie als Lehre vom glücklichen Leben', in *Philosophische Essays*, 86.

reflection' which questions the first reflection and its consequences by reflecting upon its very conditions and also its failures. Spaemann's view of philosophy is thus similar to Rousseau's in that he views philosophy as a second reflection that restores self-evident knowledge, but Spaemann does not share the latter's modernistic polarization of nature and history. As Spaemann shows, Rousseau forcefully criticized mediated knowledge and skills. He appeals to the immediate 'knowledge of the heart' in his attempt to overcome the self-alienation of humanity. This knowledge of the heart 'is immediately identical with the being of the human'.[3] For Rousseau, self-evident knowledge is not distorted by the techniques of civilization and the development of history. In Spaemann's view, however, we cannot follow Rousseau in idealizing a state of nature in opposition to the historical and social dimension of human life. This would entail a serious misunderstanding of what it means to be human. Nonetheless, criticism of the course that history has taken in modernity is in order.

As we have seen, Spaemann's embrace of the Socratic conception of philosophy as a conversational recollection along with the formal features of his thought have obvious critical implications for the appreciation of modernity. In contrast to the self-understanding of modern philosophy as an essentially creative and free enterprise, Spaemann's definition of philosophy as an anamnesis, a recollection, distinguishes philosophy sharply from the arts. The arts, Spaemann says, have 'their nature and fate in historical existence'.[4] He argues that the arts have long been the 'free play of the imagination'. The arts are future-oriented and provide an 'anticipation [*Vorschein*] of what is yet to come'. In contrast to the arts, philosophy, Spaemann suggests, does not construct and foresee its object, for its object—reality—is given.[5] However, the epoch that is characterized by a kind of division of labour between philosophy and the arts, Spaemann then observes, seems to have come to an end. In modernity, he states, philosophy increasingly takes over what has been pursued by the arts and loses its relation to reality as 'unpreconceivably' given. Consequently, not only does philosophy fail to understand reality fully, but the ambiguous and dangerous nature of persons also becomes evident, according to Spaemann, because '[h]uman personality is apparently turning against human nature'.[6] The endless process of human reflection increasingly

---

[3] 'Von der Polis zur Natur—Die Kontroverse um Rousseaus ersten "Discours"', in *Rousseau: Bürger ohne Vaterland*, 43.

[4] 'Philosophie zwischen Metaphysik und Geschichte: Philosophische Strömungen im heutigen Deutschland', in *Neue Zeitschrift für Systematische Theologie*, 1 (1959), 296.

[5] For the non-prophetic character of philosophy and its task see also Joachim Ritter, 'Über den Sinn und die Grenze der Lehre vom Menschen', in *Subjektivität: Sechs Aufsätze* (Frankfurt am Main: Suhrkamp, 1974) 36–61, esp. 59ff.

[6] *Persons*, 90 (*Personen*, 99).

undermines what cannot be totally subject to human reflection: transcendence; that is, the gift of reality beyond the reach of mere reflections of consciousness.[7] Reality, then, is ultimately understood as 'image', as something to be fashioned, to be designed, and to be created, and re-created. The difference between philosophy and the arts finally vanishes. Philosophy is no longer a 'recollection' and instead is mainly concerned with how to fashion reality autonomously and according to man-made purposes.

Modernity itself, for Spaemann, can therefore be characterized as a 'first reflection' that is in need of correction through a 'second reflection'. In his definition of philosophy as a continuous conversation, as we have seen, Spaemann implicitly rejects pervasive modern views of what philosophy fundamentally is and which methods it should employ, such as the view that philosophy needs to be new and original, critical—if not dismissive— of given traditions; that it needs to be systematic, foundational, and scientific—in a modern sense; and that it is an essentially monological enterprise, based upon a priori principles. He proves these claims inconsistent, and perilous because they tend to contribute to the abolition of freedom and human dignity. In stark contrast to these modern conceptions of philosophy, Spaemann argues that philosophy in our time ought to be an explicit or implicit 'theory of modernity'[8]—not a theoretical expression of modernity, but a critical account of it that is nonetheless still involved in, and indebted to, modernity.

In his critique of modernity and its naturalistic and historicist dimensions Spaemann thus asserts that the philosopher is not subject to the criteria and measures of modern rationality. Hence, Spaemann suggests that 'the self-consciousness of the philosopher can be compared to what the apostle Paul says about the spiritual person'.[9] Paul's statement that 'he that is spiritual judgeth all things, yet he himself is judged of no man',[10] Spaemann admits, seems to a modern audience the 'pinnacle of arrogance'.[11] The same may be true if one says this of the philosopher. For both philosophy and Christianity, Spaemann maintains, recollect a knowledge that provides a measure and criterion for 'absolute reflection' and universal judgement, particularly for a

---

[7] It is important to note once again that Spaemann is not dismissive of reflection (as was Fénelon, for instance). He considers reflection necessary and inevitable (this is why he speaks of the need for a 'second reflection'), but considers it important to find a balance between reflection and spontaneity (as the title of his examination of Fénelon suggests: *Reflexion und Spontaneität*) and thus criticizes over-reflection, as it were, as much as over-spontaneity.

[8] 'Einleitung', in *Philosophische Essays*, 6.

[9] 'Philosophie zwischen Metaphysik und Geschichte: Philosophische Strömungen im heutigen Deutschland', 290.

[10] 1 Cor. 2: 15.

[11] 'Christliche Spiritualität und pluralistische Normalität', in *Communio*, 26 (1997), 166.

critique of the scientistic and functionalistic spirit of modernity. Spaemann's philosophical (as well as his religious) writings are thus meant to recollect a knowledge that tends to be forgotten, overlooked, and undermined in part because of Christianity's (but not only Christianity's) 'progressive capitulation to the irrational pressure of modern Western civilization to conform to its forms of life and thought; that is to say, the scientific hypothesis, functionalism, the exchange of goods, and the experiment'.[12]

Modernity, in Spaemann's view, is the result of a dialectical process within the very understanding of reality; it is a complex process, characterized by inherent contradictions and antinomies rather than by a straightforward uniform development. What does this mean? For better or worse, Christianity, Spaemann forcefully argues, has contributed to a great many of the key features of modernity, such as the notion of morally responsible persons, a mechanistic view of nature, and the functionalistic account of politics. At the same time, modernity is characterized by powerful anti-Christian tendencies. Modernity saw the inversion of a teleological view of reality and the rise of the paradigm of self-preservation as well as the 'climax of teleological thought in the history of philosophy'.[13] Modernity developed the most intriguing insights into the dignity of the human person, and yet the dignity of the human person has never been so threatened as in modernity. Modernity, then, is essentially a multifaceted and very complex dialectical phenomenon that is in need of careful historical analysis.

In Spaemann's view, modernity developed dialectically because in modernity nature and freedom have become two equally abstract notions between which modern philosophy oscillates dialectically. Naturalism and transcendentalism, or scientism and hermeneutics, are therefore the two opposed yet intrinsically linked reductionistic perils to which modern reason inevitably succumbs if it does not regain a more realistic view of reality that is not based on the modern inversion of natural teleology.[14] For we 'cannot understand the natural and the rational as opposites',[15] Spaemann argues, without introducing the dialectic of naturalism and transcendentalism and its implications.[16]

The idea that modernity develops dialectically has been an important key to understanding the course of modernity ever since Jean-Jacques Rousseau

---

[12] 'Vorbemerkungen', in *Einsprüche: Christliche Reden*, 7.

[13] *Die Frage 'Wozu?'*, 179.

[14] For this dialectic see esp. Spaemann, 'Über den Begriff einer Natur des Menschen', in *Essays zur Anthropologie*, 15ff.

[15] *Happiness and Benevolence*, 159 (*Glück und Wohlwollen*, 206).

[16] For an account of this dialectic see also Ritter, *Subjektivität*, esp. 'Landschaft: Zur Funktion des Ästhetischen in der modernen Gesellschaft', 141–63.

first analysed the dialectical development of modern civilization and its contradictions.[17] Modernity, Robert Spaemann suggests along the lines of Rousseau, can be described as subject to a dialectic of emancipation and self-alienation.[18] Its problem is essentially the problem of freedom. Humanity's attempt to free itself from the constraining influences of what constitutes its very context—nature, society, history, religion, tradition, and its culture— have not, however, entailed a more pronounced realization of human freedom and human autonomy. On the contrary, according to Spaemann, modernity has brought with it the rise of a new kind of enslavement and alienation, at least in the long run and for most people. There is, therefore, on the one hand the much-hoped-for idea of creating a world civilization that overcomes all boundaries between different people, and on the other hand the impression that one's own identity is fundamentally called into question—for a universal context cannot provide us with an identity. Modernity is thus, according to Spaemann, characterized by 'a feeling of a fundamental threat to one's own identity'.[19] Imposing a universal horizon, however, tends to turn into the often arbitrary focus upon what constitutes our particular existence—religion, race, nation, etc.—in order to preserve our identity in a time when universalism challenges the very possibility of an identity of an individual.[20] Thus, humanity has alienated itself from its traditionally given sources and thus inevitably from itself. Autonomy generates its own heteronomy. The attempt to rid humanity of nature as a given and insurmountable norm that needs to be explored hermeneutically, rather than analysed scientifically and utilized technologically, has entailed a subsequent naturalization of human beings, for instance. Meaning then can only be seen as a 'variant of nonsense, reason a variant of unreasonableness, and the human being himself an anthropomorphism'.[21]

There is also the dialectic of rationalization and 'mythification'. This dialectic, Spaemann argues, underlies every other kind of dialectic of modernity:

---

[17] See Spaemann, 'Rousseaus "Emile": Traktat über Erziehung oder Träume eines Visionärs. Zum 200. Todestag von Jean-Jacques Rousseau', in *Rousseau: Bürger ohne Vaterland*, 92.

[18] 'Was ist das Neue? Vom Ende des modernen Bewußtseins', in *Die politische Meinung*, 203 (July/Aug. 1982), 13.

[19] 'Rationalität als "Kulturelles Erbe"', in *Scheidewege*, 14 (1984/5), 307. For this feature of modernity and an interesting account of modernity that has many parallels to Spaemann's see Stephen Toulmin, *Cosmopolis: The Hidden Agenda of Modernity* (New York: Free Press, 1990).

[20] See in this context also Martin Heidegger, 'Building Dwelling Thinking', in *Basic Writings from Being and Time (1927) to The Task of Thinking (1964)*, rev. and expanded edn., ed. David Farrell Krell (San Francisco, Calif.: HarperCollins, 1993), 343–63; Holger Zaborowski, 'Vorbehaltloser Vorbehalt: Zur Phänomenologie des Wohnens', in *Spielräume der Freiheit: Zur Hermeneutik des Menschseins* (Freiburg im Breisgau/Munich: Alber, 2009), 169–97.

[21] *Die Frage 'Wozu?'*, 11.

it is characteristic of modernity to emphasize the role of human rationality. The modern rationalistic approach asserted the full competence of reason to comprehend reality and its coming-to-be. Given the reductionism of modern rationality and its absolute claims, however, certain fundamental experiences, such as the experience of miracles, could no longer be made, or, at least, they could no longer be made sense of. Absolute prohibitions or absolute moral norms were increasingly challenged and questioned as though they were arbitrary conventions or impositions, because the dimension of the absolute cannot be understood from a scientific viewpoint. However, in order to make sense of many ethical insights one needs to rely on a specific kind of fundamental experience that goes beyond the reach of a modernistic misunderstanding of reason:

> The trouble is, that anyone who is genuinely unable to see a value distinction between, say, the loyalty of a mother to her child, the sacrifice of Maximilan Kolbe, the crime of his executioners, the unscrupulousness of a drug-pusher and the skill of someone speculating on the stock market is, by definition, so lacking in certain fundamental experiences and certain fundamental capacities for experience that no amount of rational argument could make up for them.[22]

Modern rationalization does not merely tend to undervalue experiences of absolute prohibitions and of absolute goods. The rationalistic scientism of modernity and its hypothetical and functionalistic outlook make it impossible even to understand absolute 'dimensions of humanity', which can only be relativized or instrumentalized at the cost of dehumanization.[23]

So modern rationality, in making itself an absolute, shows a dialectical development and turns against itself; 'rationality becomes irrational by becoming exclusive'.[24] This is why Spaemann points out that rationalization, in the long run, entails a 'mythification' of a particular kind of rationality that does not integrate its 'other' and thus does not overcome the alienation (*Entzweiung*) of modernity, but radicalizes the alienation. The archaic and irrational forces of life, Spaemann reasons, are in danger of being put 'into the service of a Utopian vision of a good life' if they are not domesticated

---

[22] *Basic Moral Concepts*, 8 (*Moralische Grundbegriffe*, 19); for Spaemann's view that not Maximilan Kolbe but his murderers lost their dignity see 'Über den Begriff der Menschenwürde', in *Grenzen*, 111.

[23] Spaemann refers to this traditional natural-law view of language, the body, and sexuality in 'Kommentar', in *Die Unantastbarkeit des menschlichen Lebens: Zu ethischen Fragen der Biomedizin*, Instruktion der Kongregation für die Glaubenslehre (Freiburg im Breisgau: Herder, 1987), 90.

[24] 'Die zwei Grundbegriffe der Moral' in *Kritik der politischen Utopie*, 13.

(*domestiziert*) but rather excluded and overcome rationally, to the extent that this is possible.[25]

Another important dialectic is the dialectic between the universal scientific system of means and the increasingly irrational nature of ends. Ends, Spaemann states, can neither be understood nor be defended from within a hypothesis-centred technological and scientific civilization. The technological civilization, he argues, is characterized by the 'consistent and radical distinction between ends and means'.[26] Such a civilization focuses upon what it claims is an objective description of reality and upon the evaluation of means, but can no longer determine meaningful and normative ends of human action. The scientistic civilization is therefore, as Spaemann reasons, 'designed as a grand universal system of means for arbitrary ends'.[27] This leads to a 'shattering of absolute prohibitions and rituals of human action'.[28] Any attempt to bridge the gap between factual and normative language is discredited as a naturalistic fallacy. Hence, modern scientific functionalism is, in Spaemann's view, incapable of conceptualizing absolute norms and the normative dimension of nature. Ends, norms, and meaning are thus reduced to hypotheses that are no longer part of the overall context of reality, but subject to the individual's choice. 'Meaning', Spaemann reasons against the utilitarian spirit of modernity, 'is not useful; meaning defines possible utility. It cannot be created intentionally. Intentional persuasions and certainties are called fanaticism'.[29]

Over against this aspect of the multivalent dialectic of modernity Spaemann defends the idea that meaning and ends are already given to us and are in need of rediscovery because we have lost touch with the ' "Tao" which is given humanity from above'.[30] For, the modern preoccupation with truth (or, to put it more precisely, *truths* that can be verified or falsified scientifically) and with the relationship between means and ends stands, according to Spaemann, no longer under the 'Tao', as it were. Anything appears valuable in so far as it can be utilized and reduced to a mere means of increasingly irrational purposes. But only if we do not abolish an 'unconditional

---

[25] 'Der Hass der Sarastro', in *Grenzen*, 187.

[26] 'Rationalität als "Kulturelles Erbe"', 308.

[27] Ibid. 309.

[28] Ibid. 308.

[29] 'Überzeugungen in einer hypothetischen Zivilisation', in Oskar Schatz (ed.), *Abschied von Utopia? Anspruch und Auftrag des Intellektuellen* (Graz: Styria, 1977), 330.

[30] 'Die christliche Religion und das Ende des modernen Bewußtseins: Über einige Schwierigkeiten des Christentums mit dem sogenannten modernen Menschen', *Communio*, 8 (1979), 252. See here also C. S. Lewis, *The Abolition of Man, or Reflections on Education with Special Reference to the Teaching of English in the Upper Forms of Schools* (Glasgow: Collins, 1982), 17, 31.

meaning . . . in the form of the modern idea of human dignity', Spaemann points out, is the technological civilization preserved from nihilism,[31] only then is civilization able to overcome the increasingly irrational nature of ends because we are able to recognize that the human person is an end in himself which is 'unpreconceivably' given and thus provides rationality and sciences with an absolute measure.

It is worth noting that Spaemann's criticism echoes those of Adorno and Horkheimer, both of whom also draw attention to the incapacity of a functionalistic modernity to understand value judgements and given ends:

The words that are not means appear senseless; the others seem to be fiction, untrue. Value judgements are taken either as advertising or as empty talk. Accordingly, ideology has been made vague and noncommittal, and thus neither clearer nor weaker. Its very vagueness, its almost scientific aversion to committing itself to anything which cannot be verified, acts as an instrument of domination.[32]

In addition to the dialectics that we have mentioned thus far there is, finally, the modern dialectic between tolerance and intolerance. Spaemann does not want to dispense with a culture of tolerance, of accepting differences between human beings; on the contrary, he defends tolerance in a manner that prevents the rhetoric of tolerance from turning intolerant itself and thus from undermining the very foundation of tolerance. The modern virtue of tolerance, he points out, is based upon an 'intolerant' presupposition. It presupposes a specific understanding of the human being, particularly of human dignity and freedom, that must not be considered a mere hypothesis. So tolerance cannot be a universal attitude. Whoever denies the presupposition of tolerance cannot be tolerated—for tolerance's sake. This is why if tolerance has been made an absolute and abstract virtue it turns into its very opposite, because in this form it is incapable of really accepting someone else's *substantial* persuasions—about the dignity of all human persons, for instance—which, from a totally relativistic or hypothetical point of view, not only evade true understanding, they are also the very *conditio sine qua non* of true tolerance.[33] An entirely hypothetical culture, Spaemann's argument therefore runs, makes true tolerance unattainable and replaces it with a power struggle of competing alternative hypotheses that ultimately involve the overthrow of tolerance and freedom. The 'conversion of all persuasions into hypotheses leads to the self-abolition of a free society'.[34]

---

[31] 'Rationalität als "Kulturelles Erbe"', 310–11.
[32] Theodor W. Adorno and Max Horkeimer, *Dialectic of Enlightenment* (London: Verso, 1986), 147.
[33] 'Rationalität als "Kulturelles Erbe"', 21–2.
[34] 'Überzeugungen in einer hypothetischen Zivilisation', 323.

This chapter will look more closely at Spaemann's detailed critique of modernity's dialectic, its rise and manifest crisis, which Spaemann frequently investigated explicitly.[35] We will mainly be concerned with the following questions. How does he characterize modernity? What are the distinct features of modern reason and its 'bourgeois ontology' of self-preservation?[36] How is modernity related to Christianity, and how is Spaemann's criticism of modernity informed by Christianity? Why does Jean-Jacques Rousseau, according to Spaemann, represent a 'paradigmatic existence' of modernity? Is there a principle feature of modernity from which all the other features that Spaemann considers characteristic of modernity can be derived, and, if so, what is it?

3.2 THE *GRANDEUR* AND THE *MISÈRE* OF MODERNITY

Among the critics of modernity there are, loosely speaking, two principal ways of analysing the history of modern thought. First, there is the Nietzschean and Heideggerian way of interpreting the history of Western philosophy as fundamentally defective more or less *ab initio*.[37] Second, there is the more limited and often also more differentiated approach of looking for specific paradigm shifts that led to, and sustained, a crisis of philosophical reasoning, an approach that can also be developed from Nietzschean and Heideggerian claims, but that does not necessarily imply a judgement about the history of Western thinking *tout court*. Particularly, the nominalist theologians and philosophers of the fourteenth century have been credited with significantly changing the presuppositions of philosophical reasoning and hence with ushering in this crisis. Critics of modernity have also referred to medieval mystics and subsequent mystical and spiritual movements, to Nicolaus Cusanus, Giordano Bruno, René Descartes, Baruch de Spinoza, or Francis Bacon as founding fathers of modern reasoning.

Robert Spaemann's understanding of the history of philosophy and its modern crisis belongs to the latter viewpoint. According to the narrative provided by his philosophy, modernity and, particularly, the problematic implications of modern thought originate from the transformations of late

---

[35] 'Unter welchen Umständen kann man noch von Fortschritt sprechen?', in *Philosophische Essays*; 'Ende der Modernität', in *Philosophische Essays*; 'Die christliche Religion und das Ende des modernen Bewußtseins'; 'Was ist das Neue?'; 'Rationalität als "Kulturelles Erbe"'.

[36] For the notion 'bourgeois ontology' see also *Reflexion und Spontaneität*, 58–71.

[37] For Spaemann's view of Heidegger's account of European philosophy see 'Philosophie zwischen Metaphysik und Geschichte', 299–300.

The dialectic of Enlightenment　　　　95

scholasticism and subsequent early modern philosophies.[38] These philosophies, as we have already seen, fostered the dichotomy between a mechanistic
notion of nature, understood as mere matter and raw object of human
exploration, exploitation, and manipulation, and a spiritualized and auton-
omized self, of which René Descartes's 'disengaged' self and John Locke's
'punctual' self, as Charles Taylor has put it,[39] are but the most prominent
examples.

As we have already seen, Spaemann does not engage modernity in a spirit of
condemnation. For him, modernity is a complex phenomenon, with both
characteristic failures and successes that ought not to be denied by anyone who
does not want to fall prey to a ludicrous anti-modern Romanticism. According
to Alasdair MacIntyre's rather fatalist account of modernity, there is no third
way between the rejection of the Enlightenment project and carrying it entirely
through to Nietzsche's destructive analysis of modern reason.[40] In MacIntyre's
view, modernity has its own cogent and inevitable logic, which is profoundly
flawed from its very beginning. Robert Spaemann evidently does not share
MacIntyre's criticism of modernity in its entirety. He permits himself to
acknowledge all the convolutedness of modernity without succumbing to a
sentimental and melancholic Romanticism or a fervent anti-modernism.
Modernity, he argues, is historically unique and irreversible,[41] and he both
resists the idea that the history of modern philosophy has *necessarily* developed
towards Nietzsche and at the same time emphasizes that modern philosophy
has a relatively continuous and consistent trajectory.[42]

Spaemann's criticism of modern reason is reminiscent of Charles Taylor's
tempered appreciation of modernity. After having proposed individualism,
the primacy of instrumental reason, and the loss of freedom as the three
fundamental malaises of modernity Taylor comes to a conclusion that strives
to do justice to both the benefits and the weaknesses of modernity. He asserts:
'There is in fact both much that is admirable and much that is debased and
frightening in all the developments I have been describing.'[43] He thus develops
a view that embraces both the *grandeur* and the *misère* of modernity, for 'only
a view that embraces both can give us the undistorted insight into our era that
we need to rise to its greatest challenge.'[44] In a similar way, Spaemann defines his

---

[38] See esp. *Die Frage 'Wozu?'*, 97 ff.
[39] See esp. Charles Taylor, *Sources of the Self: The Making of the Modern Identity* (Cambridge:
Cambridge University Press, 1998), 143–76.
[40] *After Virtue: A Study in Moral Theory* (London: Duckworth, 1985), 111.
[41] 'Ende der Modernität?', in *Philosophische Essays*, 237.
[42] cf. *Die Frage 'Wozu'?*
[43] *The Ethics of Authenticity* (Cambridge, Mass./London: Harvard University Press, 1991), 11.
[44] Ibid. 121. Here Taylor implicitly refers to Blaise Pascal's idea of a dialectic between the
grandeur and the *misère* of man.

task as thinking the presuppositions of Enlightenment 'in a consciousness which preserves the acquisitions of modernity by no longer defining itself through those acquisitions'.[45] The fact that there is a *grandeur* and *misère* of modernity finds its explanation in a fundamental ambiguity which is characteristic of modernity. Spaemann argues with respect to Leibniz's theodicy that 'the ambiguity of a great idea comes ... to light when a philosophy becomes exoteric, the ambiguity of its consequences'.[46] The same argument can be developed with respect to modernity and late modernity that has now become exoteric.

3.3 THE MAIN FEATURES OF MODERNITY AS AN AMBIGUOUS PHENOMENON

'Modern', Spaemann points out, is a formal and relative term that signifies the current culture.[47] This is why it is ambiguous, on his account, to speak of the 'end of modernity' or of 'post-modernity'. To do so, Spaemann maintains, is based on the premise that 'modern' has an absolute meaning. Modernity, on this reading, 'essentially defines itself in opposition to all previous history';[48] it is the contemporary period as opposed to past times and their ideas. Given such an understanding of 'modernity', Spaemann argues, any attempt to surpass modernity or to declare its end cannot but be read as a fundamental dismissal of modernity as such, unless one accepts two closely related premises.

The first premise is that modernity is conceived of as a substantial notion rather than as a purely formal one, so that 'modernity' stands for certain achievements of thought that may partly also deserve to be preserved. In this case modernity cannot be merely modern at root, Spaemann argues, but must contain something of timeless value. The second premise is that the end of modernity, that is to say 'post-modernity', does not imply the abolition of the positive achievements of modernity. Moving beyond modernity, Spaemann surmises, would then probably be an unspectacular, almost imperceptible change in our attitude towards modernity, not a radical rejection of its content. It rather strives to base the real insights into human self-realization

---

[45] Spaemann, 'Was ist das Neue?', 27.

[46] 'Leibniz' Begriff der möglichen Welten', in Venanz Schubert (ed.), *Rationalität und Sentiment: Das Zeitalter Johann Sebastian Bachs und Georg Friedrich Händels*, Wissenschaft und Philosophie: Interdisziplinäre Studien, 5 (St Ottilien: EOS, 1987), 9–10.

[47] For the following, see Spaemann, 'Ende der Modernität?', in *Philosophische Essays*, 232f.

[48] *Rationalität und Sentiment*.

for which we are deeply indebted to modernity upon foundations deeper than modernity. Such foundations, which safeguard the intrinsic limits of freedom and the teleological dimension of nature, can, in Spaemann's view, help to defend key ideas of modernity against their modernist interpretation and the tendency to self-abolition that is immanent within them.[49] Spaemann accepts these two premises: he does not consider modernity and post-modernity (properly understood) to be two mutually exclusive alternatives but suggests a way of appropriating modernity in a fashion that develops a material account of modernity (as opposed to a merely formal understanding of it), takes its achievements as seriously as its problems, and thus may offer a way around the dialectic of modernity.

What, then, are the main features of modernity? In the preface to his *Philosophische Essays* Robert Spaemann briefly draws attention to C. S. Lewis's *The Abolition of Man*, noting that this slim volume articulates all that Theodor W. Adorno and Max Horkheimer intended to say in the *Dialectic of Enlightenment*—more briefly, more soberly, and less dialectically (and, we might add, in a deeply Augustinian way that certainly accounts for Spaemann's fascination with Lewis).[50] *The Abolition of Man*, Spaemann holds, cannot be overestimated in the value and depth of its insights.[51] In this book C. S. Lewis mentions three main features of modernity: first of all, the value-full de-valuation of the world; second, the adoption of the natural sciences as the paradigm for reason; and, finally, the objectification of nature and of human beings. These tendencies, Lewis argues, imply a progressive deposition of human nature; the modern attempt to realize technologically what one understands to be the potentials of human beings paradoxically implies what Lewis describes as the 'abolition of Man'. Genetically designing human beings, for example, means 'abolishing' humanity and, as Spaemann argues, threatening the 'fundamental equality of all human beings upon which the solidarity of the human species is based'.[52] It furthermore ignores the 'temporal Gestalt' of human beings and the natural beginning of the person that corresponds to his dignity.[53] Modernistic strains of humanism thus seem inevitably to be in danger of turning inhumane because they

---

[49] Spaemann, 'Ende der Modernität?', in *Philosophische Essays*, 233f.

[50] 'Einleitung' in *Philosophische Essays*, 11. For Spaemann's critique of Adorno's and Horkheimer's Rousseauism see his brief remark on p. 12. For Spaemann's view of Lewis's *The Abolition of Man* see also 'Über den Begriff der Menschenwürde', in *Grenzen*, 121.

[51] 'Was ist das Neue?', 13.

[52] 'Wozu der Aufwand?', in *Grenzen*, 409.

[53] For this idea see Spaemann, 'Kommentar', in *Die Unantastbarkeit des menschlichen Lebens*, 87ff., esp. 95.

emancipate themselves from given limits that make life fully human. Human beings are begotten and not made,[54] and whoever renders human beings an object of making undermines the fundamental equality of all human beings.

All the features of Lewis's criticism of modernity are also characteristic of Spaemann's analysis of the modern age. In an essay entitled 'Ende der Modernität?' Spaemann points out that modernity, including late modernity, is characterized by seven main features: (1) it understands freedom as emancipation; (2) it develops the myth of a necessary and infinite progress; (3) it seeks a progressive dominion over nature; (4) it exhibits an objectivistic approach to reality; (5) it homogenizes experience; (6) it has lost sight of the limits of hypothetical perspectives; (7) it is characterized by a naturalistic universalism.[55]

These seven features are closely associated with one another. We will see that they ultimately reflect the modern attempt to deny original sin and, furthermore, to redefine nature, freedom, and their complementary relation so that human freedom and nature first become incommensurable and are then conflated with one another, be it in the form of spirit-centred idealism (or transcendentalism) or of naturalistic materialism (or naturalism). These characteristic features of modernity reflect the paradigmatic character of the sciences and their understanding of truth as a claim that is at once hypothetical and universal. Spaemann's interpretation of these features shows that in modernity reality has finally been rendered a product that tends to be understood in purely functionalistic terms.

The understanding of freedom as emancipation

Freedom, Spaemann argues, is related to what is not, and cannot be, subject to the *exercise* of freedom; that is to say, freedom is related to nature as its presupposition.[56] This view of nature and freedom calls into question the modern understanding of freedom as emancipation, as a 'continuous enlargement of possible options'.[57] In Spaemann's view, what is distinctive about the modern notion of freedom is the understanding of freedom as freedom *from*

---

[54] See for a discussion and examination of this 'human difference' also Oliver O'Donovan, *Begotten or Made?*, 2nd edn. (Oxford: Clarendon, 1998).

[55] 'Ende der Modernität?', in *Philosophische Essays*, 234 ff.

[56] For this section, see Spaemann, 'Ende der Modernität?', in *Philosophische Essays*, 234 f.

[57] Ibid. 235.

something.[58] This modern notion of freedom is opposed to two previous ways of understanding freedom.

In ancient Greece, Spaemann points out, freedom meant the permission to live in usual and traditional ways. The realm of freedom was a kind of 'second nature'. Under the influence of Greek philosophy and Christianity, however, the meaning of 'freedom' changed, because the traditional way of life in a city such as Athens was no longer considered the ultimate horizon of one's life. Freedom now meant 'self-determination'. The 'second nature' was no longer seen as an unquestionable given, mediated by a tradition that might be assumed unreflectively. The status quo became questionable, and in this instability human beings needed to reassure themselves of the measure of their freedom. What is true and right needed to be chosen freely while still being determined by what conforms to nature. This second meaning of freedom—self-determination within the limits of nature—still presupposed the first one, as Spaemann thinks. It was a further development based on an acknowledgement of the limits of the old understanding of freedom in a time in which what is actually the case is not always what ought to be the case.

The modern understanding of freedom, Spaemann states, no longer stands in this tradition but is very different. Modernity gives up on the idea that freedom itself entails an orientation toward a certain given measure, such as history, tradition, and nature, and the limits these involve.[59] Freedom, understood as radical and unlimited emancipation, becomes its own end, but it unmakes itself in the long run. 'For if possibilities are to be meaningful for free choice', as Oliver O'Donovan has put it, 'they must be well-defined by structures of limit.'[60] Because in modernity the idea of the limitation of freedom that makes freedom possible is no longer commonly shared, Spaemann points out, there is also no longer a commonly shared idea of a good life that could be the measure for the realization of one's freedom. Freedom becomes an abstract notion and loses its personal, social, and political context, even though there is, as he argues, 'no emancipation without solidarity'.[61] The underlying reason for this is that nature has lost its teleological implications and has been reduced to 'mere nature'. Since nature no longer

---

[58] For an account of the modern history of freedom, particularly of Hegel's understanding of freedom, see also Joachim Ritter, 'Subjektivität und industrielle Gesellschaft: Zu Hegels Theorie der Subjektivität', in *Subjektivität*, 11–35, esp. 18 ff.

[59] For a comparable account of pre-modern and modern concepts of freedom see Louis Dupré, *Passage to Modernity: An Essay in the Hermeneutics of Nature and Culture* (New Haven, Conn./London: Yale University Press, 1993), 120–44.

[60] *Resurrection and Moral Order: An Outline for Evangelical Ethics* (Grand Rapids, Mich.: Eerdmans, 1986), 107.

[61] 'Am Ende der Debatte um § 218 StGB', in *Grenzen*, 353.

provides an orientation for the understanding of human nature, of the good will, and thus of the exercise of freedom, the modern interpretation of freedom as an absolute was an almost automatic development, although, as Spaemann notes, this development has sometimes been limited on the basis of a pre-modern view of freedom. As an example of this limitation he points out that a 'tendency to self-abolition resides in the free-market economy' because of its dynamic toward absolute freedom. The constitutional state, however, limits the market economy, and such limitation is an 'enterprise against the trend' towards the progressive unmaking of freedom.[62] Spaemann accordingly argues that modernity must limit itself by remembering the 'unpreconceivable' limits of human action and human freedom. Remembering these limits shows that freedom does not need to be sacrificed to the functionalistic tendencies of modernity, that reason can remain substantial, that is to say not merely abstract, and thus 'the reason of life and not of death'.[63]

In outlining a critique of an abstract notion of freedom and the understanding of freedom as emancipation *from* given norms, Spaemann targets the prevailing moral features of modernity. These are, according to Alasdair MacIntyre, protest and indignation. In one of the most striking analyses in *After Virtue* MacIntyre associates protest and indignation with the modern focus upon the rights of the individual and upon utility. Because the notions of rights and of utility are 'a matching pair of incommensurable fictions', MacIntyre argues, protestors can never win an argument and can never lose it. In his eyes, protest cannot 'be rationally effective'.[64] The modern focus upon rights and utility, however, ultimately derives from the conviction that an emancipation from nature is the measure for the exercise of freedom, and from the dismissal of the common good and the good of each human being.

In a way that similarly criticizes this tendency of modern society Spaemann rejects the characterization of the goal of education as teaching young people 'how to stand up for their own interests'.[65] This would be the aim of an educational theory based upon the language of rights and protest and upon the principles of emancipation and increase of options. Such an education, then, is no longer a hermeneutics of what is already there. 'There is',

---

[62] 'Der Anschlag auf den Sonntag, in *Grenzen*, 275.

[63] For this idea see 'Die zwei Grundbegriffe der Moral', in *Kritik der politischen Utopie*, 18.

[64] *After Virtue*, 68–9.

[65] Spaemann, *Basic Moral Concepts*, 26 (*Moralische Grundbegriffe*, 38). For Spaemann's in-depth critique of emancipation as the goal of education see also 'Emanzipation—ein Bildungsziel?', in *Grenzen*.

Spaemann argues to the contrary, 'a much more fundamental task, which is to teach people how to have interests, that is to say, how to be interested in something'.[66] However, without a given measure, be it the traditional context of one's society as a 'second nature' or the context of nature as limiting human freedom, one cannot meaningfully discover one's true interests and their substantial reality—and it is in the mediation of this 'second nature' or our 'first nature' that the task of proper education lies.[67]

One of the main aims of Spaemann's philosophy is therefore to remember nature in freedom and thus the intrinsic bond between freedom and nature. This bond resists modernity's inherent tendency to make freedom an absolute—a tendency that inevitably eradicates freedom rather than preserving it: 'If human freedom is understood as absolute independence, then there is only one action left to us': suicide. Through committing suicide we remove ourselves from the workings of the world. This action, however, negates not only the natural condition of human life, but also freedom itself at the very moment that it seems to come into play. Freedom as an absolute, or total, concept is 'consumed by suicide because afterwards it no longer exists'.[68] In a similar way, 'a total notion of responsibility would lead to a corruption of the ethical, to the dissolution of the moral identity of the acting person',[69] because if one considers oneself to be totally and absolutely responsible, one cannot act any more in so far as action presupposes a concrete understanding of responsibility and its limits. Both infinite freedom and infinite responsibility make ethics ultimately impossible and lead to an abolition of agency and to 'moral indifference'.[70] A notion that becomes universal, as Spaemann remarks, breaks down, as 'with all notions that lose the relation to their opposite'.[71]

---

[66] *Basic Moral Concepts*, 26 (*Moralische Grundbegriffe*, 38).

[67] For this understanding of proper education see also Spaemann, *Happiness and Benevolence*, 158 (*Glück und Wohlwollen*, 205).

[68] *Basic Moral Concepts*, 81 (*Moralische Grundbegriffe*, 99); see also *Happiness and Benevolence*, 160 (*Glück und Wohlwollen*, 207).

[69] 'Die Herausforderung des ärztlichen Berufsethos', in *Grenzen*, 341. For Spaemann's critique of the idea of infinite responsibility see also 'Nebenwirkungen als moralisches Problem', in *Kritik der politischen Utopie*; *Happiness and Benevolence*, 123 ff. (*Glück und Wohlwollen*, 162 ff.); *Persons*, 97 ff. (*Personen*, 106 ff.); for his view of responsibility in general see also 'Verantwortung als ethischer Grundbegriff', in *Grenzen*; 'Wer hat wofür Verwantwortung', in *Grenzen*.

[70] 'Emanzipation—ein Bildungsziel?', in *Grenzen*, 487.

[71] 'Politisches Engagement und Reflexion: Rede zum 17 Juni 1964', in *Kritik der politischen Utopie*, 29.

The myth of a necessary and infinite progress

The modern idea that freedom is essentially an emancipation from nature and given norms entails a view of history as a progressive unfolding of autonomous freedom. In interpreting history as emancipation from nature, Spaemann points out, this modern view does not merely transform our understanding of nature. It also transforms and challenges the Christian account of salvation history. The history of the *civitas Dei* is, according to the Christian tradition as famously expressed by, for instance, Augustine, different from the history of the *civitas terrena*; salvation transcends the realm of the worldly city.[72] Modernity, however, transfers the Christian promise, valid for the *civitas Dei*, to world history and secularizes it. History turns into the object of human planning, designing, and foreseeing what appears historically necessary, be it in the idealist Hegelian way of analysing the implications of the development of the absolute spirit or in the materialist Marxist way of interpreting the implications of the dialectic of social change and development without being able to do justice to man's capacity really to transcend his nature.[73] Metaphysics thus turns into philosophy of history as *prima philosophia*. In Spaemann's view, this philosophy, in its endeavours to make statements about the future, about the necessary progress of humanity, and hence about the overall meaning of history, represents one of the major myths of modernity.[74]

Spaemann contrasts the modern understanding of history as progress with pre-modern conceptions of progress in order to examine what is typical of modernity and its understanding of history. He demonstrates that the modern notion of a universal and necessary progress is an empty and abstract notion and is thus subject to the dialectical tendency of abstract notions to turn into their opposite. Pre-modern philosophy, he argues, also had an idea of progress at its disposal. Progress, however, was then defined as the improvement of something that is teleologically structured. The *telos* provides the measure for this improvement and makes it possible to distinguish between true progress and regression.[75] The modern understanding of progress, however, no longer relies upon a teleological understanding of reality

[72] Spaemann speaks of the 'incredible actuality' of Augustine's *Civitas Dei* in his 'Über die gegenwärtige Lage des Christentums', in *Das unsterbliche Gerücht*, 243.
[73] For Spaemann's critique of Marx's position see also his 'Zur Ontologie der Begriffe "rechts" und "links"', in *Grenzen*, 265.
[74] 'Ende der Modernität?', in *Philosophische Essays*, 236. For an excellent analysis of this feature of modernity's mind-set see also Pierre Manent, *The City of Man*, trans. Marc A. LePain, foreword Jean Bethke Elshtain (Princeton, NJ: Princeton University Press, 1998).
[75] 'Ende der Modernität?', in *Philosophische Essays*, 236.

and is thus subject to the illusion of a total progress; that is to say, the idea that progress is the measure for everything and not just an aspect of reality.

This is why there are, to sum up Spaemann's argument, two significant differences between the modern and the pre-modern understanding of progress. First, pre-modern thought did not develop the idea of an absolute universal progress that is not simultaneously relativized by retrogression and by deterioration as the inevitable cost of any kind of progress. Modernity, however, uses progress in the singular (there is only one universal progress without any kind of substantial retrogression), and thus, Spaemann points out, as a 'notion of intimidation'.[76] Second, pre-modern thought did not interpret progress as necessary. The notion of historical necessity, Spaemann argues, has been modelled on a misconception of biological models and thus on the modern natural sciences.[77] It is reflective of the historicist naturalization of history. However, in Spaemann's view, progress is neither absolute nor necessary. If true progress is to happen, he thinks, 'it depends essentially upon our not simply forgetting what we once already knew'.[78] If we forget what we have already known, he makes clear, regression will ultimately be the result, because 'the finitude of human existence [*Dasein*] and the endlessness of progress are incommensurable'.[79] Thus, human beings must not simply be understood as a means towards the end of the progress of history.

The progressive dominion over nature

The myth of progress also affects our understanding of the sciences substantially. Spaemann therefore points out that 'what brings about the historical uniqueness and irreversibility of modernity is the systematic instrumental use of the sciences in the service of the human practice of life'.[80] The investigation of reality is no longer primarily pursued for its own sake. It is utilized for the sake of achieving the dominion over nature which is based upon 'systematically prescinding from the essence and nature of what is dominated'.[81]

Spaemann argues that this feature of modernity is not entirely new. It radicalizes a feature of the pre-modern approach to reality. What is distinctive about modernity is the idea that dominion over nature will progressively

[76] 'Die Herausforderung des ärztlichen Berufsethos', in *Grenzen*, 351.
[77] 'Ende der Modernität?', in *Philosophische Essays*, 237.
[78] 'Emanzipation—ein Bildungsziel?', in *Grenzen*, 489.
[79] 'Praktische Gewißheit: Descartes' provisorische Moral', in *Kritik der politischen Utopie*, 52–3.
[80] Ibid. 237.
[81] Spaemann, 'Kommentar', in *Die Unantastbarkeit des menschlichen Lebens*, 70.

increase. This dominion, Spaemann states, is a despotic dominion 'which progressively reduces the *Selbstsein* of what is dominated'.[82] Human practice no longer considers what nature as such is—'as a self-enclosed context of meaning, as monadic world which is in a sense unique and incommensurable'.[83] It develops a reductionistic view of nature so as to subject nature to its self-made purposes without an obligation to do justice to nature's own *telos*. That is to say, modernity does not attempt to understand nature hermeneutically as it shows itself to us by analogy to human self-experience; that is, by 'comprehending an intentional structure'.[84] On the contrary, modernity attempts to explain nature scientifically, as defined and objectified by human beings, because it finds 'talking with nature' in order to 'understand it in itself' to be 'useless', unempirical, and meaningless.[85]

The development of a new approach to nature, as Spaemann points out, was possible, first, because of capitalism as the 'socio-economic constellation that initiated a process of continuously accelerating revolutions of the conditions of human life'.[86] It was possible, second, because of a specific type of science which construed its results within a distinctly non-teleological mathematical framework. Modern sciences thus lost sight of final causes and of the difference between qualitative and quantitative statements, because reality was supposed to be explicable within an entirely mechanistic framework that could fully be understood by means of mathematicical calculation.[87]

Theodor W. Adorno and Max Horkheimer have also spoken of the modern dominion over nature and its context. It is noteworthy that they relate the modern dominion over nature to the cultural amnesia of modernity in a way that is reminiscent of Spaemann's idea that modernity no longer understands freedom as 'recollected nature'. The dominion over nature, Adorno and Horkheimer argue, has only become possible because we are living in a culture of oblivion. The loss of memory is, in their view, the transcendental condition for science. This is why, for them, any kind of objectification is a

---

[82] 'Ende der Modernität?', in *Philosophische Essays*, 237.

[83] '*Die Frage 'Wozu?*', 285.

[84] For Spaemann's notion of understanding see *Die Frage 'Wozu?*', 17–19.

[85] Ibid. 15.

[86] 'Ende der Modernität?', in *Philosophische Essays*, 238.

[87] For the far-reaching implications of the 'mathematization' of reality see also Robert Sokolowski, *Phenomenology of the Human Person* (Cambridge: Cambridge University Press, 2008), 115: 'The transformation of the world into a mathematical world is not an isolated philosophical issue (no philosophical issue can ever be isolated, since philosophy as such is the inquiry into the widest context of things); it is related to political philosophy and philosophical anthropology, as well as to ethics and logic'.

forgetting.[88] From this point of view, the connection among Spaemann's ideas—the notion that philosophy is recollection of self-evident knowledge, his critique of modernity, and his natural philosophy—is manifest. To remember nature means to undermine the basic principles of the modern sciences and their claims and to overcome their focus upon what is as mere objects 'presently' and observably there.

The next four features of modernity are its objectivism, its homogenization of experience, its understanding of reality as hypothesis, and its naturalistic universalism. All these features are, according to Spaemann's account, the 'consequences of the reconstruction of life, first by the modern natural sciences and subsequently by the humanities as modelled on the natural sciences'.[89]

The objectivism of modernity

According to Spaemann, modern epistemology establishes a gap between the perceiving subject and nature as the object of our perception, a gap that changes the very nature of scientific investigation. This also has significant implications for the object: 'The object of the domination of nature', Spaemann reasons, 'is essentially what is dead; sciences only know passivity, only dependent variables'.[90] The object of modern scientific research, Spaemann therefore argues, is made immobile and loses its natural direction, because the modern sciences attempt to speak of motion in exact terms, 'but . . . at the cost that natural things no longer move'.[91] Nature as an object of human manipulation is thus no longer understood, or contemplated, as life and as analogical to our own self-experience, as Spaemann argues should be the case. For, the contemplative view of nature as teleological is at odds with the methods of the natural sciences, which thus abstain by definition from interpreting nature by analogy to the personal experience of *Selbstsein*[92] because 'the form of scientific objectivity is the form of causal explanation'.[93] This makes nature alien to

---

[88] Adorno and Horkheimer, *Dialektik der Aufklärung*, in Horkheimer, *Gesammelte Schriften*, ed. Alfred Schmidt and Gunzelin Schmid Noerr (Frankfurt am Main: Fischer, 1987), 263 ('Die perennierende Herrschaft über die Natur aber . . . sie wäre durch Vergessen erst möglich gemacht. Verlust der Erinnerung als transzendentale Bedingung der Wissenschaft. Alle Verdinglichung ist ein Vergessen').

[89] 'Ende der Modernität?', in *Philosophische Essays*, 238. For what follows see esp. 'Die christliche Religion und das Ende des modernen Bewusstseins', 254 ff.

[90] 'Die christliche Religion und das Ende des modernen Bewußtseins', 255.

[91] *Die Frage 'Wozu?'*, 38. For a historical account of the 'emergence of objectivity' see Louis Dupré, *Passage to Modernity*, 65–90.

[92] *Die Frage 'Wozu?'*, 23.

[93] 'Ende der Modernität?', in *Philosophische Essays*, 239.

human persons; subject and object are polarized, and reality is no longer experienced as 'friendly', as the appropriate and fitting context of human life—in contrast to the view of classical and medieval metaphysics, for which, as Spaemann points out, 'the subject of the dominion over nature is itself part of a teleologically structured nature'.[94]

Modern objectivism, furthermore, tends to subsume everything into its ontological and epistemological framework, even though, as Spaemann argues, the 'idea of a total "scientification" of human existence is absurd because it does not consider that the subject of the sciences is infinite, but fictitious, while the real human being is finite'.[95] This contradiction between the epistemological and ontological implications of modern sciences, on the one hand, and the reality of the human being, on the other, shows that an abstract objectivism, taken to its extreme, turns inhumane. For scientific objectivism disregards the finitude of human beings and reduces them to either passive objects of the sciences or to mere parts of the universal scientific community that, in their particularity, are negligible. This, ironically, is not a truly 'objective' view of reality. Spaemann therefore calls it one of the uncorrected biases of modern thought that something seems to be the more objective the less subjective it is.[96]

So the anti-teleological objectification of nature[97] even goes so far as utterly to objectify and naturalize human beings, even though this entails a considerable misunderstanding of what it means to be human. For '*Selbstsein* is categorically inaccessible to [the sciences]'.[98] Persons who are 'at once subjects and objects'[99] freely transcend their nature. It is, Spaemann therefore argues, the 'non-identity with their nature that entitles us to call human beings "persons"'.[100] Yet if a person who is not simply identical to his nature but 'has' his nature is viewed from a scientistic perspective, the person's self-understanding will inevitably appear to be an anthropomorphism; that is, an understanding that is not based on the objectivity of the sciences but upon the prejudice of the subjective self-experience of the person.[101] And in so far as anthropomorphisms do not conform to the epistemological standards of

---

[94] *Die Frage 'Wozu?'*, 104.
[95] 'Überzeugungen in einer hypothetischen Zivilisation', 328.
[96] *Persons*, 89 (*Personen*, 99).
[97] In *Persons* Spaemann argues that this is a distinctly modern endeavour: 'Antiquity knew no way of getting behind the nature of a man or woman, no way of regarding the nature itself as an object' (*Persons*, 31 (*Personen*, 22)).
[98] *Die Frage 'Wozu?'*, 275.
[99] 'Die Herausforderung des ärztlichen Berufsethos', in *Grenzen*, 351.
[100] *Persons*, 81 (*Personen*, 91).
[101] 'Ende der Modernität?', in *Philosophische Essays*, 240.

modernity, the understanding of the person needs to be 'de-anthropomorphized'. Persons need to be understood in merely scientific terms (which implies not to understand them as persons!).

In this context, Spaemann speaks of the ' "colonialization" of our life-world by science' which 'appears to have made the concept of action, and with it the human, obsolete. There seems to be only systems without subjects, in which the human appears under different aspects, without the possibility of being able to refer to "reality"'.[102] The objectivism of modern scientism thus not only renders impossible the experience of the reality of nature, it also becomes an instrument of humanity's self-alienation and self-abolition. This can only be averted if a view of reality is recollected which maintains that, in the end, all human knowledge is anthropomorphic and that anthropomorphisms cannot and need not be entirely avoided, for they are the *conditio sine qua non* of proper knowledge about reality. As humans, we can, in the end, only attain knowledge through our human eyes.

The objectivism of modernity also has significant implications for ethics, for it does not allow for a transition from descriptive to normative language. Given the methodological premise of modern scientism, it is impossible really to make sense of the normative dimension of Being. In his epoch-making criticism of the naturalistic fallacy David Hume writes:

In every system of morality, which I have hitherto met with, I have always remark'd, that the author proceeds for some time in the ordinary way of reasoning, and establishes the being of a God, or makes observations concerning human affairs; when of a sudden I am surpriz'd to find, that instead of the usual copulations of propositions, *is*, and *is not*, I meet with no proposition that is not connected with an *ought*, or an *ought not*. This change is imperceptible.[103]

If reality is no longer teleologically structured, but only the 'mere object' of human research and planning, there can be, by definition, no transition from 'is' to a moral 'ought'. The subjective realm of freedom cannot but be strictly opposed to the objective realm of nature, in which a natural good no longer inheres.

Human beings have not only been objectified by the natural sciences; they have also been objectified by the social sciences. This is perhaps most obvious in educational theory. C. S. Lewis argues that education, which in the past had been understood as an initiation, is nowadays understood as a conditioning, that is to say as a kind of propaganda, which, as he remarks critically, will lead

---

[102] *Happiness and Benevolence*, 147–8 (*Glück und Wohlwollen*, 191–2).
[103] *A Treatise of Human Nature*, ed. L. A. Selby-Bigge, 2nd edn., with rev. text and variant readings by P. H. Nidditch (Oxford: Clarendon, 1985), 455–70 (III. I. I), esp. 469–70.

to 'men without chests'.[104] In Lewis's view this 'atrophy of the chest' characterizes modern man because he has lost touch with the Tao. Spaemann shares this critical view of modern education and explicitly draws attention to Rousseau's ridicule of the bourgeoisie and their colleges.[105] Education, Spaemann thinks, cannot be understood as a making, based on the objectification of human beings; on the contrary, it needs to be understood as education into reality. Therefore, the educator needs to take seriously the student's *Selbstsein* (and must not regard him as an object), for otherwise he cannot attain insight into reality. Walker Percy defines the task of teachers as follows: 'The highest role of the educator is the maieutic role of Socrates: to help the student come to himself not as a consumer of experience but as a sovereign individual'.[106] This finds an echo in Spaemann's idea that philosophy needs to be reminded of its Socratic roots and that the philosopher as educator as much as any other educator needs to remind his students of what they have already known. The philosopher is, in Spaemann's Socratic view, a midwife and not an architect or producer of educated people, particularly since education is, in his view, a 'by-product' of the shared life of teacher and pupil.

The scientific objectivism of modernity also makes it impossible to understand the absolute and the ultimate. While the sciences cannot understand anything ultimate, 'the practice of life is the medium of the ultimate. This is the reason', Spaemann concludes, 'for the incommensurability of science and life'.[107] This is why the metaphysical and epistemological paradigm shift towards objectivism bears significant implications also for Christianity, for Christians believe that their 'interior view of reality is the ultimate truth about the world and humanity'.[108]

Thus, in Spaemann's view, modern objectivism has serious ontological and ethical implications. In the end, objectivism and naturalism revert, ironically, to a spiritualized idealism, for there is ultimately nothing but an infinite becoming if all that we have is natural processes as understood by a scientistic metaphysics. Given this dialectic, the absolute claim of modern scientism demands a decision by humanity. In *Die Frage 'Wozu?'* Spaemann and his

---

[104] *The Abolition of Man*, 19. Walker Percy has similarly criticized modern 'colleges' and the education that they provide. They tend to reduce students to consumers of an alienating experience of reality that is 'radically devalued by theory' ('The Loss of the Creature', in *The Message in the Bottle: How Queer Man Is, How Queer Language Is, and What One Has to Do with the Other* (New York: Farrar, Strauss and Giroux, 1986), 63).

[105] 'Natürliche Existenz und politische Existenz bei Rousseau', in *Rousseau: Bürger ohne Vaterland*, 25.

[106] 'The Loss of the Creature', in *The Message in the Bottle*, 63.

[107] 'Über den Mut zur Erziehung', in *Grenzen*, 500.

[108] 'Christliche Spiritualität und pluralistische Normalität', 166.

co-author Reinhard Löw conclude that human beings must resolve to interpret nature in an anthropomorphic way that is based upon their own self-understanding, for otherwise human beings will under the influence of modern scientism inevitably become (illegitimate) anthropomorphisms and worldless subjects who cut the ground from under their own feet.[109] 'The attempt to dismiss an anthropomorphic point of view', Spaemann argues, 'can *realiter* only succeed in the way of the ultimate self-abolition of humanity on earth'.[110] This means that if human beings do not limit the claim of scientific objectivism and its tendency to render the 'friendly' alien they will no longer be able to understand themselves and what it means to live a human life. This is why the question about natural teleology leads to the practical question 'whether the familiarity in the circle of what is friendly is more desirable than the security through progressive domination over the alien'.[111] In light of this question, Spaemann and Löw's 'nice obituary of teleology' leads to the recognition that only a 'weak caricature' of teleology has died in modernity and that the true teleology 'as always, offers a rich meal, both to its persecutors and to its adherents'.[112] Otherwise, if teleology really had 'died', all its 'self-appointed heirs' would have died as well, because a policy of avoiding anthropomorphism could only be carried through with strict consistency at the price of the self-abolition of the human race.[113]

Such a policy would have manifold further implications, as Spaemann shows. He reasons, for instance, that the notion 'causality' cannot properly be understood without taking into account personal self-experience, because causality cannot be observed objectively.[114] If we speak of causes, according to Spaemann's argument, we presuppose knowledge about human action and thus not only a teleological point of view but also a reflective knowledge of ourselves. 'There are mechanisms', Spaemann argues, in the context of his discussion of Hegel's philosophy, 'only under the premise of life, and, to put it differently, teleology is the truth of mechanism'.[115] For, the perceiving subject not only determines what needs to be explained causally (B) and what explains it causally (A). We also 'impinge upon an event, A, by acting

[109] *Die Frage 'Wozu?'*, 288.   [110] Ibid. 274.
[111] Ibid. 22.   [112] Ibid. 239.
[113] Ibid. 274ff.
[114] Here Spaemann provides important arguments for a discussion of the Humean and post-Humean naturalistic understanding of causality. For Hume's two famous definitions of causality, or causation, see, for example, David Hume, *An Enquiry Concerning Human Understanding*, ed. Tom L. Beauchamp (Oxford: Oxford University Press, 1999), 146.
[115] *Die Frage 'Wozu?'*, 167. For a critical examination of mechanism see also Charles Taylor, 'How is mechanism conceivable?', in *Philosophical Papers, I. Human Agency and Language* (Cambridge: Cambridge University Press, 1985), 164–86.

on it in deed or thought, we vary it, and then we ascertain...what happens with B'.[116] For otherwise we could only determine 'what happens successively in the flux of things'.[117] That is, it is impossible to determine, as Spaemann points out, whether the regular crowing of the rooster in the morning makes the sun rise, unless one encroaches actively upon the order of things.[118] Causality, furthermore, needs to be experienced subjectively (in that we intentionally cause things to happen) before we can use it as a category to understand non-human reality. Hence, the notion 'cause' still has teleological implications.[119] This is why the dismissal of natural teleology, so Spaemann reasons, entails finally a dismissal of the notion of 'causality', which is replaced with 'accordance with the laws of nature'. Initially this occurs for theological reasons, as Spaemann points out, for God is thought to 'cause all things to follow one another according to the laws of nature'. If God is left out, however, 'only a regular succession is left, without the attempt to understand it'.[120] Hence, the modern notion of 'natural law' does not, in Spaemann's view, demand any kind of understanding (as opposed to explanation) except the understanding of the words in which the law of nature is formulated.[121]

In a comparable manner, Spaemann argues, the scientific talk of system is meaningless unless one presupposes the self-experience of the human person. Human conscious life, he reasons, is the 'the presupposition for the qualification of even the most simple system as system'.[122] Systems, Spaemann reasons, are particular arrangements of matter that ought to uphold an identical state of affairs. This is why 'they suggest...a teleological interpretation'.[123] Given this difference between systematic and non-systematic arrangements of matter, we can only speak of systems under 'the premise of the consciousness of identity'.[124] In other words, without the 'unsystematic' experience of *Selbstsein* and its identity over time we could not speak of systems, but only of random arrangements of matter. This shows that the objectivistic systematization of the whole of reality fails to account for its key notions and thus inevitably undermines itself.

The homogenization of experience

Spaemann forcefully points out that the homogenization of experience is the main characteristic of modern Enlightenment culture.[125] He states that

---

[116] *Die Frage 'Wozu?'*, 246.   [117] Ibid.   [118] Ibid. 245–6.
[119] Ibid. 21.   [120] 'Leibniz' Begriff der möglichen Welten', 35.
[121] *Die Frage 'Wozu?'*, 21.   [122] Ibid. 251.   [123] Ibid. 250.
[124] Ibid. 251.   [125] 'Ende der Modernität?', in *Philosophische Essays*, 241.

experience, properly conceived, has two implications that contrast oddly with the scientific notion of experience. Experience (*Er-fahrung*) originally refers to knowledge that we achieve by travelling (*fahren*) through the world. It also has the implication that experience can disappoint our expectations, tends to challenge our perception of reality, and changes us. This is why human beings cannot control what they experience. Experience is in its original meaning something given that affects and surprises us; it points to the openness of future, rather than to something made, prognosticated, and planned. However, the modern scientific community that sets up scientific conditions for experience cannot but misconceive the full notion of proper experience. The scientific homogenization of experience, Spaemann points out, is counter-intuitive and contradicts our human self-experience and morality. For it is, among others things, at odds with the 'immediate "vision" of what ought not to be the case'[126] in so far as it does not permit the experience of this vision in the first place.

Yet in modernity the homogenizing natural sciences have sought to explain the reality of nature and of the human person more comprehensively than philosophy appears to them to do. They even tend to replace philosophy (properly understood) and its focus on self-evident knowledge, despite the fact that, as Charles Taylor has pointed out, we cannot just leap outside the terms in which human beings live their lives 'on the grounds that their logic doesn't fit some model of "science" and that we know a priori that human beings must be explicable in this "science"'.[127] In this ambitious endeavour natural sciences challenge every other kind of experience that does not fit their concept of experience—especially the experience of contingent particular events, such as religious, mystical, or interpersonal experiences—both because of their interest in dominion over nature and because of their interest in certainty and stability.[128] Within the framework of this reductive scientific notion of experience, certain (rather unsettling and destabilizing) phenomena, such as the experience of friendship, miracles, and the reality of sacrifice, Spaemann argues, can no longer be articulated.[129] Because transubstantiation, he points out as an example, cannot be discussed in the categories of modern sciences, it turns 'either into magic or it declines in a subjectivist way

---

[126] 'Tierschutz und Menschenwürde', in *Grenzen*, 468.
[127] *Sources of the Self*, 58.   [128] *Die Frage 'Wozu?'*, 103 ff.
[129] For an examination of Francis Slade's interesting remark that for Hobbes, one of the eminent proponents of early modern scientific reasoning, 'friendship is terrible' see Thomas Prufer, 'Notes on Nature', in his *Recapitulations: Essays in Philosophy* (Studies in Philosophy and the History of Philosophy, xxvi) (Washington, DC: The Catholic University of America Press, 1993), 25–6.

to a mere "transignification".[130] Modern science is therefore, in Spaemann's view, wrongly called empirical science, because the 'concrete experience plays for it only a marginal role'.[131] In contrast to the scientific view of reality and the scientific claim to realism, Spaemann asserts that 'only he who believes in miracles is a realist'.[132] Spaemann ascertains that the underlying ontological idea of the modern scientific notion of experience is that there is nothing in particular but, at the very most, a change of the same universal substance. Radically new and unforeseeable developments such as real coming-into-existence, real passing away, and miracles can therefore no longer be experienced and thus can no longer be conceptualized. Given the homogenization of reality, 'there is nothing new, there is no new beginning; we have to explain the higher forms of reality with regard to the lower and older forms of reality; mind with regard to life; life with regard to inorganic matter'.[133]

This, again, contradicts our self-experience as persons. The fact that there are persons (which is at the heart of our self-experience), therefore, makes it necessary to question the modern tendency to make change (*alloiosis*) an absolute at the expense of utterly new coming-into-existence (*genesis*) and passing away. For the person *comes into existence* all at once, as something new: personal existence is not a mere modification of some underlying, evolving matter; and death is not 'a change of our material substratum, but a threat to our existence'.[134] The existence of persons, therefore, calls into question the viewpoint of the sciences and their reductionistic and homogenizing methodologies because the individual discloses something fundamentally novel which resists any scientific attempt to homogenize it.[135] In contrast to the modern scientific view of reality, therefore, Spaemann attempts to rehabilitate an ontological and epistemological framework within which the individual can again be understood—not simply as a specimen of a species or as an event in the universal flow of matter, but as an ever unique and species-transcending individual with his own dignity.

That there are persons, who can talk to one another, be friends, love, and even sacrifice themselves, also makes it necessary to amend the physical

---

[130] 'Die christliche Religion und das Ende des modernen Bewußtseins', 256. For a similar critique of the idolatrous (modernistic) understanding of the Eucharist see Jean-Luc Marion, *God Without Being*, trans. Thomas A. Carlson (Chicago, Ill.: University of Chicago Press, 1991), 161–82.

[131] 'Die Herausforderung des ärztlichen Berufsethos', in *Grenzen*, 342.

[132] 'Erziehung zur Wirklichkeit', in *Grenzen*, 511.

[133] 'Die christliche Religion und das Ende des modernen Bewußtseins', 259.

[134] 'Über den Begriff einer Natur des Menschen', in *Essays zur Anthropologie*, 22.

[135] According to Percy, 'science cannot utter a single word about an individual molecule, thing or creature in so far as it is an individual but only in so far as it is like other individuals' ('The Delta Factor', in *The Message in the Bottle*, 22).

understanding of a homogenous time. Human time is the subjective time of freedom as it relates to, and often radically transcends, its nature. It therefore has the character of an event rather than of a continuous chain of mutually interchangeable instants. The time of *Selbstsein* is not homogenous. It is, in Spaemann's view, the event of the disclosure of *Selbstsein* and requires, like religious belief, a 'break with the disbelief in the new'.[136]

The understanding of reality as a hypothesis

Spaemann argues that ours is a hypothetical culture. The idea that any kind of truth claim is of a merely hypothetical character and hence subject to the continuous attempt to falsify it has become characteristic of the modern approach to reality. In Spaemann's view, this is reflected even in the arts, for the modern 'artist understands himself as entertainer, as stimulator of an experimental life'.[137] According to Spaemann, modernity thus comprises cultures that have universalized the methodological claim of the natural and social sciences. It is important to note here that, as Spaemann underlines,

a hypothetical way of thinking is in practice identical with a functionalistic way of thinking. Functionalistic thought seeks equivalents. To define a thing by its function means not to ask what a thing is as such, but in which functional context it stands ... But this means at the same time to ask through which equivalent ... it can be replaced.[138]

The tendency towards functionalism and a hypothesis-centred view of reality is perhaps best exemplified by the rise of evolutionary metaphysics as a new grand narrative and by the development of what one may aptly call a 'Darwin industry'.[139] Evolutionary metaphysics has become increasingly popular be-cause a metaphysical interpretation of evolutionary theory amalgamates naturalism, nominalism,[140] scientism, and functionalism. Despite also being substantially criticized,[141] evolutionary theory has been interpreted as a metaphysical position; it has become a popular 'scientific paradigm in the sense of Thomas Kuhn'[142] and thus a *Weltanschauung*, as Spaemann

---

[136] 'Die christliche Religion und das Ende des modernen Bewußtseins', 260.

[137] 'Überzeugungen in einer hypothetischen Zivilisation', 319.

[138] 'Die christliche Religion und das Ende des modernen Bewußtseins', 265; 'Ende der Modernität', in *Philosophische Essays*, 243.

[139] Peter J. Bowler, *Charles Darwin: The Man and His Influence* (Oxford: Blackwell, 1990), xi.

[140] For discussion of Darwin's nominalism see Spaemann's *Die Frage 'Wozu?'*, 213 ff.

[141] For Spaemann's account of the critique of evolutionary theory see *Die Frage 'Wozu?'*, 239–70.

[142] *Die Frage 'Wozu?'*, 241.

claims.[143] Biology has, to some extent, become a substitute for religion and philosophy and informs the public idea about what reality and humanity ultimately are like.

One of the most prominent examples of this tendency is the thought of E. O. Wilson, whose voluminous *Sociobiology: The New Synthesis* makes the claim to provide a scientific account of the sociological significance of biology: 'It may not be too much to say that sociology and the other social sciences, as well as the humanities, are the last branches of biology waiting to be included in the Modern Synthesis'.[144] Wilson thus makes an effort to contribute to a hypothesis-centred and functionalistic explanation of society and human life, including phenomena as different as religion, philosophy, art, and literature, by means of sociobiology.[145] It is obvious that Wilson has high hopes for the future of the natural sciences. Evolutionary metaphysics—which is defended by many of its followers 'with a certain missionary pathos', as Spaemann has put it[146]—has thus become an ontological and epistemological paradigm with grave theoretical implications. With respect to this, Spaemann remarks sarcastically that 'one is inclined to add that sociobiology itself will become a branch of sociobiology'.[147] So, ironically, the attempt to make evolutionary theory a metaphysical absolute undermines its own truth claim because it cannot properly articulate its own time-transcending truth claim and must understand itself in terms of evolutionary metaphysics, as a mere event in the history of evolution.

The presentation of reality as hypothesis does not have merely theoretical implications. Like all the other main features of modernity, it also has practical ramifications that contradict the very nature of the human person and of human action. The human person who can freely relate to his being-a-part is, as Spaemann argues, not '*mere* parts, but a whole, which cannot be accounted for as a means to an end'.[148] The person cannot be understood from within a framework that does not allow an understanding of the total character of the

---

[143] For this process see esp. *Die Frage 'Wozu?'*, 220–33.

[144] *Sociobiology: The New Synthesis* (Cambridge, Mass.: Harvard University Press, 1977), 4.

[145] For important remarks about the difference between science and religion see Spaemann, 'Religion und "Tatsachenwahrheit"', in *Das unsterbliche Gerücht*, 166–7. Religion and science, Spaemann argues, are ways of dealing with our contingency. But while religion intensifies the experience of contingency, science abolishes contingency and thus trivializes reality.

[146] Spaemann, 'Sein und Gewordensein. Was erklärt die Evolutionstheorie?', in *Philosophische Essays*, 192.

[147] *Die Frage 'Wozu?'*, 232. For a critique of the universal claim of sociobiology see also Peter Koslowski, 'Evolutionstheorie als Soziobiologie und Bioökonomie: Eine Kritik ihres Totalitätsanspruchs', in Robert Spaemann, Reinhard Löw, and Peter Koslowski (eds.), *Evolutionismus und Christentum* (Civitas-Resultate, 9) (Weinheim: Acta Humaniora/VCH, 1986), 29–56.

[148] *Persons*, 38 (*Personen*, 47).

human person, for the human person is not a hypothesis, and not only a means to an end or part of a bigger whole, but an end and total entity, as it were, in itself. Human beings can relate to natural ends negatively or affirmatively. They are not entirely dependent upon nature, but can transcend it; and this 'acosmism' of the person, as Spaemann puts it, makes up the dignity of the human person, his being an end in itself.[149] Yet in modernity human dignity, like moral absolutes and morality as such, tends to be naturalized and to be made hypothetical unless one develops, like Descartes, a '*morale provisoire*' that is excluded from the view of reality as hypothesis (while ironically itself being hypothetical) in order to unburden the acting person.[150] Acts of self-transcendence are then integrated into a functionalistic framework or entirely questioned, for one can no longer understand them: 'One does not die for a hypothesis'.[151]

Far from being a remote epistemological theory, the hypothetical stand-point has become the prevailing attitude of our everyday culture—not only in the form of sociobiology or in the general form of a misunderstanding of what it means to be a person but, even more importantly, in the particular form of utilitarianism which, as Spaemann states, is 'potentially terrorist'.[152] Utilitarianism is tied to an epoch that, as Adorno and Horkheimer lay bare in *Dialectic of Enlightenment*, is characterized by a thoroughgoing tendency to reduce persons to consumers and things to objects of desire and consumption; that is, to reduce reality ultimately to a hypothesis, the hypothesis of the market, which makes everything commensurable. Thus Enlightenment culture, they argue, cuts off the incommensurable;[153] civil society reduces things to abstractions in order to render comparable what does not have the same name.[154] Bernard Williams also emphasizes the link between utilitarianism and modern economic culture. For 'utilitarianism is unsurprisingly the value system for a society in which economic values are supreme; and . . . quantification in money is the only obvious form of what utilitarianism insists upon, the commensurability of value'.[155] Spaemann shares Adorno and Horkheimer's and Williams's view of the economic underpinning of utilitarianism in a society which is, in Spaemann's language, 'entirely economized'.[156]

---

[149] For discussion of this idea see 'Sein und Gewordensein', in *Philosophische Essays*, 201; and 'Über den Begriff der Menschenwürde', in *Grenzen*, 112.

[150] For Spaemann's understanding of Descartes's provisional morality see 'Moral, provisorische', in Joachim Ritter and Karlfried Gründer *Historisches Wörterbuch der Philosophie* vi (Basle: Schwabe, 1984), 172–4; 'Praktische Gewissheit—Descartes provisorische Moral', in *Grenzen*.

[151] 'Ende der Modernität?', in *Philosophische Essays*, 244.

[152] 'Sind alle Menschen Personen?', in *Grenzen*, 427.

[153] Adorno and Horkheimer, *Dialektik der Aufklärung*, 29.

[154] Ibid. 23–4.

[155] *Morality: An Introduction to Ethics* (Cambridge: Cambridge University Press, 1993), 89.

[156] 'Es gibt kein gutes Töten', in *Grenzen*, 437.

C. S. Lewis also targets utilitarianism and its dangerous implications because its focus upon the maximization of happiness or upon future generations falls short of our basic moral intuitions. 'No parents . . . would dream for a moment of setting up the claims of their hypothetical descendants against those of the baby actually crowing and hiding in the room.'[157] Not to distinguish between real and hypothetical children, however, is characteristic of the modern tendency to reduce what is essentially incomparable to abstract comparable entities, to lose respect for given reality, and to confuse the difference between what is actual and what is merely potential.[158] Yet in a hypothesizing culture the real–actual and hypothetical–potential difference is abolished; reality as a whole is virtualized and made a hypothesis. According to Spaemann, the hypothesizing approach to reality that makes the incommensurable commensurable is linked to the inversion of teleology in modernity, because the dismissal of natural tendencies has equalized everything. This has not only led to the 'left-wing' interest in leaving behind a current state of affairs to realize more fully the potentials of mankind, but also to the rise of what he calls a 'bourgeois ontology' and a 'bourgeois rationality'[159] of self-preservation against which Spaemann recollects a largely forgotten view of nature.

Spaemann argues that within this 'bourgeois ontology' the classical Aristotelian triad of goods is substantially transformed.[160] The *bonum iucundum* is dismissed, because 'sensual happiness, pleasure cannot be legitimized vis-à-vis self-preservation'.[161] Given the focus upon the idea of self-preservation, major currents of modern philosophy also no longer consider the fundamental relation between mere life and the good life. They sacrifice the good life (*bonum honestum*) for the preservation of mere life. The *bonum honestum*, then, is at best derived from what is useful (*bonum utile*) for self-preservation, if not totally dismissed. The idea of self-preservation has thus become the man-made ontological framework within which moral norms are to be justified.[162] They are now justified as purely hypothetical and utilitarian norms that lack the dimension of being naturally given and the possibility

---

[157] *The Abolition of Man*, 26. See Hans Jonas, *The Imperative of Responsibility: In Search of an Ethics for the Technological Age*, trans. Jonas with David Herr (Chicago, Ill.: University of Chicago Press, 1985), 130 ff. for an exploration of the parent–child relation that takes this to be the 'archetype of responsibility'.

[158] See in this context also Spaemann, 'Die Herausforderungen der Zivilisation', 15.

[159] *Die Frage 'Wozu?'*, 108.

[160] See e.g. Aristotle, *Nicomachean Ethics*, 1155bff. for his discussion of the good (*bonum honestum*), useful (*bonum utile*), and pleasant (*bonum iucundum*).

[161] *Die Frage 'Wozu?'*, 107.

[162] For this development in the history of ideas see also *Reflexion und Spontaneität*, 62–3.

of being unconditional. Reality, Spaemann shows, can then no longer be understood adequately. While a scientific and hypothesizing view of reality makes universal statements about reality possible, it makes freedom impossible, for 'freedom means: to be able to be identical with oneself. But this identity cannot be an abstract identity, stripped of all content; on the contrary, it requires concrete possibilities of identification. And these cannot have the form of hypothesis'.[163] But if there are no non-hypothetical beliefs and acts of freedom, reality (and that is to say the whole of reality) cannot but be conceived of as entirely naturalistic: mere nature. Consequently, a naturalistic universalism is yet another noteworthy feature of modernity.

The naturalistic universalism of modernity

Spaemann points out that the universalism of modernity is part of the European heritage, particularly of Christianity. He distinguishes between the 'universalism of logic' and the 'universalism of the Christian faith'. While the former universalism 'is abstract . . . freeing itself at least seemingly from all historical presuppositions', the latter universalism relies upon the particularity of a historical event and, subsequently, a historical religion. Spaemann points out that from a Christian point of view history does not move towards an overcoming of the tension between the esoteric and the exoteric view of Christianity. That is to say, the tension between the particularity and the universality of Christianity will not be resolved over the course of merely human history.[164] Christian universalism thus contradicts the abstract character of modern universalism,[165] which not only is modelled on logical universalism but also, in Spaemann's view, has turned naturalistic in modernity.

Naturalistic universalism is, as we have already argued, a consequence of modern scientism. The sciences endeavour to make universal statements about reality. This tends to change the concept of truth, Spaemann argues; for, the modern consciousness 'no longer requires universality for truth, but universality is conversely the criterion for truth'.[166] In order to achieve this end, the sciences have to follow a specific methodology and have to presuppose a specific understanding of their object. Only a reductionistic view of reality makes scientific universal statements possible. Modern scientific universalism is therefore

---

[163] 'Überzeugungen in einer hypothetischen Zivilisation', 322.

[164] For the difference between Christian and logical universalism see 'Rationalität als "Kulturelles Erbe"', 308.

[165] For this see also 'Über die gegenwartige Lage des Christentums', in *Das unsterbliche Gerücht*, 235.

[166] 'Was ist das Neue?', 21.

naturalistic, dependent on a specific interpretation of reality. It presupposes a view of nature that opposes nature to freedom and spirit, and dismisses any teleological view of nature, for the universal claim of the sciences is only possible as long as nature and freedom are dichotomized and Being and meaning are polarized: 'The world of pure facticity (*Faktizität*) does not know any moral "ought"'.[167]

This universalistic and naturalistic perspective of modernity is once again paradigmatically reflected by the claims of evolutionary metaphysics and its tendency towards universalizing Darwinism. Richard Dawkins has argued in his essay 'Universal Darwinism' that 'Darwin's theory of evolution by natural selection is more than a local theory to account for the existence and form of life on Earth. It is probably the only theory that can adequately account for the phenomena that we associate with life'.[168] Darwin's naturalistic theory of natural selection thus becomes the cornerstone of a universalizing and totalizing 'evolutionary exobiology' the fictitious and reductionistic character of which is not viewed as a problem.[169]

In contrast to the universalistic claim of evolutionary metaphysics, Spaemann retrieves what he calls an 'open rationality'[170] that does not exclude what does not conform to its standards and emphasizes what cannot be reconstructed from a universalistic and naturalistic standpoint. For, the particularity of history, of the gift of nature, and of human subjectivity and freedom, of *Selbstsein* as the dignified representation of the absolute (as we will see later) cannot be comprehended from a universalistic and naturalistic point of view. These phenomena require an altogether different epistemology and ontology, which Spaemann strives to propose in his philosophy. His philosophy is thus a 'resistance against this oblivion'[171] of nature and its teleology. In this way, he contributes to the end of modernity, for to speak of the end of the modern consciousness, Spaemann says, refers to a 'consciousness which no longer defines itself in the categories of the sciences'.[172]

Spaemann's account of the naturalistic dimension of modernity is again reflective of his criticism of modernity, informed as it is by Christianity.[173]

---

[167] *Die Frage 'Wozu?'*, 259.
[168] 'Universal Darwinism', in David L. Hull and Michael Ruse (eds.), *The Philosophy of Biology* (Oxford: Oxford University Press, 1998), 15.
[169] See also Richard Dawkins, *The Selfish Gene* (Oxford: Oxford University Press, 1989), 264 ff.
[170] For his idea of the open rationality of the ancient-polis ethics see 'Die zwei Grundbegriffe der Moral', in *Kritik der politischen Utopie*, 12.
[171] 'Einleitung,' in *Philosophische Essays*, 12.
[172] 'Was ist das Neue?', 11.
[173] C. S. Lewis has in a similar way written of the naturalist doctrine that 'a great process, or "becoming," exists "on its own" in space and time, and that nothing else exists—what we call particular things and events being only the parts into which we analyse the great process or the

For, the naturalistic doctrine of reality as process does not permit a proper understanding of the particular, and above all of the individual person. It also does not allow for an ontological conceptualization of crucial Christian doctrines such as the hypostatic union and the possibility and reality of miracles. So in a milieu in which many theologians fuse Christian orthodoxy with the *Zeitgeist* of modernity without even realizing the destructive implications of doing so, Spaemann provides incisive philosophical remarks on an apologetic theology. He does not seek to demonstrate how Christian doctrines, however modified, are reconcilable with modern reason. In contrast, he strives to lay bare how constricted many ontological premises of modern reason are and to show that, therefore, remembering what is self-evident can show that Christianity is reasonable. Indeed, Christianity, as he thinks, constitutes its own understanding of reason 'within an entirely different normality'[174] and thus without requiring substantial transformations and assimilations of its doctrinal content.

3.4 JEAN-JACQUES ROUSSEAU AS A PARADIGMATIC FIGURE OF MODERNITY

Thus far we have examined Spaemann's critique of modernity and its ambiguities in a rather general way. We have been investigating general tendencies that Spaemann regards as characteristic of the spirit of modernity and have also discussed some of the alternative views of reality that he offers. In what follows we will discuss Spaemann's reading of Jean-Jacques Rousseau's life and his writings and thus provide a concrete example of a typically modern figure. Throughout his career Spaemann has eagerly engaged in conversation with this ambiguous figure of modern intellectual history, whose life and work, and their tensions and ruptures, are paradigmatic of the dialectic of modernity.[175] Spaemann has said that Bonald's thought is characterized by an 'insurmountable ambiguity'.[176] The same can be said of Jean-Jacques Rousseau, who not only significantly influenced

shapes which that process takes at given moments and given points in space' (*Miracles: A Preliminary Study* (New York: Macmillan, 1947), 19–20).

[174] 'Christliche Spiritualität und pluralistische Normalität', 168.

[175] See esp. *Rousseau: Bürger ohne Vaterland*; see also *Der Ursprung der Soziologie aus dem Geist der Restauration*.

[176] *Der Ursprung der Soziologie aus dem Geist der Restauration*, 14. For a short discussion of the ambiguity of Rousseau's thought see also *Persons*, 85 ff. (*Personen*, 95 ff.).

Bonald,[177] but is also the most self-aware of modern thinkers, fully conscious of the problems raised by the break with classical thought.[178]

Spaemann's interpretation of Rousseau's thinking is therefore sympathetic, though far from being entirely affirmative. It tries to do justice to the ambiguity of Rousseau's thought, in that he outlines trenchantly where Rousseau was doubtless right and where he went astray. In his analysis of Rousseau Spaemann deals not only with this important figure of modern intellectual history but with modern philosophy as a whole. For, modern philosophy, above all the philosophy of Immanuel Kant and the German Idealists, has been deeply influenced by Rousseau's anthropology and his understanding of nature, freedom, and history.[179] This is why Spaemann's reading of Rousseau, like his reading of Bonald, needs to be interpreted from within a considerably wider horizon than that of the discussion of one particular figure in the history of ideas. In proposing an interpretation of Rousseau, Spaemann deals with the very spirit of modernisms and anti-modernisms and their ambiguities. For Spaemann, Rousseau's thought is revolutionary in that it recalls an 'old truth' and defends a 'common-sense' view of reality.[180] Thus, Spaemann's interest in Rousseau is mainly an interest in the foundations of modernity, since Rousseau proves to be 'the father of all modern modernisms and anti-modernisms; that is, of the Revolution and the restoration, of the liberal constitutional state and of the populist dictatorship, of anti-authoritarian pedagogy and of totalitarianism, of romantic Christianity and of

---

[177] For Rousseau's influence on Bonald see esp. Jean-Yves Pranchère, 'The Social Bond According to the Catholic Counter-Revolution: Maistre and Bonald', in Richard A. Lebrun (ed.), *Joseph de Maistre's Life, Thought, and Influence: Selected Studies* (Montreal/Kingston: McGill-Queen's University Press, 2001), 207ff. For the difference between Rousseau's and Bonald's philosophies see also Spaemann, 'Zur Ontologie der Begriffe "rechts" und "links"', in *Grenzen*, 262–3.

[178] This ambiguity is well reflected in recent scholarship on Rousseau. While some interpret his philosophy as materialist 'autocritique of Enlightenment' (see e.g. Mark Hulliung, *The Autocritique of Enlightenment: Rousseau and the Philosophes* (Cambridge, Mass.: Harvard University Press, 1994)), other scholars point out that Rousseau is essentially a 'Platonist' and his philosophy characterized by a 'Platonic Enlightenment' (see for this interpretation David Lay Williams, *Rousseau's Platonic Enlightenment* (University Park, Penn.: Pennsylvania State University Press, 2007)) or even argue that his break with the Enlightenment was 'inevitable' (for this view see Leo Damrosch, *Jean-Jacques Rousseau: Restless Genius* (Boston, Mass./New York: Houghton Mifflin, 2005), 294ff.) and that he must be read as a 'counter-Enlightenment' philosopher (for this approach to Rousseau see Graeme Garrard, *Rousseau's Counter-Enlightenment: A Republican Critique of the Philosophes* (Albany: State University of New York, 2003)).

[179] For the relation between Rousseau and Kant see Richard Velkley, *Freedom and the End of Reason: On the Moral Foundation of Kant's Critical Philosophy* (Chicago, Ill.: University of Chicago Press, 1989), esp. ch. 1; Williams, *Rousseau's Platonic Enlightenment*, 207ff.

[180] 'Von der Polis zur Natur', in *Rousseau: Bürger ohne Vaterland*, 37.

structuralist ethnology'.[181] And because of its ambiguous character Rousseau's thought was almost inevitably subject to a dialectic that would become paradigmatic of modernity.[182]

In the context of his interpretation of Jean-Jacques Rousseau's thought Spaemann provides a brief summary of Rousseau's critique of modern European civilization. Rousseau's critique, he suggests, prefigures the criticisms of European civilization that have been proposed in the two centuries since Rousseau.[183] Spaemann's summary provides an overview not only of Rousseau's critique of modern civilization but also of Spaemann's way of characterizing modernity. Although Spaemann does not make his own position explicit, it is evident that he largely shares Rousseau's criticism of modern civilization, which latter, in Spaemann's view, is a 'threat to the dignity of the human being which has never before existed'.[184] Spaemann identifies five motifs of Rousseau's argument, which reflect, and partly supplement, the seven main features Spaemann emphasized in *Ende der Modernität?*, and direct us to a more detailed discussion of Spaemann's investigation of Rousseau's philosophy.

First, modern civilization is based upon an increasing generation of desires. Ever new forms of desire lead to ever new forms of enslavement. Hence, 'progress is progressive loss of freedom'.[185] Second, modern civilization presupposes the dichotomization of Being and appearance. This implies also that the public and the private, laws and morality are opposed to one another. This dichotomy can only be overcome either by absolutizing Being (or nature, in Rousseau's case, as Spaemann argues) or by absolutizing appearance (in Rousseau's case, society). It is noteworthy that this feature of Rousseau's criticism of modernity provides Spaemann with a theoretical key to understanding the unity of Rousseau's thought. Third, in modernity the claim of the political turns total and makes indifference and neutrality impossible. Every action, even in its claim not to be political, has a political dimension. Philosophical leisure—*theoria* for its own sake—is regarded as a waste of time. Very often, arbitrary opinion is substituted for thinking. The nature of philosophy is thus substantially transformed. Fourth, the only measure for one's opinions is self-affirmation of subjectivity through the negation of what

---

[181] 'Einleitung' in *Rousseau: Bürger ohne Vaterland*, 14; for discussion of the controversial character of Rousseau and the aftermath of his thought see also 'Natürliche Existenz und politische Existenz bei Rousseau', in *Rousseau: Bürger ohne Vaterland*, 15 ff. For Rousseau's relation to modern ethnology see also 'Von der Polis zur Natur', in *Rousseau: Bürger ohne Vaterland*, 51.

[182] Spaemann, 'Einleitung', in *Rousseau: Bürger ohne Vaterland*, 9.

[183] 'Von der Polis zur Natur', in *Rousseau: Bürger ohne Vaterland*, 40 ff.

[184] 'Über den Begriff der Menschenwürde', in *Grenzen*, 120.

[185] 'Von der Polis zur Natur', in *Rousseau: Bürger ohne Vaterland*, 40.

has traditionally been valid. Fifth, arts and sciences promote the differences between human beings and neglect what is common to human beings. The division of labour seems to pose significant problems and in the end undermines human freedom and the equality between all human beings.

In his interpretation of Rousseau Spaemann speaks in familiar terms of the 'indigent Jean-Jacques'.[186] Why is Rousseau indigent, deserving of our compassion rather than our antipathy? Spaemann proposes that this is because Rousseau is paradigmatically modern himself. He has understood the specific character of modernity and then drawn the consequences from it. Rousseau's option, Spaemann correspondingly argues, 'is not arbitrary, but originates from a historical discernment'.[187] In Rousseau, modernity and the ambiguity of the separation of the particular from the universal find a concrete expression that is tragic and paradoxical.

Rousseau as a paradigmatic and paradoxical character

Spaemann highlights what at first seem to be inconsistencies in Rousseau's biography.[188] Yet a closer look at Rousseau's *Confessions* will make clear that these apparent inconsistencies originate in, and are consonant with, the milieu that he typifies.[189] Rousseau, Spaemann points out, wrote a lengthy treatise on education, *Emile*, and yet he put his five children into a home for foundlings, arguing that not he but society bore the responsibility for them.[190] He then stylized himself as a paradigmatic victim of an unjust society, since this society made it impossible to pursue an education as ideally outlined in *Emile*. Rousseau, furthermore, claimed to be an enemy of the arts and of the sciences, and nevertheless, as he himself underscores, he wrote and published plays. According to Rousseau's own testimony, this should not

[186] 'Einleitung', in *Philosophische Essays*, 11. For references to Rousseau by his Christian name see also Mark Hulliung, *The Autocritique of Enlightenment*, 229–30.

[187] 'Natürliche Existenz und politische Existenz bei Rousseau', in *Rousseau: Bürger ohne Vaterland*, 24; for Rousseau's historical reflection upon the separation of natural and political existence see also p. 30.

[188] 'Einleitung' in *Rousseau: Bürger ohne Vaterland*, 9–10; and 'Rousseaus "Emile"', in *Rousseau: Bürger ohne Vaterland*, 78–9.

[189] For a wider discussion of this milieu see also Nicholas D. Paige, *Being Interior: Autobiography and the Contradictions of Modernity in Seventeenth-century France* (Philadelphia, Pa.: University of Pennsylvania Press, 2001).

[190] See Jean-Jacques Rousseau, *Confessions*, 338 ff. Rousseau does, of course, to some degree regret his decision. However, '[a]ll things considered, I chose for my children what was best, or, at least, what I believed to be best for them' (p. 340). For the biographical context see also Damrosch, *Jean-Jacques Rousseau*, 191 ff.

be held against him, but should rather be seen as a satire on his time.[191] As Spaemann makes clear, Rousseau not only anticipates Hegel, Nietzsche, and Adorno and Horkheimer in his at least implicit reference to the dialectical character of modern reason,[192] but also publicly lives this very dialectic, in an almost unprecedented way. Rousseau, Spaemann states, stylizes himself as 'victim and paradigmatic place where the antinomies of the bourgeois society take place'.[193]

In analysing the paradoxes of Rousseau's thought and life Spaemann does not limit himself to an exposition of the unity of Rousseau's thought as distinctly *modern* and thus as dialectical, but gives attention also to the dialectical implications of Cartesian philosophy. Rousseau's *Emile*, Spaemann states, presupposes an 'inverted Cartesianism': not that self-consciousness is the starting-point of all certainty, but that the intensity of (self-)feeling is the end of all knowledge.[194] The antinomies of Rousseau's thought are therefore the antinomies of his time. They have a theoretical and general significance, Spaemann contends, with reference to Rousseau's own self-assessment.[195]

According to Spaemann, paradigmatic existences are typical of modernity. He makes this observation almost in passing, yet it is an important insight about the very attitude of modernity and its tendency to go beyond traditional ontology and to undermine the truth claim of Christianity. For, the emblematic, or paradigmatic, character of individual existences, Spaemann argues, has to do, first, with the rise of the modern understanding of subjectivity and, therefore, also with the modern dismissal of a teleological understanding of nature, with implications for the understanding of human nature. It also has to do with the dismissal of an orthodox Christian anthropology in which Christ is the paradigmatic example of a truly human life as 'image of God'. According to Spaemann, modernity is an epoch that neither retains the Platonic–Aristotelian idea of a teleological essence inherent in humanity nor maintains the belief that God incarnate provides the ultimate answer to the question of who human beings are. In this age new variations on the answer to this crucial question—for instance, proposals such as Rousseau's or, under

---

[191] 'Von der Polis zur Natur', in *Rousseau: Bürger ohne Vaterland*, 47, 56.

[192] 'Rousseaus "Emile"', in *Rousseau: Bürger ohne Vaterland*, 92.

[193] 'Von der Polis zur Natur', in *Rousseau: Bürger ohne Vaterland*, 47. See also for this self-understanding the preface to Rousseau's *Confessions*.

[194] 'Natürliche Existenz und politische Existenz bei Rousseau, in *Rousseau: Bürger ohne Vaterland*, 28. For an illustration of Spaemann's interpretation see Jean-Jacques Rousseau, *Emile or On Education*, 442 ff.

[195] 'Natürliche Existenz und politische Existenz bei Rousseau', in *Rousseau: Bürger ohne Vaterland*, 19.

the conditions of a 'new non-teleological teleology',[196] Friedrich Nietzsche's
self-stylized life—are necessary.[197] These paradigmatic figures are thus important keys to understanding their periods.

There are also paradigmatic figures for Christians, as Spaemann points out.
Apart from Christ, these are the saints who reject sin, egoism, hatred, and
injustice.[198] The saint, Spaemann argues, is different from the secular hero in
that the former 'does not sacrifice his life for an idea, but for God and the
neighbour in whom God discloses himself to him, and in that he is even
willing to sacrifice his ideas to the living God'.[199] Thus, Spaemann can
conclude that the 'heroism of the saint is the highest dignity one can
achieve',[200] for 'the saints are the actual teachers of the following of Christ,
that is to say, of being a Christian'.[201] There is, therefore, another essential
difference between paradigmatic modern figures, such as Rousseau, and
saints. Because the modern paradigms of how to lead one's life are substitutes
both for the teleology of human nature and for religious ideals, both of which
are denied cultural acceptability, they do not point to anything beyond
themselves. They are self-sufficient expressions of modern subjectivity and
do not allow for radical self-transcendence. In sharp contrast to this, saints are
paradigmatic in that they deny themselves and do not provide a substitute for
dismissed world-views and examples of how to live. 'Sainthood', Spaemann
states, 'is not a luxury and not a matter of a special inner vocation, but it can
be the only possibility of corresponding to God's demand in certain situations'.[202] Saints point beyond themselves to a truly exemplary figure, as
Spaemann argues; they represent the absolute symbolically, but they do not
constitute it. Hence, the paradigmatic character of individuals like Rousseau
is itself a symptom of anti-Christian tendencies in modernity. For it is
obvious from Spaemann's understanding of Christianity that he rejects the
Enlightenment notion of Christ as merely another example of a morally good

---

[196] For Spaemann's interpretation of Nietzsche's transformation of teleology see *Die Frage
'Wozu?'*, 194–207.

[197] 'Einleitung', in *Rousseau: Bürger ohne Vaterland*, 12. For an important examination of
this dimension of Nietzsche's life see Alexander Nehamas, *Nietzsche: Life as Literature* (Cambridge, Mass.: Harvard University Press, 1985).

[198] 'Die christliche Religion und das Ende des modernen Bewußtseins', 253.

[199] 'Der heilige Franz und seine Söhne', in *Kirche und Leben*, 30 (24 July 1949). See *Persons*,
85–6 (*Personen*, 95–6) for the difference between Rousseau and Augustine.

[200] 'Über den Begriff der Menschenwürde', in *Grenzen*, 115; see also *Persons*, 204 (*Personen*,
216; trans. modified): 'Totally to renounce egoism it not totally to renounce oneself as a person,
but actually to realize oneself'.

[201] 'Christliche Spiritualität und pluralistische Normalität', 168.

[202] 'Die christliche Religion und das Ende des modernen Bewusstseins', 266.

life (and thus merely another hero or paradigmatic individual)[203] because Christ, as the Son of God, is historically and ontologically absolutely unique and different from any merely human being.

The dismissal of natural teleology

It has already been pointed out that according to Spaemann philosophy ought to remember nature as the horizon within which humanity, freedom, history, and ethics are positioned. Nature, thus conceived, needs to be re-appreciated as teleological; that is to say, as intrinsically oriented towards ends that are not fashioned by human beings, but 'unpreconceivably' given. In modernity, as we have already seen, the union of nature and freedom, or history, gives way. Modernity, in its rejection of a teleological view of nature, cannot accommodate a notion of history that is integrated into, though not ultimately subject to, the normative frame of nature; nor can history be understood as an explication of human nature or as the history of the Divine redemption (and not human self-redemption) of humanity's fallen nature. The dialectic of modernity is therefore essentially the dialectic between history, or freedom, and nature. This dialectic can be seen at work in Rousseau's thought.

In Rousseau's dismissal of a social existence as the fulfilment of man's nature we see modernity's polarization of the private and the public. Spaemann's collection of essays about Rousseau is subtitled *Citizen Without a Fatherland* (*Bürger ohne Vaterland*). The citizen Rousseau lost his fatherland, which, as he must have realized, cannot be restored. A union of the public and private, of society and the individual, is impossible under the premise of the modern 'discovery' of subjectivity and freedom and its political implications. The only answer to the separation of public and private which Rousseau seems to provide is a flight from society and public *Sittlichkeit*, a turn towards one's own inner morality, as outlined in the educational programme of *Emile*. Spaemann therefore points out that in the second discourse Rousseau 'does not interpret nature teleologically, that is from the unfolded historical and cultural existence of human beings, but through radical abstraction from it'.[204] In Rousseau's time, nature is no longer the measure according to which political or social life is to be understood.

---

[203] Rousseau's tendency to compare himself to Jesus seems to suggest such an interpretation of Christ on his side. For his identification with Christ see esp. Mark Hulliung, *The Autocritique of Enlightenment*, 226–7.

[204] 'Natürliche Existenz und politische Existenz bei Rousseau', in *Rousseau: Bürger ohne Vaterland*, 26.

Rousseau's thought, however, as Spaemann argues, oscillates between two extremes. The first one is the denaturalization of human beings: the dismissal of the individual's existence and his integration into a political totality for the sake of a political order—a well-known feature of Rousseau's political thought. The second extreme, represented in *Emile*, is the 'depoliticization' and desocialization of humanity due to an account of human nature that dismisses any teleological structure, idealizes a state of pure, prehistorical, and pre-social nature, and dismisses the doctrine of original sin.[205] Nature and *polis*, that is to say the realization of freedom within the context of the *polis*, are the two extremes between which Rousseau's philosophy thus oscillates without achieving a proper integration.

Rousseau's conception of nature is therefore, as Spaemann argues, the foundation of a new understanding of history and the philosophy of history. In modernity history is conceived of as a progressive emancipation from nature rather than as a life along the lines of nature and its laws.[206] Consequently, nature ceases to be the measure for human behaviour and for a happy life. While the teleological understanding of human nature can accommodate and integrate history without reducing history to nature, humanity is now understood in a reductively historical fashion. Thus, in accord with his paradigmatically modern character, Rousseau acutely analyses and criticizes the modern condition while at the same time sharing some of modernity's main premises. Despite his sympathy with Plato, for instance, Rousseau does not share in one of the most fundamental presuppositions of Plato's philosophy. For unlike Plato, Spaemann argues, Rousseau treats philosophy politically, and thus as an ideology, rather than subordinating politics to philosophy. For Rousseau, philosophy is subject to political purposes.[207] Detached from any consideration of the idea of the good, Athens can no longer be the political ideal for Rousseau, as Spaemann points out. Rousseau's political ideal is therefore the anti-*polis* of Sparta.[208]

[205] For Rousseau's rejection of the doctrine of original sin in the context of the philosophy of his time see Garrard, *Rousseau's Counter-Enlightenment*, 70, 104.
[206] 'Natürliche Existenz und politische Existenz bei Rousseau', in *Rousseau: Bürger ohne Vaterland*, 26.
[207] 'Von der Polis zur Natur', in *Rousseau: Bürger ohne Vaterland*, 40.
[208] Ibid. 39. See also Jean-Jacques Rousseau, *Discourse on the Sciences and Arts (First Discourse)*, ed. Roger D. Masters and Christopher Kelly, trans. Judith R. Bush, Roger D. Masters, and Christopher Kelly (Hanover, NH: University Press of New England, 1992), 23.

The truth and unworldliness of Christianity

Why does the dualism of the public and the private, of the *homme naturel* and of the *citoyen*, pose a problem for Rousseau? Why is this a specifically Christian problem, as Spaemann and Rousseau both suggest? How does Christianity resituate the political and the religious in modernity so that Rousseau must acknowledge that the ancient *polis* is a thing of the past that can no longer be restored? The dichotomy of the public and the private is particularly due to the universal character of Christianity and its truth, which no longer allows for a political 'fatherland' to which exclusive obedience is due. Early Christianity, Spaemann points out, 'did not understand itself as the continuation of ancient-*polis* religiosity, but as the continuation of ancient philosophy, as *philosophia Christi*'.[209] Christians thus essentially live in two cities. They dwell both in the universal *civitas Dei* and in the particular *civitas terrena*. Thus the *kosmos* of a particular *polis* can no longer be the universal horizon of one's life. The Greek *polis* has disappeared, apart from certain residua such as the Polish state, which Rousseau identifies as a relic from the past because of the status of Catholicism as a national religion not unlike that of an ancient-*polis* religion. In so far as Christians do indeed live in two cities and Poland is an exception, a relic of the past, the restoration of a unity of state and religion, or the public and the private dimension of one's life, is impossible in Rousseau's view.

Thus, according to Spaemann, Rousseau had to contend not only with the modern dismissal of a teleological view of nature and the modern transformation of the concepts of history and freedom, but also with the full explication of Christianity and its political implications in modernity.[210] Traditional structures of political philosophy, such as the unity of society and religion in the ancient pre-Christian *polis*, are no longer open to Rousseau. Accordingly, he argues that the words 'Christian' and 'republic' are 'mutually exclusive'.[211] Unlike Bonald, who optimistically maintained the hope that France would recover from the Revolution and finally continue the pre-revolutionary order, Rousseau dismissed the possibility of a reconciliation of the public and the private and the restoration of the ancient *polis*, as Spaemann states.[212] The *Contrat Social* is, in Spaemann's view, a farewell. The *polis* and its forms of life,

---

[209] 'Rationalität als "Kulturelles Erbe"', 313.

[210] For a discussion of Rousseau's political theology see also Peter Koslowski, *Gesellschaft und Staat: Ein unvermeidlicher Dualismus* (Stuttgart: Klett-Cotta, 1982). 155–61.

[211] *Social Contract*, in *The Collected Writings of Rousseau*, iv, ed. Roger D. Masters and Christopher Kelly (Hanover, NH/London: University Press of New England, 1994), 221.

[212] *Der Ursprung der Soziologie aus dem Geist der Restauration*, 10.

Rousseau argues, according to Spaemann, have been lost irretrievably.[213] Rousseau does not choose Bonald's restorative solution, which employs Christianity for the sake of the preservation of an established, or formerly established, political order. He acknowledges the world-transcending implications of Christianity. 'Christianity', he writes, 'is a totally spiritual religion, uniquely concerned with heavenly matters. The Christian's fatherland is not of this world. He does his duty, it is true, but does it with profound indifference for the good or bad outcome of his efforts'.[214] For Rousseau, Spaemann writes, 'the absolute truth upon which Plato wanted to found the republic has become non-political, and that in the form of Christianity'.[215] The educational programme of *Emile* and its elitist turn towards the individual's own inner morality reflect, in Spaemann's cogent interpretation of Rousseau's philosophy, the Christian focus upon inner attitudes. This is distinctly different from pre-Christian Socratic intellectualism, for which good action is based upon the knowledge of the good.[216]

Spaemann agrees with Rousseau that the non-political character of Christianity rules out the possibility of a *Christian* political theology. The historical process towards this insight, Spaemann writes, in a passage in which Rousseau's view and his own become almost indistinguishable, is irreversible because of the 'truth of this universal religion of the heart'. Christianity is a religion of the heart because it focuses upon inner attitudes that cannot be judged in terms of worldly measures. It is therefore even a politically destructive religion.[217] Christians, Spaemann writes, 'are used to relating the Christian preaching of salvation, as far as it concerns the earthly life, to an inwardness not ultimately graspable in social terms'.[218]

A reconciliation between the public and the private is not possible, according to Spaemann's summary of Rousseau's standpoint. *Rousseau: Bürger ohne Vaterland* is thus also reflective of Spaemann's own non-political view of Christianity and makes clear why, in Spaemann's view, political theology was no longer possible with the ascendancy of Christianity: Christianity does not concern the visible political order, but the inner attitudes of its

---

[213] For Spaemann's account of Rousseau's view of history and his understanding of the arts and the sciences see esp. 'Von der Polis zur Natur', in *Rousseau: Bürger ohne Vaterland*, 55–6.

[214] *Social Contract*, 220 (quoted also by Spaemann in 'Natürliche Existenz und politische Existenz bei Rousseau', in *Rousseau: Bürger ohne Vaterland*, 29).

[215] Spaemann, 'Von der Polis zur Natur', in *Rousseau: Bürger ohne Vaterland*, 39.

[216] For the difference between the Socratic and the Christian moral psychology see *Persons*, 19 ff. (*Personen*, 28 ff.).

[217] 'Von der Polis zur Natur', in *Rousseau: Bürger ohne Vaterland*, 39; for this view of Christianity see also *Persons*, 151–2 (*Personen*, 161 ff.).

[218] 'Theologie, Prophetie, Politik', in *Kritik der politischen Utopie*, 57.

believers and their citizenship, as it were, in the heavenly kingdom.[219] The Christian is not entirely without a fatherland but rather has a fatherland very different from that of non-Christians. Therefore, in calling Rousseau a citizen without a fatherland Spaemann refers not only to the political implications of Rousseau's philosophy but also to the ambiguity of Rousseau's thought vis-à-vis both Christianity and modernity.

Having investigated modernity and its main features, we can now ask what lies at the heart of the non- and anti-Christian attitudes of modernity. What is it that made the emancipation from nature, an absolute notion of freedom, the idea of necessary progress, the dominion over nature, scientism, and utilitarianism so powerful in spite of the fact that they contradict and undermine basic human experiences? Spaemann only occasionally makes an explicit statement about the reasons for this, and does so in his religious rather than in his philosophical writings.

3.5 THE TRANSFORMATION OF THE DOCTRINE OF ORIGINAL SIN

We have already discussed the implications of some of the main features of modernity for Christianity. Yet the rise of modern scientific culture is at the same time deeply influenced by Christianity. Objectification, homogenization of experience, the tendency to make truth claims universal and at the same time hypothetical, Spaemann argues, can at least partly be traced back to Christian ideas. Hence, modernity cannot be defined simply as an anti- or post-Christian epoch, since Christianity made a substantial contribution to the rise of modernity and therefore is not irreconcilable with modernity.[220]

First, the objectification of being, as we have argued, has traditionally been justified theologically within the context of the doctrine of creation. We have already seen that the transformation, or dismissal, of natural teleology has been interpreted as an act of worship because it seemed idolatrous to speak of merely natural ends. Nature could be objectified by man in the first place because it is the object of God's creative power. The ends of this world could

---

[219] For a different account of the political dimension of Christianity and of the reappraisal of pre-modern Christian political theology see esp. Oliver O'Donovan, *The Desire of the Nations: Rediscovering the Roots of Political Theology* (Cambridge: Cambridge University Press, 1996).

[220] For a discussion of the historical relation between Christianity and modernity see also Michael Allen Gillespie, *The Theological Origins of Modernity* (Chicago, Ill./London: University of Chicago Press, 2008); Louis Dupré, *Passage to Modernity*.

be found in God's consciousness.[221] Second, the homogenization and ratio-nalization of experience is also partly due to the Old and New Testament understanding of reality and its questioning of non-rationalistic ways of approaching reality, such as astrology and magic. Christ deprived 'the powers' of power, as Spaemann points out, and this is why they have ceased to be the decisive reality. A rational way of life is thus implied by the belief in the one and unconditional power of God.[222] Third, the universal claim of modernity, Spaemann states, goes back to the Christian claim that Christianity is the universally valid religion. The Christian claim of universality, however, is eschatologically modified.[223] According to its own inner self-understanding Christianity is an absolute and universal religion, whereas viewed from outside it is a particular religion as any other. The gulf between the inside and outside understanding of Christianity will not be bridged in the course of the progress of human history, since it will be realized by the eschatological event of the second coming of Christ.[224]

In spite of (or, perhaps, because of) the close link between modernity and Christianity, modernity has significantly transformed orthodox Christian theology, particularly the doctrine of original sin, which has found many different interpretations in modernity. Spaemann's close disciple Peter Kos-lowski has argued:

A thinker's way of theorizing about the whole of reality—be it the theological-philosophical, the Gnostic, or the mythological theory of the whole of reality—and his way of theorizing about how the world changes, follows from the way in which the fall is conceived. One could even go so far as to argue that the way one conceives the fall determines what kind of philosopher one is.[225]

Spaemann shares the view that one's appraisal of original sin determines what kind of philosopher one is. Although it is often implicit, the issue of how one conceives of original sin is one of the leading questions of Spaemann's analysis of modernity.

---

[221] 'Die christliche Religion und das Ende des modernen Bewußtseins', 255.
[222] Ibid. 258–9.
[223] Ibid. 261–2; see also 'Vorwort', in *Das unsterbliche Gerücht*, 9.
[224] 'Rationalität als "Kulturelles Erbe"', 308.
[225] 'Sündenfälle: Theorien der Wandelbarkeit der Welt', in Peter Koslowski and Friedrich Hermanni (eds.), *Die Wirklichkeit des Bösen: Systematisch-theologische und philosophische Annä-herungen* (Munich: Fink, 1998), 128 ('Der Typus der Theorie der Gesamtwirklichkeit, die ein Denker vertritt—sei sie die theologisch-philosophische, die gnostische oder die mythologische Theorie der Gesamtwirklichkeit—und der Typus der Theorie der Wandlung der Welt folgt aus der Art und Weise, wie der Sündenfall gedacht wird. Man könnte so weit gehen zu sagen, daß mit der Art der Sündenfalltheorie, die man hat, entschieden ist, welche Art von Philosoph man ist'). Koslowski's assertion echoes Fichte's idea that whether one is an idealist or a dogmatist depends upon which kind of person one is.

Walker Percy has argued that the novelist, 'unlike the new theologian . . . [is] one of the few remaining witnesses to the doctrine of original sin, the immanence of catastrophe in paradise'.[226] Spaemann, too, is one of the remaining witnesses to what he considers the orthodox doctrine of original sin and its rationality.[227] He thus claims to defend a rationality that goes deeper than both the rationality of the modern technological civilization and the subjectivist emphasis upon self-determination and absolute freedom, and which thus considers and integrates into itself what modern rationality tends to exclude. According to Spaemann, the 'peculiarly rational nature of the Christian understanding of humanity lies in the fact that it connects the idea of human dignity with the idea of original sin'.[228] The orthodox view of original sin resists, in Spaemann's account, modernity's tendency to make either freedom or 'mere nature' an absolute, and thus escapes its fatal dialectic. The Christian doctrine does not express an irrational and completely sectarian idea, he argues, but refers to a universal quality of humanity. For, the tendency to falsify the standards for excellence, 'which is called "original sin" in the Christian tradition, is part of the universal equipment of humanity', Spaemann states.[229]

Spaemann retrieves a philosophical conception of original sin consistent with orthodox Christian doctrine, as he claims, a view of human nature that takes seriously its being created, its finitude, its freedom, and its fall, without rendering the fall an absolute such that nature is regarded as completely corrupted. This is an important key to appreciating Spaemann's criticism of modernity more fully. Up to now we have been investigating different features of modernity and its dialectic in light of Spaemann's philosophical critique.

---

[226] 'Notes for a Novel about the End of the World', in *The Message in the Bottle*, 106.

[227] See also for this significance of the doctrine of original sin for Spaemann Richard Schenk, OP, 'The Ethics of Robert Spaemann in the Context of Recent Philosophy', in Brian J. Shanley, OP (ed.), *One Hundred Years of Philosophy* (Studies in Philosophy and the History of Philosophy, xxxvi) (Washington, DC: The Catholic University of America Press, 2001), 166: 'While Spaemann has resisted attempts to absorb the doctrine of original sin into philosophy, his religious convictions about it have both liberated and enriched his philosophy'. For Spaemann's view of the rationality of the Christian doctrine of original sin and its transformation in modernity see *Happiness and Benevolence*, 191 (*Glück und Wohlwollen*, 244): 'One easily sees how both the teaching of Kant and Schopenhauer on the choice of the intelligible character as well as Heidegger's theory of fallenness are attempts to transform the doctrine of original sin into a theory and to metamorphose the traditional contingency of the myth of the fall of humans which the Bible narrates into something like an apriori constitution of the human's essence. But one sees also that the myth explains more than the theories which are supposed to interpret it'. For his argument that all scientific or merely philosophical explanations of the reality of evil are circular and fail see also *Persons*, 218 (*Personen*, 231).

[228] 'Rationalität als "Kulturelles Erbe"', 311.

[229] 'Was ist das Neue?', 21.

We have already begun to examine what is common to all those features, and have argued that Spaemann considers one of the fundamental problems of modernity to be its misconstruals of nature, freedom, and their relation. From a merely philosophical point of view this may seem to be all that can be said. Yet if we put Spaemann's analysis of modernity into a wider context and explicate what is implicit to it we can see that the fundamental flaw of modernity is its misunderstanding of the fall and its attempt, if the fall is, in however transformed a way, recognized at all, autonomously to overcome it. In contrast to the modernistic approach to the doctrine of original sin, the orthodox version shows why human life is characterized by a fundamental rupture and alienation between nature and freedom that cannot be overcome dialectically, but can only be healed by an act of divine intervention.

Hence, what Spaemann seeks in his effort to recover, rather than to dismiss, the doctrine of original sin is the retrieval of a view of human nature in which the consequences of the fall cannot be overcome in an autonomous exercise of merely human freedom, nor by the reductive focus upon 'mere nature' that cannot countenance the sinful condition of humanity. From this point of view we can also understand more fully why Jean-Jacques Rousseau's philosophy has elicited both sympathy and criticism from Spaemann. One of the central presuppositions of Rousseau's anthropology is the loss of an original unity; he acknowledges the brokenness of humanity, but stands in the tradition of the modern transformation of the doctrine of original sin. At the centre of his philosophy is, therefore, the alienation that, in both Rousseau's and Spaemann's view, is one of the most fundamental keys to understanding the human condition. As Rousseau states, there is an insurmountable contradiction between society and the individual. In this vein, Spaemann has pointed out that in Rousseau the contradiction between *nomos* and *physis* breaks up again. Like Plato, Rousseau lays stress on educational theory and provides a comprehensive political theory. But unlike Plato he does not believe that the orders of *nomos* and *physis* are in principle reconcilable. The unity of Rousseau's thought, according to Spaemann, lies in its farewell to the ancient *polis* and to political theology. For Rousseau (as for Spaemann), political theology is ultimately impossible, as is the unity of the public and the private, of law and morality, of appearance and Being. The fatherland of the Christian, as we have seen, is not of this world. All that is left, at least from the perspective of Rousseau's ambiguous philosophy, is 'civil religion'.[230]

The understanding or transformation of original sin thus has grave implications for our understanding of the political. Carl Schmitt has pointed out that

---

[230] For Rousseau's concept of civil religion, see Rousseau, *The Social Contract*, trans. G.D.H. Cole, introd. Alissa Ardito (New York: Barnes and Noble, 2005) 137ff.

[t]he connection of political theories with theological dogmas of sin which appears prominently in Bossuet, Maistre, Bonald, Donoso Cortés, and Friedrich Julius Stahl, among others, is explained by the relationship of these necessary presuppositions. The fundamental theological dogma of the evilness of the world and man leads, just as does the distinction of friend and enemy, to a categorization of men and makes impossible the undifferentiated optimism of a universal conception of man. In a good world among good people, only peace, security and harmony prevail. Priests and theologians are here just as superfluous as politicians and statesmen.[231]

Because of the fall, the political as well as the historical and the moral have become a problem. In Spaemann's view, attempting to deal with these problems while at the same time denying, or misconceiving, the reality of the fall inevitably leads to totalitarian consequences. This impossible venture, however, not only partly contributes to the ambiguity of Rousseau's philosophy, it also largely determines the very spirit of modernity.

The main features of modernity, as discussed by Spaemann, therefore reflect why and how modernity displays a transformation of the understanding of the fall. Modernity, as we have seen, exhibits a new understanding of freedom as opposed to nature because it raises objections to the idea of a complementary relation between nature and freedom. Consequently, the fall was interpreted as the starting point of history and the very beginning of the rise of free human consciousness through the progressive emancipation from nature. The history of mankind was thus construed as the progressive overcoming of the fall through freedom. Hence, Spaemann point out, modern philosophies of history as well as modern political totalitarianisms are based upon a secularization of Christianity, particularly of the doctrine of original sin and of Christian eschatology. By contrast, the doctrine of original sin, in its orthodox sense, limits human autonomy and emancipation in that it sheds light upon an insurmountable limitation of human beings. This limitation is not tantamount to the fact that freedom relates to nature as its condition and measure. The doctrine of original sin makes a more fundamental statement about the character of both nature and freedom as fallen and in need of redemption. Redemption, however, is a gift and needs to be prayed for. It cannot be achieved autonomously. This is why the modern transformation of the doctrine of original sin fails, turning inhumane and irrational, as Spaemann compellingly shows.

Utilitarianism, one of the most significant results of the modern transformation of the doctrine of original sin, fails because there is no vantage point from which man could ultimately decide what he is to do. But utilitarianism is

---

[231] *The Concept of the Political*, trans. George Schwab (Chicago, Ill./London: University of Chicago Press, 1996), 64–5.

based upon the arrogant pretension to a divine perspective and upon an autonomous anticipation of what Christianity believes is yet to come and what philosophy generally believes to be beyond humanity's capacities: insight into the whole meaning of history. In a similar way, the modern preoccupation with universal, naturalistic, and hypothetical truths fails because it undermines the very existence of human beings as more than mere nature. The emancipation from nature fails because it turns dialectically into the dominion of nature over humanity—the 'abolition of Man' and not his redemption. The same holds true of political Utopias that, as Spaemann argues, may be based partly upon 'secularized derivatives of the Christian idea of human dignity'.[232] They express the belief that brotherhood can immediately be realized in the course of human history and thus dismiss original sin altogether or secularize the notion in the framework of a teleological philosophy of history. In doing so, according to Spaemann, they subject themselves to the dialectic of idealism, on the one hand, and cynicism and totalitarianism, on the other. In Spaemann's view, the fusion of ethics, political philosophy, and the philosophy of history undermines the rationality of the doctrine of original sin and thus the very possibility of freedom, true tolerance, happiness, and human flourishing. It also undermines the possibility of *theoria* as contemplation of substantial reality and not, in the modern sense, as 'our free creation'[233] which is subordinated to practical, or even political, goals.

Spaemann develops his critique of modernity at a time when, as he says, modernity is about to come to an end: 'Modernity has become an object about which we think; it is no longer the form in which we think about it'.[234] In this context Spaemann often refers to Hegel's view that '[t]he owl of Minerva spreads its wings only with the falling of the dusk'.[235] This stance vis-à-vis modernity gives Spaemann a kind of privileged position in comparison to earlier Christian critics of modernity. The example of the anti-modernist thought of Bonald shows how even a Christian criticism of modernity could be subject to the very principles of modernity which, naively and unconsciously presupposed, as Spaemann argues, could easily undermine the very truth claim of orthodox Christianity. This constitutes the tragedy of Bonald's restorative thought, which also shows itself to be paradigmatic of anti-modernism and manifests a dialectic that is comparable to the dialectic of Enlightenment.

---

[232] 'Rationalität als "Kulturelles Erbe"', 311.
[233] 'Überzeugungen in einer hypothetischen Zivilisation', 313.
[234] 'Ende der Modernität?', in *Philosophische Essays*, 249.
[235] *Hegel's Philosophy of Right*, trans. T. M. Knox (Oxford: Oxford University Press, 1967), 13. For Spaemann's reference to this idea in philosophy see e.g. 'Die Herausforderungen der Zivilisation', 12.

We will now turn our attention to Spaemann's examination of Bonald's political theology. His thought will once again show the 'determination of the relation between the human being and the citizen in the modern society'.[236] We will see that the dialectic of modernity cannot possibly be understood without also taking into consideration the dialectic of anti-modernism. In showing precisely this, Spaemann's philosophy—as a theory of modernity—can itself be considered paradigmatic philosophy in our time in demonstrating that philosophy must neither limit itself to examining the initial outlook of modernity nor simply establish an anti-modern attitude if it intends to provide the foundations for overcoming the problematic features of modernity. If Joachim Ritter is right in arguing that the 'revolutionary negation of the past and the restorative negation of the present are ... identical in their presupposition of the historical discontinuity of tradition and future, and this discontinuity thus becomes for Hegel the decisive problem of the age; it goes unresolved in all the tensions and antagonisms of the period',[237] the chapter that follows may not only show Spaemann's attempt to remind us of the continuity of history and the close and unsurmountable relation between tradition and future, but also a distinctly Hegelian element (not more than that, of course!) of his philosophy that was mediated through Ritter's own concern with the continuity of past and future.

---

[236] 'Der Irrtum der Traditionalisten: Zur Soziologisierung der Gottesidee im 19. Jahrhundert', in *Wort und Wahrheit*, 8 (1953), 495.

[237] 'Hegel and the French Revolution', in Joachim Ritter, *Hegel and the French Revolution. Essays on the 'Philosophy of Right'*, trans. with introd. by Richard Dien Winfield (Cambridge, Mass.: The MIT Press, 1982), 62.

4

Society, philosophy, and religion: Spaemann and the dialectic of anti-modernism

> In our own case we can see this oft-repeated process close at hand; we
> know how completely a society can lose its fundamental religion without
> abolishing its official religion; we know how men can all become agnos-
> tics long before they abolish bishops. And we know that also in this last
> ending, which really did look to us like a final ending, the incredible thing
> has happened again; the Faith has a better following among the young
> men than among the old.
>
> G. K. Chesterton

4.1 THE DIALECTIC OF ANTI-MODERNISM

An important feature of Robert Spaemann's philosophy lies in the fact that his
critique of modernity is complemented by a compelling criticism of the
dialectical logic of anti-modern developments. His interpretation of modernity shows that the dialectic of modernity is not restricted to the dialectic of
enlightened reason and the inhumane perversion of rationality, but includes
many anti-modern developments which still presuppose a polarization of
reason and reason's other. So as long as reason, Spaemann argues, does not
acknowledge and reconcile itself with what is its other, the dialectic of
modernity and its abstract and totalitarian character cannot be overcome.
Along these lines, Spaemann comments with reference to Mozart's *Magic
Flute* that the Queen of the Night should not have been eliminated, but rather
integrated, as Athens did with the Erinyes—integrated so that life in the *polis*
could flourish.[1] As we have already seen, the alternative to modernity that
Spaemann proposes is not a naive anti-modernism—however fashionable
such a position may be among some conservative thinkers.

---

[1] See e.g. 'Die zwei Grundbegriffe der Moral', in *Kritik der politischen Utopie*, 13; 'Der Hass
des Sarastro', in *Grenzen*, esp. 192 ff.; 'Ende der Modernität?', in *Philosophische Essays*, 259 ff.

We will now consider Spaemann's criticism of L. G. A. de Bonald's thought. Because of the representative character of Bonald's philosophy, this chapter will also lead us to examine Spaemann's criticism of political and sociological functionalism and their absolute claims. At stake here is 'whether sociology expresses the ultimate reality of humanity'[2] or whether there is a substantial reality that lies beyond any kind of sociological function and makes it possible to speak of functions without succumbing to the danger of nihilism. To put it slightly differently, what is at stake is the question whether there are two entirely different cities that cannot be reconciled because 'the earthly city was created by self-love reaching the point of contempt for God, the Heavenly City by the love of God carried as far as contempt of self',[3] or, alternatively, whether it is the case that there are two cities that can and progressively will be resolved into one. The latter alternative, however, would empty the Christian promise of its absolute character and instead promise a strictly earthly fulfilment.

The philosophy of the French 'traditionalist' and counter-revolutionary L. G. A. de Bonald (1754–1840) was one of the earliest objects of Spaemann's interest in the dialectic of anti-modernism. Bonald was the subject of Spaemann's (published) doctoral dissertation: *The Origin of Sociology in the Spirit of Restoration: Studies on L. G. A. de Bonald* (*Der Ursprung der Soziologie aus dem Geist der Restauration: Studien über L. G. A. de Bonald*).[4] The main body of *The Origin of Sociology* consists of a detailed and thorough survey of the centremost features of Bonald's sociopolitical metaphysics and his counter-Enlightenment 'pragmatism'.[5] Spaemann examines Bonald's philosophy of

---

[2] 'Der Irrtum der Traditionalisten: Zur Soziologisierung der Gottesidee im 19. Jahrhundert', in *Wort und Wahrheit*, 8 (1953), 497.

[3] Augustine, *City of God*, trans. Henry Bettenson (London: Penguin, 1984), XIV. 28 (p. 593).

[4] Spaemann did not at first want to publish his doctoral dissertation, until he was advised to do so with an eye to his future career as a professional philosopher. See also Jürgen Kaube,'Was ist Bonaldismus? Originelles Völkchen, diese Konterrevolutionäre: Robert Spaemann zeigt, dass die ursprüngliche Einsicht in die Wirklichkeit den großen Zerstörern gefehlt hat', in *Frankfurter Allgemeine Zeitung*, 27 Sept. 1999.

[5] For a short discussion of de Bonald's "pragmatism" see also Spaemann, Robert, 'Zur Ontologie der Begriffe "rechts" und "links"', in *Grenzen*, 264. For contemporary research on Bonald, see, e.g., Lorenz, Gabriele, *De Bonald als Repräsentant der gegenrevolutionären Theoriebildung. Eine Untersuchung zur Systematik und Wirkungsgeschichte* (Frankfurt am Main: Peter Lang, 1997) (= Französische Sprache und Literatur, vol. 216); Toda, Michel, *Louis de Bonald. Théoricien de la contrerévolution* (Étampes Cedex: Clovis, 1996); Klinck, David *The French Counterrevolutionary Theorist Louis de Bonald (1754–1840)* (New York: Peter Lang, 1996) (=Studies in Modern European History, vol. 18). Klinck, though, did not take notice of Spaemann's book; otherwise he would have modified his statement that '[a]lthough he [de Bonald] was generally recognized as a major figure in French conservative thought and in the rise of French sociology, no one had ever done a study of his ideas in the context of his life and times' (vii). See also Klinck, 'Louis de Bonald: The Foreshadowing of the Integral Nationalism of

language, of history, of religion, and of society and compares and contrasts them with those of several modern philosophers, including Joseph de Maistre, Jean-Jacques Rousseau, and Thomas Hobbes. Spaemann demonstrates that Bonald anticipated many of the philosophical turns that were yet to occur, such as those in linguistics[6] and hermeneutics,[7] and introduces his readers to Bonald's hermeneutics.[8]

Spaemann's own explicit critical remarks in the thesis are relatively rare, apart from his brief 1998 preface[9] and his unequivocal and concise critical appreciation of Bonald's thought both in the last chapter and in the afterword.[10] These remarks, however, are most revealing and will be of assistance to us in understanding Spaemann's argument more fully. He points out that the purpose of a philosophical study about a thinker cannot be either to praise or to criticize his thought because an adequate exposition of it should itself disclose both its truth and its lack of truth.[11] Thus, we need to examine his presentation of Bonald's thought very carefully. Spaemann's own standpoint is frequently hidden behind that of other critics, such as Abbé Lamennais, Charles Péguy, and G. K. Chesterton. It is important to read between the lines and to analyse meticulously the point of view from which Spaemann undertakes his own interpretative enterprise.

Spaemann uses the method of ideological criticism in order to recall a view of reality that has been camouflaged in modernity. In its intellectual rigour, its foundational proposition, and, to a certain extent, even in its language, *The Origin of Sociology* is reminiscent of Adorno and Horkheimer's *Dialectic of Enlightenment*, with which Spaemann was already familiar when he wrote his

---

Charles Maurras and the Action Française', in: *History of European Ideas*, 15 (1992), 327–32; Klinck, 'The French Counterrevolution and the Rise of Sociology. The Question of the Modernity of Louis de Bonald's Science of Society,' in *Selected Papers. Consortium on Revolutionary Europe 1750–1850* (1994), 705–13. See also Gilson, Etienne, 'French and Italian Philosophy,' in Etienne Gilson, Thomas Langhan, Armand A. Maurer, *Recent Philosophy. Hegel to the Present* (New York: Random House, 1966), 169–408, particularly 209–14; Quinlan, Mary Hall, *The Historical Thought of the Vicomte de Bonald* (Washington, D.C.: The Catholic University of America Press, 1953); Krauss, Werner, 'Bonald und die Theorie der Restauration', in Krauss, Werner, *Gesammelte Aufsätze zur Literatur- und Sprachwissenschaft* (Frankfurt am Main: Vittorio Klostermann, 1949), 369–99. For a recent scholarly examination of the French counter-Enlightenment see McMahon, Darrin M., *Enemies of the Enlightenment. The French Counter-Enlightenment and the Making of Modernity* (New York: Oxford University Press, 2001).

[6] *Der Ursprung der Soziologie aus dem Geist der Restauration*, 11.
[7] Ibid. 43.
[8] For a short discussion of Bonald's main ideas see also Lorenz, *De Bonald als Repräsentant der gegenrevolutionären Theoriebildung*, 23–47.
[9] *Der Ursprung der Soziologie aus dem Geist der Restauration*, 9–11.
[10] Ibid. 194–213.
[11] Ibid. 194.

dissertation.[12] The influence of the *Dialectic of Enlightenment* on Spaemann's thought and his cultural and philosophical criticism of modernity should not be underestimated, although Spaemann takes a rather critical stand towards the authors' Rousseauan understanding of the incommensurability of nature and history.[13] According to Spaemann's brief criticism of Adorno and Horkheimer's thought, they still presuppose a modern—that is to say, non-teleological—view of nature. In contrast to them, Spaemann recollects a view according to which nature, on the one hand, and history, society, and freedom, on the other, are not conflicting but complementary phenomena— nature, as we have argued, being the underlying normative presupposition of the exercise of freedom. Furthermore, Spaemann provides what he considers a Christian answer to the modern alienation of the public from the private, an answer that contrasts with the neo-Marxist underpinning of Adorno and Horkheimer's thought, particularly their anthropology and Utopian view of history. Spaemann rejects the synthesis of ethics and political philosophy on the one hand and history on the other; and he regards any political Utopia as fundamentally flawed, particularly because it overlooks, or even dismisses, not only the intrinsic limitations of man but also, more specifically, the implications of the Christian account of the fall of man and of man's redemption. In *The Origin of Sociology*, too, he re-appreciates philosophically a non-Utopian and non-totalitarian ethics and a political philosophy that endeavours to reconnect the drive for self-preservation with the search for happiness. Given the conditions of modernity, Spaemann thus not only reassesses reason as 'the organ that is common',[14] but also proposes a Christian ethics of inwardness and the need for a substantial belief that, he argues, makes freedom fully possible and overcomes the abstract emptiness of modern rationality and its totalitarian and nihilistic implications.

In *The Origin of Sociology* Spaemann applies Adorno and Horkheimer's analysis of the dialectic of Enlightenment reason and revolutionary thought to the French Catholic counter-revolution. Adorno and Horkheimer's thesis is that humanitarian rationality dialectically turns into inhumane irrationality. Twentieth-century totalitarianism thus is not an anti-modern phenomenon, but is rather due to the dialectical unfolding of Enlightenment rationality. With respect to Bonald's counter-revolutionary thought, Spaemann reasons, the argument can be developed in a similar way. Bonald's functionalistic defence

---

[12] Spaemann reports purchasing *The Dialectic of Enlightenment* in 1949, some years before his dissertation was finished ('Einleitung', in *Philosophische Essays*, 10).

[13] For more on Adorno's and Horkheimer's Rousseauism see 'Einleitung', in *Philosophische Essays*, 11–12.

[14] 'Einleitung', in *Kritik der politischen Utopie*, viii.

of authoritarian monarchism and Catholicism, as we will see, turns dialectically into the abolition of the French monarchy, substantial Christianity, and its truth claims.

Although he criticizes them implicitly, Spaemann does not refer to Adorno and Horkheimer in *The Origin of Sociology*. Indeed, most of the philosophers whom Spaemann criticizes are hardly mentioned in this book; when they *are* indicated by name it is most often in contexts that do not draw attention to Spaemann's critical attitude towards them. His critique, largely implicit in this work, is directed at the implications of major currents of modernity and anti-modernity for an adequate understanding of humanity, of the political, of history, and of Christianity. Informed by Christianity, Spaemann's philosophy offers a criticism of modernity, including supposedly Christian anti-modernisms. He accuses Bonald and Hegel of an 'abolition of Enlightenment' 'in that they moved away from concrete reason and subjective freedom into a realm of absolute, objective and universal reason'.[15] Hence, his criticism of modernity is at the same time a defence of modernity against the self abolition of reason which is not grounded in the 'unpreconceivable'. This chapter will therefore show once more that Spaemann's defence of modernity and his defence of an orthodox Christian point of view over against the erroneous truth claims of modernity are very closely intertwined, so as to be almost indistinguishable.

4.2 THE PARADIGMATIC CHARACTER OF BONALD'S PHILOSOPHY

Since Spaemann's historical interpretation does not follow a merely historical agenda, his investigation into Bonald's thought, like his interpretation of Jean-Jacques Rousseau and of the controversy between Fénelon and Bossuet,[16] needs to be considered in a wider context. Oliver O'Donovan has argued that in response to contemporary moral problems

the moralist has to adopt a more adventurous and wide-ranging approach to the discussion. He has to do more than analyse difficult 'cases of conscience'; his argument must aim at more than demonstrating that this or that practice is legitimate or

---

[15] 'Der Irrtum der Traditionalisten', 494.

[16] For Spaemann's interpretation of the controversy between Fénelon and Bossuet see *Reflexion und Spontaneität*. Spaemann argues that Fénelon was 'perhaps the first theologian' who saw the problem of secularization and 'posed the questions of how a Christian existence is possible under the conditions of alienation' (*Reflexion und Spontaneität*, 21; for Fénelon and the problem of alienation see also 240ff.).

illegitimate. He has to become an interpreter, who can explain how and why these decisions now come to us in these forms and present these difficulties.[17]

O'Donovan's idea of what the moralist ought to do helps us to understand the thrust of Spaemann's philosophy more deeply, particularly his interest in the history of ideas.

Spaemann, as may already have become clear, is never interested in the history of ideas for its own sake.[18] His account of the history of ideas, particularly of the rise and development of modernity, also follows a systematic agenda that has critical implications for several contemporary discussions, particularly in the field of moral philosophy. Spaemann wants, too, to grasp why particular decisions now come to us and what this entails. He shares Charles Taylor's desire 'to understand just what makes up this new age we are living in'.[19] *The Origin of Sociology*, as well as his examination of Rousseau, Fénelon, and Bossuet and their paradigmatic (and ambiguous) philosophies, displays Spaemann's desire to understand modernity, its ambiguity, and its implications more fully. Bonald's philosophy, for instance, exhibits paradigmatically how the modern attempt to preserve a traditional political and social order turns against itself due to its focus upon the very act of preservation and not upon what is to be preserved. Bonald was the first, as Spaemann points out, to develop a strictly functionalistic theory of religion, a theory which proved less interested in the truth of religious content than in its function for society.[20]

Spaemann's study on the 'maître de la contrerévolution' is, not the least because of the paradigmatic character of Bonald's philosophy,[21] a nucleus out of which his later thought, particularly his criticism of modernity, develops. Bonald, as Spaemann emphasizes, stated that his *Théorie du pouvoir politique et religieux*[22] contained the initial stages of almost everything that he would later write more densely and systematically.[23] Almost the same argument can be made about Spaemann's dissertation. In his preface to the 1998 edition Spaemann points out that he has not moved very far from the point of view

---

[17] *Begotten or Made?*, 2nd edn. (Oxford: Clarendon, 1998), vii–viii.

[18] See in this context also Louis Dupré, *Passage to Modernity: An Essay in the Hermeneutics of Nature and Culture* (New Haven, Conn./London: Yale University Press, 1993), 9: 'A reflection on past thought that is not a search for permanent meaning leaves us defenceless against cultural nihilism'.

[19] Taylor, 'Preface', in *Philosophical Papers* (Cambridge: Cambridge University Press, 1985), xi.

[20] *Der Ursprung der Soziologie aus dem Geist der Restauration*, 10.

[21] Spaemann, *Der Ursprung der Soziologie aus dem Geist der Restauration*, 13.

[22] *Théorie du pouvoir politique et religieux dans la société civile démontrée par le raisonnement et par l'histoire* (Constance, 1796).

[23] *Der Ursprung der Soziologie aus dem Geist der Restauration*, 16.

that he held at the time when he wrote *The Origin of Sociology*.[24] In this foreword Spaemann explicitly refers to his idea that in modernity the teleological view of nature and humanity was inverted, in order to illustrate to what extent this work forms a continuity with his subsequent writings.[25] The discussion of Spaemann's understanding of philosophy in Chapter 2 should have made it clear that this assertion is not the denial of an intellectual development on Spaemann's side. It is the claim to a specific kind of intellectual development that mirrors perfectly the nature of philosophy as Spaemann conceived it.

Spaemann's interest in Bonald is unquestionably influenced by the legal philosopher Carl Schmitt, whose anti-liberal thought also sheds light upon the dialectical character of modernity.[26] Spaemann occasionally characterizes Bonald's critique of the French Revolution as 'anti-Romantic'.[27] This characterization is particularly reminiscent of Schmitt's emphasis upon the distinctly anti-Romantic character of the Catholic political philosophers Bonald, Maistre, and Donoso Cortés, since they 'would have considered everlasting conversation a product of a gruesomely comic fantasy, for what characterized their counter-revolutionary political philosophy was the recognition that their times needed a decision'.[28] Unlike the German Romantics, who, roughly speaking, based their critique of the modern Enlightenment period upon the irrational and the mystical, and who thus questioned the modern preoccupation with a narrowly defined rationality, Bonald's critique and his decisionism presuppose modern enlightened reason, though in a modified way. Because Bonald is still far too modern a figure to be able truly to see through the problematic dialectic of modernity and its concept of reason, John Milbank has appropriately spoken of the 'hyper-' or 'post-'Enlightenment character of Bonald's thought.[29]

Bonald, for instance, affirms that there is no conflict between proper authority and universal reason, for he defines authority and reason circularly.

---

[24] Ibid. 9.

[25] Ibid. 10.

[26] Carl Schmitt, *Politische Theologie: Vier Kapitel zur Lehre von der Souveränität* (Berlin: Duncker & Humblot, 1996), 57–70, esp. 59–60 (*Political Theology: Four Chapters on the Concept of Sovereignty*, trans. George Schwab (Cambridge, Mass.: MIT Press, 1985), 53–66, esp. 53–4).

[27] Spaemann, *Der Ursprung der Soziologie aus dem Geist der Restauration*, 15, 123, 171.

[28] Schmitt, *Political Theology*, 53. Schmitt was extraordinarily sceptical of any Romantic ideas (see esp. his *Politische Romantik*, 3rd edn. (Berlin: Duncker & Humblot, 1968)). Spaemann is less critical of Romanticism and conversation, but his critique of Karl-Otto Apel's and Jürgen Habermas's philosophy calls to mind Schmitt's critique of the Romantic tendency to replace inevitable decisions with conversation and discursive agreements. See Spaemann, 'Die Utopie der Herrschaftsfreiheit', in *Kritik der politischen Utopie*; 'Die Utopie des guten Herrschers: Eine Diskussion zwischen Jürgen Habermas und Robert Spaemann', in *Kritik der politischen Utopie*; *Happiness and Benevolence*, 131–42 (*Glück und Wohlwollen*, 172–85).

[29] *Theology and Social Theory: Beyond Secular Reason* (Oxford: Blackwell, 1997), 55.

Bonald's defence of Catholicism proceeds *more geometrico*[30] and thus maintains the high epistemological status of that knowledge that can be reduced to a mathematical equation, while at the same time criticizing its anti-Catholic and anti-monarchical implications. His anthropology is deeply indebted to Cartesian principles, and his relation to both Jean-Jacques Rousseau and Thomas Hobbes is ambiguous, as Spaemann shows. Bonald (on whom Rousseau did have a significant influence) and Hobbes agree with regard to their anthropology—that is to say, they both affirm that the individual is fundamentally evil—while disagreeing with regard to their notion of nature. In contrast to Hobbes, Bonald defines the nature of human beings ultimately as being citizens in the French Catholic monarchy and not as being isolated individuals.[31] Bonald belongs to the non-teleological Hobbesian tradition of political philosophy[32] that understands the state with respect to its tendency to preserve itself as opposed to its duty to order itself toward the search for happiness. 'The essence of the "bourgeois society"', Spaemann points out, is defined 'as "absolute preservation"'.[33] Thus, Leo Strauss could see astounding parallels between the anti-liberal Bonaldian Charles Maurras and Thomas Hobbes;[34] this connection neatly illustrates the ambiguous and dialectical character of modern anti-liberalism.

While Bonald understood human reason from within its historical context (and thus dismissed a purely abstract notion of reason), he increasingly sought to defend an abstract order, as Spaemann points out, that evoked both violence and the abolition of ideas that he formerly held.[35] According to

---

[30] Spaemann, *Der Ursprung der Soziologie aus dem Geist der Restauration*, 209.

[31] Ibid. 105.

[32] For the relation between Bonald and Hobbes see *Der Ursprung der Soziologie aus dem Geist der Restauration*, 104–8.

[33] For the relation between Bonald and Hobbes see *Der Ursprung der Soziologie aus dem Geist der Restauration*, 66.

[34] In July 1933 Strauss writes in a letter to Carl Schmitt: 'Inzwischen habe ich mich ein wenig mit Maurras beschäftigt. Die Parallelen mit Hobbes—von einer Abhängigkeit kann wohl kaum die Rede sein—sind frappant. Ich wäre sehr froh, wenn ich ihn einmal sprechen könnte. Wären Sie in der Lage und bereit, mir ein paar Zeilen zur Einführung bei ihm zu schreiben?' See Leo Strauss, 'Drei Briefe an Carl Schmitt', in Heinrich Meier, *Carl Schmitt, Leo Strauss und 'Der Begriff des Politischen': Zu einem Dialog unter Abwesenden* (Stuttgart: Metzler, 1998), 135.

[35] *Der Ursprung der Soziologie aus dem Geist der Restauration*, 173. Spaemann's critical remarks about Bonald's abstract and elitist conservativism and his emphasis upon the need to take notice of the concrete and particular society are suggestive of Alasdair MacIntyre's communitarian critique of Herbert Marcuse's abstract and elitist disapproval of contemporary society and philosophy (MacIntyre, *Marcuse* (London: Fontana/Collins, 1970); see e.g. 21–2, 63, 74; 64 for Marcuse's elitism). The dialectic of abstraction and violence of which Spaemann speaks with regard to the political ideas of the later Bonald can also be found in modern left-wing critics of contemporary society. Spaemann's analysis of this dialectic might also be read as a critique of Adorno and Horkheimer.

his thinking, the true nature of a particular philosophy depends upon whether it is connected to atheism or religion.[36] While the French Revolution claimed to inaugurate the dominion of philosophy, Bonald argues, it effectively initiated the end of the dominion of reason because of its one-sidedly abstract and atheistic character. In contrast to the Revolution, Bonald maintains that the authority of reason is realized by the reasonable character of the given authority in a society. This view, however, also tends to defend an abstract order. Bonald's own emphasis on an abstract order shows why he is a typically modern figure while at the same time articulating opposition to modernity and its most fundamental principles.

Spaemann points out that because the Revolution not only undermined reason but also threatened Bonald's own sense of religiosity, he reluctantly became a philosopher and a political writer.[37] Although Spaemann is critical of Bonald's totalitarian notion of society[38] and his political theology, he agrees with Bonald's interpretation of modernity not only as a time of crisis but also as a time of conversion and decision. Spaemann also sympathizes with Bonald as a writer who does not give up but defends his substantial belief in the violent unrest of the French Revolution. However, despite this sympathy, Spaemann's reading of Bonald is by and large very critical. For him, Bonald's philosophy exemplifies the common ground of modernism and modernistic anti-modernism that is primarily a functionalistic transformation of traditional ontology and the inversion of a teleological view of nature. Given this paradigm shift, philosophy was increasingly pursued from an instrumentalist point of view. *Theoria* is no longer an end in itself, but becomes a kind of subdiscipline of social and political practice. The hidden and largely unintended implications of anti-modernisms, Spaemann shows, thus tend to be even more modern than modernity. 'The actual modernity', he presumes, 'begins only with the counter-revolution'.[39] Thus, in his examination of the dialectic of modernity and its consequences, above all for political philosophy and Christianity, Spaemann discovered an important stage in Bonald's thought, which has been rather neglected in spite of its influence. This is perhaps because it is still eclipsed by subsequent nineteenth-century traditionalism and its faulty epistemology, not to mention the ecclesial

---

[36] *Der Ursprung der Soziologie aus dem Geist der Restauration*, 21 ff.

[37] Ibid. 13, 16, 21.

[38] For a similar view of Bonald's 'totalitarianism' see W. Jay Reedy, 'Maistre's Twin? Louis de Bonald and the Enlightenment', in Richard A. Lebrun (ed.), *Joseph de Maistre's Life, Thought, and Influence: Selected Studies* (Montreal/Kingston: McGill-Queen's University Press, 2001), 183–4.

[39] 'Der Irrtum der Traditionalisten', 498.

reprobation of traditionalism which, Spaemann argues, did not concern Bonald's position.[40]

Because of its paradigmatic character, the thought of Bonald is not the only target of Spaemann's critique. Bonald's philosophy provides an example of specific modern tendencies that no longer see the limits of philosophy (such as Hegel's philosophy) and of the political (such as Carl Schmitt's legal philosophy). Spaemann also criticizes notions of philosophy which functionalize philosophy, whether in a rather bourgeois way in view of the needs of a modern industrial society, as in Joachim Ritter's thought, or in a neo-Marxist way, as in Adorno and Horkheimer's cultural criticism, or in a way which renders the sociological theory of society a kind of absolute, as in Niklas Luhmann's sociology. Hence, in criticizing Bonald's thought and its implications for the understanding of the individual, Spaemann criticizes an anti-human tendency of modern philosophy that subjects the individual human being to the ends of society, politics, and history. In what follows we will show why *The Origin of Sociology* can also be read as an indirect critique of Hegel, Schmitt, Ritter, and Adorno and Horkheimer. In addition to this, we will discuss Spaemann's critique of Luhmann's functionalistic sociology, which clearly stands in Bonald's tradition and is thus an indirect target *avant la lettre*.[41] Before we proceed to examine Bonald's thought, it is worth commenting on the historical context of *The Origin of Sociology*.

4.3 THE HISTORICAL CONTEXT OF *THE ORIGIN OF SOCIOLOGY IN THE SPIRIT OF RESTORATION*

When Spaemann wrote *The Origin of Sociology* most of the issues that were of importance for Bonald were also passionately discussed in post-war Germany. How is authority to be properly conceived and justified?[42] How should society be reshaped after a catastrophe as far-reaching as German Nazism and the Holocaust?[43] How can a consensus about the fundamental good be

---

[40] For the ecclesial reprobation of traditionalism see also Spaemann, 'Der Irrtum der Traditionalisten', 493 ff.; see also *Der Ursprung der Soziologie aus dem Geist der Restauration*, 175 ff., esp. 180.

[41] For the interpretation of Bonald as forefather of sociological functionalism see also Reedy, 'Maistre's Twin?', 186 ff. (p. 186 provides further secondary sources).

[42] For this question see also Spaemann, 'Der Christ und die demokratische Autorität', in *Kirche und Leben*, 39 (25 Sept. 1949).

[43] Richard Schenk also points out the importance of Spaemann's early life experience for his philosophy: 'The conviction that truth is neither guaranteed to nor impossible for any given age

achieved? What is the end of human life and of society? What is constitutive of human flourishing? How can society be unified, and overcome socially devastating individualism as well as the terror of abstract ideologies and totalitarianism? Particularly in West Germany, the 1950s are what Spaemann calls a 'breathing time' in the development of European civilization towards a world civilization.[44] It was characterized by a restorative tendency in which, for example, the Christian Churches were appealed to as sources of moral strength and revival. In this socio-historical situation *The Origin of Sociology* is also an answer to the tendency in Germany to utilize Christianity as a means of reorganizing society and of re-establishing and preserving democracy and a particular order of values.[45] Spaemann refers to the subjection of humanity's nature to the conditions of its mere preservation as Bonald's 'totalitarianism'.[46] Spaemann, it seems, conceives of a dialectic between revolutionary and restorative totalitarianisms as an imminent danger for post-war Germany and Europe and expresses his scepticism about these political tendencies, however appealing they may have appeared to many of his contemporaries. *The Origin of Sociology* is therefore an ambiguous testimony of the 'sceptical generation' of which the sociologist Helmut Schelsky has spoken.[47] Spaemann's scepticism, however, was not universal in its scope, but concerned the absolute domination of a particular political system and a particular way of defending and justifying authority.

In *The Origin of Sociology* Spaemann refers to the shift in papal teaching and to Leo XIII's readoption of the Aristotelian and Thomistic view that democracy, aristocracy, and monarchy are possible forms of government

---

will remain fundamental in Spaemann's thought' ('The Ethics of Robert Spaemann in the Context of Recent Philosophy', in Brian J. Shanley, OP (ed.), *One Hundred Years of Philosophy* (Studies in Philosophy and the History of Philosophy, xxxvi) (Washington, DC: The Catholic University of America Press, 2001), 159). For Spaemann's own reference to the atrocities committed by the Nazis see e.g. his 'Sind alle Menschen Personen?', in *Grenzen*, 426.

[44] Spaemann, 'Die Aktualität des Naurrechts', *Philosophische Essays*, 65.

[45] See here also Robert Spaemann and Hanns-Gregor Nissing, 'Die Natur des Lebendigen und das Ende des Denkens: Entwicklungen und Entfaltungen eines philosophischen Werks. Ein Gespräch', in Nissing (ed.), *Grundvollzüge der Person: Dimensionen des Menschseins bei Robert Spaemann* (Munich: Institut zur Förderung der Glaubenslehre, 2008), 123–4.

[46] Spaemann, *Der Ursprung der Soziologie aus dem Geist der Restauration*, 96 (Spaemann himself uses quotation marks).

[47] For the notion 'skeptical generation', see Schelsky, Helmut, *Die skeptische Generation. Eine Soziologie der deutschen Jugend* (Düsseldorf: Diederichs, 1963). In an interview, Spaemann says that his current state of mind is characterised by skepticism and cheerfulness, which temper one another (Fragebogen: Robert Spaemann, in *Magazin der Frankfurter Allgemeine Zeitung* (July 1985)).

provided they are just.[48] According to Aristotle, 'the true forms of government are three'. He then argues that

the best must be that which is administered by the best, and in which there is one man, or a whole family, or many persons, excelling all the others together in excellence, and both rulers and subjects are fitted, the one to rule, the others to be ruled, in such a manner as to attain the most desirable life[49]

Given this view of political constitutions, which Spaemann seems to share, he implicitly criticized tendencies to identify a particular political system as the best system from a moral, or even a religious, point of view, and to use Christianity in an attempt to restore the lost foundations of society. This use, he thinks, is a departure from Christian truth and tends to become nihilistic.

Only very rare statements in *The Origin of Sociology* explicitly demonstrate that this book is also a contribution to contemporary questions. In his discussion of the aftermath of Bonald's metaphysics of society Spaemann considers the problematic character of those restorative tendencies that are situated, as he thinks, within the dialectic between revolution and restoration that he considers typical of modern societies. G. K. Chesterton, as Spaemann argues, saw this problem clearly. His critique of modern abstract humanism refrains from defining itself as either revolutionary or restorative, since it 'transcends this dichotomy by being rooted in a 'deeper fatherland' (*Beheimatung*) which could not be uprooted by modern society and which is thus capable of convicting it of its own opposite'.[50] Chesterton's idea of fatherland is a substantial belief that is to be preserved, to be sure, but this is not a preservation for its own sake. It is this substantial belief that Spaemann, too, aims at defending; and it is against the background of this belief that a critique of both revolution and restoration is not only possible but most pertinent, as Spaemann's decision in the 1950s to write *The Origin of Sociology* suggests. The problem raised by the dialectic of revolution and restoration is 'crucial for the whole question of restoration today',[51] as Spaemann consequently

---

[48] *Der Ursprung der Soziologie aus dem Geist der Restauration*, 180. For Leo XIII's view of civil power see *Au Milieu des Sollicitudes*, § 14 or *Diuturnum*, § 7: 'There is no question here respecting forms of government, for there is no reason why the Church should not approve of the chief power being held by one man or by more, provided only it be just, and that it tend to the common advantage. Wherefore, so long as justice be respected, the people are not hindered from choosing for themselves that form of government which suits best either their own disposition, or the institutions and customs of their ancestors'.

[49] *Politics*, 1288a (in *The Complete Works of Aristotle: The Revised Oxford Translation*, ed. Jonathan Barnes (Princeton: Princeton University Press), 2044). For Thomas's view see esp. *Summa Theologiae*, Ia Iae q. 105 a. 1.

[50] Spaemann, 'Der Ursprung der Soziologie aus dem Geist der Restauration', 190.

[51] Ibid.

argues. 'State restoration cannot break through the circle of modern society; it only gets even more deeply into it'.[52]

In a way which makes his own underlying interests evident and which also demonstrates his integration of Chesterton's thought, Spaemann states that it is only possible for the historical dynamic characteristic of Europe to unfold if the absolute content of belief which transcends all historical realization (and hence also all instrumentalist interpretation) is present as such.[53] Bonald, he argues, was still aware of the old European tradition, which has the benefit of an absolute notion of perfection—that is to say, of the absolute future of the Heavenly City, the 'everlasting peace which no adversary can disturb', as Augustine put it[54]—at its disposal, and which thus could not be instrumentalized or overtaken by any kind of historical progress and relative perfection. But this did not only change soon after Bonald; it was already different in many modernistic approaches to Christianity prior to Bonald. So, borrowing from Charles Péguy, Spaemann evaluates the problem of a modernism that does not intend '"to believe what one believes", but to harness the belief of one's own and of other people as a means'.[55] By contrast, the actual substance of the old French society is, according to Péguy's anti-modernist statement, the freedom that consists of believing in what one believes in.[56] Only this substantial belief allows, in Spaemann's view, for true freedom, because a functionalistic interpretation of belief and an absolute notion of freedom, as we have already seen, lead dialectically to the abolition of belief and freedom and become totalitarian. *The Origin of Sociology* thus enables us to become more fully aware of the relation between man and citizen in modernity and of the politics-transcending impetus of substantial Christianity and its indirect political implications.

This examination of the historical background of *The Origin of Sociology* leads us now to a more detailed discussion of the anti-modernism of Bonald's philosophy as outlined in Spaemann's doctoral dissertation.

4.4 THE AMBIGUITY OF BONALD'S THOUGHT

According to Spaemann, the underlying problem of Bonald's thought is the question of how power is to be legitimized.[57] This paradigmatically modern

---

[52] Spaemann, 'Der Ursprung der Soziologie aus dem Geist der Restauration', 182.

[53] Ibid. 193.

[54] Augustine, *City of God*, XIX, 10 (trans. Henry Bettenson (London: Penguin Books, 1984), 864).

[55] Spaemann, '"Politik zuerst"? Das Schicksal der Action Française' in *Wort und Wahrheit*, 8 (1953), 660.

[56] Spaemann, *Der Ursprung der Soziologie aus dem Geist der Restauration*, 182.

[57] See esp. ibid. 76ff. For Spaemann's view of the legitimization of power and his critique of different approaches to legitimizing power see 'Die Utopie der Herrschaftsfreiheit', in *Kritik der politischen Utopie*.

problem, Spaemann states uncontroversially, began with the dissolution of the religious and political unity within Europe and with the liberation of political thought from theology.[58] The political and religious crisis that confronted Bonald brought up the issue of whether non- and anti-Christian conceptions of the political have any legitimacy at all. Bonald's answer to this question is unambiguous. In his view, it is the imaging or imitation of God through society that legitimizes political power. Non-Christian political systems and philosophies are therefore ultimately illegitimate; the political order of the French Revolution is indefensible and unjustifiable. The context of Bonald's writings is thus a time of crisis; his solution is deeply ambiguous because, as Spaemann shows, it undermines the truth claim of orthodox Christianity and also revolutionizes the insights of traditional philosophy.

Spaemann argues that Bonald hypostasizes society and its very existence without embedding the social and political in the much wider context of the question of what makes life good. According to Spaemann, Bonald thinks that 'the true philosophy in its absolute form is ... metaphysics of society and philosophy of history'.[59] Bonald also held the opinion, Spaemann further points out, that looking at politics from a theologian's point of view was essentially the same as looking at theology from a politician's point of view.[60] While Bonald's motives for the assimilation of the Heavenly City to the earthly city are orthodox beyond any doubt and lack the anti-Christian attitude of many of his nineteenth- and twentieth-century successors, the very content of his thought is subject to dialectical transformations that were originally unintended. This is why Spaemann calls Bonald's identification of Christianity and civil society and his totalitarian view of the political ambiguous and daring[61] and speaks of the 'insurmountable ambiguity' of Bonald's works. It is particularly Spaemann's anti-functionalistic attitude, his emphasis on the fallen nature of humanity, and his Christian view of history that make it impossible for him to subscribe to Bonald's idea that the absolute form of philosophy is realized in the historical unity of French absolutism and Catholicism.

As Spaemann points out, Bonald did not take into account the particular historical situation of Christianity after the French Revolution and in modernity nor the distinctly apolitical character of Christianity as a universal,

---

[58] *Der Ursprung der Soziologie aus dem Geist der Restauration*, 83–4. Spaemann's brief acount of the history of the problem of sovereignty is very close to Carl Schmitt's account in *Political Theology*.

[59] *Der Ursprung der Soziologie aus dem Geist der Restauration*, 38.

[60] Ibid. 201.

[61] *Der Ursprung der Soziologie aus dem Geist der Restauration*, 123.

world- and history-transcending religion for which the salvation of one's soul
is more important than any change in the worldly state of affairs.[62] Spaemann, as we have shown, agrees with Rousseau's interpretation of Christianity
as 'the absolute truth and at the same time politically destructive',[63] and
accordingly accuses Bonald of overlooking this important implication
of Christianity. This is why Bonald's political theology implies, in the end,
as Spaemann makes clear, a more fundamental secularization of society than
the revolutionary critique and disapproval of Christianity because he defends
religion in terms of its political and social function; that is to say, religion
becomes ultimately an instrument of politics and thus politically constructive.
Bonald thus unwittingly attenuates the position that Christianity is substantially true, apart from its instantiation in any particular society, function, or
end, except God.

Hence, Bonald's thought shows the genesis of a new functionalistic metaphysics and, consequently, the sociological transformation of metaphysics in
modernity because society is for him the 'a priori reality of humanity'.[64] For
Bonald, society, as the expression of the objective spirit, is the fundamental
dimension from which everything else is to be derived. Sociology has become
prima philosophia; genealogy and functionalism being its primary methods.
Already a brief look at the development of nineteenth- and twentieth-century
thought confirms Spaemann's thesis. The question as to what something
essentially is, is replaced by the functionalistic analysis of how something
affects a given context with respect to man-defined purposes. Substantial
truth is transformed into hypothetical truth statements, valued for their
applicability. Freedom (and often also the political order and history) has
become total and has relinquished nature and its teleology as its normative
point of reference.

Spaemann argues that the ontological functionalism of Bonald's defence
of Christianity has the tendency to turn into what he calls the nihilism of
the right,[65] which, unlike Aristotle's and Thomas Aquinas's political philosophies, subordinated the good life to the preservation of its mere existence.
Given this non-teleological view of reality, actions of self-transcendence—
theoria as the highest form of activity, worship of God for God's sake,
amor Dei usque ad contemptum sui,[66] care for one's soul, the sacrifice, the

---

[62] 'Theologie, Prophetie, Politik', in *Kritik der politischen Utopie*, 67.

[63] Spaemann, 'Von der Polis zur Natur—Die Kontroverse um Rousseaus ersten "Discours"',
in *Rousseau: Bürger ohne Vaterland*, 39.

[64] '"Politik zuerst"? Das Schicksal der Action Française', 657.

[65] *Der Ursprung der Soziologie aus dem Geist der Restauration*, 10, 186, 188–9.

[66] For this notion, frequently referred to by Spaemann, see Augustine, *De Civitate Dei*,
XIV. 28; for Spaemann's reference to it see e.g. *Happiness and Benevolence*, 113 (*Glück und*

Sabbath,[67] and the feast,[68] for instance—do not make sense and are subject to the logic of functionalistic interpretation for the sake of political ends. Bonald no longer appreciates activities that cannot be integrated into a political framework, because these activities are, by his definition, antisocial and revolutionary attitudes.

Because of the French Revolution, which has 'made manifest the dialectic of the abstract formalism' of modern philosophy,[69] Bonald envisioned the need to reconcile reason and authority and to overcome the horrible 'neutral thought' of the Revolution.[70] For him, there is no third alternative beyond politically destructive atheism and society-guaranteeing Catholicism, since even liberalism is the transition towards a totalitarian dictatorship.[71] The proper understanding of reality is in his view ultimately based upon a political decision which does not circumvent reason but rather does justice to it by subjecting it to society and its authority. This is characteristic of nineteenth-century Catholic philosophy, as Carl Schmitt emphasizes: 'Wherever Catholic philosophy of the nineteenth century was engaged, it expressed the idea in one form or another that there was now a great alternative that no longer allowed of synthesis. No medium exists, said Cardinal Newman, between Catholicism and atheism. Everyone formulated a big either/or.'[72]

Bonald's philosophy also has obvious repercussions in Carl Schmitt's own thought, to which Spaemann stands in an ambiguous relationship.[73] This is

---

Wohlwollen, 150); Spaemann, *Persons*, 202 (*Personen*, 214); 'Frieden—utopisches Ideal, kategorischer Imperativ oder politischer Begriff?', in *Grenzen*, 27.

[67] For Spaemann's view of the Sunday see 'Der Anschlag auf den Sonntag', in *Grenzen*; see also 'Der Sonntag christlich verstanden', in *Kirche und Leben*, (11 Sept. 1949). See also 'Zur Ontologie der Begriffe "rechts" und "links" ', in *Grenzen*, 268: 'Und wenn ein Volk den Sabbat oder den Sonntag in einem bestimmten Stil begeht, dann wird ein öffentliches Gut realisiert, das sich nicht in private Befriedigungsfunktionen zurückübersetzen läßt'.

[68] For Spaemann's view of the feast as the 'image for "rational happiness" 'see *Happiness and Benevolence*, 89 (*Glück und Wohlwollen*, 118).

[69] Spaemann, *Der Ursprung der Soziologie aus dem Geist der Restauration*, 33.

[70] Ibid. 29.

[71] Spaemann upholds the idea that there is a link between liberalism, on the one hand, and collectivism and totalitarianism on the other. He mentions, for instance, a dialectic between liberalism and collectivism ('Funktionale Religionsbegründung und Religion', in *Philosophische Essays*, 225) and a proximity between liberalism and totalitarian theories with regard to their reductionistic understanding of the state (*Persons*, 191 (*Personen*, 202)).

[72] *Political Theology*, 53. Spaemann also refers to the fact that Cardinal Newman saw the same alternative (*Der Ursprung der Soziologie aus dem Geist der Restauration*, 29).

[73] For a very brief critique of Schmitt's position see Spaemann, 'Die Sendung der Jeanne d'Arc', in *Wort und Wahrheit*, 8 (1953), 376–8. Carl Schmitt draws attention to Spaemann's *Der Ursprung der Soziologie aus dem Geist der Restauration* as an interesting book about Bonald in *Politische Theologie, II. Die Legende von der Erledigung jeder Politischen Theologie*, 4th edn. (Berlin: Duncker & Humblot, 1994), 39.

particularly because Schmitt's philosophy continues and justifies the totalitarian notion of the political that is typical of Bonald.[74] In the 1934 preface to *Political Theology* Schmitt points out that '[w]e have come to recognize that the political is the total, and as a result we know that any decision about whether something is unpolitical is always a political decision, irrespective of who decides and what reasons are advanced'.[75] However, his epoch is, Schmitt argued in 1932, the time of liberal neutralizations, 'depoliticizations', as it were, and denaturalizations of political conceptions.[76] It is the time of the manifest crisis of the modern state that has ceased to be truly a 'clear and unequivocal eminent entity confronting non-political groups and affairs'.[77] The state no longer 'poses the monopoly on politics'.[78] In this situation, Schmitt thinks, a decision is necessary. And this leads him to the fundamental 'semi-Hegelian'[79] distinction of friend and enemy, between which no mediation is possible.

It is not too difficult to see the Bonaldian elements of Schmitt's philosophy. Both Bonald and Schmitt criticize the contemporary state of affairs and deal with the problem of modernity. Bonald targets the French Revolution and its outcome. Schmitt criticizes the Weimar Republic and the rise of modern technology and mass culture. According to Bonald, individuals are at war with one another, and the restoration of the *ancien régime* and the Catholic Church as an important element in historical progress can provide a remedy for this turmoil. In Schmitt's philosophy, a pseudo-eschatological ontology of history, too, is lurking behind his ontology of the friend and enemy, that led to his extremely problematic identification with, and support of, National Socialism. Leo Strauss has therefore rightly drawn attention to the fact that Schmitt's main interest in *The Concept of the Political* is not the critique of modern liberalism: 'The polemic against liberalism can therefore only signify a concomitant or preparatory action: it is meant to clear the field for the battle of decision between the "spirit of technicity," the "mass faith that inspires an

---

[74] *Der Ursprung der Soziologie aus dem Geist der Restauration*, 172–3. For an interpretation and critique of Schmitt's thought that is indebted to Spaemann see Peter Koslowski, *Gesellschaft und Staat: Ein unvermeidlicher Dualismus* (Stuttgart: Klett-Cotta, 1982), 108–18.

[75] *Political Theology*, 2.

[76] *The Concept of the Political*, trans. George Schwab (Chicago, Ill./London: University of Chicago Press, 1996), 69.

[77] *The Concept of the Political*, 22.

[78] Ibid.

[79] See Tracy B. Strong, 'Foreword', in Carl Schmitt, *The Concept of the Political*, xx. Strong also draws attention to the proximity between Schmitt's thought and Alasdair MacIntyre's anti-liberalism, which, as he points out, has similarly been stressed by Stephan Holmes (see p. xxi of Strong's foreword). Holmes emphasizes the differences between MacIntyre's 'soft anti-liberalism' and Schmitt's rather militant anti-liberalism; see Holmes, *The Anatomy of Antiliberalism* (Cambridge, Mass.: Harvard University Press, 1993), 88.

antireligious, this-wordly activism", (93) and the opposite spirit and faith, which, as it seems, still has no name'.[80] Strauss further concludes that in Schmitt 'the affirmation of the political as such is not his last word. His last word is "the order of the human things"'.[81] Schmitt's main concern is with 'morality',[82] but in a transformed way: like Bonald's philosophy, his thought exhibits an apocalyptic narrative of history which substitutes philosophy of history, that is to say the future 'battle of decision', for substantial morality and which, in so doing, moralizes politics as well as history and provides a kind of ontological account of them. Both Bonald and Schmitt aim at the reconciliation of the public and the private in order to overcome the modern alienation between society and the free subject as well as the modern rupture between politics and religion. But the private, religion, and the inwardness of one's conscience have become the function of a highly moralized politics in the process of this transformation of political philosophy. Spaemann's critique, then, targets Bonald's and Schmitt's totalizing and monistic conception of the political while at the same time sympathizing with their criticism of modernity; he also shares their view that conversation and mediation cannot be the solution to the problem of modernity and that there are enemies who cannot be turned into friends nor even be neutralized. This, Spaemann argues, is far from being an implication of Christianity. 'The Christian command to love', he reasons, 'does not prohibit us from having enemies and from fighting against them. It prohibits us from hating them.'[83]

The main reason for Spaemann's explicit critique of Bonald and his implicit critique of Schmitt lies in their misconception of the substantial truth of Christianity. Schmitt's language, as well as Bonald's, is indebted to Christianity because of the analogy between theology and jurisprudence. 'All significant concepts of the modern theory of the state', Schmitt argues, 'are secularised theological concepts not only because of their historical development . . . but also because of their systematic structure.'[84] Unlike modern liberalism, Schmitt takes his historical analysis seriously and theorizes about the sovereign 'who decides about the exception'[85]—and whose concept is dependent

---

[80] Strauss, 'Notes on *The Concept of the Political*', in Schmitt, *The Concept of the Political*, 106.
[81] Ibid.
[82] Ibid. 104.
[83] 'Theologie, Prophetie, Politik', in *Kritik der politischen Utopie*, 68–9.
[84] *Political Theology*, 36. It is important to note that Spaemann does not deny the relation between some political and theological concepts, but he is much more aware of the problems that are closely related to this secularization than Schmitt. For him, the concept of 'positive peace', developed by the peace movement, is a secularized theological concept ('Frieden—utopische Ideal, kategorischer Imperativ oder politische Begriff?', in *Grenzen*, 327).
[85] *Political Theology*, 5.

on the secularization of the concept of God. 'The exception in jurisprudence', he further argues, 'is analogous to the miracle in theology'.[86] Yet the political thought of Bonald and Schmitt is not limited to analogies to Christianity or to the realization that there is a close historical link between political and theological concepts. In both Schmitt's and Bonald's philosophies, as we have already seen, the universal claim of Christianity has been *transformed* from within a political context. Political philosophy has not only become analogous to theology, it even seems to replace it, providing its own messianic account of salvation.[87]

This is why Spaemann could formulate an explicit critique of Schmitt's thought along the lines of his critique of Bonald's revolutionary transformation of metaphysics into a 'sociological ontologism' (*soziologischer Ontologismus*). For in *The Origin of Sociology* Spaemann develops the thesis that the political order is not, as Bonald and Schmitt both maintained, 'the most intense and extreme antagonism'.[88] Schmitt's idea that '[e]very religious, moral, economic, ethical, or other antithesis transforms into a political one if it is sufficiently strong to group human beings effectively according to friend and enemy'[89] is called into question by Spaemann's idea that there is a crucial distinction between the public and the private, the external and the internal, between law and morality, and hence between religion and the political. The most intense and extreme antagonism, according to Spaemann, is not a political but a religious and world-transcending antagonism. This antagonism does not comprise an ontological category, nor is it an individual-transcending antagonism, as Carl Schmitt envisaged his friend–enemy distinction: 'The enemy is not merely any competitor or just any partner of a conflict in general. He is also not the private adversary whom one hates. An enemy exists only when, at least potentially, one fighting collectivity of people confronts a similar collectivity'.[90] This most intense antagonism, as Spaemann conceives it, is a relation between friend and enemy as individuals who are fallen, but cannot autonomously 'make' their redemption happen, as it were. In this situation the main aim cannot be not to have enemies at all, he thinks, but to love one's enemies, for it is not up to us 'to decide whether we have enemies or not'.[91]

[86] *Political Theology*, 36.
[87] See here also Peter Koslowski, *Gesellschaft und Staat*, 110ff.
[88] *Political Theology*, 29.
[89] *Political Theology*, 37
[90] Ibid. 28.
[91] For this and Spaemann's view on enemies see also his 'Der Hass des Sarastro', in *Grenzen*, 183–4.

The ambiguity of Bonald's thought, particularly with respect to Christianity, is also manifest in the way Bonald's philosophy was adopted in France. Abbé Lamennais's Christian Socialism[92] goes back to Bonald's understanding of the relation between religion and society (even though Lamennais did not adopt the monarchist strand of Bonald's thought). So too does Charles Maurras's *action française*,[93] which is rooted in Bonald's idea that religion is necessary for the preservation of the French monarchy. Maurras, for instance, did not take the substantial truth claim of Christianity seriously, although he gave credence to its external social function and expression, particularly in its liturgical form. Bonald also had a considerable impact upon Saint-Simon,[94] Auguste Comte,[95] and the traditionalist Joseph de Maistre.[96] Positivist thought, even in its anti-metaphysical tendency, can adopt Bonald's thought, his hypostatization of society, and his functionalistic view of religion—it has, indeed, become paradigmatic of modern thought. Some scholars, such as David Klinck, therefore also point out the resemblance between Bonald's anti-individualism and German Romantic nationalism and twentieth-century fascism,[97] as well as between Bonald's 'anti-humanism' and his 'depersonalization' of the state and twentieth-century structuralism.[98]

4.5 THE FUNCTIONALISTIC INTERPRETATION OF CHRISTIANITY

Before we give attention to the thought of some of Bonald's immediate heirs, we can now briefly summarize Spaemann's critique of his sociological

[92] *Der Ursprung der Soziologie aus dem Geist der Restauration*, 175 ff. For Bonald's influence on Lamennais see also Lorenz, *De Bonald als Repräsentant der gegenrevolutionären Theoriebildung*, 51–69.
[93] *Der Ursprung der Soziologie aus dem Geist der Restauration*, 183 ff; see also his '"Politik zuerst"? Das Schicksal der Action Française'; Lorenz, *De Bonald als Repräsentant der gegenrevolutionären Theoriebildung*, 168 ff.
[94] For his influence on Saint-Simon see Lorenz, *De Bonald als Repräsentant der gegenrevolutionären Theoriebildung*, 70–82.
[95] See ibid. 83–100 for Bonald's influence on Auguste Comte.
[96] *Der Ursprung der Soziologie aus dem Geist der Restauration*, 83–4. For the relation between Bonald and Maistre see also Reedy, 'Maistre's Twin?', 173–89; Jean-Yves Pranchère, 'The Social Bond According to the Catholic Counter-Revolution: Maistre and Bonald', in Richard A. Lebrun (ed.), *Joseph de Maistre's Life, Thought, and Influence: Selected Studies* (Montreal/Kingston: McGill-Queen's University Press, 2001), 190–219; Lorenz, *De Bonald als Repräsentant der gegenrevolutionären Theoriebildung*, 47–9.
[97] Klinck, *The French Counterrevolutionary Theorist Louis de Bonald*, 6.
[98] Ibid. 59.

functionalism. In Bonald's philosophy, Spaemann argues, functionalism replaced a teleological understanding of reality as proposed by the Aristotelian–
Thomistic tradition, and significantly transformed the understanding of
religion and philosophy. Bonald, as Spaemann points out, renders 'theology
a mere tautology of sociology'.[99] In Spaemann's view, this contradicts the self-
understanding of Christians, who 'from the very beginning . . . did not understand their religion as a continuation of ancient political religion, but as a
continuation of ancient philosophy'.[100] Christianity, as we have seen, has a
truth claim with only indirect political implications. Bonald's interpretation
of the *conditio moderna* thus differs substantially both from that of orthodox
Christianity and from that of Jean-Jacques Rousseau,[101] because Bonald
interprets the modern separation between the public realm and the private
realm as historical progress.[102] In Bonald's judgement, this break shows how
the public and the private can be brought into a new relation (the proper one,
Bonald would say) and how metaphysics ought to be redefined within a
sociological context. Bonald defines the metaphysics of society as *prima
philosophia*, entailing not only philosophical but also theological implications; this shows that he does not sufficiently differentiate between the
external and public life of the *civitas terrena* and the utterly inward life
of the *civitas Dei*. In his view, the *ancien régime* has realized what orthodox
Christianity believes to be an absolute future that is yet to come. Bonald's
functionalistic political theology, as Spaemann's argument goes, cannot but
turn nihilistic. 'Functionalism', Spaemann argues, 'to cut a long story short, is
the dissolution of the substance of faith'.[103] The consequence of functionalism, ironically, is that religion loses its function.[104]

According to Spaemann, the political theologies of Jürgen Moltmann and
Johann Baptist Metz also reflect a functionalistic approach to religion that has
similarities to the style of Bonald's political theology, differences notwithstanding.[105] Spaemann's critical appreciation of Metz's and Moltmann's
political theology is contained in the collection of essays *Zur Kritik der
politischen Utopie: 10 Kapitel politischer Philosophie* (*On the Critique of*

[99] Spaemann, 'Der Irrtum der Traditionalisten', 497.
[100] 'Rationalität als "Kulturelles Erbe"', in *Scheidewege*, 14 (1984/5), 313.
[101] For a comparison between Bonald's and Rousseau's views of education see Spaemann,
Der Ursprung der Soziologie aus dem Geist der Restauration, 108 ff.
[102] Ibid. 10.
[103] 'Die Existenz des Priesters: Eine Provokation in der modernen Welt', in *Communio*, 9
(1980), 491.
[104] See Spaemann, 'Christliche Religion und Ethik', in *Einsprüche: Christliche Reden*, 57.
[105] For an English translation of important texts by Metz and Moltmann see Metz and
Moltmann, *Faith and the Future: Essays on Theology, Solidarity, and Modernity*, introd. Francis
Schüssler Fiorenza (Maryknoll, NY: Orbis, 1995).

Political Utopia: 10 Chapters of Political Philosophy), rather than the collection entitled *Einsprüche: Christliche Reden* (*Objections: Christian Speeches*). This fact is significant because it shows how Spaemann views the political theologies of Metz and Moltmann. In his view, political theology is not a religious enterprise, but rather a political and philosophical enterprise. According to Spaemann, political theologies leave behind the opportunistic tradition of Christianity vis-à-vis politics and Christianity's focus upon eternal salvation and justify political ideas religiously. In their failure to uphold the separation between the heavenly and the earthly city, modern political theologians are in danger of undermining an eschatological view of history, and in so doing of transforming our view of reality. In spite of evident differences between Metz's and Moltmann's theologies and Hans Küng's 'world-ethos project', Spaemann also formulates a comparable criticism of Küng, though in a more acerbic and polemical way.[106] We will not discuss Spaemann's criticism of Küng's thought here, but will focus upon his examination of Metz's and Moltmann's political theologies.

At the start of his essay 'Theologie, Prophetie, Politik: Zur Kritik der politischen Theologie' Spaemann summarizes his critique of modern political theology. He argues, first, that 'the eschatological justification of politics proposed by political theology is based upon an ambiguity and indecision with respect to the content of the Christian preaching of salvation'. Spaemann points out that 'it is impossible to derive political maxims from theological statements'. He then reasons that 'a revolutionary politics and its humanitarian variant are in need of a theological justification just as little as other modern forms of politics'.[107] So the 'new political theology' as conceived of by Metz and Moltmann is, according to Spaemann, strictly speaking, untenable and does not do justice to the essence of Christianity.

In the course of his argument Spaemann refers to an essay by the canon lawyer and legal philosopher Hans Barion to demonstrate that one can derive principles from Christian eschatology that are opposed to the principles derived by the new political theology. Spaemann points out that in an essay entitled 'Kirche oder Partei?'[108] Barion argues for a pragmatic, 'utterly positivistic, relativistic, historical' relation between Church and State as typified by the opportunistic use of the State for the sake of ecclesial interests and,

---

[106] 'Weltethos als "Projekt"', in *Grenzen*. For Küng's 'project' see esp. his *Global Responsibility: In Search of a New World Ethic* (New York: Crossroad, 1991). For further discussions and developments of his global ethic/responsibility see also Hans Küng and Helmut Schmid, *A Global Ethic and Global Responsibilities: Two Declarations* (London: SCM 1998); Hans Küng, *A Global Ethic for Global Politics and Economics* (New York: Oxford University Press, 1998).

[107] Spaemann, 'Theologie, Prophetie, Politik', in *Kritik der politischen Utopie*, 59.

[108] In *Der Staat*, 4 (1965), 131–76.

ultimately, eternal salvation. It is important to note that Spaemann's own position is largely Barion's position. According to Barion's and Spaemann's view, Christian eschatology is apolitical and about an absolute non-worldly future. Christianity, Spaemann points out, clearly has a universal and absolute claim, but this claim is based upon a view from within which differs notably from the view from outside which takes Christianity to have only particular claims. The overcoming of the gap between these two views of Christianity is, according to Spaemann, 'expected . . . as an apocalyptic event, not as the result of an evolution, of an immanent historical progress'.[109] This character of Christian eschatology leads, as Spaemann reasons, only indirectly to a political, that is to say an anti-totalitarian, effect. In this context Spaemann speaks of a 'certain affinity of the Christian faith to the liberal principle of the rule of law'.[110]

Spaemann then claims that the new political theology significantly transforms Christian eschatology in comparison to an ecclesial political opportunism which may or may not include an affinity to a certain kind of liberalism, and the emphasis upon indirect political consequences of Christianity. Political theology, as Spaemann's argument runs, therefore transforms both the object of Christian hope and the 'qualitative structure of hope'.[111] The optimistic talk about the inner-worldly future of humanity, he reasons, is either naive or cynical and scornful vis-à-vis the victims of the 'progress' of history. To render the absolute future of hope a relative future also makes it impossible adequately to conceive of the coexistence of future and present eschatologies. The dialectic of the presence and the future fulfilment of the kingdom of God that is crucial to any orthodox Christian theology is not possible, Spaemann suggests, if the future of the kingdom of God is no longer understood to be absolute and beyond time, but rather can in principle already be present in time. This has considerable metaphysical implications for our understanding of reality, too. 'Where the "beyond time" disappears', Spaemann argues, 'the "now" also disappears in so far as it is different from the disappearing intersection between past and future on the objective scale'. The disappearance of the present as the 'actual dimension of reality',[112] Spaemann further explains, implies the disappearance of time and of reality. One cannot fully describe reality by means of scientific or sociological categories,[113] but a theology, he argues, that maintains the radical eschatological

[109] 'Rationalität als "Kulturelles Erbe"', 308.
[110] 'Theologie, Prophetie, Politik', in *Kritik der politischen Utopie*, 61; for this view see also his 'Über die gegenwärtige Lage des Christentums', in *Das unsterbliche Gerücht*, 244.
[111] 'Theologie, Prophetie, Politik', in *Kritik der politischen Utopie*, 63.
[112] 'Christliche Religion und Ethik', in *Einsprüche: Christliche Reden*, 61.
[113] Spaemann, 'Theologie, Prophetie, Politik', in *Kritik der politischen Utopie*, 64.

character of future fulfilment and resists accommodating itself to scientific and sociological methods can recollect an adequate view of time, presence, and reality as they disclose themselves to us. For in contrast to a scientific understanding of time, we do not experience reality as a mere temporal process from past to future, but as time in which the present opens up the horizon of what is beyond time and what cannot be understood as process. This is why the Christian who still maintains this view of reality and the promise of an absolute future must not primarily plan the future (or at least cannot do so with a theological justification) but rather finds 'through joy in the presence of God a qualitatively different relation to the present that contradicts the spirit of the age'.[114]

Over against what he considers the transformation of orthodox Christian eschatology (and the 'de-presentation' of reality), Spaemann defends his own position that the future with which Christianity is concerned is absolutely transcendent of time and history, both by outlining what he considers the orthodox view of Christianity and also by examining the ontological implications of the alternative view. Only because there is a 'beyond time' is it the case that what is, is ultimately not a non-substantial flux of becoming, but substantial Being. An anti-metaphysical political theology thus turns not only anti-theological, but also anti-realistic. The new political theology, Spaemann thinks, can at best be ambiguous with respect to the character of Christian hope. In the worst case it becomes entirely self-contradictory and undermines its own very possibility. In the face of such tendencies Christianity needs to become critical of modernity and its understanding of reality; and modernity itself, if it does not intend to abolish itself, needs to recall the knowledge about reality and time which has been preserved by Christianity and its belief in an absolute future that resists any attempt to turn it into something relative.

It is important to note that Spaemann does not seek to establish a quietist and completely anti-political account of Christianity. What he wants to do is to distinguish sharply between Christian eschatology and its understanding of future on the one hand and Christian social ethics and moral theology on the other. His critique of political theology is thus essentially a critique of the fusion of categories and disciplines, which he sees at work in Metz's and Moltmann's theologies. It is also very important to note that he does not deny that both Metz and Moltmann still maintain the idea of an absolute future— he speaks of the 'ambiguity of the eschatological position in Moltmann and Metz'.[115] In spite of this, Spaemann (who, as it seems, does not really do full

---

[114] 'Christliche Religion und Ethik', in *Einsprüche: Christliche Reden*, 62.
[115] 'Theologie, Prophetie, Politik', in *Kritik der politischen Utopie*, 64.

justice to the ambiguity of Metz's and Moltmann's positions) finds it necessary to criticize the long-term implications of their political theology and its
political transformation of Christian eschatology.

4.6 THE FUNCTIONALISTIC INTERPRETATION OF PHILOSOPHY

Bonald's critique of the philosophy of his contemporaries particularly targets
philosophers whom he categorizes as part of the Aristotelian tradition. He
accuses them of complicity in the Revolution and of a fundamentally wrong
understanding of the relation between religion, philosophy, and society. Their
main misunderstanding is the nominalist denial of the existence of general
ideas independently of merely human generalizations. The universalism and
nominalism of modern Enlightenment philosophy have the same roots, as
both Bonald and Spaemann argue: the paradigmatic role of abstraction as
conceived of by natural sciences.[116] There is also, Bonald points out, the
tradition of a true philosophy that cannot be charged with the shortcomings
of the Aristotelian tradition. Bonald refers to Plato, Augustine, Descartes
(in a rather ambivalent way), Pascal, Malebranche, Bossuet, Fénelon, and
Leibniz[117] as eminent exceptions, though, from a historical perspective,
transitional figures. These philosophers stand for a true, spiritual, and religious philosophy which aims at taking universal reason into account and
which gives an answer to the question of the origin of the *idées generales* (as
opposed to *idées generalisées*) that does not reflect modern reductionism. In
contrast to Locke, Hume, and Voltaire, among others, the true philosophers
stand for the tradition of a philosophy that is reconcilable with Catholic
Christianity as realized by the *ancien régime*. However, the tradition of
true philosophy, according to Bonald, failed to preserve the *ancien régime*
because it did not yet fully understand the connection between truth and
society. The answer to the question why the Revolution was possible in
spite of the Platonic tradition of spiritual and religious philosophy leads to
the very heart of Bonald's sociological and functionalistic transformation of
metaphysics. Bonald states that in all these true philosophical systems truth
can be found, but not yet in its ontologically absolute, that is to say its social
and historical, form.

---

[116] *Der Ursprung der Soziologie aus dem Geist der Restauration*, 80.
[117] Ibid. 35. For Malebranche's influence on Bonald see also Jean-Yves Pranchère, 'The Social
Bond According to the Catholic Counter-Revolution', 195–6.

Bonald's understanding of modern philosophy thus exhibits a 'historical consciousness that believes it can position philosophy within a wider context than the one which is opened up by philosophy itself'.[118] Philosophy, for him, was no longer mere *theoria* and 'absolute reflection', but rather the theoretical justification of social and political practice and, therefore, a function of society and particularly of Christianity.[119] In a culture such as ancient Greece, in which the common religion lost sight of morality and was preoccupied with superstitious beliefs, philosophers such as Socrates and Plato were, according to Bonald, important figures to counterbalance the social influence of a dubious religion. In a Christian society, which Bonald interprets as the realization of the Platonic dominion of reason, however, only Christianity, and, that is to say, a Christian metaphysical theory of society, can be the acceptable form of philosophy.

Spaemann criticizes this functionalistic interpretation of philosophy because it contradicts his understanding of philosophy—as *theoria* that cannot be functionalized but, rather, critically examines functional relations and rationally reflects upon what precedes any function; that is, substantial reality. In his view, the Socratic conversation about ultimate questions must not be made subject to external purposes, for it is an end in itself and also explicitly challenges the view that purposes are only defined subjectively. This is why it contemplates the teleological structure of nature and the substance of reality that exists not only 'for me' (and is thus utilizable), but also 'in itself'—as *Selbstsein* with its own intrinsic ends. If philosophy is pursued in this way and resists making ideological claims, there can be no tension between philosophy and Christianity, in Spaemann's view. Christianity does not need to functionalize philosophy, nor does philosophy need to affirm the strictly speaking theological truth claim of Christianity.

Spaemann's critique of Bonald's functionalistic view of philosophy may also be read as an indirect criticism of Joachim Ritter, who supervised the writing of Spaemann's dissertation[120]. In 1963 Ritter wrote an essay on the

---

[118] Spaemann, 'Philosophie zwischen Metaphysik und Geschichte: Philosophische Strömungen im heutigen Deutschland', in *Neue Zeitschrift für Systematische Theologie*, 1 (1959), 291.

[119] In his *laudatio* of Niklas Luhmann, Spaemann mentions that already the *philosophes* of the Enlightenment understood themselves in terms of their social function; that is, the function of *enlightening* their society; see *Paradigm Lost*, 72. Spaemann, as we have already seen, thinks that it is possible and necessary to look at philosophy from outside). But this does not necessarily entail a functionalistic understanding of philosophy.

[120] Joachim Ritter (b. 4 Mar. 1903; d. 3 Aug. 1974), German philosopher, studied at the universities of Heidelberg, Marburg, Freiburg, and Hamburg. Appointed professor first at the University of Kiel in 1943, subsequently at the University of Münster; head of the so-called Ritter-Schule and of the cross-disciplinary Collegium Philosophicum, to which, among others, the philosophers Hermann Lübbe, Odo Marquard, Robert Spaemann, Ernst Tugendhat,

task of the humanities (*Geisteswissenschaften*) in modern society entitled 'Die Aufgabe der Geisteswissenschaften in der modernen Gesellschaft'[121] which contributed to an ongoing debate to which he had already provided many contributions as Chancellor of Münster University. In this essay Ritter deals with the self-understanding of speculative philosophy and its crisis, with the Humboldtian and modern mass university and its crisis, and with the modern *Geisteswissenschaften*. Ritter points out that Humboldt's ideal of the university is in a structural crisis because there is a contradiction between the needs of the modern industrial society and this ideal, exemplified in the freedom and loneliness of the scholar with his entirely theoretical interests. Ritter agrees with both Max Scheler[122] and Helmuth

---

Friedrich Kambartel, and Ludger Oeing-Hanhoff and the lawyers and legal philosophers Ernst-Wolfgang Böckenförde and Martin Kriele belonged (see also Böckenförde (ed.), *Collegium Philosophicum: Studien. Joachim Ritter zum 60. Geburtstag* (Basle/Stuttgart: Schwabe, 1965)). Ritter was a disciple of Ernst Cassirer. He is well known for his early work on Nicholas of Cusa (*Docta ignoranta: Die Theorie des Nichtwissens bei Nikolaus Cusanus* (Leipzig: Teubner, 1927)) and Augustine (*Mundus intelligibilis: Eine Untersuchung zur Aufnahme und Umwandlung der neuplatonischen Ontologie bei Augustinus* (Frankfurt am Main: Klostermann, 1937)), for his later work on Aristotle and Hegel (published collectively in Metaphysik und Politik (Frankfurt am Main: Suhrkamp, 1969)), for his interest in the rise of modern subjectivity and its endangerment (see the essays of Ritter published in *Subjektivität: Sechs Aufsätze* (Frankfurt am Main: Suhrkamp, 1989)), and for the *Historische Wörterbuch der Philosophie*, of which he was the first editor-in-chief. The renewed interest in practical philosophy in Germany since the 1960s is also, to a huge extent, due to Ritter's influence. See *Gedenkschrift Joachim Ritter zur Gedenkfeier zu Ehren des am 3. August 1974 verstorbenen em. ordentlichen Professors der Philosophie Dr. phil. Joachim Ritter* (Münster: Aschendorff, 1978) for biographical and bibliographical information about Joachim Ritter (esp. pp. 9 ff. and *passim* and 59–72 respectively); see also Ulrich Dierse, 'Joachim Ritter und seine Schüler', in Anton Hügli and Poul Lübcke (eds.), *Philosophie im 20. Jahrhundert, i. Phänomenologie, Hermeneutik, Existenzphilosophie und Kritische Theorie*, 3rd edn. (Hamburg: rororo, 1998), 237–78, esp. 236 ff.; Henning Ottmann, 'Joachim Ritter', in Nida-Rümelin, *Philosophie der Gegenwart in Einzeldarstellungen: Von Adorno bis Wright*, 504–9. For Odo Marquard's philosophy see Peter Kampits, 'Odo Marquard', ibid., 402–5; for Hermann Lübbe see Volker Steenblock, Hermann Lübbe', ibid. 354–6.

[121] Ritter, Joachim, 'Die Aufgabe der Geisteswissenschaften in der modernen Gesellschaft', in Ritter, *Subjektivität. Sechs Aufsätze*. In our analysis of Ritter's thought, we will focus on this essay even though it was published more than ten years after Spaemann finished *Der Ursprung der Soziologie aus dem Geist der Restauration*. This is justifiable (i) in that this essay expresses his understanding of the modern university and of philosophy in the most advanced and comprehensive way, and (ii) in that his thought regarding these issues has not significantly changed, as his earlier work shows. See also Ritter, Joachim, 'Wesen der Philosophie', in *Aufgaben deutscher Forschung*, vol. 1, ed. Leo Brandt (Köln/Opladen: Westdeutscher Verlag, 1956), 65–71; 'Die Universität vor den Ansprüchen der Zeit. Zur gesellschaftlichen Funktion freier Forschung und Lehre', in *Strukturprobleme unserer wissenschaftlichen Hochschulen*, edited by the Friedrich-Naumann-Stiftung (Bonn, Köln/Opladen: Westdeutscher Verlag, 1965), 49–61.

[122] Ritter refers to Scheler, 'Universität und Volkshochschule', in *Die Wissensformen und die Gesellschaft* (Leipzig: Der Neue-Geist Verlag, 1926).

Schelsky[123] that a new context makes it necessary to reform university education and its self-understanding. Ritter calls the contemporary crisis of the
university a 'salutary and necessary disillusionment'.[124] The *Wissenschaften*,
he argues, increasingly lay the foundation for practice such that Humboldt's
ideal of the university, particularly his idea that philosophical speculation is
not necessary and an end in itself, was increasingly questioned in the course of
the nineteenth century.[125]

According to Ritter, the nineteenth-century history of the university of
Berlin, particularly its development after the death of Hegel, reveals the failure
of traditional speculative philosophy to unify the diversity of the positive
Wissenschaften.[126] In this context, he argues, the *Geisteswissenschaften* developed. They are not relics of a pre-modern world, Ritter argues, but developed
within the modern industrial society,[127] where they balance its ahistoricity
and abstractness and remind it of what would otherwise be forgotten: the
historical and the spiritual.[128] Ritter therefore interprets the development of
the modern *Wissenschaften* as an emancipation from speculative theory.
Wissenschaft has become autonomous and independent of philosophical
speculation,[129] and as such the function and substance of social praxis.[130]
Ritter further argues that in modernity it is no longer human practice and
experience that yield the coordinates for theoretical speculation. The *Wissenschaften* and their understanding of reality have been substituted for
natural and historical experience and make modern praxis possible.[131] This
not only leads to a new understanding of experience as quantifiable and
commensurable (an implication Spaemann considers characteristic of modernity), but also implies a new understanding of the function of the university and an inversion of the traditional relation between theory and practice.

While there is a certain proximity between Ritter's view of the development
of the modern university and its crisis and Spaemann's criticism of modernity, *The Origin of Sociology* represents an implicit criticism of Ritter's view
of philosophy, as we have already indicated. Spaemann criticizes Ritter's

---

[123] Schelsky, *Einsamkeit und Freiheit: Zur sozialen Idee der deutschen Universität* (Schriften
der Gesellschaft zur Förderung der Westfälischen Wilhelms-Universität zu Münster, 45)
(Münster: Aschendorf, 1960).
[124] Ritter, 'Die Aufgabe der Geisteswissenschaften in der modernen Gesellschaft', 119.
[125] For Ritter's account of (Hegel's) speculative philosophy see also Ritter, 'Subjektivität und
industrielle Gesellschaft: Zu Hegels Theorie der Subjektivität', in *Subjektivität*, 13.
[126] Ritter, 'Die Aufgabe der Geisteswissenschaften in der modernen Gesellschaft', 118.
[127] Ibid. 120–1.
[128] Ibid. 131.
[129] Ibid. 112–13.
[130] Ibid. 108.
[131] Ibid. 137.

failure to defend the ideal of theoretical speculation that must not be functionalized, and his view of the crisis of theory as a kind of historical necessity that indispensably entails the inversion of the traditional understanding of theory and practice. While Ritter's view of philosophy claims to be anti-functionalistic, his interpretation of the modern *Wissenschaften*, including the *Geisteswissenschaften*, as theoretical constituents of social reality reflects the *tendency* to utilize philosophy, to define it with respect to its function, and to render modern society an absolute—and precisely this tendency is explicitly criticized by Spaemann with regard to Bonald's writings. No 'misunderstood sense of responsibility' ought to cause philosophy to concern itself with its social consequences, according to Spaemann; mere truth is philosophy's concern. 'Thinking can fulfil its responsibility only by thinking.'[132] Philosophy needs to be based upon social practice and common experience, to be sure (for it is first of all an examination of what we all immediately know, or have once known), but it must not, Spaemann thinks, understand itself as *essentially* having a function for society. Its very essence is *not* to have a function. And thus philosophy, rightly understood, may serve as the basis for a fundamental critique of any given society, particularly the modern society, but may well also—secondarily—be interpreted from a standpoint that thematizes the purpose of this 'non-functionalism'.

In *The Origin of Sociology* Spaemann develops another implicit critique of Ritter's thought.[133] Ritter's thought is indebted to T. S. Eliot, about whose poetry he wrote an essay in 1945, when the issue of how to reshape political and social life in Germany after the catastrophe of war and National Socialism was most urgent.[134] Ritter's reading of Eliot interprets his poetry as disclosing a deep spiritual dimension of reality which the modern industrial culture tends to forget, and without which life cannot flourish but becomes inhumane. For Ritter, Eliot's work discloses the religious and divine dimension of Being that cannot fully be grasped by the modern functionalistic and technological mind. Eliot's poetry is, in Ritter's view, characteristic of a time of crisis.

At first sight it seems that if Eliot's aim was to recollect a forgotten knowledge, Ritter's indebtedness to Eliot cannot have been an object of criticism to Spaemann. However, a closer look at the nature of Eliot's thought explains why Spaemann's critique of Bonald's functionalistic defence of Catholicism represents an indirect critique of Eliot and of Ritter, who appropriates Eliot's ideas.

---

[132] Spaemann, 'Philosophie zwischen Metaphysik und Geschichte. Philosophische Strömungen im heutigen Deutschland', 305.

[133] Spaemann explicitly mentions this in Spaemann and Nissing 'Die Natur des Lebendigen und das Ende des Denkens', 122.

[134] 'Dichtung und Gedanke: Bemerkungen zur Dichtung T. S. Eliots', in *Subjektivität*, 93–104.

The reason lies in the proximity between T. S. Eliot and Charles Maurras, significant differences between the two notwithstanding—for Eliot doubtless believed in Christianity and did not simply utilize it as a political means. Yet T. S. Eliot, one biographer has convincingly argued, was at one point in his life on the road to becoming an 'Anglo-Saxon Maurras'.[135] Eliot's conversion may 'have been profoundly affected by Charles Maurras and the *Action Française*';[136] he even wanted to write a book about Charles Maurras, although in the end he did not.

At the start of his essay 'Dichtung und Gedanke' ('Poetry and Thought') Ritter quotes from Eliot's 'The Idea of a Christian Society'[137] and notes his interest in the Christian foundations of State and society. Ritter stresses that Eliot's question is different from nineteenth-century ideas about religion; in the nineteenth century, he argues, considerations about religion were premised on the rational system of reality. In Eliot's thought, Ritter holds, the foundational character of religion is at stake. Without ever drawing explicit attention to this, Ritter's affirmative account of Eliot's political thought and his poetry envisages them as somehow close to Bonald's political theology and his 'nihilism of the right'. For Eliot, as Ritter points out, religion means 'preservation'. Ritter, therefore, attributes to Eliot's understanding of religion a sense of preservation that leaves behind mere traditionalism and instead entails the 'attempt to counteract what is lost through disregard and forgetfulness'.[138] This has become necessary because the relation between present and past has not always been preserved, as Ritter's allusion to Nietzschean thought (and the Nazi period) implies: we all come out of a time in which the relation between our past and our present has been cut off. The real destruction,

---

[135] Peter Ackroyd, *T. S. Eliot* (London: Hamilton, 1984), 156: 'After *The Hollow Men* and the abandonment of *Sweeney Agonistes*, it was conceivable that he would never write poetry again, and he was outlining a possible future career as an intellectual historian in the European mould—an Anglo-Saxon Maurras, perhaps'.

[136] Ibid. 173.

[137] 'The Idea of a Christian Society', in *Christianity and Culture* (New York: Harcourt, Brace, 1949), 1–77. For a discussion particularly of Eliot's political thought see Stefan Collini, 'The European Modernist as Anglican Moralist: The Later Social Criticism of T. S. Eliot', in Mark S. Micale and Robert L. Dietle (eds.), *Enlightenment, Passion, Modernity: Historical Essays in European Thought and Culture* (Stanford, Calif.: Stanford University Press, 2000), 207–29. Collini interprets Eliot's oeuvre as being subject to a dialectic between *Gesellschaft* in his modernist poetry and *Gemeinschaft* in his anti-modern social criticism. This interpretation of Eliot's writings reinforces our view that Ritter's very affirmative reading of Eliot was a very plausible object for an indirect criticism from Spaemann via his interpretation of Bonald's anti-modern modernism. If Eliot's position is subject to a dialectic, so may Ritter's be—and Spaemann may well have been aware at least of the ambiguity of Ritter's position.

[138] Ritter, 'Dichtung und Gedanke', 95.

Ritter writes with respect to his own life context, shows the inner loss.[139] In this context Eliot's religious poetry symbolizes for Ritter a culture of recollection which is now being sought everywhere.[140] It seeks the divine in a culture that is preoccupied with the useful and the pragmatic.[141] Poetry thus discloses, on Ritter's account, what an utterly modern point of view hides and covers up.

Spaemann's implicit critique of Eliot's and Ritter's answers to the crisis of modernity as a period of cultural loss and amnesia targets the role that poetry ought to play. Spaemann would probably agree with Ritter's analysis of the contemporary situation, but sees a possible danger in Ritter's solution. He would disagree with the way Ritter aims to re-establish a social and political order and to bind society and human beings to their severed roots by appealing to the spirit of the religious and the divine as expressed in Eliot's poetry. In spite of Ritter's anti-functionalistic convictions, he strangely tends to fall back into a functionalistic understanding of religion and is in danger of making a case for a merely poetical and philosophical religion that may well restore human memory while at the same time having lost sight of the unpoetical truth of Christianity. But, in Spaemann's view, neither a theory of society nor poetry, however politically useful, can comprehend the Christian difference that is immediate 'love, nothing else!'.[142] That is to say, Christianity does not have a political or social function in the first instance, but is concerned with the inner attitude of the believer and his eternal salvation. And it cannot be mediated politically, poetically, and socially.

4.7 THE TOTALITARIAN CLAIM OF SOCIOLOGY IN NIKLAS LUHMANN'S PHILOSOPHY

As far as contemporary thought is concerned functionalism and its nihilistic implications are perhaps best reflected in the sociology of Niklas Luhmann.[143]

---

[139] Ritter, 'Dichtung und Gedanke', 95.

[140] Ibid. 104.

[141] Ibid. 95, 104.

[142] 'Wenn die Liebe auf Widerspruch stößt', in *Caritas: Zeitschrift für Caritasarbeit und Caritaswissenschaft*, 57 (1956), 278–9; for the 'Christian difference' see also 'Über die gegenwärtige Lage des Christentums', in *Das unsterbliche Gerücht*, 237–8.

[143] For a helpful introduction in English to Luhmann's thought see Hans-Georg Moeller, *Luhmann Explained: From Souls to Systems* (Chicago/La Salle, Ill.: Open Court, 2006.) (See pp. 227 ff. for a list of translations of Luhmann's works and a bibliography of his writings.) For a volume with important essays by Luhmann in English see Luhmann, *Theories of Distinction: Redescribing the Descriptions of Modernity*, ed. and introd. William Rasch (Stanford, Calif.: Stanford University Press, 2002).

Spaemann thus characterizes Luhmann's thought as the most important challenge to contemporary philosophy, particularly because it compels philosophy to rethink the relation between immediacy and mediation with regard to the absolute.[144] In so far as Luhmann's thought has significant similarities to Bonald's, Spaemann's critique of Bonald can also be read as foreshadowing his critical remarks on Luhmann's functionalistic sociology and its modernistic reinterpretation of reality.

In an address in honour of Luhmann, Spaemann states that Luhmann is what he calls an anti-philosopher who, because of his stature, inevitably becomes a philosopher himself.[145] In Spaemann's view, Luhmann is currently the most representative philosopher of a 'reflective modernity' which has ceased to believe that faith, morality, and the immediacy of values (*Wertbezüge*) can structure the responses of complex social systems to real problems.[146] Spaemann regards Luhmann's supposedly comprehensive sociology as most comparable to Hegel's systematic philosophy.[147] Attempting to take into account all the possible standpoints of external viewers, Luhmann claims to provide an alternative to the philosophical way of developing theories about the 'symbolic understanding and communicative representation of the whole of reality'.[148] Luhmann's sociology thus claims to be a definitive functionalistic 'enlightenment' about society and reality,[149] without noticing its own limits.[150] There is,

---

[144] *Paradigm Lost*, 71. For Spaemann's critique of the political implications of Luhmann's thought see 'Die Utopie der Herrschaftsfreiheit', in *Kritik der politischen Utopie*, 125.

[145] *Paradigm Lost*, 62.

[146] Ibid. 63. For the modern character of Luhmann's thought see also William Rasch, *Niklas Luhmann's Modernity: The Paradoxes of Differentiation* (Stanford, Calif.: Stanford University Press, 2000). This volume contains an interesting interview with Luhmann on 'Answering the Question: What is Modernity?' (pp. 195–221). Moeller shows convincingly that Luhmann can be interpreted as a post-modern thinker, not least because of his interest in difference and postmodern theory (Moeller, *Luhmann Explained*, 193ff.)—it seems that Luhmann's modernity, too, is an ambiguous modernity that is subject to its own dialectic.

[147] *Paradigm Lost*, 62. Jürgen Habermas makes a similar observation about the proximity between Hegel and Luhmann in *The Philosophical Discourse of Modernity*, trans. Frederick Lawrence (Cambridge, Mass.: MIT Press, 1987), 370; for the 'Hegelianism' of Luhmann see also Michael Welker, 'Die neue "Aufhebung der Religion" in Luhmanns Systemtheorie', in Welker (ed.), *Theologie und funktionale Systemtheorie: Luhmanns Religionssoziologie in theologischer Diskussion* (Frankfurt am Main: Suhrkamp, 1985), 93–119; Moeller, *Luhmann Explained*, 173ff. For an interesting interpretation of Luhmann's thought see also Stephan Körnig, *Perspektivität und Unbestimmtheit in Nietzsches Lehre vom Willen zur Macht: Eine vergleichende Studie zu Hegel, Nietzsche und Luhmann* (Basler Studien zur Philosophie, 9) (Bern: Francke, 1999).

[148] *Paradigm Lost*, 52ff.

[149] For this claim on Luhmann's side see, for example, Luhmann, Niklas, *Soziologische Aufklärung. Aufsätze zur Theoric sozialer Systeme* (Köln und Opladen. Westdeutscher Verlag, 1970), particularly the essay 'Soziologische Aufklärung' (66–91).

[150] *Paradigm Lost*, 56–7.

of course, a similar dialectic in Bonald's thought. While Bonald claims to be a philosopher, he turns into an anti-philosopher, into a theorist of society who changes, as we have seen, the traditional notion of philosophy. In contrast to Bonald, however, Luhmann does not develop a metaphysical account of society, for he radicalizes the functionalism of modernity and attributes metaphysics to a past epoch of human history.

Luhmann, Spaemann accordingly emphasizes, does not limit himself to developing hypotheses but provides a new scientific paradigm which is difficult to call into question and for this reason is comparable to evolutionary metaphysics and its paradigmatic claim.[151] For, Luhmann's sociology, which (like Bonald's thought) has been accused of anti-humanism,[152] aims to understand reality in terms of functional relations within the dialectic of system and environment, or, more recently, as Spaemann points out, within the traditional philosophical dialectic of identity and difference.[153] It thus strives to substitute sociology for philosophy. According to Luhmann, philosophy belongs to what he calls the 'old-European epoch' (*alteuropäische Epoche*) and needs to be surpassed by functionalistic sociology.[154] This echoes Bonald's substitution of political and sociological analysis for philosophy and is also considered critique-worthy by Spaemann.

Luhmann's treatment of religion and theology[155] is also of interest to Spaemann, who outlines a critique of Luhmann's theoretical 'totalitarianism'

[151] Ibid. 57; for the proximity between system theory and the theory of evolution see also *Happiness and Benevolence*, 45 ff. (*Glück und Wohlwollen*, 67 ff.). Luhmann explicitly develops his theory from within the framework of evolutionary theory (see e.g. Luhmann, *The Differentiation of Society*, trans. Stephen Holmes and Charles Larmore (New York: Columbia University Press, 1982), 8, 251 ff., 322, and *passim*). For an analysis of the role of evolutionary theory in Luhmann's thought see Christian Schmidt-Wellenburg, *Evolution und sozialer Wandel: Neodarwinistische Mechanismen bei W. G. Runciman und N. Luhmann* (Opladen: Budrich, 2005).

[152] *Paradigm Lost*, 64. For this critique of Luhmann, see Habermas, *The Philosophical Discourse of Modernity*, 377–8.

[153] *Paradigm Lost*, 60–1. See for Luhmann's earlier position Luhmann, *The Differentiation of Society*, 257–8, 262 ff., and *passim*; see for his later position Luhmann, 'Identity—What or How?', in *Theories of Distinction*, 113–27.

[154] *Paradigm Lost*, 53.

[155] For Luhmann's sociological discussion of religion and theology see his *Funktion der Religion* (Frankfurt am Main: Suhrkamp, 1977); for an English translation of chapter 2 see Luhmann, *Religious Dogmatics and the Evolution of Societies*, trans. and introd. Peter Beyer (Studies in Religion and Society, ix) (New York/Toronto: Mellen, 1984); see also *Die Religion der Gesellschaft*, ed. André Kieserling (Frankfurt am Main: Suhrkamp, 2000). For further discussion of Luhmann's theory of religion and theological responses to his thought see also Welker (ed.), *Theologie und funktionale Systemtheorie*; Matthias Woiwode, *Heillose Religion? Eine fundamentaltheologische Untersuchung zur funktionalen Religionstheorie Niklas Luhmanns* (Studien zur systematischen Theologie und Ethik, x) (Münster: LIT, 1997); Andreas Kött, *Systemtheorie und Religion: Mit einer Religionstypologie im Anschluss an Niklas Luhmann* (Würzburg: Königshausen

from a perspective informed by Christianity.[156] Philosophy, Luhmann says, is characterized by an aprioristic method and is thus different from theology because theology relies on the dual historical gift of revelation and reality. But Luhmann's 'philosophical' thought, particularly in its aprioristic presuppositions, we can argue, following Spaemann, fails to do full justice to the concrete gift upon which substantial belief is based, and indeed undermines substantial belief in that its functionalistic framework does not allow for absolutes of any kind and subjects religion to theories about its evolutionary development.[157] Philosophy, however, is concerned with 'ultimate thoughts' (*Abschlussgedanken*), as Spaemann says with reference to Dieter Henrich;[158] it is concerned with the thinking of the absolute,[159] which does not necessarily contradict any concrete religious relation to the absolute. Luhmann, however, does not think the absolute; according to Spaemann's analysis, he intends to think more radically than philosophers by deriving the idea of the absolute in a functionalistic way,[160] and this makes his view of religion deeply problematic.

Thinking, as Spaemann points out, is for Luhmann no longer the paradigm for self-reference, as it was even for Hegel. For Luhmann, thinking can be reconstructed from a naturalistic point of view, for instance, which lies beyond thinking and from which thinking as well as the fundamental dialectic between difference and identity can be understood. But if he were right, philosophy as 'absolute reflection' and 'continuous conversation about ultimate questions' would no longer be possible. Philosophy would no longer be allowed to reflect absolutely, and the ultimate answers which it seeks would be reduced to objects of scientific examination and thus deprived of their ultimacy. There would no longer be ultimate questions or thoughts, let alone philosophy as traditionally understood.

& Neumann, 2003); Günther Thomas and Andreas Schüle (eds.), *Luhmann und die Theologie* (Darmstadt: Wissenschaftliche Buchgesellschaft, 2006).

[156] *Paradigm Lost*, 54–5.

[157] For Luhmann's view of the evolution of religion see his *Die Religion der Gesellschaft*, 250–77.

[158] *Paradigm Lost*, 65. See Henrich, 'Was ist Metaphysik, was Moderne? Thesen gegen Habermas', in *Merkur*, 40 (1986), 495–508. (For an English translation see Peter Dew (ed.), *Habermas: A Critical Reader* (Oxford: Blackwell, 1999]) 291–319; the translator of this essay translates 'Abschlußgedanken' as 'thoughts of a resolving closure'.) See for Henrich's understanding of philosophy also his 'Warum Metaphysik?' and 'Bewußtes Leben und Metaphysik', in his *Bewußtes Leben: Untersuchungen zum Verhältnis von Subjektivität und Metaphysik* (Stuttgart: Reclam, 1999), 81ff. and 194ff.

[159] *Paradigm Lost*, 65.

[160] Ibid. 66. For a discussion of the radical character of Luhmann's philosophy see also Paul R. Harrison, 'Niklas Luhmann and the Theory of Social Systems', in David Roberts (ed.), *Reconstruction Theory: Gadamer, Habermas, Luhmann* (Melbourne: Melbourne University Press, 1995), 65–90.

Thus, in a radical way, Luhmann's functionalism, as Spaemanns shows, calls into question both theoretical and practical philosophy (as did Bonald's functionalism), because philosophy is of its essence in need of ultimate thoughts, whether about the absolute or about the way to act in a given situation, which then re-establishes immediacy.[161] This is why philosophy, Spaemann argues, must not refrain from ultimate thoughts; they make it, he further argues, even possible to take seriously one's sense of self as acting person even if one thinks about the function of philosophy.[162] Therefore, philosophy can only be overtaken by sociological theory if it accepts the idea of modernity rather than dealing with it as a problem.[163] That is to say, philosophy can only be dispensed with if human beings are willing not only to abolish philosophy, ethics, and ultimate thoughts but also to subject themselves to modernisms such as Luhmann's and thus to relinquish what is self-evident about reality and their self-esteem—that is, if they are willing to abolish themselves as persons.[164] Here, again, mankind is required to make a decision. Over against Luhmann's view of reality (which inevitably loses sight of reality as it is disclosed to us), Spaemann recalls a substantial view of reality that still knows why ends are ends (and not merely purposes) and that functions can only be understood within the horizon of what cannot be understood from a functionalistic point of view.

4.8 THE FUSION OF MORALITY AND PHILOSOPHY OF HISTORY

Bonald can, in Spaemann's view, be charged with fusing morality and the philosophy, or theology, of history—a fusion which entails the corruption of morality: 'To gather the maxims of our action from philosophy and theology of history', Spaemann points out, 'would be the corruption of all morality'.[165] We have already pointed out that, in Spaemann's view, Hegel's philosophy, for instance, is not immoral, but simply amoral, as long as his endeavour remains purely retrospective.[166] If, however, 'the philosophy of history claims to anticipate the goal of history and thus the whole of history, it tends generally

[161] *Paradigm Lost*, 68–9.
[162] Ibid. 71.
[163] Ibid. 73.
[164] For a similar criticism of Luhmann's sociology and its claims see Welker, 'Die neue "Aufhebung der Religion" in Luhmanns Systemtheorie', 111–12.
[165] 'Theologie, Prophetie, Politik', in *Kritik der politischen Utopie*, 66.
[166] *Persons*, 132 (*Personen*, 142).

to replace the moral perspective'.[167] Spaemann considers the tendency to reduce morality to philosophy of history to be typical of modernity. The inversion of teleology has separated reflection on the natural *telos* inherent in human society from reflection on the conditions of its preservation; the idea of natural perfection has been reinterpreted from within a historicist context; ends have become purposes. It is furthermore typical of a time in which the difference between world history and salvation history has increasingly been attenuated. But from an ethical point of view, maintaining the difference between world history and salvation history is crucially important because the disregard of the difference between these two histories has, among other things, promoted the rise of utilitarianism, according to which actions can only be justified with reference to a realizable purpose, rather than with reference to the inward attitude of one's conscience. If there is no eschatological view of mankind, Spaemann's philosophy shows, ethics tends to focus upon the consequences of one's actions and loses insight into moral absolutes. Ethics then ignores the fundamental difference, as Spaemann repeatedly recalls, between the absolute providential will of God (with its historical implications) and what God wants *us* to will (with its ethical implications).[168]

It is important to note that the fusing of morality and history also results in a new understanding of theodicy. If the progress of history is the measure according to which the moral quality of human action is discerned, history becomes the progressive justification of God or, in a secular context, of humanity. Modern historicism is, in its focus on historical progress, therefore a Gnostic theodicy. The reason for the fusion of morality and philosophy of history lies in the misconception of reason, religion, society, and history and, according to Spaemann, originates in the transformation of Christian eschatology and of the doctrine of original sin.[169] It reflects the (inevitably futile) attempt—characteristic not only of modernity, but also of postlapsarian mankind—to overcome the alienation of humanity autonomously.

---

[167] 'Zur philosophisch-theologischen Diskussion um die Atombombe', in *Grenzen*, 283.

[168] See e.g. *Reflexion und Spontaneität*, 101, 177; *Happiness and Benevolence*, 113 (*Glück und Wohlwollen*, 150).

[169] For Spaemann's account of the transformation of the doctrine of original sin see 'Über einige Schwierigkeiten mit der Erbsünde', in Christoph Schönborn, Albert Görres, and Robert Spaemann (eds.), *Zur kirchlichen Erbsündenlehre: Stellungnahmen zu einer brennenden Frage*, 2nd edn. (Einsiedeln/Freiburg im Breisgau: Johannes, 1994), 37–66; 'Christentum und Philosophie der Neuzeit', in Herrmann Fechtrup, Friedbert Schulze, and Thomas Sternberg (eds.), *Aufklärung durch Tradition: Symposion der Josef Pieper Stiftung zum 90. Geburtstag von Josef Pieper, Mai 1994 in Münster* (Münster: LIT, 1995), 132ff; see also, 'Was ist das Neue?', 21; for this view of the doctrine of original sin see also 'Die Zerstörung der naturrechtlichen Kriegslehre: Erwiderung an P. Gustav Gundlach S. J.', in *Grenzen*, 314.

The transformation of the doctrine of original sin is therefore also an important interpretative key for a proper understanding of Bonald's thought, the main problem of which concerns the relation between immediate and mediated knowledge. Bonald, Spaemann argues, saw that this is one of the fundamental problems of philosophy; however, he reformulates the ontological problem of how to relate immediacy and mediation as a sociological question. Bonald's answer failed because he strove to resolve the antinomy by anticipating counterfactually a harmony of immediacy and mediation that Christians can only hope for. Bonald's gross overestimation of the external power of the Catholic Church[170] and the French monarchy led him to revise Christian eschatology. He envisaged the concrete unity of monarchical state and Christian religion, Spaemann points out, as characterized by the intention to be the *communio sanctorum* of Christian theology.[171] Like Metz and Moltmann, Bonald shows a tendency to immanentize the absolute eschatological future for which orthodox Christianity hopes.

Bonald's view of history as progressive theodicy finds striking similarities in the philosophy of Hegel, whose philosophy is another of the indirect targets of *The Origin of Sociology*.[172] Although Hegel would have been critical of Bonald's Catholic philosophy, there are evident parallels between Hegel's and Bonald's philosophies.[173] Both may appear as revolutionaries and reactionaries at the same time.[174] Spaemann even labels Bonald's philosophy as 'perhaps nothing other than the French and Catholic parallel of Hegel's philosophy of the objective Spirit itself'.[175] The most fundamental parallel

---

[170] In a very early essay on the Jesuits Spaemann argues that the temporary suspension of the Jesuits might have been a blessing for the order, for the Jesuits might otherwise have lost sight of the difference between the kingdom of God within the heart of the people and the external power of the Catholic Church; see 'Die Jesuiten', in *Kirche und Leben*, 39 (29 Sept. 1949).

[171] *Der Ursprung der Soziologie aus dem Geist der Restauration*, 64.

[172] For the similarity between Hegel's and Bonald's philosophies see also Reedy, 'Maistre's Twin?', 185.

[173] *Der Ursprung der Soziologie aus dem Geist der Restauration*, 147. Franz von Baader, Spaemann points out, is the only contemporary of Hegel's and Bonald's who was aware of the proximity between both (*Der Ursprung der Soziologie aus dem Geist der Restauration*, 82).

[174] According to Joachim Ritter's interpretation of Hegel, this would be a misunderstanding of Hegel. See Ritter, 'Hegel and the French Revolution', in his *Hegel and the French Revolution: Essays on the Philosophy of Right*, trans. and introd. Richard Dien Winfield (Cambridge, Mass.: MIT Press, 1982), 62 for Ritter's interpretation of Hegel as trying to counter the dialectic of revolution and restoration without being subject to it. Because Hegel faces a dual challenge—the challenge of revolution as well as the challenge of restoration—his philosophy is 'almost out of necessity', as Ritter argues, subject to 'dual misinterpretation as a reduction of the religious substance to what is political and historical, and as a reactionary idealistic veiling of the revolutionary liberation of man from theological and metaphysical heaven' (p. 62). It seems that Spaemann would at least put more emphasis on the ambiguity of Hegel's philosophy.

[175] 'Der Irrtum der Traditionalisten', 494.

between Hegel and Bonald lies in their understanding of philosophy and of society and in their reinterpretation of metaphysics as metaphysics of society. Hegel's *Philosophy of Right*, Joachim Ritter correctly points out, provides a metaphysical account of society in times of a crisis of speculative philosophy. Ritter writes:

The age which philosophy has to grasp in thought is its own epoch, because this epoch for itself no longer seems to have anything in common with the One Philosophy or with what it had preserved in previous history. The present has emancipated itself from the philosophical tradition; the question of the essence of the historical-political present and its truth becomes in this time and hour a question of metaphysics in which the continuity of its history and tradition has become broken and problematic.[176]

This can, as we have seen, be said *mutatis mutandis* of Bonald's philosophy. Paradoxically, both Bonald's and Hegel's theories of society tend to turn into merely sociological arguments and transform the understanding of philosophy. Their philosophies have an ambiguous character, which neither thinker recognized; this ambiguity resulted in right-wing and left-wing tendencies in the aftermath of both men's thought. Hegel's and Bonald's answer to the crisis of their respective social and cultural contexts is structurally similar in that they assume that truth is objectively represented in society. One cannot understand society without reference to the presence and realization of the absolute within it. Hegel views history from an ontological point of view and ontology from a historical point of view; the absolute unfolds historically. In Bonald's dialectical philosophy there is a link, similar to Hegel's thought, between society, history, religion, and truth that blends history, morality, and eschatology from a political point of view. Bonald, for instance, argues in a manner comparable to Hegel that the French revolution was a necessary step towards the development of a theory of society as a truly spiritual philosophy. Atheism is, according to Bonald, God's absence from society; political philosophy is part of his political theology.[177] Bonald no longer sees the difference between Christianity and philosophy on the one hand and politics and history on the other because the political order has become total and world history is interpreted as salvation history. But outside of Eden, Spaemann thinks, it is impossible to overcome the tension between history and politics, on the one hand, and religion and Christianity, on the other, as if nature were not fallen and as if humanity's nature could immediately be made identical with freedom. Fallen humanity cannot redeem itself, whether by radically

---

[176] 'Hegel and the French Revolution', 41.
[177] See Spaemann, *Der Ursprung der Soziologie aus dem Geist der Restauration*, 122.

opposing itself to nature in order to emancipate itself from nature, or by radically naturalizing itself in order to emancipate nature. It is obvious that this view of original sin also has critical implications for Spaemann's understanding of Adorno's and Horkheimer's philosophies: it is not only the Marxist and Hegelian elements of their philosophy that he views very critically, but also their Rousseauan historicism and their Bonaldian focus on society.

Spaemann asserts that the doctrine of original sin explains the 'derangement that the divine order of the world in its unbroken state and harmony has undergone through the fall of humanity'.[178] As we have already seen in our interpretation of Spaemann's reading of Rousseau, an orthodox understanding of this doctrine precludes a totalizing of the political or social order. There remains a fundamental distinction between the private and the public, between religion and politics. In Spaemann's view, Christianity provides a distinctly unworldly account of salvation and contradicts the modern (as well as anti-modern) tendency to theologize secular history as did Bonald and, *mutatis mutandis*, Hegel (and as some political theologians, such as Metz and Moltmann, according to Spaemann, still tend to do). Spaemann criticizes this view of history, questions the programmatic *politique d'abord* of the *action française*, that is to say of Bonald's influential successors, and wonders 'if the political order can be built on nothing without presupposing a foundational order of Being'.[179] This leads us further to explore the theological and philosophical alternative, the ' foundational order of Being', as it were, that Spaemann proposes to Bonald's political theology.

4.9 PHILOSOPHY AS *THEORIA* AND RELIGION AS SUBSTANTIAL BELIEF

The Origin of Sociology is an important contribution to the history of ideas in that it re-evaluates a largely neglected philosopher to whom the title of father of modern sociology and modern social sciences belongs more properly even than to Auguste Comte. In addition to this, it also outlines a substantial critique of political theologies, of the modern paradigm of self-preservation, and of the sociological and functionalistic transformation of metaphysics in modernity. It questions the understanding of history as either emancipation of nature or emancipation from nature, both of which tendencies can be

---

[178] 'Die Zerstörung der naturrechtlichen Kriegslehre', in *Grenzen*, 314.
[179] Spaemann, '"Politik zuerst"?', 660.

found in Bonald's thought. Without naively longing for a pre-modern ideal, Spaemann recollects a complementary view of nature and freedom that does not find its foundation in the modern dismissal of natural teleology. Given the fallen situation of humanity, he also provides us with a sketch of a fatherland beyond both restoration and revolution, a conception that challenges anti-modern Romantics as well as modernists because it is not of this world and questions any self-preservation for the sake of mere preservation as well as any political Utopia. At this point it also becomes evident why *The Origin of Sociology* presents us with a Christianly informed critique of modernity and a philosophical alternative to the modern transformation and distortion of the doctrine of original sin. It is because Spaemann brings back into consciousness the fact that human nature is fallen and that politics cannot lead to a paradisiacal fulfilment of humanity, but rather needs to be understood within the context of the enduring consequences of the fall of man.

How can one deal with the modern separation of the private from the public, of religion from politics and society, without diminishing, or even abolishing, the fundamental difference between them? How can one live in a world in need of redemption without undermining the idea of substantial morality in a cynical, anti-humanist way, on the one hand, and without falling prey, on the other hand, to the dialectic of Rousseau's and Bonald's attempt to set aside any notion of the alienation of humanity? How is *theoria*—philosophy that finds its end in itself and 'disembogues, as contemplation of what always is, into prayer',[180]—still possible in the face of the utilitarian tendency to question ends in themselves and increasingly to utilize all dimensions of human life? How can self-preservation and self-transcendence be reconnected? Spaemann offers an answer to these questions by defending a notion of philosophy as a search for substantial wisdom which resists the questionable spirit of the technological civilization of modernity, and a notion of freedom which lies 'in believing what one believes', in the words of one of Charles Péguy's 'deepest sentences', in Spaemann's estimation.[181] In delineating the historical and natural conditions of human reason Spaemann does not constrain humanity, but rather provides the outline of a philosophy of freedom. In so doing, he takes the modern idea of freedom more seriously even than many modern thinkers, whose disregard for the limits and the context, as it were, of freedom eventually leads to the abolition of freedom.

---

[180] Spaemann, 'Christliche Religion und Ethik', in *Einsprüche: Christliche Reden*, 59; for Spaemann's understanding of prayer see 'Über die gegenwärtige Lage des Christentums', in *Das unsterblicheGerücht*, 241: 'Das Gebet ist die Erhebung des Menschen in die Sphäre der Einmaligkeit'.
[181] '"Politik zuerst"?', 657.

Spaemann defends the believer who still believes in what he claims to believe in, that is to say who believes in God who cannot be functionalized,[182] and who in so doing realizes and vindicates his freedom as one of the ' "mystical" ideas that are not constituted by reason, but rather make up its very substance as the simple and likewise mystical idea of truth'.[183] This 'mystical idea' 'precedes', as it were, the 'moral idea' of freedom and is a more fundamental idea about the nature of human beings.[184] Thus, Spaemann defines freedom not simply as an 'absence of external coercion' but as the more fundamental 'unity of the will with oneself'.[185] He does so against the backdrop of a culture in which substantial persuasions tend to be hypothesized and functionalized and in which friendship with oneself, that is to say the unity of one's will with oneself, as well as substantial belief appear increasingly impossible.[186] He does not allow for modifications of the belief that he defends by means of considerations of its private usefulness or political function because the freedom which he remembers as 'knowing in whom one believes'[187] is informed by the absolute primacy of the love of God[188]—the Augustinian *amor Dei usque ad contemptum sui*,[189] which is one of the keys to understanding Spaemann's philosophy as a whole. This belief reveals the 'principle of honour', which finds its orientation in the immediacy of a 'value'[190] and which stands in a tension with rationality which 'cannot be overcome without overcoming morality'.[191]

---

[182] See here also 'Das unsterbliche Gerücht', in *Das unsterbliche Gerücht*, 28, where Spaemann argues that it belongs 'to the function of God' that he is not 'definable through any kind of function'.

[183] ' "Politik zuerst"?', 662.

[184] In Spaemann's 'Einzelhandlungen', in *Grenzen*, 62 he distinguishes between a 'moral' and a more fundamental 'mystical' idea of universal responsibility. It appears that the same distinction can be made between a moral and a mystical idea of freedom.

[185] Spaemann, 'Moral und Gewalt', in *Kritik der politischen Utopie*, 81.

[186] For the concept of 'friendship with oneself' see also Spaemann, 'Was ist philosophische Ethik?', in *Grenzen*, 20 ff.

[187] Spaemann, 'Der Irrtum der Traditionalisten. Zur Soziologisierung der Gottesidee im 19. Jahrhundert', 498.

[188] For the ethical implications of the primacy of the love of God see Spaemann, 'Christliche Religion und Ethik', in *Einsprüche: Christliche Reden*, 60.

[189] For an account of Augustine's understanding of self-love, particularly in its relation to the love of God, see Oliver O'Donovan, *The Problem of Self-Love in St Augustine* (New Haven/London: Yale University Press, 1980), esp. 93 ff., where O'Donovan points out that Augustine's 'idea of a self-love diametrically opposed to the love and worship of God is a late arrival in Augustine's pages . . . It is in the context of the doctrine of the Fall that Augustine's perverse self-love first makes it appearance'. Spaemann does not distinguish between different stages in Augustine's intellectual development, but emphasizes the opposition between self-love and the love of God. This shows once again not only that his primary interest does not lie in historical analysis, but also that the doctrine of the fall occupies a central role in Spaemann's thought.

[190] Spaemann, 'Die zwei Grundbegriffe der Moral', in Kritik der politischen Utopie, 14.

[191] Ibid. 15.

The issue of how a substantial life can be both lived and philosophically defended—in the first place precisely by living it—is thus another of the implicit leitmotifs of Spaemann's criticism of modernity and of his retrieval of an integral relation between nature and freedom and between self-preservation and self-transcendence, which humanity cannot dispense with without abolishing itself.

5

Nature, freedom, and persons: Spaemann's philosophy of *Selbstsein*

PHAEDRUS: Tell me, Socrates, isn't it somewhere about here that they say Boreas seized Orithyia from the river? . . .
SOCRATES: I should be quite in fashion if I disbelieved it, as the men of science do. I might proceed to give a scientific account of how the maiden while at play with Pharmacia, was blown by a gust of Boreas down from the rocks hard by, and having thus met her death was said to have been seized by Boreas, though it may have happened on the Areopagus, according to another version of the occurrence. For my part, Phaedrus, I regard such theories as no doubt attractive, but as the invention of clever, industrious people who are not exactly to be envied, for the simple reason that they must then go on and tell us the real truth about the appearance of centaurs, Gorgons and Pegasuses and countless other remarkable monsters of legend flocking in on them. If our skeptic, with his somewhat crude science, means to reduce every one of them to the standard of probability, he'll need a deal of time for it. I myself have certainly no time for the business, and I'll tell you why, my friend. I can't as yet 'know myself,' as the inscription at Delphi enjoins, and so long as that ignorance remains it seems to me ridiculous to inquire into extraneous matters.

Plato

5.1 THE PERSON IN CONTEMPORARY PHILOSOPHY

The notion of the person is widely discussed in contemporary philosophy and theology.[1] Peter Geach has argued optimistically that '[i]n the West even

---

[1] See for important examples for this discussion Robert Sokolowski, *Phenomenology of the Human Person* (Cambridge: Cambridge University Press, 2008); Spaemann, *Persons (Personen)*; Derek Parfit, *Reasons and Persons*, 2nd edn. (Oxford: Clarendon, 1987); John F. Crosby, *The Selfhood of the Human Person*, (Washington, DC: The Catholic University of America Press, 1996); Theo Kobusch, *Die Entdeckung der Person: Metaphysik der Freiheit und modernes Menschenbild* (Darmstadt: Wissenschaftliche Buchgesellschaft, 1997); Stanley Rudman,

infidel philosophers are not tempted to reject the concept of a person'.[2] But, contrary to Geach's judgement, the notion of the person is in a considerable crisis in modernity. It is no longer contentious to call into question the concept of 'person' or to deny that each human being, regardless of whether he has self-consciousness and memory, is a person with absolute and inalienable dignity. Contemporary philosophy displays a 'genuine theoretical dilemma'[3] about the notion of the person, as Spaemann emphasizes. In times of decreasing agreement about previously undoubted foundations, recovery of which is one of the chief principles of Spaemann's philosophy, we need to reassure ourselves, as he argues, of the tradition and its conceptual achievements.[4]

This modern crisis of the notion of person is all the more striking because modern philosophy has also had profound insights into the dignity of the human person. The history of this notion may thus provide us with the best demonstration of the modern dialectic of nature and freedom and of the related and ultimately totalitarian dialectic of abstract notions set loose from any relation to reality as self-evidently given. For the modern conception of the person, which dichotomizes nature and freedom, tends to oscillate between a 'spiritualized' person (and thus a fuller understanding of freedom at the cost of the person's nature) and a 'materialized' person (and thus an understanding of the natural basis of being a person at the cost of freedom and subjectivity).

At present there are two chief tendencies in the philosophical treatment of the person. The first is to ask whether all human beings are persons. Philosophers wonder: Are there human beings who either are not persons at all or, alternatively, persons only to a certain degree? This tendency is closely connected to the contemporary increase in scientific and technological knowledge, which generates manifold problematic issues that have never been heard of before, such as those connected with *in vitro* fertilization and genetic engineering, not to mention the issues of abortion and euthanasia.

Concepts of Person and Christian Ethics (New Studies in Christian Ethics, xi) (Cambridge: Cambridge University Press, 1997); Richard Schenk, OP (ed.), *Kontinuität der Person: Zum Versprechen und Vertrauen* (Stuttgart/Bad Cannstatt: frommann-holzboog, 1998); Mechthild Dreyer and Kurt Fleischhauer (eds.), *Natur und Person im ethischen Disput* (Freiburg im Breisgau/Munich: Alber, 1998); Charles Taylor, 'The Concept of a Person', in *Philosophical Papers, I. Human Agency and Language* (Cambridge: Cambridge University Press, 1985), 97–114.

[2] *The Virtues: The Stanton Lectures 1973–74* (Cambridge: Cambridge University Press, 1977), 41.

[3] Spaemann, *Persons*, 3 (*Personen*, 10).

[4] Ibid. 3 (11).

The second tendency is to ask whether some species of animals[5] or machines[6] are persons and whether at least some animals have, therefore, the same dignity as human beings.[7] In this context it is telling to look at how Peter Singer, following the tradition of the post-Lockean philosophy of person-hood, rephrases this question:

It sounds odd to call an animal a person. This oddness may be no more than a symptom of our habit of keeping our own species sharply separated from others. In any case, we can avoid the linguistic oddness by rephrasing the question in accordance with our definition of 'person'. What we are really asking is whether any non-human animals are rational and self-conscious beings, aware of themselves as distinct entities with a past and a future.[8]

In arguing this way Singer defines personhood empirically without taking into account the long and significant philosophical and theological tradition that does not connect being a person to actually being rational and self-conscious.[9] These two chief tendencies often overlap because both of them are likely to presuppose an empiricist and naturalistic notion of personhood and they are also likely to deny that 'person' is a fundamental notion, as Derek Parfit does in his *Reason and Persons*.[10]

In Parfit's opinion, one can pursue ethics from an entirely 'impersonal' point of view: 'We could therefore describe a person's life in an impersonal

---

[5] See e.g. Karin Blumer, 'Sind Tiere Personen? Eine Analyse terminologischer Kontroversen in der gegenwärtigen bioethischen Diskussion dargestellt am Beispiel der Position von Peter Singer', in *Theologie und Philosophie*, 73 (1998), 524–37; U. Kohlmann, 'Überwindung des Anthropozentrismus durch Gleichheit alles Lebendigen?', in *Zeitschrift für philosophische Forschung*, 49 (1995), 15–35.

[6] See e.g. Christopher Cherry, 'The Possibility of Computers Becoming Persons: A Response to Dolby', in *Social Epistemology*, 3 (1989), 337–48; Cherry, 'Machines as Persons?', in David Cockburn (ed.), *Human Beings* (Cambridge: Cambridge University Press, 1991), 11–24; John L. Pollock, *How to Build a Person? A Prolegomenon* (Cambridge, Mass.: MIT Press, 1989).

[7] On the discussion of whether or not animals should be considered and treated as persons see Holger Zaborowski and Christoph Stumpf, 'Menschenwürde versus Würde der Kreatur: Philosophische und juristische Überlegungen zur Personalität und Würde des menschlichen und des nicht-menschlichen Lebens', in *Rechtstheorie: Zeitschrift für Logik und Juristische Methodenlehre, Rechtsinformatik, Kommunikationsforschung, Normen- und Handlungstheorie, Soziologie und Philosophie des Rechts*, 36 (2005), 91–115. For Spaemann's comments on the necessary protection of animals and the difference between the dignity of animals and the dignity of human beings see 'Tierschutz und Menschenwürde', in *Grenzen*.

[8] *How Are We to Live? Ethics in an Age of Self-Interest* (Oxford: Oxford University Press, 1997), 110–11.

[9] For Spaemann's explicit critique of Peter Singer's (and Norbert Hoerster's) position, see also 'Sind alle Menschen Personen?', in *Communio*, 19 (1990), 108–14.

[10] *Reasons and Persons*, 217. For a discussion of *Reasons and Persons* see also Jonathan Dancy (ed.), *Reading Parfit* (Oxford: Blackwell, 1997).

way, which does not claim that this person exists'.[11] In Spaemann's view, Parfit is thus pleading for 'a Buddhist view of the world for which individuality is a mere appearance'.[12] Are individual persons qualitatively different from things? How can we recognize and conceptualize persons? Do persons need to be treated specifically—that is to say, differently from 'things'? Can a 'somebody' gradually 'recede' into a 'something'? Can this process be reversed? Can one be partly 'somebody' and partly 'something'? The answer to these questions has considerable ethical implications, which Parfit does not conceal. Because there is no sharp borderline within the development of an embryo, he argues, the embryo *becomes* a human being and a person. This is why '[w]e can believe that there is nothing wrong in an early abortion, but that it would be seriously wrong to abort a child near the end of pregnancy.... The cases in between we can treat as matters of degree'.[13] He argues similarly with regard to euthanasia. 'We can plausibly claim that, if the person has ceased to exist, we have no moral reason to help his heart to go on beating, or to refrain from preventing this.'[14] Parfit explicitly states that he finds 'liberating' and 'consoling' the notion of personhood in which 'our continued existence is not a deep further fact, distinct from physical and psychological continuity'.[15] Furthermore, he points out, death 'seems to me less bad'[16] because we either continuously die or—what amounts to the same thing—'we' cannot die at all because 'we' lack a time-transcending identity.

The discussion of the person has thus ceased to have a purely 'theoretical and academic character', as, Spaemann argues, used to be the case.[17] It has become a discussion with significant implications for ethics, politics, technology, and the natural and social sciences. Even tendencies that first seem to be an affirmation of personhood can, in the long run, undermine the idea that every human being is a person. In a striking remark Spaemann briefly draws attention to the tendency to 'personalize', as it were, the non-personal elements of everyday culture in order to mimic personal relationships—to an Internet customer, for instance. An impersonal vocabulary, he suggests, would be more appropriate to computerized communications than programming computers so that monitors read 'Hello' or 'Thank you' as if the

---

[11] For the critique of the ethical implications of Parfit's thought see *Reasons and Persons*, 323 and also Vinit Haksar, *Equality, Liberty, and Perfectionism* (Oxford: Clarendon, 1979), 111; Geoffrey Madell, *The Identity of the Self* (Edinburgh: Edinburgh University Press, 1981), 116.

[12] Spaemann, 'Sind alle Menschen Personen?' *Grenzen*, 422.

[13] *Reasons and Persons*, 322.

[14] Parfit, *Reasons and Persons*, 323.

[15] Ibid. 281.

[16] Ibid.

[17] *Persons*, 2 (*Personen*, 10).

machine were a human person.[18] The increase of 'pseudo-persons', Spaemann
holds, undermines the person and manipulates our understanding of the
reality of persons. This is similar to the paradoxical tendency of 'scientific
diction to become all the more teleological the further away one gets from
creatures, with respect to machines, elementary particles, and hurricanes. It is
only consistent that they get proper names, too'.[19]

In what follows we will examine Spaemann's philosophy of the person,
which has been crucial to his thought from its very beginning.[20] In Spaemann's view, it does indeed matter whether a person is in reality there or
not—it has a significant effect on our understanding of reality. His philosophy of the person is an education into reality, in that it recollects how we
experience reality in its most intense form. In so doing, he recollects a self-
evident knowledge about the fundamental difference between 'something'
and 'somebody'. We will focus particularly on Spaemann's magisterial *Persons*.
In this book Spaemann seeks to read both the Anglo-American and the
Continental discussion of 'person' with philosophical seriousness. He criticizes the post-Lockean discussion about personal identity on the one hand
and examines on the other the idealist as well as the phenomenological
philosophy of freedom and of the free recognition of the other person.
Plato, Aristotle, Augustine, Thomas Aquinas, F. W. J. Schelling, Max Scheler,[21]
Martin Heidegger, Theodor W. Adorno, Max Horkheimer, and Emmanuel
Levinas are important, although not necessarily explicit, sources for Spaemann's thought about who a person is and how we can understand the
'mystery . . . that we call "person"'.[22] *Persons* also articulates an in-depth
critique of modernity and of such philosophical presuppositions as the
anti-Aristotelian inversion of natural teleology and the misconceptions of
the notions 'life', 'motion', and 'possibility', as paradigmatically manifest in
John Locke's and Derek Parfit's philosophies.

From a Spaemannian point of view, we will criticize Derek Parfit for
denying the fundamentality of the notion of person and for failing to see
that an entirely impersonal viewpoint is impossible because it is self-contradictory. First, we will ask why the notion of person has become such
a controversial notion in modernity even though modernity contributed

[18] Ibid. 195–6 (207).
[19] Spaemann, *Die Frage 'Wozu?'*, 239.
[20] For one of the earliest documents of Spaemann's personalist philosophy see 'Das
Vertrauen als sittlicher Wert', in *Die Kirche in der Welt*, 1 (1947/8).
[21] For Scheler's ethical personalism see John F. Crosby, 'The Individuality of Human
Persons: A Study in the Ethical Personalism of Max Scheler', in *Review of Metaphysics*, 52
(1998), 21–50.
[22] 'Sind alle Menschen Personen?', in *Grenzen*, 425.

considerably to the 'discovery' of subjectivity, human dignity, and freedom. In examining the controversy over the notion of person we will provide the background to the discussion of Spaemann's and Parfit's philosophies and will begin a critique of Parfit's position by showing that he does not rely on unaided reason, but on significant and contestable ideological presuppositions. Second, we will examine the style and method of Parfit's philosophy and show how questionable several of his ontological and epistemological premises are. Third, we will discuss the relation between person, life, and nature in order to develop the argument that the notion of person is indispensable and serves to undermine the dualism of spirit and matter, in both its ontological and its epistemological forms. We will then go on to examine more closely Spaemann's philosophy of *Selbstsein* and his philosophy of religion.

5.2 MODERNITY AND THE CRISIS OF THE 'PERSON'

A major reason for the modern crisis of the concept 'person' lies in the crisis of Christianity and of traditional metaphysics. The notion of the person originates particularly from the controversies about the nature of Christ and the Trinity in the early Church.[23] Although its later development was not so greatly influenced by doctrinal speculations, the manifest crisis of Christianity in modernity entailed not only the crisis of the Christian understanding of the human being as created, fallen, and in need of redemption, but also the crisis of the philosophical notion of person.[24] This is especially the case because many modern approaches to the person, such as Kant's, are still at least partly deeply indebted to a Christian viewpoint, even though one must carefully distinguish the context of ideas out of which a notion arose from the context of ideas in relation to which it is justified. Precisely because of the influence of Christianity on the history of the person, Derek Parfit has

---

[23] See e.g. Spaemann, *Persons*, 19 ff. (*Personen*, 28 ff.). For the relation between the crucifixion of Christ and the radical internalization of the notion of dignity see Spaemann, 'Über den Begriff der Menschenwürde', in *Grenzen*, 111. See also Kobusch, *Die Entdeckung der Person*; Geach, *The Virtues*, 41–2; M. Fuhrmann et al. 'Person', in Joachim Ritter and Karlfried Gründer (eds.), *Historisches Wörterbuch der Philosophie*, vii (Basle: Schwabe, 1989), 269–338. For a contrasting view see Dieter Henrich, 'Trinität Gottes und der Begriff der Person', in Odo Marquard and Karlheinz Stierle (eds.) *Identität*. (Munich: Fink, 1979), 612–20.

[24] For the theological dimension of 'person' see Helmut Hoping, 'Göttliche und menschliche Personen: Die Diskussion um den Menschen als Herausforderung für die Dogmatik', in *Theologie der Gegenwart*, 41 (1998), 162–74.

argued for an explicitly non-religious utilitarian ethics that no longer relies upon the notion of person.[25]

Similarly, the crisis of traditional metaphysics, specifically the inversion of natural teleology and the understanding of reality as process, has reinforced the crisis of the concept 'person'. Because of the underlying scientism of their philosophies, many modern thinkers no longer understand nature by analogy to personal self-experience, as Spaemann argues; rather, personal self-experience is increasingly understood by analogy to a non-teleological understanding of nature. Given this tendency, it is difficult to understand that persons are not instances of a species 'person' and that *Selbstsein* is not a sortal, that is to say generic, term. From a scientistic point of view, 'human being' and 'person' are at best synonyms; at worst, 'person' is an outmoded and superfluous notion, because it still carries implications that the reductionistic spirit of some important strands of modernity is incapable of understanding. For being a person is not dependent upon qualitative traits, such as self-consciousness, that could somehow be objectified, observed, and measured such that 'the identity of consciousness then is the consciousness of identity'.[26] Self-consciousness, Spaemann counters, 'is the consequence of being a person and not its origin'.[27]

Cartesian epistemology, too, has implications for the understanding of the person. Once the Cartesian ideal of certainty[28] and of clear and distinct knowledge[29] began to dominate philosophy, the emphasis upon objectivity and certainty led to the methodological exclusion of a personal point of view and hence of the self-experience of persons. The Cartesian ideal of certainty as immediate *Bei-sich-Sein*, Spaemann thus states, cannot be reconciled with the idea of the identity of living *Selbstsein*, because 'life is not a *clara et distincta perceptio*, but can be given definition from the point of view of consciousness only by way of negation'.[30] The crisis of the notion of a person is thus in the first place a crisis of philosophical categories that fail to describe reality fully while nonetheless claiming to do so. There are other aspects to this failure of

---

[25] *Reasons and Persons*, 443 ff.

[26] 'Wir dürfen das Euthanasie-Tabu nicht aufgeben', in *Grenzen*, 414. For Locke's view that 'whatever has the consciousness of present and past Actions, is the same person' see his *An Essay Concerning Human Understanding*, ed. and foreword Peter H. Nidditch (Oxford: Clarendon, 1979), 340–1 (II. 27. § 16).

[27] 'Kommentar', in *Die Unantastbarkeit des menschlichen Lebens: Zu ethischen Fragen der Biomedizin*, Instruktion der Kongregation für die Glaubenslehre (Freiburg im Breisgau: Herder, 1987), 85.

[28] *The Philosophical Writings of Descartes*, trans. John Cottingham, Robert Stoothoff, and Dugald Murdoch (Cambridge: Cambridge University Press, 1984), 126–7.

[29] Ibid. 120.

[30] *Persons*, 57 (*Personen*, 66).

modern philosophy. Cartesian philosophy, Spaemann reasons, is also characterized by a timeless methodological solipsism and by what Spaemann calls
an 'instantialism' (*Momentanismus*).[31] These characteristics are incompatible
with an adequate notion of person, Spaemann argues. For the person is only
conceivable within a plurality of persons—as an active, free, and temporal
person among other persons.[32] 'Real Being', Spaemann argues, 'is Being-with
(*Mitsein*), or it is not real'.[33] The person therefore cannot correspond to the
scientific 'ideal' of timeless, self-contained, and passive objects. Cartesian
philosophy also fails to understand the notion 'life', which is, as Spaemann
argues with reference to Aristotle,[34] the being of persons.[35] This is why
whoever abolishes the notion 'life' and reduces reality to the dualism of nature
and freedom cannot but misinterpret the phenomenon of the person who as a
living being actively 'has' his nature in freedom and always already 'bridges'
the gap between *res cogitans* and *res extensa*. In sum, Spaemann argues that to
abolish the self-transcendence and life of the person, the reality of time, and
the paradigmatic character of the person as being with other persons—that is
to say, to understand Being as *Bei-sich-sein* (rather than as *Selbstsein*)—makes
the idea of personal identity as self-objectification impossible.[36]

A phenomenology of the human person such as Spaemann's shows that the
Cartesian dichotomization of the subjective and the objective does not really
reflect reality as it is, but is based upon ideological presuppositions and
preliminary methodological decisions and is subject to dialectical 'transformations'. Derek Parfit's philosophy is a good example of this, even though he
explicitly rejects Cartesianism. For Parfit's philosophy of the person, like a
great deal of post-Cartesian modern philosophy, is characterized by a dialectic
of transcendentalism and materialism which shows the intrinsic problems of a
non-person-centred account of reality. The materialist underpinning of his
philosophy, as we will see, inevitably turns into a transcendentalist view of the
person. Parfit's argument that 'person' is not a fundamental notion and his
defence of an 'impersonal point of view' are based upon a critique of more

---

[31] *Persons*, 37 (*Personen*, 45).

[32] Ibid. 40 (49). For important considerations about 'intersubjectivity' see also Robert
Sokolowski, 'The Christian Difference in Personal Relationships', in his *Christian Faith and
Understanding: Studies on the Eucharist, Trinity, and the Human Person* (Washington, DC: The
Catholic University of America Press, 2006), 199–213, esp. 205 ff.

[33] 'Wirklichkeit als Anthropomorphismus', in Oswald Georg Bauer (ed.), *Was heißt 'wirklich'? Unsere Erkenntnis zwischen Wahrnehmung und Wissenschaft* (Waakirchen/Schaftlach:
Oreos, 2000), 29; see also *Persons*, 66 (*Personen*, 75): '*Selbstsein* implies that being is radically
plural'.

[34] Aristotle, *De anima*, 415b13.

[35] Spaemann, *Persons*, 4 (*Personen*, 11).

[36] Ibid. 147 (157).

than one view of personhood. He rejects both the *purely* physical and the *purely* psychological criterion of personal identity over time and criticizes as indefensible non-reductionistic views such as the Cartesian dualism that upholds that 'a person is a purely mental entity',[37] and what he calls the 'further-fact theory'. Parfit argues against the dualist idea of a Cartesian ego that '[w]e are not separately existing entities, apart from our brains and bodies, and various interrelated physical and mental events'.[38] The 'further-fact theory' agrees that we do not exist apart from our bodies, yet at the same time refuses to accept that personal identity is entirely dependent upon either physical or psychological continuity.[39] For Parfit, on the other hand, the physical and psychological criteria are sufficient. This allows him to question the continuity of our personal identity; persons are in the course of their lives persons to differing degrees, dependent on the observable and measurable state of affairs of what constitutes being a person in Parfit's eyes. This comprises the materialist aspect of Parfit's philosophy. Yet there is a spiritual aspect as well, less prominent, though certainly detectable and as such a clear sign of the dialectical character of post-Cartesian philosophy. It has to do with a 'gradualization', as it were, of the person. In order to understand this, we need to look at Parfit's examination of what it means to be a person more closely.

Parfit maintains that neither the unity of consciousness at any time nor the unity of a whole life can 'be explained by claiming that different experiences are had by the same person',[40] because the 'subject' of a whole life of different moments could be different persons. Parfit therefore criticizes the 'determinacy theory', which says that personhood is only either wholly present or wholly absent, for failing to allow a third possibility for such cases as people enduring agony: '[T]he person in agony will be partly me. I can imagine being only partly in agony, because I am drifting in and out of consciousness. But if someone will be fully conscious of the agony, this person cannot be partly me'.[41] On the basis of this view, he concludes, personal identity is not what matters. He suggests that this is 'the most important claim in the Reductionist View'.[42] Personal identity is indeterminate because personal identity is not a further fact.[43] Persons are not separately existing entities, apart from their

---

[37] *Reasons and Persons*, 210.

[38] Ibid. 216.

[39] For a self-critical revised account of possible criteria of personal identity see Parfit, 'Persons, Bodies, and Human Beings', in Theodore Sider, John Hawthorne, and Dean W. Zimmerman (eds.), *Contemporary Debates in Metaphysics* (Oxford: Blackwell, 2008), 177–208.

[40] *Reasons and Persons*, 217.

[41] Ibid. 233.

[42] Ibid. 241.

[43] Ibid. 240, 243.

brain and body. Parfit consequently concludes that '[o]rdinary survival is about as bad as being destroyed and replicated'.[44] It is important to see that Parfit's materialism is here trading in transcendental contraband. Who, for instance, is the ego who/that is 'drifting in and out of consciousness'? From which point of view and for whom is 'ordinary survival as bad as being destroyed'? Who, or what, survives or is being destroyed? On what basis can we even speak of 'a whole life', if different persons have the experience of it—including, perhaps, the experience of being destroyed and replicated? How is destruction and replication possible (and not simply change within one and the same underlying substance) if there is no such thing as non-gradual identity over time? We encounter here a fundamental problem of Parfit's philosophy. It is impossible to develop a consistent non-person-centred point of view because of the structure of reality. However much we deny the fundamental category of personhood, a 'ghostly' person keeps coming back—most unavoidably perhaps also in the figures of the writer and his audience. Nevertheless, Parfit denies that there are individual substances which, because of their ability to transcend themselves, are not merely static substances and which are identical with themselves over the course of time, whether they are conscious of this identity or not. In this denial Parfit shares key presuppositions of modern atomistic scientism, which no longer takes human freedom in its relation to nature—that is to say, the subjective time of persons among other persons—as the paradigm for understanding reality.[45]

According to sociobiology, which also displays the atomistic tendencies of modern scientific reasoning, the individual is part of an all-encompassing and all-embracing development of genes which transcends the individual. In Richard Dawkin's words: 'It is not success that makes good genes. It is good genes that make success, and nothing an individual does during its lifetime has any effect whatever upon its genes'.[46] Human bodies as well as animal bodies and the physical structure of plants are nothing but 'temporary vehicles' for genes.[47] Dawkins calls this 'anti-substantialist' anthropology 'total embryology', for 'the whole growth of the individual past adulthood into old age should be seen as an extension of the same process of embryology'.[48] Hence, Dawkins 'de-substantializes' the individual, as it were, and reduces him to a temporary carrier on the ever-flowing river of genes. Dawkins therefore also argues that 'the individual body, so familiar to us on

---

[44] Ibid. 280.
[45] For this see also Kobusch, 'Die Entdeckung der Person', 263.
[46] *River out of Eden: A Darwinian View of Life* (London: Weidenfeld & Nicolson, 1995), 3.
[47] Dawkins, *River out of Eden. A Darwinian View of Life*, 7.
[48] Ibid. 30.

our planet, did not have to exist. The only kind of entity that has to exist in order for life to arise anywhere in the universe is the immortal replicator'.[49] The individual body, be it conscious or not, is solely a function of genetic information and its replication, which, in Dawkins's account, is the goal of the universe. This explains why the notion of a 'subject', as well as the much broader notion of 'person', is criticized, 'punctualized', as it were, and in the end abolished. The claim, often linked to the scientific method, to provide a comprehensive *genealogical* account of reality, thus not only dissolves Being into becoming, but also makes it impossible to comprehend that there could be persons who do not become and are not merely part of an overarching flux of becoming, but *are* substantially persons, and who not only 'are' their nature, but 'have' their nature in freedom.

This is why one of the key criticisms in Spaemann's analysis of evolutionary metaphysics, such as sociobiology, concerns the confusion of change (*alloiosis*) with coming-into-existence (*genesis*). In his view, evolutionary metaphysics does not sufficiently distinguish between these two, but subsumes coming-into-existence and passing away under the changing of one universal substance. But given the understanding of reality as pure process, it no longer makes sense that there is such a thing as a human individual substance that comes into existence and passes away, that is subject to change and development while it is alive, and that freely relates to its nature while having, or, better, living, its own time. This is why the scientistic logic of Parfit and Dawkins not only ignores the temporal direction of existence[50] and hence the identity of the person over time; the naturalistic understanding of Being as evolution makes it also impossible to understand itself and its own claims. But evolutionary metaphysics, Spaemann concludes, fails to realize that it understands evolution as a succession of situations that, in the end, are nothing. The failure of evolutionary metaphysics to acknowledge its own nihilistic dialectic makes it inferior even, Spaemann states, to Buddhism, which fully acknowledges its nihilism and the negativity of suffering, of the non-ego, and of the absolute.[51]

However compelling the new views of the person may seem at first, they fail, and commit the elementary logical fallacy of a *petitio principii*. It is obvious to argue that philosophies which exclude a priori the categories and methods which are essential for a proper understanding of the notion

---

[49] *The Selfish Gene* (Oxford: Oxford University Press, 1989), 266. It needs to be asked why the replicator is immortal for Dawkins. Is it not just as plausible that the universe should continue to exist while life ceases to exist?

[50] Spaemann, 'Sein und Gewordensein: Was erklärt die Evolutionstheorie?', in *Philosophische Essays*, 204 ff.

[51] Ibid. 206–7. See for Spaemann's interpretation of Buddhism also 'Über den Sinn des Leidens', in *Einsprüche: Christliche Reden*, 123.

'person' cannot but significantly transform, if not entirely dismiss, the notion of a person. Given these tendencies, Spaemann interprets modern ontology as a forgetfulness of what Plato and Aristotle already achieved in their teleological philosophies of nature. This development of modern ontology, Spaemann suggests, means to dispense with the common and self-evident view of nature as the precondition and 'unpreconceivable' measure of human freedom in analogy to which we understand ourselves. Spaemann thus points out that modern natural philosophies can be construed as a revival of Heraclitus' and Parmenides' philosophies.[52] Depending upon whether one focuses upon the process of becoming or upon the universal substance of becoming, Heraclitus or Parmenides appears as forefather of the spirit of modern philosophies of nature. Spaemann makes an interesting point in underscoring that their views of reality finally amount to the same thing and turn into one another, depending upon one's perspective. Heraclitus' and Parmenides' views—as well as the modern evolutionary view of the world— coincide in that they do not acknowledge the reality of individual substances as opposed to one single substance of which individual 'substances' are mere parts. This is why the difference between the substantial and the accidental also vanishes in many modern ontologies, as in Leibniz's nominalist philoso- phy, such that 'the individual is defined through the sum of his predicates'.[53] That is to say, many modern philosophies (and, consequently, any philosophy of the person that is based upon them) are based upon a 'radically unfamiliar and alien' view of reality.[54] For what Spaemann calls the natural and self- evident view of the world presupposes that there are individual substances and substantial differences.[55] Hence, he reverses Hegel's idea that 'everything turns on grasping and expressing the True, not only as *Substance*, but equally as *Subject*',[56] and concludes that subjects must be thought of as substances.

---

[52] Here, and with respect to what follows, see Spaemann, *Die Frage 'Wozu?'*. For Spaemann's interpretation of Plato's philosophy in comparison to Heraclitus' and Parmenides' philosophies see *Persons*, 113 (*Personen*, 122). It is noteworthy at this point that the title of Richard Dawkin's *River Out of Eden* is reminiscent not only of the biblical account of paradise but also of Heraclitus' philosophy.

[53] See Spaemann, 'Leibniz' Begriff der möglichen Welten', in Venanz Schubert (ed.), *Ratio- nalität und Sentiment: Das Zeitalter Johann Sebastian Bachs und Georg Friedrich Händels* (Wissenschaft und Philosophie: Interdisziplinäre Studien, v) (St Ottilien: EOS, 1987), 18; for Spaemann's view of Leibniz's ontology see also 'Religiöse Identität', in *Das unsterbliche Gerücht*, 123–4; see also *Happiness and Benevolence*, 163 (*Glück und Wohlwollen*, 211) for a short discussion of Leibniz's metaphysics and *Reflexion und Spontaneität*, 210–36 for a discus- sion of Leibniz's position in the controversy about 'pure love'.

[54] *Die Frage 'Wozu?'*, 29.

[55] 'Sein und Gewordensein', in *Philosophische Essays*, 206.

[56] Hegel, *Phenomenology of Spirit*, trans. A. V. Miller (Oxford: Oxford University Press, 1979), 10.

Spaemann further states that if human beings want to continue to think of themselves as free agents, nature as such needs to be interpreted from a teleological viewpoint.[57]

The questioning of the idea of personal identity in modernity (as much as the so-called death of the subject in late modern philosophy) is thus due to the subjectivist abolition both of substances and of the teleological account of nature, whether by sociobiology and analytic logic or by different kinds of functionalism and structuralism. The fundamental crisis of the person, Adorno and Horkheimer have argued, also needs to be read against the background of a complete economization of reality because the crisis of the subject is intimately intertwined with the logic of economization and 'scientification'.[58] This economization is only the end of a development within which all the vestiges of traditional conceptions of nature were methodologically rejected as mythological.[59] Adorno and Horkheimer's analysis of the modern tendency to abolish differences within reality also sheds light on the modern crisis of the idea of personal identity, for '[t]he identity of everything with everything else is paid for in that nothing may ... be identical with itself'.[60] The utilitarian paradigm for the exchange of goods makes everything identical and thus exchangeable. In consequence, it finally turns against human beings and their self-experience of identity, and subjects persons to the totalized process of the market, for instance. From this point of view, we can further understand why Spaemann recommends letting be (*Gelassenheit; désintéressement*) as a key virtue.[61] For this notion is opposed to the economic notion 'interest' that has taken a central position in the modern philosophy of self-preservation.[62]

5.3 HISTORICISM AND SCIENCE FICTION AS PHILOSOPHICAL METHODS

In the following section we will provide a critique of two prominent features of Parfit's philosophy. The first is Parfit's historicism. The second is the role

---

[57] *Die Frage 'Wozu?'*, 288.

[58] Theodor W. Adorno and Max Horkheimer, *Dialektik der Aufklärung*, in Horkheimer, *Gesammelte Schriften*, ed. Alfred Schmidt and Gunzelin Schmid Noerr (Frankfurt am Main: Fischer, 1987), 40.

[59] Ibid. 29.

[60] Ibid. 12.

[61] For Spaemann's understanding of *Gelassenheit* see e.g. *Basic Moral Concepts*, 80–9 (*Moralische Grundbegriffe*, 98–109); *Persons*, 77 (*Personen*, 87).

[62] For the notion 'interest' and its significance see Spaemann, *Reflexion und Spontaneität*, esp. 63 and 81–2.

played by 'science fiction' considerations in his argument. We will also draw attention to Peter Singer's popular ethics, on which Parfit's thought has arguably had an impact. Singer draws the practical consequences from the post-Lockean and post-Humean debate about personhood more explicitly (and possibly more influentially) than any other philosopher, though without achieving the philosophical rigour and quality of Parfit. His arguments, Spaemann maintains, are 'extremely weak; they are only impressive to people who do not accept any rational argument that could lead to a notion such as sanctity'.[63]

The inversion and revision of historicism

Parfit's and Singer's philosophies, as we have already seen, are based upon historicist presuppositions. Both of them suggest that things have somehow never been worse and problems have never been more difficult. Parfit, for instance, refers to the disturbingly impersonal life in big cities,[64] which seems to necessitate an impersonal ethics as outlined in *Reasons and Persons*. This attitude is typical of a great deal of contemporary ethical theory.[65] It is an inversion of the modern Enlightenment optimism and derives its doctrine from the change in modern technology and from the widening field of scientific research. Yet this inversion of Enlightenment optimism is intended to prepare for a reaffirmation of Enlightenment optimism with respect to the prospects for the future of mankind. Parfit emphasizes that how we affect future generations 'is the most important part of our moral theory, since the next few centuries will be the most important in human history'.[66] The optimism of this view also embraces scientific ethics. When ethical problems become increasingly difficult, non-religious and scientific ethics will gradually be more successful, Parfit thinks. Because non-religious ethics, according to Parfit, is 'the youngest and least advanced' science, he rejects the claim that there is no progress in ethics and that there are no new arguments in ethics. Peter Singer argues similarly: 'We are only now breaking with a past in which

---

[63] 'Geleitwort', in Till Bastian (ed.), *Denken—schreiben—töten: Zur neuen 'Euthanasie'-Diskussion und zur Philosophie Peter Singers* (Stuttgart: Wissenschaftliche Verlagsgesellschaft, 1990), 8.

[64] *Reasons and Persons*, 444.

[65] See Karl-Otto Apel, 'The *A Priori* of the Communication Community and the Foundation of Ethics: The Problem of a Rational Foundation of Ethics in the Scientific Age', in *Towards a Transformation of Philosophy*, trans. Glyn Adey and David Frisby foreword Pol Vandevelde (Marquette Studies in Philosophy, xx) (Milwaukee, Wis.: Marquette University Press, 1998), 225–300.

[66] *Reasons and Persons*, 351.

religion and ethics have been closely identified. It is too early to tell what changes may lie ahead, once we have a better understanding of the nature of ethics, but they are likely to be profound'.[67] This is why there really are, in Parfit's and Singer's views, indeed new ethical questions, whereas Spaemann, as we have pointed out, argues at the very beginning of *Happiness and Benevolence* that there are no new ethical questions.[68]

Parfit's optimistic projections for the future of non-religious ethics give the concluding paragraph of *Reasons and Persons* a kind of pathetic appeal, in which the abolition of freedom becomes clear in the comparison of ethics to mathematics:

> But the progress could be greatest in what is now the least advanced of these Arts and Sciences. This, I have claimed, is Non-Religious Ethics. Belief in God, or many gods, prevented the free development of moral reasoning. Disbelief in God, openly admitted by a majority, is a recent event, not yet completed. Because this event is so recent, Non-Religious Ethics is at a very early stage. We cannot yet predict whether, as in Mathematics, we will all reach agreement. Since we cannot know how Ethics will develop, it is not irrational to have high hopes.[69]

We may raise the question whether it is true that non-religious ethics has actually been studied systematically only since the 1960s, as Parfit suggests. For anyone even remotely familiar with the history of modern philosophy, it is a perplexing suggestion: utilitarianism goes back to the eighteenth century; the 'moral science' conception to the seventeenth.

Parfit's emphasis on the scientific character of ethics and his view of the future of scientific ethics are closely connected to his attempt to question strong everyday beliefs[70] and to lay the foundations for a change in those beliefs. In the introduction to *Reasons and Persons* Parfit reveals the leitmotif of his philosophical undertaking and the often implicit interests of his ontology and ethics. 'Philosophers should not only interpret our beliefs; when they are false, they should change them.'[71] The reference to Karl Marx's understanding of philosophy, as expressed in his eleventh thesis on Feuerbach, is obvious and hence, one can presume, intended.[72] Parfit is

---

[67] Singer, *How Are We to Live? Ethics in an Age of Self-interest* (Amherst, NY: Prometheus, 1995), 16.

[68] *Happiness and Benevolence*, vii (*Glück und Wohlwollen*, 9).

[69] *Reasons and Persons*, 454.

[70] An interesting parallel is Hume's argument that 'this small attention (i.e. to the fundamental difference between *is* and *ought*) wou'd subvert all the vulgar systems of morality' (*A Treatise of Human Nature*, ed. L. A. Selby-Bigge, 2nd edn., with rev. text and variant readings by P. H. Nidditch (Oxford: Clarendon, 1985), 470).

[71] Parfit, *Reasons and Persons*, 10.

[72] Marx, 'On Feuerbach', in *Early Political Writings*, trans. and ed. Joseph O'Malley and Richard A. Davis (Cambridge: Cambridge University Press, 2006), 118: 'The philosophers have only interpreted the world in different ways; the point is to *change* it'. For Spaemann's

concerned with changing our world; and this change is considered necessary for historical progress. Ethics is thus not only confused with the philosophy of history, but also treated as a scientific enterprise undertaken by experts with considerable practical implications. This understanding of philosophy is, as we have already argued, very much at odds with Spaemann's view that philosophy recollects the self-evident. Parfit's modernistic philosophy, however, has no conception of the self-evident and of the gift of reality that precedes any logical and scientific deductions of it; Parfit, one could say, is not fully 'awakened to human being'.[73] For Parfit, whether or not 'someone' is a person depends not only on certain characteristic features, but also on the philosophical, that is to say scientific, definition of these features. On the contrary, Spaemann contends, human dignity as manifest in the person and his identity can only *freely* be respected and recognized; it cannot be scientifically proved.[74] '*Selbstsein* means emancipation from the conditions of one's coming-to-be.'[75] One cannot fully understand it from a genealogical or scientific point of view because the event of the person brings 'something' radically new into the world. However, the fact that it is impossible to provide a genealogical scientific account of human dignity or personal identity does not say anything about whether all human beings are continuously and fully persons or not. It says a great deal, though, about the intrinsic constraints of a genealogical and scientistic account of reality.

Science fiction as argument

At the beginning of *The Selfish Gene* Richard Dawkins blurs the distinction between science and science fiction. He suggests that 'this book should be read almost as though it were science fiction. It is designed to appeal to the imagination. But it is not science fiction: it is science'.[76] In Parfit's philosophy, too, the difference between science and science fiction vanishes because his argument is at least partly based on entirely impossible scenarios. It is not possible in this forum to discuss the scientific validity of his proposals

comment on this conception of philosophy see 'Der Anschlag auf den Sonntag, in *Grenzen*, 277: 'Marx once said that the philosophers have only contemplated the world and that it is important to change it. In response to this one can only say: No change changes the world for the better that does not change it in such a way that it is worthwhile to contemplate it in the first place'.

[73] See Spaemann, *Happiness and Benevolence*, 173f. (*Glück und Wohlwollen*, 222f.) for Spaemann's comments on the relation between "awakening to human being" and "understanding reality as gift".

[74] 'Über den Begriff der Menschenwürde, in *Grenzen*, 122.

[75] Spaemann, *Persons*, 90 (*Personen*, 51; translation modified).

[76] *The Selfish Gene*, v.

concerning teletransportation,[77] neurosurgery, and brain transplantation,[78] which seem highly questionable and perhaps entirely fictional. Instead, we will focus on the philosophical problem of using as yet entirely hypothetical arguments.

Parfit admits that some of his hypothetical cases 'remain impossible'.[79] But what difference does impossibility make? Parfit introduces a distinction between 'ontological' and 'technical' possibility, and denies that technical impossibility has any bearing on his ethical argument: 'Since I use these [currently infeasible] cases only to discover what we believe, this impossibility does not matter'.[80] In his attempt to clarify our existing moral intuitions—with questionable outcomes; for his philosophy, we will argue, is counter-intuitive—Parfit, however, does not restrict himself to what he calls merely technically impossible given the state of our technological capacities. He frankly admits that some of his imaginary cases are merely technically impossible, while others are even 'deeply impossible'.[81] Yet the concession that 'impossibility may make some thought-experiment irrelevant'[82] remains pure lip service, for his further argument does not reflect critically upon the reasons for this irrelevance, or upon its implications.

The specific understanding of possibility (and of impossibility) that is presupposed here changes not only our understanding of actuality, but our understanding of possibility, too. The important difference between actuality and possibility is undermined if technical possibility is dealt with as if it does not matter. For Parfit, things are necessary, necessarily impossible (that is to say, ontologically or deeply impossible and therefore self-contradictory), actual, or simply not yet actual (because possible or, to use Parfit's term, merely technically impossible). If we follow Parfit, then, possibility needs to be understood as a subcategory of actuality. Contingency—that is to say, what *may* be the case but *does not actually need to* be the case (most prominently and importantly, one can argue, the person)—can then no longer *adequately* be understood *as* contingency. Given this view of reality, neither history, nor freedom, nor the irreversible character of time, nor a person's relation to his nature and to other persons in freedom—as manifestations of contingency—has full validity and intelligibility. All these phenomena are interpreted in a reductionist manner from within a framework that subjects possibility, or

[77] *Reasons and Persons*, 199 ff.
[78] Ibid. 220–1, 229–30, and *passim*.
[79] Ibid. 234.
[80] Ibid.; similarly on 238: 'Since our psychological features depend on the states of our brains, these imagined cases are only technically impossible'.
[81] Ibid. 219.
[82] Ibid.

contingency, to actuality without being able properly to understand what is contingent. Reality, then, is reduced to what conforms to the methodological norm of the sciences that presuppose not only the passivity of their objects but also that their respective object is, as a timeless object, actually and observably there.

We also have to assess the value of purely hypothetical considerations for ethical theory. This will show that Parfit's philosophy, too, is subject to the dialectic of abstract concepts: the dismissal of a proper concept of possibility, or contingency, seems to have the reduction of reality to a hypothesis as its dialectical other. What does this mean? Parfit is certainly right in saying that ethics ought to take modern sciences into careful consideration. This implies also anticipating and evaluating future problems and future arguments in the sciences and in philosophy. But Parfit's thought goes beyond mere foresight, transforming the very nature of ethics by reducing ethics to an intellectual pastime, a kind of fictitious enterprise, even though ethics cannot wholly rely upon virtual reality without losing its practical, action-focused dimension, as we have indicated. Technical impossibility does indeed matter, at least for ethics as ordinarily understood.

Seen from a Spaemannian point of view this virtualization of reality[83] betrays both a dismissal of life in its character as an 'unpreconceivable' gift and a drive to simulate it technologically as a mechanism. But virtual reality, Spaemann argues, can never truly take the place of reality; it can, though, replace art as the fictional and simulated 'other' of reality. If simulated reality replaces art, then, as Spaemann suggests, it can possibly be taken for reality itself. This is possible if reality, which is to say life, has first been misunderstood as a technological simulation, rather than as an unpreconceivable given reality.[84] So the mechanistic character of modern philosophy makes it possible for virtual reality to be made the paradigm for all reality. It is important to note that Parfit's philosophy stands in this modern tradition of rendering reality virtual; that is to say, of making reality ultimately a product of human invention. Against this tendency, Spaemann endeavours to alert his readers to reality itself, which, he argues, is not even an observable 'quality', because it is similar to ourselves as persons and thus needs to be freely recognized. 'To understand reality as such means to look at it from the angle of its greater or lesser similarity with ourselves.'[85]

---

[83] For Spaemann's critical discussion of 'virtual reality' see *Persons*, 90–1 (*Personen*, 100–1).

[84] Ibid. 91 (101).

[85] Spaemann, 'Wirklichkeit als Anthropomorphismus', 22; for the idea that reality is not a quality, see 15.

It is important to emphasize at this point in our argument that Parfit effectively inaugurates 'virtual ethics' or 'science-fiction ethics' as a new philosophical discipline, with serious implications; for not even in the area of science fiction, Spaemann points out, does it make no difference 'what someone considers beautiful and what he considers repugnant'.[86] This new discipline deals with such questions as how to define human identity if teletransportation were to become a possibility. But ethical categories, such as 'good' and 'evil', and ontological categories, such as 'true' or 'identical', become hypothesized if the ethical or ontological quality of a particular action or phenomenon depends entirely upon such unreal presuppositions. Whether I will remain the same responsible agent when teletransported or, alternatively, whether someone yet to be generated will be the responsible agent (who then seems to be the human being who I have been) will depend on what the lived reality of teletransportation is like—which cannot be judged or imagined from this remote distance, but can only be known by a future civilization with the actual experience of teletransportation (if it be possible at all). Any description of the ethics and ontology of this situation must be arbitrary and fanciful, and thus wide open to exploitation in the service of reinforcing existing prejudices. Because we do not know what it would be like to be teletransported, Parfit's hypothesis is useless with respect to contemporary ethical problems.

Such intellectual pastimes anticipate the answer to the question, so that ethics as a deliberative enquiry is trivialized in a manner expressive of the hypothetical spirit of modernity. One could ask, for the mere sake of the argument, how one is to think about decapitation in a world where people live happily, perhaps even more happily, without a head. However, such an enquiry falls short of what ethics must be vis-à-vis the brevity of life—*ars longa, vita brevis*. Ethics is about how to act now or in the immediate future with regard to the good.[87] Since it is about moral truth and thus about reality, as Spaemann holds, ethics cannot abstract from reality as commonly experienced without abolishing itself. Ethics without some kind of metaphysical realism is, according to Spaemann, impossible. This is precisely what Spaemann insists on, as we have seen. To consider teletransportation and full-brain transplantation may be the task of a future ethics, but it will have to be undertaken by future people who have lived in forms that allow them to conceive of meaningful analogies to these experiences. The science-fiction

[86] 'Wozu der Aufwand?', in *Grenzen*, 409.

[87] For this view see Spaemann, *Happiness and Benevolence*, 138 (*Glück und Wohlwollen*, 181): 'Ethics is not an *ars longa*; ethics has to do with *vita brevis*'. See also in this context 'Wie praktisch ist die Ethik?', in *Grenzen*.

style of Derek Parfit's philosophy therefore illustrates how a culture built on hypothesis loses its capacity to engage in a practical form of moral reasoning. This criticism does not imply a general dismissal of hypothetical arguments. Counterfactual arguments can indeed illuminate ethical queries. One of the most fundamental imaginary arguments in ethics is the question of 'what I would do if I were you'. Parfit, however, does not draw on counter-factual arguments in order to clarify moral intuitions. His 'deep' counterfactual arguments are meant radically to subvert self-evident intuitions. He uses these arguments not so much to clarify as to legitimize the counter-intuitive character of his philosophy of personhood. There are therefore limits to basing an ontological and ethical argument on imaginary cases.[88] The most important limit is the self-evident gift of a person.

Parfit's philosophy is also reflective of the scientific dismissal of activity and moral agency, because if there is no such 'thing' as personal identity over time, the idea of moral agency loses its meaning. The nominalism of Parfit's philosophy—that is to say, the denial of universals and the idea of a constant flux of becoming—makes it simply impossible to identify both individual entities and individual actions.[89] Given Parfit's naturalistic idea of the person, the person is reduced to the passivity of a scientific object and, finally, eradicated. For on the basis of his assumptions one can no longer meaning-fully distinguish between human action and merely natural events and is thus incapable of 'discovering' persons. By contrast, Spaemann's criticism of the ontological implications of modern scientism implies a reassessment of the idea of moral agency in contrast to scientific knowledge, which, as he argues, only knows passivity.[90]

---

[88] See also W. V. Quine's critique of how Shoemaker criticizes Wiggins: 'the reasoning veers off in familiar fashion into speculations on what we might say in absurd situations of cloning and transplanting. The method of science fiction has its uses in philosophy, but at points in the Shoemaker-Wiggins exchange and elsewhere I wonder whether the limits of the method are properly heeded' (review of Milton K. Munitz (ed.), *Identity and Individuation*, in *Journal of Philosophy*, 69 (1972), 4901). See also Parfit, *Reasons and Persons*, 200, and Fuhrmann et al., 'Person'. One can also criticize Parfit's method from a Wittgensteinian point of view (see Wittgenstein, *Zettel*, ed. G. E. M. Anscombe and G. H. von Wright, trans. G. E. M. Anscombe (Oxford: Blackwell, 1967), 64e (§ 350), and also Parfit, *Reasons and Persons*, 200, and Fuhrmann et al., 'Person', 321). Wittgenstein writes: '"It is as if our concepts involved a scaffolding of facts." That would presumably mean: If you imagine certain facts otherwise, describe them otherwise than the way they are, then you can no longer imagine the application of certain concepts, because the rules for their application have no analogue in the new circumstances.'

[89] For Spaemann's view of individual actions and the implications of nominalism for a theory of action see 'Einzelhandlungen', in *Grenzen*, esp. 51 ff.

[90] 'Was ist das Neue?', 13.

5.4 LIFE, MOTION, POSSIBILITY, AND THE PARADIGM
OF THE PERSON

Nature, freedom, and life

Another important feature of Spaemann's ontology is that he recollects that
without an adequate notion of life the notion of the person cannot be
understood, nor can the modern dialectic of nature and spirit be overcome.
In what follows we will explore more closely the relation between 'person',
'nature', 'freedom', and 'life'. Nature, as we have argued, underlies freedom, in
Spaemann's view, and provides it with an 'unpreconceivable' measure. The
existence of a person does not precede his essence, as Jean-Paul Sartre
thought.[91] Things and animals 'are' their nature, but persons are preceded by
their nature and 'have' their nature in freedom.[92] Accordingly, Oliver O'Donovan speaks of the natural substrate as a presupposition for human freedom.[93]
Persons can therefore differentiate between their nature and themselves; they
can transcend themselves; they can overcome self-centredness; they can distinguish between inside and outside. Unlike animals, which cannot pass judgement on their own natural appetites and cannot choose whether to behave in
accord with them or not, the nature of persons is not identical to their being a
person. Difference belongs essentially to the world of the person.

In order to understand more fully how the person relates to his nature in
freedom, we have to consider the notion of life. Spaemann argues that
personal identity is a function of the identity of a *living* being.[94] So without
the notion of life, personal identity cannot be adequately conceived. However,
it has become increasingly difficult in modernity to understand the notion
'life'. The classical philosophical tradition, as Spaemann points out, presupposed the analogous unity of being and developed a threefold understanding
of being as lifeless, living, and thinking.[95] In contrast, post-Cartesian philosophy fails to conceptualize 'life', because its foundations are laid upon the
sharp ontological distinction between *res extensa* and *res cogitans*, so that it no

---

[91] Sartre developed this position most famously in his 'Existentialism Is a Humanism',
trans. Carol Macomber, ed. John Kulka, notes and preface Arlette Elkaim-Sartre, introd.
Annie Cohen-Solal (New Haven, Conn.: Yale University Press, 2007).
[92] For the difference between animals and human beings see also Spaemann, *Happiness and
Benevolence*, 180 (*Glück und Wohlwollen*, 231): 'The animal is not awakened to reality, to being.
It does not know the antagonism between being and non-being, only that of being as such and
such or being other'.
[93] *Begotten or Made*, 2nd edn. (Oxford: Clarendon, 1998), 5.
[94] *Persons*, 137 (*Personen*, 147).
[95] Ibid. 136 (146).

longer understands the fundamental analogy of Being, but rather perceives Being as dialectical. That is to say, material being, on the one hand, and thinking being, on the other, have been set in direct opposition to each other. This is why, despite the increasing success of the so-called life sciences, there is in modernity no longer an appropriate notion of life as the 'link' between mind and matter. The scientific 'life sciences' fail to understand fully what life is, presenting us with a reductionistic understanding of life as mechanism. The history of the destruction of the notion 'life', Spaemann argues, is the history of the destruction of the notion of the person as 'having one's nature in freedom'. Once body and mind are defined in opposition to one another— that is, once life has been interpreted as mechanistic system—there are inevitably different criteria for being a free person and belonging to the natural species 'human being'[96] such that it is no longer the case that all human beings are considered persons.

In order to examine more closely why modern sciences fail to understand what life is, and what the implications of this failure are, we will now turn to Spaemann's interpretation of John Locke's philosophy, and observe how the atomization of motion and the abolition of possibility are symptomatic of a nominalist and non-teleological philosophy of life which ultimately abolishes these notions altogether. In examining Locke's understanding of life, motion, and possibility we will keep in mind the difference between Locke's definition of the person and Boethius' definition of a person as a *naturae rationabilis individua substantia.*[97] Locke's definition of a 'person'—'a thinking intelligent Being, that has reason and reflection, and can consider itself as itself, the same thinking thing in different times and places; which it does only by that consciousness, which is inseparable from thinking, and as it seems to me essential to it: It being impossible for any one to perceive, without perceiving, that he does perceive'[98]—is reflective of the empiricist and mechanistic atomization of reality and, unlike Boethius' ontological definition, entails a flawed conceptualization not only of individual substances, but also of motion and possibility. Locke can no longer understand the unity and identity of the life of a person over time because he presupposes that mechanistic and systematic knowledge is the paradigm of all possible knowledge and that the self-identical actual atom— and not the human person, as in Spaemann's thought—is the paradigm of Being. The person is no longer an 'individual substance' the nature of which is rational, as Boethius thought, but actualized consciousness. Here, once again, Spaemann's

[96] *Persons*, 137 (147).
[97] *Contra Eutychen et Nestorium*, 3. 74.
[98] Locke, John, *An Essay Concerning Human Understanding*, 355 (II, 27, § 9). See also Hume, *A Treatise of Human Nature*, ed. L. A. Selby-Bigge, 331; and Hobbes, *Leviathan*, 111.

defence of the person-centred view leads him to criticize major presuppositions of modern philosophy and to lay bare their hidden axiomatic structure.

John Locke's atomization of motion

Spaemann argues that Locke,[99] like several other modern philosophers, failed, despite his best efforts, to understand motion scientifically, and that the atomization of motion in Locke's philosophy leads to an atomization of life and thought. Locke failed because there is, as Spaemann argues, 'in the strict sense no scientific knowledge about what is moved. This [i.e. scientific knowledge] can only refer to [timeless] identical structures'.[100] The primary thrust of Spaemann's criticism is that despite his interest in a precise under-standing of motion Locke cannot conceive of an identity that transcends time—which is, of course, required if motion is to be understood. For, the underlying empiricist principle of Locke's philosophy does not allow for a conception of identity as the overarching unity which embraces a motion; rather, it leads Locke to accept only atomistic sense experiences as ontolog-ically original. In this view, any kind of synthesis appears as a mere a poster-iori construction of the viewer. Accordingly, Locke conceptualizes motion by means of infinitesimal mathematics; that is to say, he conceives of motion not as motion but as a succession of infinitely short distinct events. Yet Aristotle and Leibniz,[101] Spaemann points out, already argued that motion cannot be explained with reference to mathematics but only (in a non-scientific way) with reference to human action, its intentionality—that is to say, by analogy with human experience. To conceptualize motion, Spaemann reasons, one needs teleological notions such as 'anticipation' and 'possibility'. From a purely impersonal point of view, motion, analysable only as a succession of distinct events, cannot be understood as motion proper.

---

[99] In this and the following section, we shall mainly focus on Spaemann's reading of Locke as emblematic of an important tendency of modern epistemology and ontology to dismiss the classical teleological understanding of motion, and refrain from a detailed examination of Spaemann's interpretation with regard to Locke's philosophy, its context, and its adoption. For Locke's criticism of the Aristotelian and Thomistic understanding of motion see Locke, John, *An Essay Concerning Human Understanding*, 422f. (III, IV, § 8f.); for his discussion of slow and fast motion, see *An Essay Concerning Human Understanding*, 184f. (II, XIV, § 7ff.).

[100] Spaemann, *Die Frage 'Wozu?'*, 34.

[101] Spaemann, *Persons*, 139 (*Personen*, 149); Spaemann refers to Aristotle, *Physics* 201a11-12, but very generally to Leibniz. Spaemann may have thought of Leibniz's early *Theoria motus abstracti*. For a discussion of Leibniz's view of motion see Mercer, Christia, *Leibniz's Metaphysics. Its Origins and Development* (Cambridge University Press, 2001). For Spaemann's more detailed interpretation of Leibniz's philosophy, see 'Leibniz' Begriff der möglichen Welten'.

According to Spaemann, Locke attributes a merely epistemological and pragmatic value to the concept 'motion' and thus also to the idea of an identity over time. According to his view, Spaemann points out, only atoms are really identical. They are immobile in themselves, do not change, and are absolutely simple. On this basis it is obvious that Locke's view of motion ultimately atomizes the identity of one continuous motion into a succession of changeless and absolutely simple atoms. Hence, life as *Aus-sein-auf* ('striving after') can no longer be understood, either. The intentionality of living beings (that is, their teleology and movement) is reduced to elementary physics.

John Locke's abolition of possibility

The dismissal of personal being as the paradigm for our understanding of reality has a second aspect, which lies in the abolition of 'possibility', a turn closely related to the modern attempt, which we have just described with reference to Locke, to make motion scientifically predictable by dissolving it into a chain of successive events. The modern scientific concept of motion, Spaemann argues, makes 'the notion of possibility . . . dispensable because it is only an infinite succession of *real* statistical states'.[102] Because there is no longer natural motion and thus no intentional structures or 'anticipation' in nature, whatever is left can only be actual. In Locke's definition, we recall, a person is an actualized consciousness, not a member of a species the ordinary and adult members of which *normally* have consciousness and self-consciousness.[103] Therefore, actualized self-consciousness and memory constitute personal identity. According to this logic, Spaemann argues, 'possibility' loses its significance, for persons are simply chains of distinct events of the memorizing consciousness, but not human beings whose typical traits may either be actualized or still be potentials. This is why, for Parfit's Lockean position, difference in degree in the actualization of personal traits determines the degree of someone's or something's being a person. So Locke and Parfit both reject the view that the reason that it is possible to actualize certain potential traits lies in the fact that someone *is* actually already a person.

In contrast to Locke and Parfit (whose thought, as we have seen, also entails a dismissal of possibility properly conceived), Spaemann reasons that the person is the paradigm for the understanding of possibility and that being a

---

[102] *Die Frage 'Wozu?'*, 115.
[103] See also Spaemann, *Persons*, 140 (*Personen*, 150).

person does not mean to be a potential or actual person (in which case being a person would depend upon being accepted, or recognized, by other persons according to certain criteria) but to have actual or potential characteristics. The person, he points out, makes the experience of possibility possible and not the other way around. Even if there were such a thing as 'potential persons', as Parfit thinks, one would need to maintain that 'person' is a fundamental notion in order properly to understand possibility or potentiality. For otherwise there would only be what actually is the case; this, however, cannot be thought without self-contradiction. Whoever thinks that all that is, is what is actually the case—that is to say, whoever utterly dismisses a teleological view of reality—contradicts himself, for he himself, as a person, is always more than what is actually the case, and this is evident even given the very fact that he is making a counter-intuitive statement. The complete dismissal of a teleological view of reality and of possibility would thus lead to, and presuppose, the abolition of humanity. This leads us to turn our attention back to Parfit's philosophy and to examine further the ontologically fundamental character of the person.

5.5 THE ONTOLOGY OF IDENTITY AND THE LOGICAL INDISPENSABILITY OF THE PERSON

It is, from a point of view such as Spaemann's, a grave defect in Parfit's argument that he does not reflect upon the epistemological, ontological, and ethical infeasibility of an entirely impersonal point of view. Spaemann has frequently pointed out that our appreciation of reality can only be by way of analogy to the experience of the person. Spaemann's person-centred realism, therefore, shows a contradiction within Parfit's thought; for unless 'person' is treated as a fundamental notion one can understand neither 'causality' nor 'system', as we have already argued (in Ch. 3), nor, for instance, 'identity', which is crucially important for Parfit's thought. In this section we will demonstrate that one cannot develop an impersonal concept of identity but that, on the contrary, to employ the notion in a more than merely formal sense presupposes that there is indeed personal identity over time.

First distinguishing qualitative and numerical identity,[104] Parfit minimizes the significance of this difference, as we see in the following statement, because he makes one kind of identity a species of another—numerical identity is

---

[104] *Reasons and Persons*, 201.

understood as a special case of qualitative identity: 'If certain things happen to me, the truth might not be that I become a very different person. The truth might be that I cease to exist—that the resulting person is someone else'.[105] To be the *same* person is, for Parfit, an extreme instance of being of the *same kind*. Yet to speak of qualitative and numerical identity requires criteria, which cannot be established objectively but need to be experienced by the person. That is to say, from an 'impersonal' point of view such as Parfit's one cannot speak of identity, other than perhaps of merely formal, or logical, identity. From an entirely impersonal point of view, based upon sensory experience, it is not possible to speak of the identity of a thing but only of different degrees of the similarity of things. For it is by analogy to our own experience as persons—not, strictly speaking, by way of 'scientific' experience—that we suppose that the tree we saw in the garden before we fell asleep is the same as the tree we see after we have woken up. It is not even possible to distinguish between different things such as different trees if we do not presuppose personal identity. In the context of his discussion of Hegel's view of teleology Spaemann points out that in a world of pure objectivity there is no negativity. It is 'the world of differenceless (*differenzlose*) identity'.[106] In other words, the objectifying world-view characterized by the modern sciences cannot capture the distinction between identity and difference because 'negativity, the consciousness of possible difference, belongs to the definition of identity'.[107] Given modern objectivism, everything becomes identical and part of a single universal substance. Identity thus signifies, at the very most, the sum total of observable things.

According to Spaemann, it is indeed possible to speak of identity and difference, because we do not in fact limit ourselves to a strictly scientific methodology, even in the sciences. We experience ourselves as identical with ourselves over time even though we are not conscious of ourselves all the time, and we also experience negativity—for instance, the experience that we are different from what is outside ourselves. We presuppose then *per analogiam* that the tree in the garden which we see now is identical with the tree we saw yesterday and that it really exists. 'The idea of there being something', Spaemann argues, 'is inseparable from the idea of the identity of that thing. And precisely this thought is a fundamental anthropomorphic idea.'[108] The identity and existence of some given entity is, therefore, not something that we can scientifically demonstrate. If we were as keen on imaginary worlds as Derek Parfit, we could (in an atheist transformation of George Berkeley's

[105] Ibid. 202.
[106] *Die Frage 'Wozu?'*, 166.
[107] *Die Frage 'Wozu?'*, 251.
[108] Spaemann, 'Wirklichkeit als Anthropomorphismus', 24.

idealism) even think of a universe the parts of which are constantly reorga-
nized and reassembled in dependency upon the actual experience of them. We
could also conceive of a universe in which there is no continuous time,
but only distinctly different instants without relation or connection to one
another. Our experience of time's continuity could simply be caused by the
human incapacity to notice the successive instants that make up what seems
to be a continuous stream. But what can assure us that reality is not, in the
end, a chain of unconnected events, if not our awareness that we ourselves
are not such a chain? Only because there is personal identity, that is to say
the person's experience of negativity and difference, can we speak of the
'impersonal identity' and existence of a tree, for instance. 'For identity
presupposes difference. It is a self-relation. In a world of pure factual
being, however, there is no "self"'.[109] Because we, as persons, experience
ourselves as both different and identical, process alone cannot be the truth
of Being. Spaemann therefore points out that for impersonal entities such as
computers there is not really a difference between inside and outside; they
do not stand in the tension between self-transcendence and self-centeredness.
This difference only exists if it is translated into an inner and experienced
difference[110]—by the person.

Identity, therefore, cannot be understood from a purely impersonal point
of view. Human beings, Spaemann consequently argues, cannot take such a
purely impersonal point of view. He illustrates this not only with respect to
the notion 'identity', but also with respect to the notions 'here' and 'now'. The
indexical notions 'here' and 'now' cannot be understood without a personal
point of view. It is only because there are persons, as Spaemann's argument
goes, that space ('here') and time ('now') are identifiable.[111] If there were no
persons, there would be no point of reference for notions such as 'here' and
'now'. The homogenization of time and space as interpreted by the modern
sciences is thus intrinsically tied to their impersonal methodologies, rather
than to how reality discloses itself to us.

There is yet another notion which cannot be understood without the
fundamental experience of persons. According to Spaemann's interpretation,
the phenomenal basis of the notion of contingency is also personal experience.[112] Contingency, he states, is rooted in the distinction between essence
and existence as experienced by the person. Because there is a difference
between what a person *actually* is and what a person *essentially* is, between

[109] *Die Frage 'Wozu'?*, 166.
[110] *Persons*, 44 (*Personen*, 52–3).
[111] Ibid. 164 (175).
[112] Ibid. 29 ff. (38 ff.) and 81 ff. (71 ff.).

the free having of one's nature-existence and nature-essence, persons experience contingency. A person could somehow also be a different person or not exist at all. He can consciously and freely relate to what and who he is. Unlike animals, the person knows of, and experiences, the contingency of his existence. This means that from an impersonal point of view (such as a modern scientific view) contingency, and thus reality, cannot be understood. The empiricism of an impersonal philosophy (we have already discussed this with respect to Derek Parfit's philosophy) that is deeply indebted to the methodological maxims of modern sciences thus turns into an unrealistic idealism which has a priori determined what reality ultimately is.

Parfit's argument thus proves to be fundamentally flawed because it undermines both the very premises upon which it is built and fundamental human experience. Parfit derives personal identity from formal, or logical, that is to say 'impersonal', identity and not, as he ought to have done (and cannot help doing), vice versa. Parfit's focus upon 'impersonal' logical identity is also one of the reasons why the temporal character of identity plays only a minor role in his thought; for formal, or logical, identity is based upon an abstraction from time and thus from human agency and freedom. While an abstraction from time can be epistemologically defensible in certain contexts, this undertaking is not defensible and undermines itself once one starts to apply to persons the results of a train of thought based upon time-objectifying, or time-neglecting, premises. Personal identity, as Spaemann emphasizes, lies in the temporal self-realization of the life of a person. To neglect the temporal dimension of personhood is, like any solipsistic approach to the notion of the person, infeasible. 'To be a person', Spaemann states, 'is the form in which "rational natures" exist'.[113] 'Existence', though, here does not simply mean that a person is observably there as if he was merely a member of a species. It means that a person's nature is something that a person freely relates to. This is not a static structure, but a dynamic and temporal relation. For the person strives for something beyond himself, because, as a finite being, he 'is fundamentally defined through lack of Being. Its existence is therefore *Sorge* [anxiety]', Spaemann says with reference to Heidegger; it is 'desire for Being'— desire for reality.[114] So when Parfit wonders what the nature of a person is, and seeks for certain characteristic features which make up the nature of a person,[115] he overlooks that 'person' is not the name of a class of beings that have acquired, or are characterized by, certain qualitative traits. Being a person means to have one's very own nature in desire for Being; the actual

---

[113] *Persons*, 31 (40).
[114] Spaemann, *Die Frage 'Wozu?'*, 37.
[115] *Reasons and Persons*, 202.

non-actualization of certain characteristic traits, therefore, does not say anything about the being of a person. Therefore, Spaemann considers it one of the most significant shortcomings of Derek Parfit's solipsistic position that it makes being a person dependent upon the acquisition of characteristic traits, contrary to normal intuition. Persons need to be recognized in freedom by other persons, Spaemann thinks, and this is why he also criticizes Parfit that he, like his predecessors, dismisses the 'I–Thou relation between persons as the intrinsic place of the discovery of the person'.[116] Thus, against the tendency to dismiss a person-centred understanding of reality, Spaemann defends a non-reductive and truly empirical position in that he rehabilitates our everyday experience of life, time, space, freedom, motion, possibility, and contingency and its basis in the self-evident self-experience of the person. This shows that 'person' is indeed a fundamental notion which cannot be abolished without implying major shifts in our understanding of reality.

5.6 WHO IS A PERSON?

The main thrust of Spaemann's *Persons* is not only to show why the concept of person is fundamental for all thought, but also to demonstrate why every human being is a person, as opposed to a mere subset of human beings: characterized by features such as self-consciousness and memory. In what follows we will first examine what, in Spaemann's view, is characteristic of persons. We will then investigate the reasons why, for Spaemann, every human being is a person, and discuss whether or not Spaemann's argument is based upon speciesistic premises.

The inner difference of persons

Human beings, Spaemann suggests, are not just members of their species as 'something' is a specimen of a particular species; they are persons who do not immediately instantiate a species. There is, Spaemann suggests, an 'inner difference' that characterizes persons. Spaemann illustrates this 'inner difference' with three examples.

He first draws attention to the fact that we use the word 'human' as a normative as well as a descriptive term. 'Human' is not simply everything that belongs to human beings. There are certain actions, for instance torture,

---

[116] 'Sind alle Menschen Personen?', in *Grenzen*, 422.

violence, and murder, that are called 'inhuman' despite their being quite typical of human beings. Animals do not torture and murder one another. Hence, Spaemann argues, there is a difference between what humans are actually like and who they ought to be.[117]

In the second example Spaemann analyses the first-person pronoun 'I'. To say 'I', he argues, does not rely on qualitative characteristics (nor on time–space coordinates), for it merely expresses numerical identity. We can, at least theoretically, distinguish between a person and his qualitative appearance and manifestation. Spaemann mentions, for example, fairy tales, Ovid's *Metamorphosis*, and our own dream experience to provide illustrations of this.[118] We can somehow imagine (without subjecting being a person to science-fiction criteria!) what it means to be a tree or to live in another persons' body, for instance. There is, Spaemann points out, a difference between *who* we are and *what* we are.[119]

In the third example Spaemann investigates the fact of intentional structures and teleology. This example is by far the most important. Life, he maintains, is characterized by a teleological structure. It is characterized by the tension between the potential and the factual existence of living beings (*Lebewesen*), or, as Aristotle says, by the tension between *eu zen* and *zen*.[120] Human beings are aware of this tension. They know that the ultimate goal of their life is not their survival, the mere preservation of life, but the good life.[121] Thus, the teleology of human life shows that human beings are 'more', so to speak, than mere instantiations of their species; they not simply 'are' their nature, they 'have' their nature. To speak of persons, Spaemann argues, thus recalls a view of the individual that calls into question the opposition of nature and freedom, of facts and norms, and of self-preservation and self-transcendence.

The inner difference that is characteristic of persons shows that persons are not persons because of certain qualitative characteristics. Unlike 'human being', 'person' is not, Spaemann stresses, a generic term. It already presupposes the identification of a given being as, for instance, a human being. Because of the qualitative traits of human beings, Spaemann points out, one is

---

[117] Ibid. 8 (16).
[118] Ibid. 10 (18).
[119] Ibid. 11 (19).
[120] This is the key idea of Aristotle's *Nichomachean Ethics*.
[121] See Benedict de Spinoza, *Ethics*, trans. W. Hale White, rev. trans. Amelia Hutchison Stirling (Oxford: Oxford University Press, 1937), 195. See also Hobbes's definition of the right of nature (*jus naturale*) in *Leviathan*, 91, and Dieter Henrich, 'Die Grundstruktur der modernen Philosophie', in his *Selbstverhältnisse: Gedanken und Auslegungen zu den Grundlagen der klassischen deutschen Philosophie* (Stuttgart: Reclam, 1993), 83–108 and 'Über Selbstbewußtsein und Selbsterhaltung: Probleme und Nachträge zum Vortrag über die "Grundstruktur der modernen Philosophie"', in *Selbstverhältnisse*, 109–30.

able to perform an abstraction and thus to speak of numerical personal identity. But a person is not a person because of these traits, for 'to reduce the person to specific actual conditions of self-consciousness and rationality ultimately dissolves the notion of something like a person'.[122] This is why Spaemann refers approvingly to David Wiggins's non-speciesistic and non-empiricist definition of 'person': '[A] person is any animal the physical make-up of whose species constitutes the species' typical members' thinking intelligent being, with reason and reflection, and typically enables them to consider themselves the same thinking things, in different times and places'.[123] A philosophy of personhood therefore challenges the objectifying tendency of the sciences and recalls a different, though more fundamental, epistemology. '"Person" is not', Oliver O'Donovan has argued, 'a genetic or a biological category; to observe a gene is not to observe a person... It remains for another mode of knowledge to discern the hypostasis behind the appearance'.[124] We now have to ask why members of a particular species who, for instance, are not consciously aware of the inner difference of persons are also persons.

Why each human being is a person

In *Persons* Spaemann offers six reasons why every human being is a person and why being a person cannot be defined with reference to certain criteria, but only with reference to what he calls primary recognition through other persons. These six reasons belong very closely together and, taken together, make a very strong case for the view that all human beings are persons. Spaemann refers, first, to the ethical fact that each human being belongs to a community of other human beings that is always already a community of persons. Second, there is, as he argues, no logical transition from 'something' to 'somebody'. 'Somebody', he suggests, is not a subcategory of 'something' and is never transformed into something. The gulf between impersonal entities and persons, therefore, cannot be bridged, because there is no continuity from 'something' to 'somebody'. Only because we treat other human beings from the very beginning not as 'something' but as 'somebody', so Spaemann reminds us, do most of them actualize the features which justify a posteriori our treatment and recognition of them as persons.[125] And the

---

[122] 'Sind alle Menschen Personen?', 111.

[123] David Wiggins, *Sameness and Substance* (Oxford: Blackwell, 1980), 188; see also Spaemann, *Persons*, 247 (*Personen*, 264; in the German original, Spaemann refers here to Wiggins's book and cites his definition of the person).

[124] *Begotten or Made?*, 57.

[125] *Persons*, 240–1 (*Personen* 258).

reason why we treat them as persons is that they already belong to a community of persons.

Third, Spaemann argues that the lack of intentionality is difficult to detect, important though it is for the full understanding of personal being. It is not simply an observable characteristic but an intrinsically personal performance, which links the inner and the outer dimensions of a person and makes it possible for persons to transcend themselves.[126] It would thus be impossible to argue without error that somebody is in fact something.

Fourth, recognition is not the scientific observation of certain characteristic traits, but the recognition of the *Selbstsein* of persons. '*Selbstsein*', Spaemann argues, 'essentially cannot be found in the language of the sciences'.[127] The free recognition of someone does not constitute but rather acknowledges personal identity, as something that is already given. Persons, Spaemann argues, need to be recognized, but they do not need to be recognized to be a person. 'To know a person', as Oliver O'Donovan has put it, 'I have first to accept him as such in personal interaction'.[128] That we are capable of recognizing persons—that is to say, of transcending ourselves—is 'the nucleus of what we call human dignity', Spaemann argues.[129] Thus, one's dignity can ultimately only be 'questioned' by oneself—by not freely recognizing another person as person.

Fifth, there are, as Spaemann points out, no potential persons. Because it does not depend upon certain criteria whether someone is a person or not, and because there is no transition from things to persons, there are no potential persons 'who' could, or could not, develop these criteria. Persons have certain potentials that they may or may not be be able actually to develop, but persons themselves 'are always persons or they never become persons'.[130] It is important to note that this position is more consistent than Derek Parfit's. Parfit, in defining the notion 'person' through qualitative criteria, thus speaking of personhood as potential or alternately developing and ceasing while still seeking to maintain a kind of moral understanding of the person, falls into a biologistic position and commits a naturalistic fallacy—although this is precisely what he intends to reject. This nicely illustrates the dilemma of the post-Lockean definition of person. Either the normative character of 'person' is inevitably dismissed and 'person' simply stands for a species or class defined by having, or not having, certain traits; or

---

[126] Ibid. 48–61 (57–70).
[127] 'Was ist das Neue?', 14.
[128] *Begotten or Made?*, 60.
[129] *Die Frage 'Wozu?'*, 294.
[130] 'Es gibt kein gutes Töten', in *Grenzen*, 436.

'person' remains a normative notion, though at the cost of an illegitimate naturalistic fallacy. However, to argue that each human being is a person does not necessarily entail a naturalistic fallacy, because this assertion can rely on a different ontology altogether. Because the 'person', according to Spaemann, is a *modus existentiae*, and not the subject of certain actualized traits, the definition of 'person' does not depend on whether these traits are potential or actualized, because the 'having' of a nature, that is to say the being a person, cannot be potential or actual. Persons relate to their nature both in its potentialities and in its actualized potentialities.

Sixth, Spaemann argues that the recognition of a person is an answer to an unconditional demand. Because there are no potential persons, recognition cannot be dependent upon the actualization of these potentials. Hence, recognition is not a question of co-optation, of a majority decision or of a scientific definition for instance, but an answer to a demand that is always already there. To argue that whether someone is a person or not and, therefore, 'has' human dignity is dependent upon the decision of the current members of the human society is, in Spaemann's eyes, reflective of a 'totalitarian misconception of society'[131] and undermines the idea of universal human rights,[132] because they would lose their universality if they depended on certain prejudgements about which human being can be considered a person or not. The origin of being a person, Spaemann consequently reasons, is a 'mystery' and 'unpreconceivable'[133]; it is not dependent on acceptance by other persons and cannot fully be explained or examined.

The supposed speciesism of Spaemann's philosophy

A common criticism of the understanding of the person as proposed by Spaemann brings up the charge of a speciesism (and therefore biologism) with which we have already implicitly dealt. In what follows we will investigate why Spaemann's philosophy is not only *not* speciesist but calls into question the very premises of this accusation. Before we discuss the question of whether Spaemann's argument is speciesist we need to investigate why

---

[131] 'Verantwortung für die Ungeborenen, in *Grenzen*, 382.
[132] 'Technische Eingriffe in die Natur als Problem der politischen Ethik, in *Grenzen*, 454. For the relation between human rights and human dignity see also Robert Spaemann and Ernst-Wolfgang Böckenförde (eds.), *Menschenrechte und Menschenwürde: Historische Voraussetzungen—säkulare Gestalt—christliches Verständnis* (Stuttgart: Klett-Cotta, 1987).
[133] For the "unpreconceivable" character of the person's origin, see Spaemann, 'Kommentar', in Instruktion der Kongregation für die Glaubenslehre, *Die Unantastbarkeit des menschlichen Lebens. Zu ethischen Fragen der Biomedizin*, 87.

speciesism is, for many philosophers, a position to be rejected. By showing that the anti-speciesist argument depends upon presuppositions that Spaemann does not share, one can easily demonstrate why Spaemann is not a speciesist, but is able to mount an even more radical critique of speciesism than his critics.

The main reason why speciesism ought to be avoided, as many modern philosophers argue, is that it is based upon a naturalistic fallacy. *Factual* reality, such as belonging to a particular biological species, does not justify *normative* conclusions, for the gulf between what is the case and what ought to be the case appears to be logically unbridgeable.[134] To be a member of a particular biological species does not per se justify a treatment different from the treatment that members of other species deserve. Peter Singer argues as follows:

> The only position that is irredeemably speciesist is the one that tries to make the boundary of the right to life run exactly parallel to the boundary of our own species. To avoid speciesism we must allow that beings who are similar in all relevant respects have a similar right to live—and mere membership in our own biological species cannot be a morally relevant criterion for this right.[135]

In order to avoid speciecism, Peter Singer's pathocentric ethics focuses on suffering in general, be it animal or human suffering, rather than on *each* human being as a person (and thus as deserving a right to life) qua human being.[136]

It is important to note that the accusation of speciesism, or alternatively anthropocentrism, is based upon significant presuppositions, including not only the definition of 'all relevant respects' but also an empiricist and non-teleological understanding of reality. If there were indeed a gap between nature and freedom, it would indeed be illegitimate—and possibly also speciesist—to derive normative conclusions from factual statements. The modern dismissal of a teleological view of reality precludes the natural species to which an animal belongs from serving as the basis for any normative statement. However, if there is indeed a natural teleology, if reality is ultimately not dichotomized into 'is' and 'ought', if meaning and Being, freedom and nature, are ultimately inseparable, then the accusation of speciesism does not pertain per se, because nature and freedom are not necessarily in opposition. The being of a human being is then 'more than', or different from, 'mere

---

[134] See Hume, *A Treatise of Human Nature*, ed. L. A. Selby-Bigge, 455–70 (III. I. I), esp. 469–70; see also e.g. G. E. Moore, *Principia Ethica* (Cambridge: Cambridge University Press, 1954), 17 ff.

[135] *Animal Liberation*, 2nd edn. (London: Thorsons, 1990), 18–19; see also 213 ff.

[136] *Animal Liberation*, 2nd edn. (London: Thorsons, 1990), 9 ff., 220, and *passim*.

being'. It is the paradigm of being on which every understanding of 'mere being' as a reductionist understanding of being is based—and not vice versa. There is, therefore, a certain kind of 'biologism', as Spaemann points out, which is 'in reality the condition of freedom'.[137] It is a 'biologism' which develops a full account of what human life as the life of a person is. This account would emphasize that being a person always already consists in having, and not simply being, one's nature (even though this may be difficult to detect at times), and that every approach to the person that does not do justice to this insight (including many truly speciesist accounts of the person or of human dignity), developed on the basis of a description of how the person has his nature, cannot but fail to understand the person and his dignity as always already given disclosure of the full meaning of being.

How does Spaemann further justify his assertion that being has a normative dimension that one must not overlook if one does not want to fall prey to the modern dialectic of nature and freedom? He not only retrieves a view of freedom as 'remembered nature',[138] as we have pointed out, but also argues that suffering and pain in particular indicate that there is no unbridgeable gulf between what is and what ought to be: 'The consideration of pain falsifies Hume's assertion that Is and Ought belong to two incommensurable realms, unless—that is—we deploy a strictly "positive" sense of "Is", meaning "in front of our noses", out there in the world of objects and waiting to be stumbled over, in which case pain and negativity no longer count among things that "are"'.[139] Suffering and pain do indeed exist, and yet they should *not* exist. Pain is not just a physiological status, but has a normative dimension. Hence, the factual *being* and the normative *ought (not) to* cannot be strictly separated, unless one interprets pain as by definition non-existing. This also shows that while Peter Singer claims to take pain seriously, he undermines the understanding of pain and its negativity that corresponds to human experience. For we experience pain not as nothing, but as something that exists, but ought *not* to exist. Hence, Spaemann's philosophy proves even more pathocentric, as it were, than Singer's because it allows us to take seriously pain as we experience it.[140]

This illustrates once again that the reductionistic and supposedly empirical scientism of Parfit's and Singer's philosophies makes it impossible to understand reality fully because their thought is based upon aprioristic

---

[137] 'Haben Ungeborene ein Recht auf Leben?', in *Grenzen*, 365.
[138] 'Die Aktualität des Naturrechts', in *Philosophische Essays*, 78.
[139] Spaemann, *Persons*, 46 (*Personen*, 55).
[140] For Spaemann's view of the Christian understanding of suffering see his 'Die christliche Sicht des Leidens', in *Das unsterbliche Gerücht*.

presuppositions that do not conform to reality as it discloses itself to us. They do not consider how reality fully appears to us: as meaningful *Selbstsein*, above all in the other person, and neither as simply objective being nor as mere process. The natural sciences cannot, therefore, provide the ultimate anwer to the question as to who a person is, for persons, in their very being, need to be recognized in freedom by another person.[141] This is why the philosophy of the person does not require a scientific methodology; it requires a 'not merely metaphorical nor poetical hermeneutics of nature'[142] which remembers the complementary relation between nature and freedom and appeals to our own freedom to recognize other human beings as persons. That is to say, one needs a philosophy of *Selbstsein* as the paradigm for our understanding of reality in order to understand more fully what it means to be a person and why all human beings are persons, whether they are self-conscious or not.

5.7 ROBERT SPAEMANN'S PHILOSOPHY OF *SELBSTSEIN*

Spaemann's philosophy, as we have seen, is not limited to a critique of the failures of modernity; he retrieves and justifies the notion of self-evident knowledge.[143] His philosophy thus brings to mind what the Greeks called *aidos*; this it to say, a fundamental awe, an unwillingness 'to cross the limits which have been set for human beings'.[144] In retrieving, or recollecting, a teleological view of nature as the 'unpreconceivable' presupposition, measure, and limit of free human action and in developing a philosophy of the human person Spaemann proposes an alternative to modernity that allows us to retain the important insights of modernity without falling prey to the dialectic of nature and freedom and the 'forgetfulness of persons'[145] (*Personvergessenheit*) that it imposes. In Spaemann's view, it is this oblivion of the person,

[141] For Spaemann's understanding of recognition see his *Persons*, 180–96 (*Personen*, 192–208).

[142] For this notion, see 'Über den Begriff einer Natur des Menschen', in *Essays zur Anthropologie*, 23.

[143] For this idea see *Persons*, 3 (*Personen*, 11).

[144] Spaemann, 'Einleitung', in *Grenzen*, 9; see in this context also *Happiness and Benevolence*, 125 (*Glück und Wohlwollen*, 165), where Spaemann argues that the utilitarian 'conception of morality allows no room for something which was characteristic of all hitherto existinc ethics, that which the Greeks calles *aidos*, shyness or shame, the feeling that humans have when there are boundaries set to their pursuit of goals'. For Spaemann's reference to *aidos* see also *Happiness and Benevolence*, 180 (*Glück und Wohlwollen*, 230).

[145] *Persons*, 97 (*Personen*, 106).

of *Selbstsein*, that is the problem of modern philosophy, rather than the Heideggerian *Seinsvergessenheit*—oblivion of Being in the sense of an abstract non-personal 'Being'.

In this and the following sections we will further consider Spaemann's philosophy of *Selbstsein* as the paradigm for understanding reality. This will entail an examination of his attempt to go beyond the dichotomy of Kantian duty and pre-modern virtue ethics, as well as a discussion of his philosophy of religion, which is intimately tied up with his philosophy of the person. Spaemann develops his philosophy of *Selbstsein* not only in *Persons*, but also in *Happiness and Benevolence*, which focuses on the 'precarious balance'[146] of human happiness and on the reality-disclosing dimension of benevolence. *Happiness and Benevolence* provides an outline of Spaemann's ethics oriented towards a 'syn-vision'—as opposed to dialectical synthesis—of what one will and what one ought to do; that is to say, of the search for one's happiness and the ideas of moral obligation. He wants to overcome the 'victory of "Fénelonism"'[147] that he sees in the moral rigorism of Kant's ethics; this position, he argues, fails to see the fundamental significance of benevolence because it presupposes an ontological and ethical paradigm that does not make it possible to conceptualize benevolence adequately. Within the limits of the present endeavour we cannot fully discuss the richness and complexity of the argument of *Happiness and Benevolence*, which ranges from an in-depth analysis of the antinomies of eudaimonistic ethics,[148] to profound interpretations of the relation between life and reason[149] and the *ordo amoris*,[150] and to substantial criticisms of naturalism, hedonism, and discourse ethics.[151] Nor can we fully discuss Spaemann's criticism of utilitarianism, or consequentialism,[152] and his understanding of responsibility and its limitations. We have to confine ourselves to an examination of the central argument about the gift of *Selbstsein* and the nature of benevolence.

Spaemann's philosophy of benevolence is preceded by an examination of happiness. This examination discloses the complex character of happiness.

---

[146] *Happiness and Benevolence*, 73 (*Glück und Wohlwollen*, 99).

[147] *Reflexion und Spontaneität*, 59; for a discussion about the differences and similarities between Kant and Fénelon see pp. 242 ff. For the relation between Fénelon and Kant see also Mary Bernard Curran, 'What Is Pure, What Is Good? Disinterestedness in Fénelon and Kant', in *Heythrop Journal*, 50 (2009), 195–205.

[148] *Happiness and Benevolence*, 61–9 (*Glück und Wohlwollen*, 85–95).

[149] Ibid. 82–91 (110–22).

[150] Ibid. 106–18 (141–56).

[151] Ibid. 131–42 (172–85).

[152] Ibid. 119–130 (157–71). For an overview of contemporary theories of consequentialism and their critics see also Samuel Scheffler (ed.), *Consequentialism and its Critics* (Oxford: Oxford University Press, 1988).

Happiness, Spaemann points out, is not the 'result of a poiesis . . . but a whole praxis'[153] because 'the *telos* of humanity is not some finite purpose, but the beautiful life as a whole'.[154] Happiness is, he further argues, a deeply ambiguous notion: one's subjective happiness is not necessarily objective happiness; one cannot even make a statement about one's own life as a whole. Moreover, the reflection upon happiness as *a life which turns out well* (*Gelingen des Lebens*[155]) fails to be sufficient for practical philosophy, Spaemann acknowledges. 'One does not enter into practical philosophy without reflection on one's own happiness, and with this reflection one goes no farther.'[156]

This is why one needs a more comprehensive horizon for ethical reflection than happiness or, alternatively, moral obligation. This conclusion leads us to his interpretation of the *amor benevolentiae* and its ethical and ontological implications. For it is within the universal horizon of reality opened up by benevolence that moral obligation and the search for happiness originate. Benevolence discloses reality in a way both prior to and more fundamental than either the insight into moral obligation or the search for happiness. It 'is a function neither of instinct nor of the drive to preserve the self or the species, since it is precisely these which it relativizes. It is as universal as the horizon which it opens'.[157] In the act of benevolence, therefore, a universal horizon opens up, and human beings lose their self-centredness and transcend themselves towards the reality of the other person. The benevolent experience of *Selbstsein*, Spaemann argues, is therefore an experience of reality which 'we cannot reduce to a functional interpretation'[158] by making it dependent on a horizon different from itself.

In his philosophy of benevolent love Spaemann is deeply indebted to Augustine and his theological understanding of benevolence, which Oliver O'Donovan has summarized as follows. Benevolence (*benevolentia*) is

the will that something which has its existence from God should fulfil its existence for God. Benevolent love is a possibility only between creature and creature, for God has no fulfilment to which he strives . . . [I]t is . . . a feature of *all* relations of love between man and man. It is not one kind of human love but a partial analysis of the whole of human love.[159]

[153] *Happiness and Benevolence*, 24 (*Glück und Wohlwollen*, 40; my own trans).
[154] *Die Frage 'Wozu?'*, 46.
[155] *Happiness and Benevolence*, 39 (*Glück und Wohlwollen*, 59).
[156] This is Jeremiah Alberg's translation of *Gelingen des Lebens* (in Spaemann, *Happiness and Benevolence*, 8 and *passim*; *Glück und Wohlwollen*, 21 and *passim*).
[157] Ibid. 106 (*Glück und Wohlwollen*, 141; trans. modified).
[158] 'Die Existenz des Priesters: Eine Provokation in der modernen Welt', in *Communio*, 9 (1980), 490.
[159] O'Donovan, Oliver, *The Problem of Self-Love in St. Augustine* (New Haven and London: Yale University Press, 1980), 33f.

This interpretation of Augustine's understanding of benevolence captures well what Spaemann means by the word—apart, perhaps, from Spaemann's wider ontological understanding of benevolence; that is, his idea that we ought to be benevolent also to, for instance, animals and things and so respect their *Selbstsein*.[160]

If *Selbstsein* fully discloses itself when we encounter the person with a benevolent disposition, a philosophy of benevolence is necessary that is characterized by 'attention', by gratefulness for the gift of reality and its glory. In developing this much-needed philosophy Spaemann discloses a dimension of the life of persons that not only calls into question modern functionalist ontologies but also goes beyond the dichotomy of ethics and ontology—not, however, because his philosophy has an anti-ethical and anti-ontological thrust. Rather, he provides the outline of an 'existential Reason'[161] which underlies, or precedes, both theoretical and practical Reason as distinctly different faculties.[162] In so doing, Spaemann also remembers a love that precedes the difference between self-love and selfless love and, if properly understood, makes a new 'synthesis' of these two kinds of love possible, a 'synthesis' that was impossible within the framework of an inversion of teleology.[163]

It is important here to note that Spaemann's ethics is directed against a dominant strand of contemporary philosophy for which Being has become problematic, with the result that ontology has been kept strictly separate from ethics. Emmanuel Levinas, for instance, developed an 'ethics beyond Being', many of the basic ideas of which Spaemann shares.[164] Yet Spaemann criticizes

---

[160] Spaemann's view is (unsurprisingly) also different from David Hume's utilitarian view of benevolence as the chief 'social virtue', although Hume (unlike Hobbes and Locke) sees not only the categorical difference between self-love and benevolence (as does Spaemann), but also a close connection between benevolence and happiness: 'a part, at least, of its [i.e. benevolence's] merit arises from its tendency to promote the interests of our species, and bestow happiness on human society' (*An Enquiry Concerning the Principles of Morals*, ed. L. A. Selby-Bigge, 181). It also differs from Kant's categorical imperative; for this difference see Spaemann, *Happiness and Benevolence*, 177 (*Glück und Wohlwollen*, 1227): 'Kant's statement: "Act so that you never use the humanity in your person or in the person of another merely as a means, but rather always at the same time as an end" needs to be expanded: Nothing real ought to be reduced to the status of mere means for an individual goal, whose being is not already of itself merged in such a function'.

[161] Spaemann, *Happiness and Benevolence*, 187 (*Glück und Wohlwollen*, 239).

[162] Ibid. ix (11). According to Spaemann, ethics and ontology are originally one in the conscience (*Happiness and Benevolence*, 149 (*Glück und Wohlwollen*, 194)).

[163] According to Spaemann, we find such a 'synthesis' (not in the sense of Hegelian dialectic, of course) in Thomas's understanding of love. (See *Reflexion und Spontaneität*, 88–106 for Spaemann's discussion of Thomas's view of the *amor perfectus* in comparison to modern theories of love that are based on the inversion of teleology.)

[164] See *Autrement qu'être ou au-delà de l'essence* (Paris: Librairie Générale Française, 1990) for Levinas's move 'beyond' Being. See *Persons*, 126–7 (*Personen*, 136) for Spaemanns own view

the supposition that the epiphany of the 'other' comes from 'beyond Being';
for 'Levinas understands "being" in a modern sense as objectification'.[165] In
contrast to Levinas, Spaemann retrieves what he considers a more fundamental notion of Being, one which goes beyond the distinction between the
subjective and the objective and so overcomes the modern dialectic of spirit
and nature. This implies neither that there is no clear difference between
ontology and ethics nor that there is a hierarchical relation between them.
'There is', Spaemann states, 'no ethics without metaphysics, but ethics no
more precedes ontology, understood as "first philosophy", than the latter does
the former'. Spaemann further argues that '[o]ntology and ethics—the one as
much as the other—are constituted *uno actu* through the intuition of being as
Selbstsein'.[166] One of the most fundamental arguments Spaemann proposes
for the connection between ethics and ontology is the fact that we need to
conceive the other as real, as a 'thing-in-itself', not as an image of ourselves or
as a fiction, in order to have the experience of obligation towards the other.[167]
To describe the encounter with the human person requires, therefore, a realist
philosophy; for '[u]nconditional respect for the human', Spaemann argues, 'is
equivalent to affirmation of reality'.[168]

But what precisely does he mean by *Selbstsein*? This notion is of relatively
recent origin. It is characteristic particularly of Martin Heidegger and
Karl Jaspers;[169] the idea is also crucial to Kierkegaard's thought, though
he does not use the actual word.[170] The question of how to translate
Selbstsein appropriately in English is debatable. For Heidegger the rendering

of his relation to Levinas; and see 'Sind alle Menschen Personen', in *Grenzen*, 417 for another
explicit reference to Levinas. See Richard Schenk, OP, 'The Ethics of Robert Spaemann in the
Context of Recent Philosophy' for an important observation about the difference between
Spaemann's and Jonas's philosophies which has a bearing on Spaemann's reading of Levinas
(in Brian J. Shanley, OP (ed.), *One Hundred Years of Philosophy* (Studies in Philosophy and the
History of Philosophy, xxxvi) (Washington, DC: The Catholic University of America Press,
2001), 166–7).

[165] *Happiness and Benevolence*, ix (*Glück und Wohlwollen*, 11); for Spaemann's interpretation
of Levinas and the alternative that he proposes see also *Reflexion und Spontaneität*, 13–14.
According to Spaemann, Levinas, like Fénelon, presupposes the 'paradigm of self-preservation'
precisely by radically opposing it, but does not attempt to go beyond it. Such an attempt,
however, lies at the very heart not only of Spaemann's moral philosophy but of his whole
philosophy.

[166] *Happiness and Benevolence*, ix (*Glück und Wohlwollen*, 11). Spaemann seems to use
'ontology' and 'metaphysics' synonymously.

[167] *Happiness and Benevolence*, 113 (*Glück und Wohlwollen*, 150).

[168] Ibid. 103 (137).

[169] See e.g. Jaspers, *Philosophie* (Berlin: Springer, 1948), 333 ff.

[170] For the notion 'Selbstsein' see esp. Anton Hügli, 'Selbstsein', in Ritter and Grüner (eds.),
Historisches Wörterbuch der Philosophie, ix. 520–8.

'Being-one's-Self' is appropriate,[171] though not absolutely transparent. Spaemann, however, is far from using this word merely in an existentialist or Heideggerian sense. *Selbstsein* does not imply that the Being of the self is a temporal process beyond substance and nature.[172] It is the Being *of the person*, that is to say the dynamic having-of-one's-nature, not *Bei-sich-sein*. It cannot be derived from the conditions of its genesis precisely because it opens up a completely new horizon: the horizon of freedom. But it also cannot be understood without proper regard for its natural dimension.

This implies a certain anti-subjectivist thrust in Spaemann's thought, although he does not at all discount the importance of the subject. He endeavours, on the contrary, as we have already seen, to preserve the subject against any functionalistic and naturalistic dismissal because the current crisis of humanity is reflective of a 'profound crisis of the autonomous subject'.[173] In Spaemann's view, the problem lies not in the notion of the subject as such, but in the abstract idea of an absolutely autonomous and free subject that no longer recognizes the frontiers of nature as showing a 'basal normality'.[174] Aristotle's teleological view of nature, Spaemann argues, 'found its orientation in our everyday talk about nature' and in 'an unprejudiced eye for the natural phenomenon'.[175] In a similar way, as we have discussed, Spaemann considers his philosophy of *Selbstsein* to be a defence of an everyday understanding of reality and of freedom and the natural in particular, obscured in modernity by the totalitarian claims of scientific reductionism and different kinds of anti-humanism and, closely related to this, by the dichotomization of nature and freedom. Spaemann claims hereby to retrieve an Aristotelian understanding of substance, for the 'paradigm of substance for Aristotle is the living being, and the paradigm of a living being is the human'.[176] While post-Cartesian philosophy, as we have already pointed out, developed a dialectical understanding of Being and

---

[171] Jeremiah Alberg translates *Selbstsein*, as 'being a self' (Spaemann, *Happiness and Benevolence*, ix (*Glück und Wohlwollen*, 11)) and, very literally, as 'self-being' (Ibid. 132 (173)); O'Donovan in a somewhat Kantian way as 'being-in-itself'. Given that this notion is reminiscent of Heidegger's use of *Selbstsein*, 'Being-one's-Self' (see Martin Heidegger, *Being and Time*, trans. John Macquarrie and Edward Robinson (Oxford: Blackwell, 1983), 149 ff.), would be another translation. However, all these translations, even though they express important elements of what *Selbstsein* is, do not wholly capture the meaning of *Selbstsein* and are, at least partly, misleading, which is why we will continue to use the German word *Selbstsein* for the very Being that, as the being of the nature-having person, is the paradigm of being both in itself and for us.

[172] Spaemann seems to consider *Selbstsein* to be a reappropriation of Boethius' *individua substantia* (see *Persons*, 27–8 (*Personen*, 38–9)).

[173] 'Emanzipation—ein Bildungsziel?', in *Grenzen*, 484.

[174] *Grenzen*, 10.

[175] Spaemann, *Die Frage 'Wozu?'*, 79.

[176] *Happiness and Benevolence*, 102 (*Glück und Wohlwollen*, 135). For a comparable idea (the person as the highest form of substance) see e.g. Dietrich von Hildebrand, *Metaphysik der*

dichotomized nature and freedom, the philosophy of *Selbstsein* understands Being analogically.[177] Hence, the philosophy of *Selbstsein* can be considered *prima philosophia* with ethical, ontological, and epistemological implications. It also puts an end to the modern predominance of poiesis, because *Selbstsein* is human praxis, not a product of human making. In addition, it sets a limit to the enterprises of abstract and universalizing reasoning. For the disclosure of *Selbstsein* is a concrete 'gift (*Gabe*) which underlies every possible task (*Aufgabe*)'.[178] Connected to it is the experience of guilt, for we realize that we should have woken up earlier in order to respond to the *Selbstsein* of the other.

Thus, Spaemann attempts to reinvigorate a view of reality that appreciates the gift and 'glory' of reality.[179] The glory of reality is, in its fullest sense, the given glory of '*Selbstsein* which grounds all objectivity'[180] and which discloses itself in an event which needs to be, and can be, freely recognized: the encounter with the face of the other person.[181] By speaking of *glory* he avails himself of a notion that does not appear to belong in a philosophical context.[182] The term calls to mind scriptural and liturgical language as well as Levinas's idea of the *gloire de l'infini*[183] and Hans Urs von Balthasar's theological aesthetics.[184] It is important to shed light on the implications of this notion, for Spaemann does not delineate it explicitly. In speaking of the

Gemeinschaft: Untersuchungen über Wesen und Wert der Gemeinschaft (*Gesammelte Werke*, ed. the Dietrich von Hildebrand Legacy Project, iv) (Regensburg: Habbel, 1975), 19–20.

[177] For the difference between an analogical and a dialectical understanding of Being see Spaemann, 'Über die Bedeutung des "sum" im "cogito ergo sum"', in *Zeitschrift für Philosophische Forschung*, 41/3 (1987), 374–5.

[178] *Happiness and Benevolence*, 103 (*Glück und Wohlwollen*, 137).

[179] *Happiness and Benevolence*, 175 (*Glück und Wohlwollen*, 224).

[180] Spaemann, *Happiness and Benevolence*, 84 (*Glück und Wohlwollen*, 112; translation modified).

[181] For Spaemann's reference to the 'human face' as opening up the 'incommensurable' see *Persons*, 126, 144 (*Personen*, 136, 154).

[182] Consequently, most philosophical dictionaries and encyclopaedias do not have an entry for 'glory'. The exceptions prove the rule. See U. Theissmann and F. Niewöhner, 'Herrlichkeit', in *Historisches Wörterbuch der Philosophie*, iii (Basle/Stuttgart: Schwabe, 1974), 1079–84. These authors deal with 'Herrlichkeit' with respect to the Old Testament, the New Testament, and post-biblical Judaism; very brief attention, though, is drawn to Hegel's, Schelling's, and Herman Cohen's usage of 'Herrlichkeit'. E. Balducci focuses upon the 'gloria' (i.e. fame), of human beings and the glory of God (see his 'Gloria', in *Enciclopedia Filosofica*, iii (Firenze: Sansoni, 1967), 264–5). See also 'Gloire', in *Encyclopédie Philosophique Universelle*, ii. *Les Notions Philosophiques. Dictionnaire*, i (Vendôme: Press Universitaires de France, 1990), 1073, which focuses upon the moral and religious meaning of 'gloire' as 'un état de conscience integral'.

[183] See e.g. his *Autrement qu'être ou au-delà de l'essence*, 220 ff.

[184] *Herrlichkeit: Eine theologische Aesthetik*, i–iii (Einsiedeln: Johannes, 1961–9), esp iii. II. 943 ff. and 964 ff. (Hans Urs von Balthasar, *The Glory of the Lord: A Theological Aesthetics*, trans. Erasmo Leiva-Merikakis, ed. Joseph Fessio and John Riches (San Francisco, Calif.: Ignatius, 1983–91), v. 613 ff. and 635 ff.). Hans Urs von Balthasar has certainly influenced Robert Spaemann. A discussion of this influence lies outside the dimensions of this book.

glory of reality he transfers a genuinely theological notion into a philosophical context, but does not thereby secularize the theological notion by providing it with a new meaning or imply that the theological and religious usage of *glory* is unimportant for the philosophical purposes that he has in mind. Why, then, does he speak of the 'glory of reality' as disclosed in the experience of *Selbstsein*? Reality is glorious because we cannot produce or make it. It does not arise simply as the object of our observations and interferences, but is 'unpreconceivably' given. In characterizing reality as glorious, Spaemann reminds us that the abstract dichotomy of *res extensa* and *res cogitans* does not do justice to the paradigmatic way in which we experience reality as an interrelation of meaning and being. The seemingly infinite regress of the reflection of consciousness—that is, the problem of whether or not there is really something at all apart from our pure consciousness—comes to an end when the reality of the person is recognized. The *amor benevolentiae* vis-à-vis the *Selbstsein* of the other person is therefore the 'spanning of an infinite space between the negativity of reflection and the positivity of being'.[185] While the search for happiness cannot escape the intrinsic antinomies and ambiguities of happiness, the reality of *Selbstsein* leaves antinomy and ambiguity behind. It is simply cynical and deeply immoral not to conceive of the other human being as a real and 'glorious' gift.

The factual gift and glory of Being shows the limits of aprioristic philosophy and of merely reflective thought. In the human person, we encounter, as he further argues, a 'representation of the absolute';[186] that is to say, the person is a 'representation of the glory of God' to which we are 'premorally' obliged to respond. In speaking of the glory of reality, Spaemann therefore seems to presuppose that reality has been created by God and cannot be derived from a priori principles. Yet his philosophical analysis implies that this statement can be understood initially, though not fully, from a purely philosophical point of view. Spaemann would not deny that a *full* understanding of what it implies to speak of the glory of reality can only arise if the theological origin and dimension of this notion is taken into account, and if one acknowledges that God is 'an "unpreconceivable" unity of Being and meaning'.[187] Yet he speaks of the glory of reality not because of a specific divine revelation, but because of his insight into what he considers

---

[185] *Happiness and Benevolence*, 113 (*Glück und Wohlwollen*, 149).

[186] Ibid. 114 (151). See also Spaemann, *Persons*, 73 (*Personen*, 82): 'Personality hovers at a point between being and kind, between absolute and finite'.

[187] 'Die Frage nach der Bedeutung des Wortes "Gott"', in *Einsprüche: Christliche Reden*, 33; see also Spaemann, 'Christliche Religion und Ethik', in *Einsprüche: Christliche Reden*, 59, where Spaemann defines God as an 'original unity of Being and meaning'.

self-evident—the disclosure of the dignity of the person—and this is why he does not feel the need to leave the context of philosophical argument.[188]

Happiness and Benevolence begins with a quotation from Heraclitus that '[w]hile awake, we have one common world. But dreamers turn each to their own'.[189] Awakening, a metaphor for the essential movement of human beings towards the reality of *Selbstsein*, a description of reason properly under-stood,[190] is central to Spaemann's philosophy and to his Socratic understand-ing of the nature of philosophy. 'Philosophy', he argues, 'has no reason to promote hopelessness as long as it has not lost the power of recollection',[191]— that is to say, as long as it can still wake people up and educate them in reality. Awakening, however, is an infinite process. Full awakening can never be achieved. Spaemann argues that in contrast to the Buddhist conception of awakening, which he interprets as awakening to mere nothingness, awakening to reality remains essentially unfulfilled. It remains 'in its essence' desire for Being.[192] The idea that reality is inexhaustible and that we are always in need of Being is another feature of Spaemann's philosophy that shows, once again, considerable similarities to the thought of Emmanuel Levinas, who also points out that the desire for the other cannot be fulfilled.[193] Human beings cannot fully awaken, and full happiness thus cannot be achieved. The reason for this is that human beings cannot autonomously overcome the antinomy of 'for me'and 'as such'. The subjective and the objective dimension of happiness cannot be unified: 'Happiness names that of which we have here only momentary presentiments, but that is unable to give form to our finite existence'.[194] The person, however, is a person not only for me. He is a person also as such—as the gift of Being. This leads us to examine the dignity of the human person more closely.

---

[188] See for this also Holger Zaborowski, 'Göttliche und menschliche Freiheit: Zur Möglich-keit einer Kriteriologie von Religion', in *Spielräume der Freiheit: Zur Hermeneutik des Mensch-seins* (Freiburg im Breisgau/Munich: Alber, 2009), 99–130, esp. 111–12.

[189] *Happiness and Benevolence*, 1 (*Glück und Wohlwollen*, 12); see Heraclitus, fr. 89, in Walter Kranz (ed.), *Die Fragmente der Vorsokratiker* (Dublin/Zürich: Weidmann, 1972), 171. See also Spaemann, 'Wirklichkeit als Anthropomorphismus', 16–17.

[190] See *Happiness and Benevolence*, 175 (*Glück und Wohlwollen*, 225): 'Reason as awakening to reality'. For a short discussion of Spaemann's view see also Sokolowski, *Phenomenology of the Human Person*, 95.

[191] 'Die zwei Grundbegriffe der Moral', in *Kritik der politischen Utopie*, 22.

[192] *Happiness and Benevolence*, 187 (*Glück und Wohlwollen*, 239).

[193] See e.g. Levinas, *Autrement qu'être ou au-delà de l'essence*, 239 ff.

[194] Spaemann, *Happiness and Benevolence*, 68 (*Glück und Wohlwollen*, 94).

5.8 'PERSON' AS A *NOMEN DIGNITATIS*

The dignity of the person, Spaemann argues, requires a special 'ontology' and 'epistemology' because it is 'a non-definable, simple quality' which can only be experienced intuitively, not scientifically or on the basis of a transcendentalist or naturalist philosophy. This quality is, he argues, an *Urphänomen*.[195] It is self-evident, but easily misunderstood or misconceived.

   'Person', it is important to have in mind, is not, as many think, the name of a species, Spaemann argues, but a general proper name for each member of a species,[196] including perhaps even the species 'dolphins'.[197] This name says who we are, and this 'is evidently not simply identical with *what* we are'.[198] Nor is the life of the person simply the sum total of his actions. The person, Spaemann points out, 'is always present as a whole in his single actions'.[199] 'Person', therefore, is the name of every human being as a unique, incommensurable, and absolute Being; persons are in an 'unparalleled sense' individuals,[200] because of their freedom and their capacity to transcend themselves—'no longer *mere* parts, but a whole, which cannot be accounted for as a means to an end'.[201] And this is why human beings have a special dignity; why 'person' is a *nomen dignitatis*: to speak of persons brings the dimension of the absolute and unconditional into play, but without thereby losing the relation to nature. 'To speak of "person"', Spaemann points out, 'is to take cognizance of the fact that human nature *as* nature realizes itself only when it "awakens", when it transcends its centrality, or, put more precisely, when it consciously grasps the self-transcendence which is essential to it and does not "turn it back" into an instrument of a merely natural self-preservation'.[202]

   It belongs particularly to the dignity of the person that the person can radically transcend himself and overcome the self-centredness characteristic of non-personal life for which it suffices to say that the whole is the sum total of the moments of its life. For human persons, by contrast, as Spaemann points out, there are cases in which human persons freely give up their nature in order to maintain their moral integrity. He refers, as we have already seen,

---

[195] 'Über den Begriff der Menschenwürde', in *Grenzen*, 109.
[196] *Persons*, 32 (*Personen*, 41); see also 6 (14).
[197] Ibid. 248 (264).
[198] Ibid. 11 (19).
[199] 'Einzelhandlungen', in *Grenzen*, 51.
[200] *Persons*, 3 (*Personen*, 11); see also 35 (44).
[201] *Persons*, 38 (*Personen*, 47).
[202] *Happiness and Benevolence*, 194 (*Glück und Wohlwollen*, 248).

to the martyrdom of Maximilian Kolbe, who 'preserved the honour of the human race, in spite of its being besmirched by his murder'.[203] For Spaemann, 'sacrificial death' is not meaningless, it 'can, if it happens voluntarily, be the highest fulfilment of the human being'.[204] Clearly, then, the human person cannot be understood on purely naturalistic premises. He is 'an absolute end in itself' because he can make his natural inclinations relative, transcend his nature, and even sacrifice himself.[205]

It is obvious, as we have already argued, that a technological civilization that is characterized by 'the tendency to make ends irrational or even to efface them altogether'[206] fails to understand the dignity of the human person and his ability to transcend himself, even unto self-sacrifice. By contrast, Spaemann's philosophy attempts to retrieve the dignity of the person and the person's capacity for radical self-transcendence. Politics and the process of history, as we have already seen, are thus not the ultimate truth of, or framework for, morality. For the moral sacrifice of oneself, Spaemann makes clear, does not have some goal in view, not even a better world order or future. Kolbe simply wanted to do what was absolutely right, irrespective of its consequences.[207] Human beings are thus not 'survival machines—robot vehicles blindly programmed to preserve the selfish molecules known as genes',[208] as Richard Dawkins has suggested. Genetics and evolutionary theory cannot provide us with the ultimate truth about the human person because the highest act (and thus the dignity) of the person does not consist in an act of survival, but in an act of sacrifice.

In reassessing the dignity of the human person along these lines Spaemann overcomes the modern dichotomy of freedom and nature. 'The natural growth of the human', he argues, 'and the dignity of the human are indissolubly connected, and the humanizing of natural appetites does not consist in denaturing them, but in their conscious integration in a human and social life-context'.[209] He thus rejects the naturalistic interpretation, or often dismissal, of freedom as well as the existentialist idea that freedom is self-realization beyond and outside nature.[210] The person is the free 'having' of one's nature; he is constituted by the complementary relation between nature and freedom, between self-centredness and self-transcendence. This relation

[203] *Basic Moral Concepts*, 5 (*Moralische Grundbegriffe*, 15).
[204] 'Die Zerstörung der naturrechtlichen Kriegslehre', in *Grenzen*, 316.
[205] 'Über den Begriff der Menschenwürde', in *Grenzen*, 27.
[206] Spaemann, 'Rationalität als "Kulturelles Erbe,"' 309.
[207] See Spaemann, 'Weltethos als Projekt', in *Grenzen*, 526.
[208] *The Selfish Gene*, v.
[209] *Happiness and Benevolence*, 168 (*Glück und Wohlwollen*, 217).
[210] *Persons*, 231 (*Personen*, 247).

grounds the dignity of the human person as the 'symbolic representation of the unconditioned',[211] that cannot empirically be observed. For, subjectivity, Spaemann points out, is not 'positivity but negativity, not a found fact, but reflection'.[212] It becomes manifest in personal action, most fundamentally in the action 'as which' the person always already exists. Spaemann's philosophy of *Selbstsein* thus invites further reflection on his 'ontology' of promise and forgiveness.[213]

5.9 THE 'ONTOLOGY' OF PROMISING AND FORGIVING

'To promise',[214] Spaemann argues, 'causes that form of time-transcending personal identity which is the sign of the highest intensity of life: of the spirit'.[215] Anyone who freely makes a promise makes himself independent of his nature and transcends it. By anticipating the future and establishing a strangely unconditional claim upon it, he creates a new reality.[216] Promises are, as Spaemann argues, acts of self-relinquishment which confer on another person a claim upon oneself. Promises are thus acts of liberation from the accidents, processes, and laws of nature, because they presuppose freedom. In so far as we 'have' our nature, Spaemann argues, we can freely restrict the development of it by promises such as marital or religious vows.[217] So the highest expression of *Selbstsein* lies not in absolute freedom, but in free self-limitation, or self-transcendence.

If there is one way of 'proving' personal identity, it may well be to give and to keep a promise, because to promise makes a radical change of identity over time morally impossible. To doubt that promises can be kept at all, then,

---

[211] *Happiness and Benevolence*, 127 (*Glück und Wohlwollen*, 167).

[212] Ibid. 103 (137). For Spaemann's definition of negativity, or the negative, see *Persons*, 47 (*Personen*, 56): 'The negative, as distinct from what simply is, arises only where there is life, i.e., where interests are in play, *already* in play, that is, before a choice is made, a goal is set, or some conscious act of will takes place'.

[213] *Persons*, 221–35 (*Personen*, 235–51); *Happiness and Benevolence*, 187–99 (*Glück und Wohlwollen*, 239–54).

[214] For the philosophical dimension of promising, see also Chretien, Jean-Louis, *La voix nue. Phénoménologie de la promesse* (Paris: Minuit, 1990); Schenk (ed.), *Kontinuität der Person. Zum Versprechen und Vertrauen*.

[215] Robert Spaemann, 'Person und Versprechen. Eine Einführung', in Schenk (ed.), *Kontinuität der Person. Zum Versprechen und Vertrauen*, 6. For Spaemann's view of promises see also Spaemann, Robert and Zaborowski, Holger, An Animal That Can Promise and Forgive', translated by Lesley Rice, in: *Communio*, 34 (2007), 511–521.

[216] *Persons*, 222–3 (*Personen*, 236–7).

[217] Ibid. 226 ff. (242–3).

means to doubt personal identity; and to deny that there is such a phenomenon as personal identity is to make promising impossible. The person who makes a promise recognizes the other's personhood and confirms his own, thereby transcending his nature: 'Only in their mutual recognition and release do natural beings transcend nature'.[218] One can, however, only recognize another person after having been recognized by the other person as a person, so that there is no natural starting point of recognition in time. We are always already obliged to recognize the other person who (normally) always already recognizes us as a person. This is why it is possible to say that we, as persons, are always already a promise to the other person that we must keep.

Promises, however, can be broken; and this, Spaemann maintains, is a failure to actualize one's personal identity, not a denial of one's identity. Broken promises show the abyssal and ambiguous character of freedom, because it is through freedom that entropy destroys freedom and that promises are broken. This ever-present possibility, the possibility that freedom will fail, shows why forgiveness as an act of self-transcendence is necessary.[219]

Promising and forgiving are therefore two complementary phenomena, Spaemann states.[220] Forgiveness, however, is characterized, Spaemann argues, by a paradoxical situation. On the one hand, it must precede the other's change of heart, for otherwise he presumably will not change. On the other hand, forgiveness cannot precede conversion but presupposes it. This sheds light on the dialectic of forgiveness. To forgive means to anticipate the other person's change of attitude, which then makes this very change possible. This is possible because of what Spaemann calls 'ontological' forgiveness. To forgive 'ontologically' means, as Spaemann points out, to accept that persons are finite beings who need to be forgiven for the fact that they are as they are.[221] Persons, he further states, are in need of clemency and reconciliation because of who they are. That is to say, they are always already in need of forgiveness to restore the symmetry of mutual recognition and abolish the asymmetry caused by guilt. Whoever rejects reconciliation, then, rejects the possibility of self-transcendence and the restoration of reality made possible by forgiveness. Forgiveness is therefore an eminently creative act in that it 'restores' the identity of the person.

Spaemann wonders whether we are promises only for other people or also for ourselves. Are we responsible to ourselves? He argues that it makes sense to think that we are responsible to ourselves only 'if we think of the human as

---

[218] Spaemann, 'Natur', in *Philosophische Essays*, 37.
[219] *Persons*, 232 (*Personen*, 248).
[220] Ibid. 235 (251).
[221] See *Happiness and Benevolence*, 187 ff. (*Glück und Wohlwollen*, 239 ff.).

an image and a representative of an unconditioned being.[222] Then, we do not belong exclusively to ourselves. Furthermore, if the absolute is conceived of as subject and thus as—possibly—forgiving, we can forgive ourselves. So the ontology of promising and forgiving leads to a theory of the absolute forgiving subject who created us as the promise that we are, and to whom we are accountable. This is why the examination of Spaemann's philosophy of *Selbstsein* is best elucidated by an examination of his philosophy of religion, which is closely linked to his understanding of reality as creation.

5.10 THE HUMAN PERSON AND THE TRANSCENDENCE OF BEING

Robert Spaemann develops the most comprehensive account of his philosophy of religion in *Persons*.[223] This shows that the rehabilitation of a non-reductionistic notion of substance and the defence of the person—which, as we have seen, serve as a leitmotif of Spaemann's general philosophy—have a significant bearing on his philosophy of religion, which, as he acknowledges, originates from the paradigm of Christianity.[224] This section will examine more closely how in *Persons* Spaemann thinks about the concept of a person not only with respect to the relation between nature and freedom, but also with respect to what he identifies as the relation between transcendence and reflection. In so doing, he applies the principles of a 'speculative empiricism'[225] that, as a philosophy of freedom, focuses contingently upon the contingent. Here we once again encounter the fundamental problem of how to interpret adequately the relation between mere human consciousness and what is given to it but not produced by it—that is to say, how to relate immediacy and mediation, the centrality of life and the eccentricity of reason and freedom.[226]

By 'transcendence' Spaemann means the self-transcendence of the subject, its movement towards what it has not produced, and cannot produce: the substantial reality of Being as such. By 'reflection' Spaemann means the reflection of the subject upon its own subjectivity and upon the genesis of its

---

[222] Ibid. 198 (253); see also *Happiness and Benevolence*, 184 (*Glück und Wohlwollen*, 236).

[223] See esp. pp. *Persons*, 93–101 (*Personen*, 102–10).

[224] Ibid. 94 (103).

[225] Spaemann, 'Christentum und Philosophie der Neuzeit', 135.

[226] For what follows see also Holger Zaborowski, 'Ethik, Metaphysik und die Frage nach Gott', *Jahrbuch für Religionsphilosophie*, 1 (2002), 120–37; 'Göttliche und menschliche Freiheit', 99–130, esp. 113 ff.

thought within and for itself. Transcendence and reflection, he observes, stand in an unstable relation to one another,[227] for they are complementary, and yet each thought act tends to claim to be ontologically more fundamental, and so capable of integrating the other thought act into itself. Spaemann goes on to explore the relation between transcendence and reflection in one of the most important passages of *Persons*, a passage that contains most of the key insights of his philosophy *in nuce*.[228] Reflection upon what is given 'for me', Spaemann states, formally presupposes Being as such. Otherwise, reflection would be trivial, tautological, and empty. There must be an 'as such' that corresponds to any 'for me'. That is why true reflection transcends itself towards what is not the product but the presupposition of reflection. However, transcendence towards an 'as such', towards what is not produced by the subject, also seems to be a function of the act of reflection. For the thought about the 'as such' beyond mere thought is always a thought. Self-transcendence and reflection thus stand in a balance that can easily be destabilized. To exemplify the delicacy of this balance Spaemann offers an interpretation of Hegel's *Phenomenology of Spirit* with the dialectical tension between reflection and self-transcendence as its constructive principle. Hegel believed the dialectical tension would come to a complete rest in an absolute synthesis of 'as such' and 'for me'—that is to say, in the speculative thought which is only possible because the absolute spirit is already present while still developing.

Spaemann interprets the Hegelian dialectic between self-transcendence towards the gift of Being and reflection as 'putting the notion "person" into motion'.[229] In Spaemann's eyes Hegel defines the self-possession of a person as the process of appropriating what we have always already been. In the remainder of his chapter on religion Spaemann leaves Hegel's philosophy and its ambiguities behind, setting aside the question whether or not Hegel succeeded in overcoming the difference between Being and the thought of Being. He seems to believe that Hegel's project ultimately fails. Rather than focusing on Hegel, Spaemann draws attention to the later Schelling. It is not contentious to assert that Schelling found a less ambiguous way of examining the relation between transcendence and reflection than Hegel did—in what was considered at their time impossible;[230] that is to say, a positive philosophy which reflects upon the 'unpreconceivable' and contingent gift of reality. The later Schelling was right, Spaemann seems to think, to argue that the attempt to overcome the dialectical tension between Being and the thought of Being

---

[227] Spaemann, *Persons*, 93 (*Personen*, 102).
[228] Ibid.
[229] *Persons*, 94 (*Personen*, 102).
[230] See Spaemann, 'Christentum und Philosophie der Neuzeit', 135.

by means of mere (human) thinking is itself a thought and cannot possibly succeed in overcoming the antinomy of transcendence and reflection.[231] This kind of negative philosophy, as Schelling called it, cannot find an easy way out of the danger of an aprioristic philosophy of mere consciousness—short of a fundamental change in its notion of Being and of how Being becomes an object of our thought. Here Spaemann refers to Schelling's argument that 'Being always remains "unpreconceivable"'.[232] Schelling coined this notion to convey that Being cannot be thought of prior to its actual being-given. If Being is 'unpreconceivable', it is, in Schelling's view, *freely* created. It cannot be 'necessary', nor can it be merely 'hypothetical'. It is contingently there—as a matter of sheer fact. So in his attempt to overcome the short-sightedness of transcendental philosophy Schelling reassessed philosophically the doctrine of creation and the idea of divine freedom in order to answer the question whether transcendence is the final truth of reflection or not. Spaemann thinks along these lines: 'In conceiving of God and of its own creation, reflection comes to a standstill, confronted with itself as Being'.[233] Spaemann, however, does not follow a fideistic trajectory. For religion, philosophically understood as it is here, is based upon the self-understanding of the person, without being entirely dependent on it. 'The inexpressible sense that in saying "I" we refer to something unique but inexpressible and incommunicable', he argues, 'is one of the most powerful sources of religion'.[234] It is one of various sources—certainly *a* source of being religious, as one might say, but manifestly not the only source, on Spaemann's account. He is, therefore, far from subjecting religion to a philosophy of the person.[235]

---

[231] *Persons*, 94 (*Personen*, 103).

[232] Ibid. (trans. modified). Schelling first develops this idea in his *Of Human Freedom*. For his understanding of unvordenklich see also his *System der Weltalter: Münchener Vorlesung 1827/ 28 in einer Nachschrift von Ernst von Lausaulx*, ed. and introd. Siegbert Peetz, 2nd edn. (Frankfurt am Main: Klostermann, 1998), 131 and *passim*.

[233] *Persons*, 94 (*Personen*, 103). For Spaemann's view of God as 'unconditional freedom' and free subjectivity see also his 'Religion und "Tatsachenwahrheit"', in *Das unsterbliche Gerücht*, 176. For an important comment on the *philosophical* significance of the concept of creation see also Jürgen Habermas, *Glauben und Wissen* (Frankfurt am Main: Suhrkamp, 2001), 30.

[234] *Persons*, 159 (*Personen*, 149).

[235] In recent years Spaemann has developed a philosophical *ad hominem* argument for the existence of God that is based on his understanding of the person as oriented towards reality and truth: Everything that is real, Spaemann argues, is 'eternal'. He explains this through an examination of the *futurum exactum*, or 'future perfect tense'. There will never be a time, as he points out, 'when it will no longer be true that someone has experienced the pain or joy that he now experiences'. This 'past reality' (or the pastness, the having-been, of reality), he argues, cannot be dependent on our human memory; for, if this were the case, past reality would at some point be forgotten and would not be eternal. So if '[o]ur present consciousness of what is now implies the consciousness of a future "having-been", or it annihilates itself', as Spaemann points out, we are required to think of a non-human 'place' 'where everything that happens, is forever preserved'.

A philosophy such as Schelling's, which accepts the limits of what is historically contingent and of what human thought cannot derive transcendentally,
does not try to integrate the absolute, and religion with it, into its own
framework. It presupposes a free gift that is the *prius*, so to speak, to any a
priori, and so is prior to any reflection of consciousness. Schelling's philosophy
of creation, while still philosophy, thus opens up a space for religion as
distinctly different from philosophy, though not contradicting it. The dialectic
of reflection and transcendence, then, can be overcome if religion, or a
religious view of reality, is taken philosophically seriously, because 'religion
is . . . undialectic'.[236] Spaemann's philosophy of *Selbstsein* is therefore critical,
and shows the failure of any reductionist or dialectical attempt to bridge the
gap between the 'subjectivity' of reflection and the 'objectivity' of transcendence. In his view, this can only lead to abstract reductionisms with totalitarian
and inhumane implications, for every attempt to dissolve the tension between
reflection and transcendence by means of philosophy alone must lead either to
transcendentalist idealism or to a naturalistic materialism.

5.11 *SELBSTSEIN* AND THE END OF THE DIALECTIC OF MODERNITY

Persons as *Selbstsein*, we have argued, 'have' their nature 'freely'. And religion
allows us fully to understand this 'having' of one's nature, as Spaemann points
out, because from a religious point of view 'nature is not the last horizon, but
something we "have". Taken as a whole, nature is "creation", and its teleological structures allow us to discern the creator's will for humankind'.[237] In
Persons Spaemann therefore suggests that it is possible fully to understand
the subject as a person 'if subjectivity is understood from a religious point of
view'.[238] At this point he does not make it his first concern to defend the
Christian point of view. His argument simply intends to show that every

---

And this 'place' is what we call God. For this argument see Spaemann, 'Das unsterbliche Gerücht',
in *Das unsterbliche Gerücht*, 35–6 and also 'Gottesbeweise nach Nietzsche', in *Das unsterbliche
Gerücht*, esp. 50 ff.; for a nucleus of this argument see *Persons*, 120–1 (*Personen*, 130–1). For a
discussion of Spaemann's argument see Thomas Buchheim, 'Erkannt, aber nicht aufbewahrt: Die
Person, die Erfassung des Wahren und Robert Spaemanns Gottesbeweis aus dem *futurum
exactum*', in Hanns-Gregor Nissing (ed.), *Grundvollzüge der Person: Dimensionen des Menschseins
bei Robert Spaemann* (Munich: Institut zur Förderung der Glaubenslehre, 2008), 37–53.

[236] Spaemann, *Persons*, 95 (*Personen*, 104).
[237] Ibid. 96 (105).
[238] Spaemann, *Persons*, 93 (103; trans. modified).

philosophy that does refrain from taking the absolute or God into account cannot grasp the notion of the person, and that a philosophy of the person which takes reality, nature, history, freedom, and personhood seriously—that is to say, that takes fundamental human experience seriously—cannot but somehow acknowledge its own limits vis-à-vis what is not made but unpreconceivably given. There is, therefore, need for a philosophical reassessment of the concept of givenness, of creation, he thinks. With respect to the characteristically 'unreal' modern tendency to take definite possession of human life on the basis of naturalist premises or to develop a merely idealist (and equally unreal) account of reality, Spaemann points out that the 'idea of creation has never been more important than today'.[239] But he also realizes that 'this notion has never been more at odds with the mainstream of the predominant civilization'.[240]

In taking the gift of creation seriously Spaemann rediscovers, and re-appreciates, the importance of the contingent, and questions the epistemological and ontological claims of any philosophy that fails to do justice to the dignity of the concrete individual human person. The question that is at stake here is, as we have seen, not a merely theoretical one. A free, existential decision to recognize the gift of a person as free *Selbstsein* must be made. Spaemann's philosophy is thus, as we have already pointed out, a philosophy of freedom. 'The idea of the person', he argues, 'is inseparably bound up with the idea of freedom'.[241] It is, as we have seen, also a philosophy of nature in that it takes the teleological dimension of nature seriously because it is only in light of his end that the dignity of the person can be fully understood. And, as we have seen, freedom and dignity constitute, in Spaemann's eyes, 'the only interest which motivates us to do philosophy'.[242]

Spaemann's philosophy of *Selbstsein* centres, as should have become clear by now, around the notion *oikeiosis*[243]—the 'becoming familiar with' reality in which 'what is alien ceases to be alien'.[244] 'Reality', Spaemann states, 'is any event of *oikeiosis*, however ephemeral, in which an objective content is appropriated through a subjective pole'.[245] This happens most fundamentally

---

[239] 'Sind alle Menschen Personen?', in *Communio*, 19 (1990), 114; for the realism of the doctrine of creation see Spaemann, 'Die Zerstörung der naturrechtlichen Kriegslehre: Erwiderung an P. Gustav Gundlach S. J.', in *Grenzen*, 316–17.

[240] See Spaemann, 'Sind alle Menschen Personen?', 114.

[241] *Persons*, 196 (*Personen*, 209).

[242] 'Philosophie als institutionalisierte Naivität', in *Philosophisches Jahrbuch*, 81 (1974), 141.

[243] This is the title of the Festschrift for Robert Spaemann (Reinhard Löw, *Oikeiosis: Festschrift für Robert Spaemann* (Weinheim: Acta Humaniora/VCH, 1987)).

[244] *Die Frage 'Wozu?'*, 16.

[245] 'Wirklichkeit als Anthropomorphismus', 31.

in the experience of the person, who, as we have pointed out, is himself the paradigm for the understanding of reality as familiar, friendly, and, ultimately, given. This insight also makes friendship with oneself and with the other and thus happiness possible.[246] Spaemann's philosophy therefore demonstrates how (and why) one may uphold that the person is a fundamental notion and that basic features of the religious understanding of the person as created are *philosophically* understandable and defensible. If this were not the case, philosophy would—paradoxically—mount a refutation of religion only by becoming a pseudo-religion itself; but this would ultimately make it impossible to understand who a person is. That all human beings are persons can be understood from a merely philosophical point of view, Spaemann thinks, but not from an anti-religious point of view that denies the concept of creation and its philosophical significance. For through religion, Spaemann argues, subjectivity achieves reality and substantiality without the need to abolish itself as subjectivity. Religion, for Spaemann, is therefore not a further dimension of the person that merely supplements other traits. To be a person means to transcend oneself and to experience oneself and the other person as created and, therefore, as always already given. And this is why human beings are neither made nor declared persons by other human beings, although they are *recognized* as such by other human beings.

If Spaemann is right in arguing that the notion of a person not only arose under the influence of Christian doctrinal speculation but may be inconceivable in a non-Christian culture for which, amongst other concepts, creation is nothing but a mere myth of times past, then the doctrine, or idea, of creation—that is to say, of the gift of reality—needs to be revisited also from a philosophical point of view.[247] For this idea particularly challenges and provides an alternative to one of the fundamental implications of modernity, namely the predominance of poiesis, or making and producing, because 'creation is different from human production in that it establishes substantial reality, "*Selbstsein*".[248] If this is not done, late modernity will lose sight of one

---

[246] For the idea that this is the end of education see Robert Spaemann and Hanns-Gregor Nissing, 'Die Natur des Lebendigen und das Ende des Denkens: Entwicklungen und Entfaltungen eines philosophischen Werks. Ein Gespräch', 125. For a view of friendship that is very close to Spaemann's philosophy of the person see Sokolowski, *Phenomenology of the Human Person*, 267ff.

[247] *Persons*, 17–18 (*Personen*, 27): 'Without Christian theology we would have had no name for what we now call "persons", and, since persons do not simply occur in nature, that means we would have been without them altogether. That is not to say that we can only speak intelligibly of persons on explicitly theological suppositions, though it is conceivable that the disappearance of the theological dimension of the idea could in the long run bring about the disappearance of the idea itself'.

[248] *Die Frage 'Wozu?'*, 94.

of the fundamental insights of the pre-modern and modern tradition: the idea that *Selbstsein*, rather than objectivity or process, is the paradigm for Being; that all human beings are persons; that they are created and not produced; that human dignity is universal; and that the notion of the person matters (and indeed matters above all other categories, on Spaemann's account). So Spaemann's philosophy may indeed help us to regain 'a normal human way of talking about the human and the world'.[249]

This view of reality may help us successfully to overcome the dialectic of Enlightenment thought without endlessly reconstituting it, as modernists as well as anti-modernists have done and continue to do. It also shows how Spaemann's criticism of modernity and its dialectic of spirit and nature are informed by a religious understanding of reality. His approach is informed by a Christian understanding of reality as given (created) and of freedom as limited, to be sure, but his philosophy that explores the rationality of the Christian position (and therefore does not betray philosophy and its claims) also makes it possible to gain a new appreciation of many Christian doctrines that have come to seem dubious in modernity.

---

[249] For Spaemann's idea that it could be an important contribution of Christianity in our culture to help to regain such a view see also his 'Über die gegenwärtige Lage des Christentums', in *Das unsterbliche Gerücht*, 256.

6

Christianity, philosophy, and the end of modernity

> Since, then, the life of mortals is afflicted now more gently, again more
> harshly, by the death of those very dear to us . . . nevertheless, we would
> rather hear of or behold the death of those whom we love than perceive that
> they have fallen from faith or virtue, that is, that the soul itself has suffered
> death . . . The result is that we feel thankful at the death of good men among
> our friends, and that, though their death brings sorrow, it is the more surely
> mitigated in that they have been spared those evils by which in this life even
> good men are crushed or contaminated or at least are in danger of either fate.
>
> Augustine

The examination of Robert Spaemann's philosophy of *Selbstsein* has led us to
his philosophy of religion. This invites a more systematic treatment of
Spaemann's view of the relation between Christianity and philosophy, and
of the implications of his thought for truly post-modern philosophies.

6.1 THE APOLOGETIC CHARACTER OF SPAEMANN'S PHILOSOPHY

George Marsden has suggested reading Charles Taylor's *Sources of the Self*[1] as
a study in apologetics, one that conceives modernity as the prodigal son of
Christianity. Taylor, Marsden argues,

is probably right that talking about sin is not the best place to start our Christian
witness to the more progressive of our contemporaries. Letters to alienated children
that condemn everything in their lifestyle are going to get tossed away in anger. Better
to sympathetically consider their interests and aspirations in their own terms and
gently lead them to see their emptiness . . . *Sources* is an extended essay on the

[1] Charles Taylor, *Sources of the Self: The Making of the Modern Identity* (Cambridge:
Cambridge University Press, 1998).

particular genius of modern sinfulness, but it may have alienated many potential readers to make explicit Christian teaching integral to the story.[2]

Marsden's interpretation of Taylor's philosophy provides a key also to the thought of Spaemann who, like Taylor, directs his readers to see the abstract emptiness, the paradoxical and self-contradictory character, and the intrinsic dialectic of many of the key notions of modernity without dismissing its intellectual achievements or utterly alienating its adherents. Like the prodigal son of Christianity, he thinks, modernity is not a period that can be understood as wholly legitimate on its own terms. We have seen that, according to Spaemann, Christianity is not without responsibility for modernity's ascendancy; many of modern philosophy's distinctive features, however problematic, are deeply indebted to Christianity and to specific Christian theological and doctrinal developments. Modern natural philosophy, modern political philosophy, the understanding of the dignity of the person, the emphasis upon one's inward attitude, and even Sartre's ethics of 'commitment',[3] Spaemann shows, could not have developed without Christianity.

Spaemann's proposal of a truly post-modern reconciliation between philosophy and Christianity can thus be read as an account of how the prodigal son returns to his parent without losing his relative independence. In this, Spaemann formulates a paradigmatic challenge for modern and late-modern philosophy and for Christianity. His is a particular way of engaging modernity without being entirely submersed in it. As we have seen, he concedes that a pre-modern view of reality has been irretrievably lost. This does not prevent him from initiating a philosophical conversation between modernity and the legacy upon which it is based in order to defend what is positive about modernity against its own self-understanding.

In this concluding chapter we will show how Spaemann understands Christianity and demonstrate that his understanding of philosophical reason, which both limits the claim of autonomous reason and restores a suitable metaphysical framework, is reconcilable with Christianity. Before we go on to examine Spaemann's explicit view of Christianity, we will briefly summarize his notion of the relation between religion and philosophy. We will then outline Spaemann's view of the relation between Christianity and philosophy

---

[2] 'Matteo Ricci and the Prodigal Culture', in James L. Heft (ed.), *A Catholic Modernity? Charles Taylor's Marianist Award Lectures* (New York/Oxford: Oxford University Press, 1999), 86–7. The relation of Taylor's philosophy to (his) religion has been controversially discussed among scholars of his thought. For a brief overview of this discussion see Ruth Abbey, *Charles Taylor* (Princeton, NJ/London: Princeton University Press, 2000), 31–3.

[3] See Spaemann, 'Politisches Engagement und Reflexion: Rede zum 17 Juni 1964', in *Kritik der politischen Utopie*, 24 ff.

both historically and systematically and discuss the relation between modernity and Christianity with respect to evolutionary theory. This examination will lead us to his idea of truly post-modern philosophies and his recollection of a relation between nature and freedom that not only is reconcilable with Christianity but truly overcomes the shortcomings of modernity.

6.2 SPAEMANN'S VIEW OF CHRISTIANITY

Religion and philosophy

Spaemann, as we have shown, is aware of and accepts the distinction between philosophy and theology and resists any temptation to fuse them. He holds that philosophy needs to be prevented from abolishing theology or subjecting it to philosophy's own goals and intentions. According to Spaemann, we cannot recognize God speculatively by means of reason alone. In *The Origin of Sociology in the Spirit of Restoration* he draws attention briefly to Thomas Aquinas's assertion that revelation is not absolutely necessary for the knowledge of God. It is, however, *morally* necessary, because only very few people are able to recognize God speculatively.[4] According to Spaemann, theology must not eradicate the authentic possibilities of philosophical search for truth either. He thus explains that the Roman Catholic magisterium does not favour any particular philosophical theory, but only criticizes philosophical theories if there is need to criticize them.[5] 'Neither is faith permitted to deny its rational roots without "not believing what it believes"', he consequently argues, 'nor is reason permitted to deny its *natural* and *mystical* roots without becoming historically sterile'.[6]

John Paul II provides an outline of a model for the harmonious and mutually beneficial coexistence of faith and reason as distinctly different, though intrinsically related, human faculties in his encyclical letter *Fides et Ratio*. In this letter he asserts that 'the desire for truth is part of human nature itself'.[7] 'Theology's source and starting point must always be the word of God revealed in history', the Pope argues. 'Yet, since God's word is Truth . . . the human search for truth— philosophy, pursued in keeping with its own rules—can only help to understand

---

[4] *Der Ursprung der Soziologie aus dem Geist der Restauration*, 199. See Thomas Aquinas, *Summa Theologiae*, Ia q. 1 a. 1 for Thomas's discussion of his view.

[5] 'Kommentar', in *Die Unantastbarkeit des menschlichen Lebens: Zu ethischen Fragen der Biomedizin*, Instruktion der Kongregation für die Glaubenslehre (Freiburg im Breisgau: Herder, 1987), 80.

[6] '"Politik zuerst"? Das Schicksal der Action Française', in *Wort und Wahrheit*, 8 (1953), 662.

[7] *Fides et Ratio* (Washington, DC: United States Catholic Conference, 1998), 6.

God's word better.'[8] The important task, then, is to outline an understanding of reason that does not undermine the truth claim of Christianity by violating the limits of reason itself. And this is what Spaemann attempts to do.

The key to Spaemann's reconciliation of Christianity and philosophy, as we have seen, lies in his philosophy of the person, which conceptualizes how a transcendent, absolute, and unconditional horizon is always already present in human life. We have seen that Spaemann's philosophy, like the philosophy of the later Schelling, endeavours to understand history, human freedom, and the intrinsic limits of mere reflection vis-à-vis the gift of the person.[9] This 'aposter-ioristic philosophy', as it were, has implications for the understanding of the relation between philosophy and religion, particularly between philosophy and Christianity. An aprioristic philosophy cannot state that there *is* something prior to, and irrespective of, there actually *being* something. But a philosophy such as Spaemann's recognizes the gift of the person and of nature as the 'unpreconcei-vable' condition of human freedom, which the person can remember because he is more than nature and different from it.[10] It recognizes that human self-consciousness does not establish itself. It is, Spaemann argues with implicit reference to Schelling, 'part of the phenomenology of self-consciousness that it is established in the unpreconceivable".'[11] This view of reality opens up the horizon for religion and the absolute, of which the person, in Spaemann's view, is an image.

Spaemann's contributions to Christian issues

Spaemann frequently reflects on the self-understanding of Christianity in modernity;[12] he concedes that he defends a position that belongs, in our

---

[8] John Paul II, *Fides et Ratio*, 107. For the understanding of philosophy in this encyclical letter see also Sokolowski, Robert, 'The Autonomy of Philosophy in *Fides et Ratio*', in Soko-lowski, Robert, *Christian Faith and Understanding. Studies on the Eucharist, Trinity, and the Human Person* (Washington, D.C.: The Catholic University of America Press, 2006), 9–24.

[9] For Spaemann's understanding of creation see also 'Zur Frage der Notwendigkeit des Schöpfungswillens Gottes', in *Philosophisches Jahrbuch*, 60 (1950), 88–92.

[10] For the idea that the person is more than, and different from, nature and can therefore remember nature see *Persons*, 98 (*Personen*, 106).

[11] 'Verantwortung für die Ungeborenen', in *Grenzen*, 368.

[12] See esp. Spaemann, *Einsprüche: Christliche Reden*; see also his 'Christentum und Philosophie der Neuzeit', in Herrmann Fechtrup, Friedbert Schulze, and Thomas Sternberg (eds.), *Aufklärung durch Tradition: Symposon der Josef Pieper Stiftung zum 90 Geburtstag von Josef Pieper, Mai 1994 in Münster* (Münster: LIT, 1995); 'Das unsterbliche Gerücht', in *Das unsterbliche Gerücht*; 'Die Existenz des Priesters: Eine Provokation in der modernen Welt', in *Communio*, 9 (1980), 481–500; 'Die christliche Religion und das Ende des modernen Bewußtseins: Über einige Schwierigkeiten des Christentums mit dem sogenannten modernen Menschen', *Communio*, 8 (1979), 251–70;

modern civilization, to a 'rather small cognitive minority'.[13] Many of his earliest essays and articles, for instance, were written for the weekly church magazine of the diocese of Münster in Westphalia, *Kirche und Leben*. Although Spaemann also studied theology he is not a theologian and explicitly emphasizes that his contributions are made from a theological lay person's point of view.[14] It must be of interest to the 'Christian non-theologian', he thinks, 'when the theology of the Christian proclamation of salvation is given a sociologically and politically manifest and describable content as in false modernist theologies'.[15] His remarks and considerations about, among other things, the character of moral theology, the notion of God, and the countercultural role of the priest as a 'provocation' and a 'foreign substance'[16] in contemporary society (simply by virtue of *being* a priest, as opposed to performing the duties of a priest) have always proved theologically challenging, and even controversial among theologians. However, he writes in the preface to *Objections: Christian Talks* (*Einsprüche: Christliche Reden*) that 'the following "occasional texts"... do not claim theological competency. This is why they do not share with theology the problem of becoming contemporary and secular'.[17]

Spaemann's position as a layman implies that he addresses such issues only when he feels obliged to, either as a Christian or, professionally, as a philosopher who is a Christian. This commitment parallels that of Bonald, as we have already argued, who, as Spaemann points out, only engaged in philosophy when he 'found himself immediately threatened in his religious substance'.[18] The title of Spaemann's *Objections: Christian Talks* reflects the underlying agenda of Spaemann's contributions to religious and theological issues: 'objections' tend to be ad hoc. Against the currents of contemporary theology and contemporary religious life that he thinks naively assimilate Christianity to modernity, Spaemann intends to recollect Christian orthodoxy

'Theologie, Prophetie, Politik', in *Kritik der politischen Utopie*; 'Weltethos als Projekt', in *Grenzen*; 'Christliche Spiritualität und pluralistische Normalität', in *Communio*, 26 (1997), 63–70; 'Das neue Dogma und die Dogmentheorie', in *Münchener Theologische Zeitschrift*, 3 (1952), 151–60.

[13] Spaemann, 'Christliche Spiritualität und pluralistische Normalität', 164.

[14] 'Wovon handelt die Moraltheologie? Bemerkungen eines Philosophen', in *Einsprüche: Christliche Reden*, 65; see also Spaemann, 'Über die gegenwärtige Lage des Christentums', in *Das unsterbliche Gerücht*, 225–6.

[15] 'Theologie, Prophetie, Politik', in *Kritik der politischen Utopie*, 57.

[16] 'Die Existenz des Priesters: eine Provokation in der modernen Welt', 481.

[17] 'Vorbemerkungen', in *Einsprüche: Christliche Reden*, 7.

[18] *Der Ursprung der Soziologie aus dem Geist der Restauration*, 16. In *Reflexion und Spontaneität* Spaemann emphasizes several times that Fénelon and Bossuet, too, thought of themselves as dealing with questions that concern the very substance of their Christian belief (pp. 39, 58). If not only Bonald's philosophy but also the controversy between Fénelon and Bossuet are paradigmatically modern, as Spaemann argues, we find here important examples for the genesis of modernity out of the spirit of Christianity.

as he thinks it was before its transformation by the principles and maxims of a modernistic reinterpretation. This is why his 'speeches' are explicitly characterized as Christian. They are Christian as opposed to modernistic, and they challenge a 'soft version of Christianity' such as that of Hans Küng, as Spaemann argues.[19]

It would be entirely wrong to read these theological and religious writings as mere by-products of his philosophy or as independent of his philosophical thought. Although Spaemann's philosophy can be understood without taking them into account, it cannot be appreciated fully. William J. Hoye concluded his review of Spaemann's *Happiness and Benevolence* by stating that he knows of 'no living theologian who has come as far with the theological question as the philosopher Robert Spaemann'.[20] This is why it is sometimes not easy to categorize Spaemann's writings. The chapter 'Souls' ('Seelen') in *Persons*, for instance, is explicitly targeted not only at a philosophical dismissal of the soul but also at a Christian theology that 'has more or less declined to put up a defence. Unwilling, for one thing, to accept ontological commitments at variance with those of its contemporaries—for theology more often than ever today leans towards pastoral opportunism at the cost of intellectual and religious substance—neither does it want to obscure the biblical message of bodily resurrection with a philosophical doctrine of the soul's immortality'.[21]

If there is a God, then, in Spaemann's eyes, no theology, nor life as such, is possible as though he did not exist, for he is always already there and commands humanity's transcendence of itself and its nature. Spaemann's view of Christianity is thus radically theocentric and questions both theological anthropocentrism and tendencies to define the task of theology without sufficient regard to what lies fundamentally at the heart of any Christian theological endeavour: the revelation of God.

Spaemann's criticism of the modernization of Christianity

Spaemann criticizes modernity from a Christian point of view. This criticism extends to theology wherever it assimilates itself to the spirit of modernity. The attitude of Spaemann's religious writings is therefore often the Socratic position of 'knowing ignorance'. Spaemann questions the currents of the day in order to recollect a knowledge that is in danger of being inappropriately criticized, of being undermined, and of getting lost, because Christianity, as he thinks, is different from the cognitive and prescriptive normality of

---

[19] 'Weltethos als Projekt', in *Grenzen*, 533.

[20] Review of *Glück und Wohlwollen: Versuch über Ethik*, in *Theologische Revue*, 87/2 (1991), 153.

[21] *Persons*, 148 (*Personen*, 158). For Spaemann's critique of 'pastoral' transformations of Christian teaching see also his brief remark in 'Einzelhandlungen', in *Grenzen*, 51.

our contemporary civilization.[22] Christianity, Spaemann argues, presupposes its own genuine norm that is regarded as a *skandalon* by the non-Christian and particularly the modern periphery, so that the Christian, as Spaemann shows, is a 'stranger' in the modern pluralist society. Spaemann intends a fundamental questioning of the modern ontological, ethical, and epistemological framework that makes orthodox belief a 'pathological pigheadedness'[23] when viewed from the outside, and which has hence made it increasingly difficult, if not entirely infeasible, for the contemporary culture to understand central doctrines of Christianity such as the possibility and historical actuality of divine revelation, the Incarnation, miracles, and divine providence.

Under these circumstances, he argues, *aggiornamento*, the famous idea of John XXIII and of the Second Vatican Council, can only mean 'to put oneself into a real relation to the contemporary age . . . into a relation of contradiction'.[24] It is the 'actualization of being different'.[25] Otherwise, only a modernized version of Christianity is possible, a rendition that seems incapable of discerning that its very foundation is so undermined by modern presuppositions that, in the long run, it will be progressively watered down and finally disappear. Like John Milbank, who speaks of Christianity's 'interruptive character', which differs 'from *both* modernity *and* antiquity',[26] Spaemann is engaged in a search for the distinctly Christian. Milbank's project would, no doubt, by and large attract Spaemann's interest, but with the caveat that it would be yet impossible for him to go 'beyond' modernity, because the relation between modernity and Christianity is, in his view, more complex than most critical accounts of modernity suggest. He seeks to show that faith and reason—and, to some extent, even the shape that reason has found in modernity—can coexist peacefully as independent, though intrinsically related, human faculties.

Spaemann would not deny that certain valuable achievements of modernity are to be affirmed by and integrated into the Christian tradition. His critique of modernity does not intend to recapitulate the anti-modernism of the nineteenth and twentieth centuries. As we have seen, he shows how a certain strand of Catholic anti-modernism, beginning with the restorative ideas of Bonald and Joseph de Maistre, was itself modernistic and, in the long run,

---

[22] 'Christliche Spiritualität und pluralistische Normalität', 163. As Walker Percy said, Christianity brings 'news from across the seas, the very news [man] has been waiting for' ('The Message in the Bottle', in *The Message in the Bottle: How Queer Man Is, How Queer Language Is, and What One Has to Do with the Other* (New York: Farrar, Strauss and Giroux, 1986), 147).

[23] 'Christliche Spiritualität und pluralistische Normalität', 165.

[24] Spaemann, 'Vorbemerkungen', in *Einsprüche: Christliche Reden*, 8.

[25] Spaemann, 'Die Existenz des Priesters', 485.

[26] *Theology and Social Theory: Beyond Secular Reason* (Cambridge, Mass: Blackwell, 1997), 399.

served to undermine the very essentials of Christianity. Spaemann also approves of Dietrich Bonhoeffer's negative theology as a correction of misconceptions of God, while at the same time warning against radicalizations of Bonhoeffer's impetus—for instance, in 'death of God' theologies.[27] Modernism cannot be the last word and must not overlook its limits. Hence, Spaemann proposes that the Christian point of view calls for a correction, not a dismissal, of modernity. From a Christian point of view, he even presumes that 'in the end, it may be the task of Christianity to uphold the dimension of rationality'[28]—and here he is also thinking of the shape that rationality has taken in modernity.

The substantial character of Christianity

According to Spaemann, one of the crucial features of the self-understanding of Christianity is the idea that Christianity must not be instrumentalized either politically or philosophically but must be lived, with a faith that still freely believes in its substantial contents as such and not in relation to an external end. Religion, as we have seen, must not be understood as a function of its society or of the progress of history. This would contradict substantial Christian belief, which presupposes the tension between world history and salvation history and refuses to anthropologize distinctly theological categories such as salvation or providence by applying them to the ways in which history may be shaped by humans. There is a fundamental difference between futurology and prophecy or eschatology, Spaemann states.

We have seen that Spaemann does not limit himself to a critique of left-wing and liberal theological tendencies but also criticizes their right-wing alternative, which lies in attempts to preserve the visible Church and its power for the sake of institutionalized Christianity: 'There is a responsibility of the Christian for life, freedom and even the salvation of the souls of those people who are entrusted to him, yet strictly speaking there is no responsibility for Christianity... Christians have to take care of their neighbours, only God can take care of Christianity'.[29] This explains his polemic against many pastors and bishops to whom 'anti-communism, social market economy and loyalty to the Christian Democratic Party' were 'for a good Catholic more important than the faith in

---

[27] 'Vorbemerkungen', in *Einsprüche: Christliche Reden*, 8–9.

[28] 'Die christliche Religion und das Ende des modernen Bewusstseins', 257; for Spaemann's view that faith is not opposed to rationality, by the "highest form of rationality" see Spaemann, Über die genwärtige Lage des Christentums, in *Das unsterblich Gerücht*, 254; see in this context also Spaemann, Religion und "Tatsachenwahrheit", in *Das unsterbliche Gerücht*, 170f., where Spaemann examines the Christian understanding of truth.

[29] 'Weltgeschichte und Heilsgeschichte, in *Hochland*, 50 (1957/8), 311.

the Holy Trinity'—because of their 'ecclesial interest'.[30] 'The future of the Church', Spaemann argues, 'is God's task and not ours'.[31] Hence, the Church, as a *potestas indirecta*, needs to be detached in its relations with a current government because eternal salvation is more important than temporal happiness and any political commitment of the Church, as Spaemann points out. For him, it is the salvation of the soul that is the primary interest of the Church, rather than even the preservation of life for the mere sake of preserving it; for 'there is *sub specie aeternitatis* no premature dying'.[32] The life of the Christian, Spaemann argues, is ultimately not about improving the world or being concerned with the course of history. It is, in an entirely non-utilitarian way, about saving one's soul and thus preserving one's true freedom.

The historical character of Christianity

Christian theology, Spaemann holds, cannot be assumed into a philosophical logic that, by definition, does not take into account the objectivity of the subjective, the universality of the particular, and the transcendence of the historical. 'Christian faith', Spaemann writes, 'understands itself as ultimate truth, but it is—as Scripture says—"a light that shineth in the darkness,"[33] "a lamp unto my feet"'.[34] In spite of its universal claim, Christianity's particularity will not be superseded in the course of human history. And Christianity does not explain away all the mysteries of the world; it is not a speculative philosophy. Spaemann said that for Fénelon there was only a real and not a speculative resurrection from the speculative Good Friday.[35] This clearly echoes Spaemann's own understanding of Christianity's 'unspeculative' and historical character. Christianity, therefore, transcends the realm of merely secular reason because it presupposes an anthropology and an understanding of history that cannot be integrated into a merely philosophical discourse and conversation.

Christianity, Spaemann argues, presupposes first that the moral problem also lies in reason and in the rational will itself. This implies a devaluation of classical moral philosophy because, given this anthropology, moral betterment depends not upon simply knowing what is good, but upon metanoia. This leads us to the second difference between Christianity and philosophy. Christianity presupposes, as Robert Spaemann points out, the 'infinite significance of the history of the life, death, and resurrection of

---

[30] 'Theologie, Prophetie, Politik', in *Kritik der politischen Utopie*, 58.
[31] 'Christliche Spiritualität und pluralistische Normalität', 170.
[32] 'Die schlechte Lehre vom guten Zweck, in *Grenzen*, 396.
[33] 2 Pet. 1: 19.
[34] Ps. 119: 105.
[35] *Reflexion und Spontaneität*, 307.

Jesus as the Christ'.[36] Christians thus bear witness to a person, to 'a historical fact',[37] as their incommensurable foundation and not to 'some abstract opinions'. The first martyrs, Spaemann points out, 'did not die for the truth of a book, but for Jesus Christ'.[38] This view of Christianity as originating from the transformative power of a historical event, however, does not imply a fideistic conception of faith, but rather entails that faith does have reason and is intrinsically oriented to the full exercise of freedom and reason for the sake of God. 'Faith for the sake of faith', Spaemann argues, is 'nihilistic' because 'the "blind" decision is neither free nor undertaken for God's sake. God is "produced" only as a result of the decision'.[39]

In Spaemann's view, Christianity, unlike philosophy, provides a definite answer to ultimate questions in that it makes a statement about the ultimate character of reality, about the nature of good and evil, the meaning of history, and the destiny of humanity. St Paul's assertion that 'he that is spiritual judgeth all things, yet he himself is judged of no man'[40] is of crucial significance for Spaemann's understanding of Christianity. Philosophy, history, psychology, and sociology cannot understand the spiritual person, but the concrete thinker—Spaemann himself, for example—can make a religiously informed judgement about everything because, for the Christian believer, an answer to ultimate questions has been given historically, in Jesus Christ. For Spaemann, then, Christ himself determines to what extent Christianity can be modernized, and to what extent Christianity is beyond any modernization, since it is not a matter of human design, but of God's revelation in history as unfolded and preserved by the tradition of the Church.[41] Therefore, history as well as human action can only be understood adequately from a Christological point of view that, at the same time, explicates original sin as one of the main presuppositions of any Christian anthropology and theology of history. Christianity remains open to philosophy, however, provided that philosophy (like Spaemann's, for example) does not pretend to present a comprehensive system of reality.[42]

---

[36] 'Wovon handelt die Moraltheologie? Bemerkungen eines Philosophen', in *Communio*, 6 (1977), 294; for the significance of the resurrection of Christ for Spaemann see also his 'Vorwort', in *Das unsterbliche Gerücht*, 8; Spaemann, 'Religion und "Tatsachenwahrheit"', in *Das unsterbliche Gerücht*, 180 ff.

[37] See also Spaemann, 'Das neue Dogma und die Dogmentheorie', 156.

[38] 'Christliche Spiritualität und pluralistische Normalität', 168.

[39] 'Der Irrtum der Traditionalisten: Zur Soziologisierung der Gottesidee im 19. Jahrhundert', in *Wort und Wahrheit*, 8 (1953), 498.

[40] 1 Cor. 2:15.; see, for example, Spaemann, 'Vorwort', in *Das unsterbliche Gerücht*, 9, for Spaemann's reference to this Pauline view.

[41] For Spaemann's understanding of the teaching authority of the Catholic Church see 'Kommentar', in *Die Unantastbarkeit des menschlichen Lebens*, 75–8.

[42] Spaemann, 'Christentum und Philosophie der Neuzeit', 138.

6.3 THE RELATION BETWEEN PHILOSOPHY AND CHRISTIANITY FROM ANTIQUITY TO MODERNITY

It is uncontroversial to argue that the relation between philosophy and Christianity has been problematic in modernity. The philosophy of modernity followed many different, though often converging, trajectories—which were often first to transform, and subsequently to undermine, the truth claim of Christianity based upon the 'faith in a real revelation of God about his own nature, about the origin and the end of man and his fall and redemption'.[43] In a lecture entitled 'Christianity and Modern Philosophy' ('Christentum und Philosophie der Neuzeit'), which Spaemann presented at a symposium in honour of Josef Pieper,[44] he interpreted the modern relation between Christianity and philosophy in light of the ancient and the medieval ways of relating philosophy to Christianity, and proposed a new definition of the relation in late modernity.

He first reminds us in an uncontroversial manner of the relationship between philosophy and Christianity before modernity. In late antiquity the relation was competitive despite Christianity's dialogue with pagan philosophy and integration of certain aspects of it. In the Middle Ages, following the decline of the ancient philosophical schools and because of the culture-forming influence of Christianity, a hierarchical relation between philosophy and Christianity and thus a division of labour came about, as Spaemann argues. While theology was concerned with ultimate questions and their authentic interpretation through the Church, philosophy was de-ideologized, as it were, and could flourish, and speculate, in relative freedom.[45] Spaemann emphasizes that the philosopher was only allowed to teach about the possible, necessary, and impossible, but not about what is contingently the case. Philosophy, by being limited to what Schelling has called 'negative philosophy', was restrained from providing people with a *Weltanschauung* that could possibly have competed with Christianity.

---

[43] Ibid. 123.

[44] For an English translation of this lecture see 'Christianity and Modern Philosophy', in Brian J. Shanley, OP (ed.), *One Hundred Years of Philosophy* (Studies in Philosophy and the History of Philosophy, xxxvi) (Washington, DC: The Catholic University of America Press, 2001), 169–80. For a brief appreciation of Josef Pieper's philosophy and its style see Spaemann, 'Philosophie zwischen Metaphysik und Geschichte: Philosophische Strömungen im heutigen Deutschland', in *Neue Zeitschrift für Systematische Theologie*, 1 (1959), 292; Odo Marquard, 'Der Philosoph als Schriftsteller: Bemerkungen über Søren Kierkegaard und Josef Pieper', in his *Philosophie des Stattdessen: Studien* (Stuttgart: Reclam, 2000), 124–34. It is worth pointing out that Pieper's and Spaemann's philosophical style and their understanding of philosophy and its aim show a certain similarity that would merit further investigation.

[45] Spaemann, 'Christentum und Philosophie der Neuzeit', 125–6.

Philosophy was entirely embedded in a well-ordered intellectual universe of essentially Christian character.

Late scholastic nominalism, Spaemann argues, was characterized by the attempt to emancipate philosophy from theology by expanding the realm of the contingent almost indefinitely.[46] This tendency makes the contingent an abstract notion. Given the late scholastic view of reality, Spaemann argues, moral norms can be understood as due either to human convention or to gracious divine revelation, but not as following from the very nature of reality. Spaemann also points out that this philosophy entails a positivism with reference to the content of revelation. Subsequently, he argues, philosophy takes over the business of providing humanity with *Weltanschauungen*. It has then emancipated itself from Christianity. Modernity, Spaemann therefore argues, is 'on the one side the product of Christianity, on the other the product of an emancipation from Christianity'.[47]

Against the background of this very brief *tour d'horizon* Spaemann analyses the course of modern philosophy. There are, in his view, four main strains of modern philosophy, though he mentions only three of them in this lecture. The first is the scepticism and agnosticism of David Hume and of French Enlightenment thinkers, who explicitly conceive of philosophy as an alternative to ecclesial Christianity.[48] Spaemann does not elaborate upon these philosophies, seeming by this silence to indicate that their influence has not proved as threatening for Christian orthodoxy as that of the second group of philosophies.

Philosophers of this second group pretended to understand Christianity much better and more fully than it could possibly understand itself without philosophical assistance. This is the path taken by the rationalists, by Jean-Jacques Rousseau, and particularly by German transcendental philosophers. Spaemann points out that these philosophers took seriously the fact that Christianity makes a universal claim. However, they attempted to rid this claim of its positive—that is to say, historically and contingently given—foundation because philosophy was meant to be 'negative' in their views. It was supposed to rely on the necessary, the hypothetical, and the impossible, not upon what is positively given. History, tradition, society, even intersubjectivity and nature *as given* were generally understood to be philosophically negligible. To deal with them as always already given meant to fall prey to heteronomy. From an orthodox Christian point of view, the cost of this speculative 'sublating', as it were, of Christianity was very high. Traditional Christian doctrines were transformed by being reformulated in, and integrated

[46] Ibid., 127.
[47] 'Die christliche Religion und das Ende des modernen Bewusstseins', 252.
[48] Spaemann, 'Christentum und Philosophie der Neuzeit', 129.

into, an aprioristic context, and thus were undermined. The ontological and historical uniqueness of Christ could no longer be understood; Christ was reduced to just one paradigmatic example of a good life, for example. Christianity, however, challenges modernity's preoccupation with a manifoldness of paradigmatic figures, which arose in the face of the modern dismissal of a teleological account of human nature and of a Christian understanding of sainthood, as we have already pointed out.

Before Spaemann goes on to sketch an alternative view, he mentions almost in passing a third modern way of interpreting Christianity in its relation to philosophy: the tendency to understand Christianity as a 'natural religion', which had repercussions on Christian theology and led to a conception of religion that focused upon religious feelings. In both cases—whether the philosophical or the theological 'naturalization' of Christianity—the traditional doctrinal truth claim, or truth dimension, of Christianity was no longer considered of central significance. It is obvious that when referring to the theological naturalization of Christianity Spaemann is thinking of Protestant pietism, of Schleiermacher, and of liberal Protestantism.

There is, furthermore, a fourth and very ambiguous way of relating philosophy to Christianity in modernity, which Spaemann does not mention in this lecture. That is the functionalistic critique and defence of Christianity. The functionalistic defence of religion, as we saw in Chapter 4, undermines the unique and absolute character of the Christian truth claim because a functionalistic view of religion not only makes it possible to conceive of 'functional equivalents', but also subordinates the substantial content of Christianity to whatever whole it serves as a function to—the political constitution, for instance, which it is meant to stabilize as a 'civil religion'. In contrast to this, the quintessence of Christianity is in Spaemann's view 'the proclamation of a joy which cannot be violated because its reason lies beyond all possible disadvantageous facts of the matter'.[49]

6.4 CHRISTIANITY AND EVOLUTIONARY METAPHYSICS

Spaemann's view on the proper relation between Christianity and modernity—a relation that can leave the truth claim of Christianity intact—is also expressed in his discussion of Christianity and evolutionary metaphysics, the latter being a distinctly modern theory because of its underlying scientism

---

[49] 'Theologie, Prophetie, Politik', in *Kritik der politischen Utopie*, 75.

and functionalism. Since its beginning, evolutionary theory has often been offered as a new metaphysics, challenging the traditional role of philosophy, theology, and religion. As we have already pointed out, becoming has then become the paradigm for understanding reality, genealogy being its method.

Spaemann has distinguished four ways of regulating the relation between Christianity and evolutionary theory, and in particular evolutionary metaphysics.[50] These four ways exemplify his view of Christianity's positions towards modernity. We will now examine Spaemann's view of the relation between Christianity and evolutionary theory, which will lead us to a discussion of his vision of a truly post-modern relation between philosophy and Christianity, as developed in 'Christianity and the Philosophy of Modernity'.

Spaemann mentions first the theological interpretation of evolutionary theory that sees evolution as history and saving event. Paradigmatic examples, in his view, are Pierre Teilhard de Chardin's thought[51] and Karl Rahner's 'Christology within an Evolutionary View of the World'.[52] Spaemann speaks of their 'pseudo-teleology' and singles out for special criticism the idea that increasing structural complexity is to be adored as such. The integration of human beings into an unconscious all-embracing unity that transcends humanity itself, he argues, must be judged critically if it can be judged at all.[53] Spaemann wonders if it can be judged at all because one does not know, he argues, whether the integration of mankind into the evolutionary process as a new whole does not entail also the abolition of those human standards by which this integration can be considered positive. The pseudo-biological integration of humanity into a unity that transcends humanity (which is, by the way, comparable to Bonald's sociological integration of the single person into the all-embracing structure of society) particularly undermines, Spaemann thinks, the dignity of individual human persons for the sake of a supposedly superior entity.

---

[50] For a view similar to that of Spaemann see Hans-Eduard Hengstenberg, 'Evolutionismus und Schöpfungslehre', in Robert Spaemann, Reinhard Löw, and Peter Koslowski (eds.), *Evolutionismus und Christentum* (*Civitas-Resultate*, ix) (Weinheim: Acta Humaniora/VCH, 1986), 75–89.

[51] See also Spaemann's criticism of Teilhard de Chardin's (and Carsten Bresch's) 'pseudo-teleology' in 'Sein und Gewordensein: Was erklärt die Evolutionstheorie', in *Philosophische Essays*, 202. For Carsten Bresch's adoption of Teilhard's thought see e.g. his *Zwischenstufe Leben: Evolution ohne Ziel?* (Frankfurt am Main: Fischer, 1979).

[52] In his *Theological Investigations*, v, trans. K.-H. Kruger (Baltimore, Md.: Helicon, 1966), 157–92. See also his *Foundations of Christian Faith: An Introduction to the Idea of Christianity*, trans. William V. Dych (New York: Crossroad, 1982), 178–203.

[53] 'Sein und Gewordensein', in *Philosophische Essays*, 202. See also 'Theologie und Pädagogik', in *Einsprüche: Christliche Reden*, 115 for Spaemann's implicit criticism of Teilhard de Chardin's thought (with reference to von Balthasar's critique of Teilhard). In 'Die Frage nach der Bedeutung des Wortes "Gott"' (in *Einsprüche: Christliche Reden*, 34), we find a positive reference to Teilhard's idea that whatever happens is to be adored. Spaemann thinks that this shows Teilhard's 'letting be' (*Gelassenheit*) and his religious understanding of reality.

Spaemann then mentions the 'immunization' against the religious and moral self-understanding of humanity. By this he means the rejection of any religious or moral notion that cannot be reconciled with evolutionary theory. Spaemann mentions that because of the debate about Galileo Galilei's cosmology biblical revelation had been reinterpreted in accord with scientific theory, such that revelation was no longer concerned with the results of scientific research. He sees this reinterpretation of revelation as the reason for the trivialization of the world with which we are confronted today. This trivialization is less trivial than it claims to be, Spaemann argues, for the self-understanding of humanity is at odds with the notion of a vast and entirely trivial universe which, according to Richard Dawkin's fatalist narrative, has 'precisely the properties we should expect if there is, at bottom, no design, no purpose, no evil and no good, nothing but blind, pitiless indifference . . . DNA neither cares nor knows. DNA just is. And we can dance to its music'.[54] Spaemann argues, to the contrary, that the laws that structure this trivialized universe and make it possible for human beings to exercise dominion over it do not allow for an interpretation of non-personal entities by analogy to *Selbstsein*.[55] And he considers such an interpretation to be intuitively evident and, indeed, necessary: 'Analogy is the only possible way of perceiving non-human life'.[56] This is to say that the 'immunization' against our traditional, pre-modern religious and moral self-understanding and the acceptance of the scientific view of reality can be, at best, very limited, such that it does not entail the abolition of our self-understanding.

The third way is radically opposed to the first and second ways. It is the fundamentalist dismissal of modern evolutionary theory as fundamentally defective.

Spaemann, however, places himself within a fourth way of defining the relationship between religion and evolutionary theory: a critique of the epistemological and ontological status of scientific paradigms and genealogical hypotheses in relation to reality. He criticizes evolutionary metaphysics to the extent that it is a variant of reductionism.[57] The very notion 'development' is based upon a serious preliminary decision, Spaemann argues, for it obscures

---

[54] *River out of Eden: A Darwinian View of Life* (London: Weidenfeld & Nicolson, 1995), 155. It almost goes without saying that Dawkin's mythologization of science is self-contradictory, for otherwise his appraisal of Darwinism and modern science would be meaningless: 'Not only does the Darwinian theory command superabundant power to explain. Its economy in doing so has a sinewy elegance, a poetic beauty that outclasses even the most haunting of the world's origin myths' (*River out of Eden*, xiii).

[55] 'Sein und Gewordensein', in *Philosophische Essays*, 187–8.

[56] *Happiness and Benevolence*, 179 (*Glück und Wohlwollen*, 229).

[57] 'Einführung', in Spaemann, Löw, and Koslowski (eds.), *Evolutionismus und Christentum*, 3–5.

the Aristotelian distinction between coming-into-existence (*genesis*) and change (*alloiosis*).[58] In Spaemann's view, the notion 'evolution', like the notion 'development', shows a metaphorical interpretation of the history of nature by means of a concept that is properly applied to the development of an individual organism. Evolution thus implies for Spaemann that there is some kind of universal substance that continuously develops but cannot be reconciled with our own experience of *Selbstsein*. Human beings, in his view, are not simply a material transformation and modification of their ancestors or part of an underlying substance. They are 'more' than just the product of the evolutionary development of a universal substance that is continuously identical with itself and, furthermore, is the only 'thing' that is identical, and identifiable, during the whole process of evolution. And in arguing so Spaemann does not develop an abstract theory about reality, but reminds us of a very concrete self-evident knowledge that we tend to forget.

This is why, in contrast to Richard Dawkins, who argues that 'Darwinism's triumph over alternative explanations of existence . . . is usually portrayed as evidence',[59] Spaemann interprets evolutionary metaphysics as lacking sufficient evidence to support its extensive metaphysical claims. Spaemann claims that his criticism of the metaphysical interpretation of evolutionary theory and of the non-teleological world-view of modernity is a defence of what is always already evident. On the basis of this criticism of evolutionary metaphysics, he favours what he calls a conservative pluralism of theories. Spaemann maintains, for instance, that the Kantian dualism of the noumenal and the phenomenal worlds indicates a path for preserving human subjectivity and freedom against the reductionistic claim of scientism. This dualism and Kant's 'immunization' against scientism do not make the sciences impossible (because they merely show their epistemological and ontological limits). However, as Spaemann argues, they do entail an indifference toward the theories and results of the sciences because Kant did not articulate an adequate notion of the free recognition of the reality of the other as similar to oneself.[60] This Kantian view, he therefore thinks, needs to be complemented by a philosophical re-appreciation of a 'natural view of the world' that, on the one hand, exhibits a more adequate idea of the freedom of recognition with respect to the existence of individual substances and, on the other hand, considers personal Being the paradigm of our understanding of life and of reality (in the tradition of Leibniz and Whitehead—and in some sense

[58] Ibid. 3. See also Aristotle, *Physics*, 201ª.
[59] 'Universal Darwinism', in David L. Hull and Michael Ruse (eds.), *The Philosophy of Biology* (Oxford: Oxford University Press, 1998), 15–37.
[60] 'Sein und Gewordensein', in *Philosophische Essays*, 189–90.

also of Kant, as Spaemann thinks).[61] Spaemann holds that this pluralism provides an alternative to evolutionary metaphysics, to the religious and theological reinterpretation of Christianity's fundamental beliefs, and to its self-'immunization' against modern science. Over against these tendencies, Spaemann critically examines the truth claims of evolutionary theory, recollects the self-evident, and proposes that reality cannot be fully understood simply according to one monistic system (including the monism of Christian fundamentalism) that makes the pseudo-religious claim to offer an ultimate explanation of the whole of reality and to provide an answer to *all* questions. This leads us to an examination of Spaemann view of the relation between Christianity and philosophy in post-modernity.

6.5 CONCLUSION: CHRISTIANITY, POST-MODERN PHILOSOPHIES, AND THE GLORY OF GOD

Spaemann's view of a truly post-modern relation between Christianity and philosophy is reflective of his preference for a pluralism of theories. He favours philosophies that contingently consider the contingent without making pseudo-religious claims and without transforming, or distorting, orthodox Christianity in a typically modern attempt to develop a systematic account of reality, such as in modern nominalism and utilitarianism as '"theologization" of ontology'[62] and of ethics. Leibniz's nominalist philosophy, Spaemann argues, 'is the heyday of a view of the world as system. It attempts to develop an ontology from God's standpoint'[63] and arrogates divine knowledge to itself in claiming to know the individual in its individual essence, making 'each individual its own species'. A similar assumption is made by utilitarianism, because it takes God's point of view, so to speak—systematically analysing the course and meaning of history, and thus transforming, if not altogether dismissing, the doctrine of original sin. However, modern philosophy, in its attempt to take God's position and to understand humanity, history, and society without relying upon positive given knowledge, Spaemann points out, tends to read the doctrine of original sin at best metaphorically as an account of the dichotomy of freedom and nature, and

---

[61] See Spaemann, 'Sein und Gewordensein. Was erklärt die Evolutionstheorie?', in *Philosophische Essays*, 189, for his reading of Leibniz and Whitehead with regard to evolutionary metaphysics. For an interpretation of Kant's understanding of life, see Löw, Reinhard, *Philosophie des Lebendigen. Der Begriff des Organischen bei Kant, sein Grund und seine Aktualität* (Frankfurt am Main: Suhrkamp, 1980).

[62] 'Leibniz' Begriff der Möglichen Welten', 35.

[63] Ibid., 34ff.

understands history and the rise of society as a progressive autonomous emancipation from nature. This denaturalization, as it were, of mankind by explaining
humanity's current state with reference to a merely historical event that does not
primarily affect humanity's relation to God entails a wholly historical view
of humanity. This also entails an anthropocentric transformation of eschatology;
for history is understood simply as an autonomous and self-redemptive
progression towards the fulfilment of humanity. For Spaemann, this contradicts
the *conditio humana*, which is characterized by an 'unpreconceivable' guilt, as
he argues in a manner reminiscent of Schelling's ontology.[64] Truly post-modern
philosophies, then, must refrain from assuming God's position and from
dichotomizing nature and freedom, and must limit themselves so as not to
contradict the truth claim of Christianity and the self-understanding of ourselves
as finite persons who have their nature in freedom.

In his lecture 'Christianity and the Philosophy of Modernity' Spaemann
sketches the direction in which truly post-modern philosophies will move. It
is telling that Spaemann does not explicitly draw attention to contemporary
'post-modern' philosophers, even though the title of his lecture may seem to
indicate this. He is critical, it seems, of post-modernity's pretension to have
surpassed modernity.[65] In setting those philosophical strands aside, he implies that 'post-modernity' stands still in substantially the same relation to
Christianity as modern philosophy; that is, it tends to generate a relation of
sceptical agnosticism, the subsumption of Christianity into philosophy, the
naturalistic reduction of doctrinally substantial faith to doctrinally uncom-
mitted feelings, and a functionalistic and non-substantial interpretation of
Christianity. What, then, is Spaemann's alternative?

According to Spaemann, Søren Kierkegaard's rediscovery of the Christian
difference is not the only alternative to the modern way of determining the
relation between philosophy and religion. The historically less successful
philosophy of Schelling and the theosophical tradition, represented by Baader
and the Russian philosopher Vladimir Solov'ev, also offer an alternative
understanding of Christianity.[66] In contrast to many anti-idealist philosophies—most prominently Kierkegaardian existentialism, Marxism, hermeneutics, and scientific positivism—the later Schelling, as we have already
pointed out, developed an intra-idealist critique of German idealism which

---

[64] 'Das unsterbliche Gerücht', in *Das unsterbliche Gerücht*, 19.

[65] For a similar view see Louis Dupré, *Passage to Modernity: An Essay in the Hermeneutics of
Nature and Culture* (New Haven, Conn./London: Yale University Press, 1993), 6, 250: 'Moreover, we are still living in the modern age and, however critical we may be of the principles
established at its beginning, we continue to share many of them. Critics of modernity implicitly
accept more of its assumptions than they are able to discard' (p. 6).

[66] Spaemann, 'Christentum und Philosophie der Neuzeit', 135–6.

allows us to conceive of the gift of Being, nature, creation, history, and freedom without necessarily undermining the truth claim of Christianity through philosophical reflection. Schelling achieved this by elaborating the intrinsic limits of any negative philosophy of mere consciousness. According to Schelling's 'positive' or 'historical' philosophy, the 'unpreconceivable' gift of Being in nature, history, revelation, and both human and divine freedom cannot be understood by an aprioristic transcendental philosophy because the essential features of reality are neither necessary nor merely hypothetical. Christianity, Schelling argues, therefore resists integration into an aprioristic system of logical truths, which is why a new way to understand it needs to be developed without dismissing transcendental philosophy entirely. Schelling's solution lies in a 'speculative empiricism'—a 'new beginning of philosophy', as Spaemann points out—the main feature of which is that it reflects upon the factual and the contingent.[67] It is evident that Schelling's philosophy parallels Spaemann's philosophy of *Selbstsein* and his attempt to rehabilitate a philosophy of substance without dismissing what he considers indispensable in the modern philosophy of subjectivity and freedom.[68]

In order further to understand why Spaemann's philosophy too provides us with a 'speculative empiricism' we must enquire into the meaning of 'speculative'. Speculation, according to Hans-Georg Gadamer,

means the opposite of the dogmatism of everyday experience. A speculative person is someone who does not abandon himself directly to the tangibility of appearances or to the fixed determinateness of the meant, but who is able to reflect or—to put it in Hegelian terms—who sees that the 'in-self' is a 'for-me'. And a thought is speculative if the relationship it asserts is not conceived as a quality unambiguously assigned to a subject, a property to a given thing, but must be thought of as a mirroring, in which the reflection is nothing but the pure appearance of what is reflected, just as the one is the one of the other, and the other is the other of the one.[69]

Spaemann's 'speculative empiricism' not only shows that philosophical speculation does not need to contradict the gift of reality (thus being empirical in a non-dogmatist way), it also shows how the 'in-self' and the 'for-me' are brought together and reconciled in the experience of the absolute, most importantly in the 'experience' of God and of the person. For in the person the 'in-self' discloses itself as contingently and 'unpreconceivably' given 'for-me' and as an 'image' of the absolute. A speculative empiricism of *Selbstsein*

---

[67] Ibid. 135.

[68] For this see also Thomas Buchheim, *Eins von allem: Die Selbstbescheidung des Idealismus in Schellings Spätphilosophie* (Hamburg: Meiner, 1992), 11, 103.

[69] *Truth and Method*, 2nd, rev., edn., trans. and rev. Joel Weinsheimer and Donald G. Marshall (London: Continuum, 2006), 461–2.

is therefore the alternative that Spaemann proposes to modernity and its dialectic of objectivism and subjectivism. In his discussion of the Thomistic philosophies of Karl Rahner, Max Müller, Gustav Siewerth, and Josef Pieper, Spaemann remarks critically that 'to my knowledge none of these philosophers has made explicitly the object of his thought the question why belonging to a specific religious confession is, as a matter of fact, evidently a condition for the truth of this philosophizing'.[70] But Spaemann's concept of a philosophy that thinks the contingent contingently can provide an answer, because it is more radically historical than the twentieth-century revival, and transformation, of Thomism was and manages at the same time to avoid a historicist reduction of reality.

Schelling's 'positive turn' of philosophy also has theological implications. While Karl Rahner's transcendental Thomism is still, in Spaemann's view, indebted to an aprioristic paradigm, Hans Urs von Balthasar's theological aesthetics and his dramatic theology stand in the tradition of Schelling, in that in them he tries to understand the history of salvation in its character as gift and from its foundation in God's inner-Trinitarian life.[71] Christian theology, Spaemann therefore argues, would benefit from a dialogue with Schellingian and post-Schellingian positive thought that treats the contingent contingently[72] and leads to a renewed appreciation of the historical and the particular—an important enterprise given the naturalistic and positivistic threat to Christianity. Because of the proximity between Schelling's and Spaemann's philosophies, theology, one can argue, can also benefit considerably from engaging in a discussion with Spaemann's thought. But Spaemann also shows how philosophy can benefit from a dialogue with the Christian view of reality as free creation. The notions of 'person', 'contingency', and 'freedom' could not, according to Spaemann, have been philosophically fully

---

[70] 'Philosophie zwischen Metaphysik und Geschichte', 293.

[71] 'Christentum und Philosophie der Neuzeit', 137. For an implicit reference to Balthasar's dramatic view of the history of salvation see Spaemann, 'Zum Sinn des Ethikunterrichts in der Schule', in *Grenzen*, 523. For a discussion of Balthasar's dramatic theology see my 'Mythos und Geschichte: Hans Urs von Balthasar und die griechische Tragödie', in Walter Kasper (ed.), *Im Dialog—Die Logik der Liebe Gottes* (Mainz: Grünewald, 2006), 45–63; 'Tragik und Erlösung des Menschen: Hans Urs von Balthasars "Theodramatik" im Kontext', *Communio*, 34 (2005), 128–35. For Spaemann's brief discussion of Rahner's Thomism see also 'Philosophie zwischen Metaphysik und Geschichte', 291–2.

[72] Spaemann briefly mentions that important recent works on Schelling have been produced by theologians such as Walter Kasper (*Das Absolute in der Geschichte: Philosophie und Theologie der Geschichte in der Spätphilosophie Schellings* (Mainz: Grünewald, 1965)). Spaemann could also have mentioned the Catholic theologian, philosopher of religion, and later bishop Klaus Hemmerle (see his *Gott und das Denken nach Schellings Spätphilosophie* (Freiburg im Breisgau/ Basle/Vienna: Herder, 1968)) and his interest in Franz von Baader (see his *Franz von Baaders philosophischer Gedanke der Schöpfung* (Freiburg im Breisgau/Munich: Alber, 1961)).

appropriated and developed without biblical revelation and Christian theology. For, the idea that reality could not be at all, or could be essentially different from the way it is, could only develop on the basis of belief in a freely creating God.[73] Christianity and philosophy thus stand in a very complex relation to one another. They can benefit from one another, Spaemann argues, as long as they work symbiotically on common themes 'without this endeavour being coordinated through a preliminary methodological decision'.[74] Spaemann is sceptical of a prior methodological regulation of the relation between Christianity and philosophy because this would undermine the categorical difference between faith and reason and integrate them into a common framework, whether of a theological or a philosophical character.

So it is possible to argue that Spaemann's understanding of philosophy provides us with a sound alternative to the shortcomings of a great deal of modern and late modern philosophy. This is the case because his philosophy shows the limits of secular reason and prevents it from abolishing itself and humanity, while refusing to dismiss secular reason altogether. Such a rejection of reason could never be an intellectually satisfying solution because it entails an attempt to establish another comprehensive 'grand narrative' according to the same failed method of much modern thinking.

Spaemann's philosophy as a 'recollection' thus allows us to understand categories such as meaning and freedom, which, he points out, cannot be constructed from an a priori point of view.[75] They are 'always already given' and do not fit into the historicist and naturalist categories of the universalizing, homogenizing, and hypothesizing mind. It is not only meaning and freedom, but also dignity, history, nature, pain, the other human being, and the absolute that need to be recollected—and thereby a notion of reality as it discloses itself to us. Substance and subject, being and meaning, nature and freedom, reflection and spontaneity, mediation and immediacy, as well as Being and becoming, therefore, need to be thought of together without being dialectically synthesized or understood in a reductive manner. For this would be an attempt to overcome the dichotomy of nature and freedom and thus a bold attempt to undo the fall and to secularize eschatology.

In contrast to the modern polarization of nature and freedom, the orthodox doctrine of the fall does not deny the complementary relation between nature and freedom, but contributes to a deeper understanding of

---

[73] 'Das unsterbliche Gerücht', in *Das unsterbliche Gerücht*, 24; see also Spaemann, 'Religion und "Tatsachenwahrheit"', in *Das unsterbliche Gerücht*, 174, where Spaemann speaks of an unsurpassable 'radicalization' of the experience of contingency due to the Jewish and Christian belief in creation.

[74] 'Christentum und Philosophie der Neuzeit', 138.

[75] 'Die zwei Grundbegriffe der Moral, in *Kritik der politischen Utopie*, 22.

it in a non-philosophical context. There is, according to Spaemann, 'nothing more rational than this idea' of original sin.[76] It shows that human beings are fallen and that what they ought to do is not simply what they are naturally inclined to do or what they want to do in their exercise of freedom. It also shows that human beings are given freedom, but have not been 'redeemed' from their nature. Nature is created and is the very condition of freedom. Hence, human beings are neither mere nature nor mere freedom and must freely relate to their nature—and this Christian anthropology also shapes the Christian view of history and the idea that people cannot and must not arrogate to themselves God's own position. This Christian standpoint, as we have seen, forms Spaemann's metaphysical realism and its implications.

In a way that is reminiscent of Heidegger[77] Spaemann recommends the virtue of letting be (*Gelassenheit*) as the 'highest expression of freedom.'[78] This virtue is a kind of placidity, sceptical about the pretensions of modernity, fitted not only for our late modern age, but for all human beings, who, despite their finitude, strive for infinity and are thus in danger of abusing their freedom and of turning the relation between nature and freedom upside down.[79] Letting be is, further-more, in its fullest sense, the attitude of the believer, because for him 'the reality with respect to which we fail is the will of God as well as the command to act.'[80] In the face of the homogenizing universalism of modern rationality that levels any kind of difference (and thus abolishes both freedom and responsibility in their concreteness) Spaemann also recollects the idea of an *ordo amoris*, 'which is founded in the finite relations of closeness and distance'. In Spaemann's view, human beings who in order to accept their finitude acknowledge the limitations of their responsibility, and thus live in dignity, also need the 'virtue of a new teleological thought' and the capacity to 'let what is be.'[81] This, he reasons, is what the freedom of *Selbstsein* requires. In our time of crisis Spaemann there-fore suggests 'a new view of what morality means' and reformulates Kant's

---

[76] Spaemann, 'Rationalität als "Kulturelles Erbe"', 311; see for Spaemann's understanding of original sin also Spaemann, 'Über den Sinn des leidens' (*Einsprüche. Christliche Reden*), 126.

[77] See e.g. Heidegger, 'Gelassenheit', in his *Reden und andere Zeugnisse eines Lebensweges 1910–1976* (*Gesammelte Werke*, 16) (Frankfurt am Main: Klostermann, 2000), 517–29.

[78] 'Über den Begriff der Menschenwürde, in *Grenzen*, 115; see also Spaemann, *Persons*, 77 (*Personen*, 87).

[79] For Spaemann's scepticism and his critical attitude see also Robert Spaemann and Hanns-Gregor Nissing, 'Die Natur des Lebendigen und das Ende des Denkens: Entwicklungen und Entfaltungen eines philosophischen Werks. Ein Gespräch', in Nissing (ed.), *Grundvollzüge der Person: Dimensionen des Menschseins bei Robert Spaemann* (Munich: Institut zur Förderung der Glaubenslehre, 2008), 133; Spaemann, 'Über die gegenwärtige Lage des Christentums', in *Das unsterbliche Gerücht*, 226.

[80] Spaemann, 'Christliche Religion und Ethik', in *Einspruch: Christliche Reden*, 63.

[81] *Die Frage 'Wozu?'*, 287.

categorical imperative: 'there is nothing at all that we can and may use only as a means to an end'.[82] Otherwise, if we do not rediscover some kind of 'natural normality' and natural ends and, thereby, learn to let persons and things be what they are, Spaemann holds, the human species is in danger of abolishing itself.

This does not mean, as we have seen, that he naively defends the 'normal' in the sense of what is presently customary. A customary state of affairs, he admits, can be perverse.[83] He remembers nature and 'natural tendencies' in order to show how one can meaningfully conceive of freedom and human dignity, preserving the achievements of modernity and criticizing its errors. In so doing, Spaemann also defends the unconditional and absolute character of reality, particularly of moral absolutes, over against a hypothetical and relativistic genealogy, for 'if one speaks of the phenomenon of morality (*Sittlichkeit*), genesis and validity are *necessarily* separated'.[84] Faced with the crisis of modern rationality, philosophy ought to summon up what is self-evident in making a strong case for a realist understanding of truth, with its 'sociological uselessness and thus its liberating character'.[85] He concedes that the 'idea of an objective science without any presuppositions and the ethos which lies in taking note of facts without resistance'[86] and the modern 'discovery' of subjectivity, freedom, and universal human rights must not be undone. In his essay 'Hegel and the French Revolution' Spaemann's teacher Joachim Ritter argued that according to Hegel's philosophy of freedom one cannot go beyond what has been both positively and negatively concluded by the French Revolution: 'Every present and future legal and political order must presuppose and proceed from the Revolution's universal principle of freedom'.[87] Spaemann assesses modernity in a similar way, whilst also defending Christianity as 'a truth that alone can give pluralism an absolute basis and can hence prevent it from abolishing itself'.[88]

This also has political implications. If Europe exports the modern technological civilization, Spaemann argues, it has also to export modern values such as the idea of the dignity of the person and the constitutional state and the separation of powers, of which he thinks very highly, for they at once

---

[82] 'Nebenwirkungen als moralisches Problem', in *Kritik der politischen Utopie*, 182.

[83] See e.g. 'Sind alle Menschen Personen?', in *Communio*, 19 (1990), 109.

[84] *Die Frage 'Wozu?'*, 260.

[85] 'Der Irrtum der Traditionalisten', 497.

[86] See Spaemann, 'Die christliche Religion und das Ende des modernen Bewusstseins', 269.

[87] 'Hegel and the French Revolution', 52 ('Hegel und die französische Revolution', in *Metaphysik und Politik* (Frankfurt am Main: Suhrkamp, 1969), 201. Hermann Lübbe has drawn attention to the influence of Ritter's *Hegel and the French Revolution* as a key text for important debates about the history of ideas in the early 1960s; see his 'Laudatio', in *Gedenkschrift Joachim Ritter zur Gedenkfeier zu Ehren des am 3 August 1974 verstorbenen em. ordentlichen Professors der Philosophie Dr. phil. Joachim Ritter* (Münster: Aschendorff, 1978), 18).

[88] 'Die christliche Religion und das Ende des modernen Bewusstseins', 269.

respect and mistrust human beings; they are thus reflective of the ambivalence of persons and do justice both to the creation of human beings in God's image and to the fallenness of mankind.[89] The acknowledgement of 'the smallness and ugliness of humanity' which is of central significance for Spaemann also prevents the dialectic of idealism and cynicism[90] and thus the attitude of a familiar figure of late modernity; namely, the mocker who, disappointed by the modern idealization of humanity, 'sees that the world is not alright and thinks that this is excellent'.[91] In contrast to idealist, cynical, totalitarian, and Utopian views of politics, Spaemann characterizes political action as mediation between what is already there and what is to be achieved: 'Political action always means doing whatever makes most sense given the conditions, even if we did not choose them, or in other words, doing the best possible thing under the circumstances. Of course this may involve trying to change the circumstances'.[92] Spaemann refers occasionally to how his experience in Nazi Germany formed his philosophy and its anti-totalitarian outlook. In the preface to the *Philosophische Essays* he mentions that growing up during the Nazi period he developed an opposition to the idea—typical of many progress-focused modernistic approaches—that 'one can no longer think this way today'.[93] As we have seen, Spaemann is to be credited with an interpretation of contemporary culture that discloses often well-hidden totalitarian tendencies along the lines of 'one can no longer think this way today'. At the centre of his criticism of every kind of totalitarianism is the idea of human dignity, which, he argues, is 'in its origin and in its nucleus not political. It presupposes that the political organization of human life does not coincide with the realm of the fulfilment of a meaningful life'.[94] Such fulfilment must be sought elsewhere—far beyond the framework of politics and of modernity.

Spaemann once argued that philosophy needs to rethink the relation between immediacy and mediation vis-à-vis the functionalistic dissolution of reality into becoming.[95] This leads us, from yet another and more direct perspective, to see once again the key problem of modernity, which may well be understood to be the epistemological problem of how to understand the relation between immediacy and mediation or the ontological problem of how to relate identity to

---

[89] 'Rationalität als "Kulturelles Erbe"', 312.

[90] See Spaemann, 'Der Spötter', in *Frankfurter Hefte*, 7/3 (1948), 643. For the similar dialectic of fanaticism and cynicism see his *Basic Moral Concepts*, 84–5 (*Moralische Grundbegriffe*, 102–3).

[91] 'Der Spötter', 641.

[92] *Basic Moral Concepts*, 81 (*Moralische Grundbegriffe*, 99).

[93] 'Einleitung', in *Philosophische Essays*, 8. See also his 'Politisches Engagement und Reflexion: Rede zum 17 Juni 1964', in *Kritik der politischen Utopie*, 33–4.

[94] 'Rationalität als "Kulturelles Erbe"', 312.

[95] Here Spaemann is writing with regard to Niklas Luhmann's sociology; see *Paradigm Lost*, 71.

difference. Classical philosophy, Spaemann argues, provided an answer to this question by conceiving of unity as substance, modern philosophy by replacing substance with unity-creating subjectivity.[96] The modern understanding of subjectivity, however, oscillates dialectically between transcendentalism and naturalism, the absolutization of immediacy or of mediation. This is also why Christianity could no longer be understood fully in modernity, because Christian faith is not possible without mediation through biblical revelation, the history of the Church, its teaching tradition, the history of theological research and reflection, the witness of saints, and life in a Christian community. Yet faith is also about the immediate relation between oneself and God and depends, in the end, upon a solitary decision. Christianity and its history are therefore based upon a balanced relation between the immediacy of grace and the mediation of nature (as a creation) and of a given tradition. To dismiss this relation would mean counterfactually to anticipate a situation that Christians hope for, but must not strive to realize by themselves. This may be even the main reason for the dialectic of modernity.

Over against the dialectic of modernity, Spaemann awakens his students to reality as a creation, both fallen and good, and he recollects the complementary relation of immediacy and mediation, of freedom and nature. This makes it possible for human beings to acknowledge their limitations, to be thankful for what is, and therefore, in an always anticipatory way, to become happy.[97] Where no merely philosophical answer is forthcoming, and should not even be sought, religion, as we have seen, comes into play. Spaemann's philosophy of *Selbstsein* therefore leads to a religious point of view, for 'religion makes it possible for human beings to understand themselves as natural beings without cancelling themselves out as persons, and, correspondingly, to perceive themselves as subjects without being forced to disavow their nature as an *adiaphoron*.'[98] Spaemann concludes that it is not the case that reflection is the truth of transcendence, while the gift disclosed in the act of transcendence is the truth of reflection. Being is 'unpreconceivable'. The very gift of reality—most prominently, the reality of *Selbstsein*—is the *prius* of all transcendental a priori knowledge. It is the glory of the human person in which we realize that the 'in-self' is a 'for-me' and in which we thus encounter an unconditional command and the image of God.[99] As human beings, we always already have

---

[96] Ibid. 55.

[97] For the relation between happiness and thankfulness see Spaemann, 'Über den Sinn des Leidens', in *Einsprüche: Christliche Reden*, 119.

[98] *Persons*, 98 (*Personen*, 107).

[99] See in this context also Holger Zaborowski, 'Ikonisches Existieren: Zur Hermeneutik des Menschseins', in *Spielräume der Freiheit: Zur Hermeneutik des Menschseins* (Freiburg im Breisgau/Munich: Alber, 2009), 19–58.

to respond to this command—by being benevolent and by glorifying God. For the glorification of God, Spaemann states, is the only thing that human beings can be good for[100] without being reduced to fulfilling a function.[101] 'In fact, the earthly city glories in itself, the Heavenly City glories in the Lord'[102]—and thus finds its true happiness.

---

[100] 'Vorbemerkungen', in *Einsprüche: Christliche Reden*, 10.
[101] For this idea see 'Die Existenz des Priesters: Eine Provokation in der modernen Welt', 490.
[102] Augustine, *City of God*, XIV, 28, trans. Henry Bettenson (London: Penguin Books, 1984) 593.

Select bibliography of primary and secondary sources

For the most recent bibliography of Robert Spaemann's writings that also contains a comprehensive list of Spaemann's journal essays, book chapters, and newspaper articles, and lists the translations and reprints of his works, see Hans Gregor Nissing, 'Robert Spaemann: Schriftenverzeichnis 1947–2007', in Nissing (ed.), *Grundvollzüge der Person: Dimensionen des Menschseins bei Robert Spaemann* (Munich: Institut zur Förderung der Glaubenslehre, 2008), 137–98. This book is available online at <http://www.denken-im-glauben.de/Downloads/Spaemann.htm>.

Monographs and collections of essays by Spaemann

Der Ursprung der Soziologie aus dem Geist der Restauration: Studien über L. C. A. de Bonald (Munich: Kösel, 1959; 2nd edn., Stuttgart: Klett-Cotta, 1998).

Reflexion und Spontaneität: Studien über Fénelon (Stuttgart: Kohlhammer, 1963; 2nd edn., Stuttgart: Klett-Cotta, 1990).

Einsprüche: Christliche Reden (Sammlung Horizonte, NS, xii) (Einsiedeln: Johannes, 1977).

Zur Kritik der politischen Utopie: Zehn Kapitel politischer Philosophie (Stuttgart: Klett-Cotta, 1977).

Rousseau—Bürger ohne Vaterland: Von der Polis zur Natur (Munich: Piper, 1980; 2nd edn., Munich/Zürich: Piper, 1992).

Die Frage Wozu? Geschichte und Wiederentdeckung des teleologischen Denkens (Munich/Zürich: Piper, 1981; 2nd edn., Munich/Zürich: Piper, 1985; 3rd edn., Munich/Zürich: Piper, 1991); repr. with a new preface under the title *Natürliche Ziele: Geschichte und Wiederentdeckung des teleologischen Denkens* (Stuttgart: Klett-Cotta, 2005) (written with Reinhard Löw).

Moralische Grundbegriffe (Munich: Beck, 1982). *Philosophische Essays* (Stuttgart: Reclam, 1983; 2nd edn., 1993).

Moralische Grundbegriffe (Munich: Beck, 1982). *Philosophische Essays* (Stuttgart: Reclam, 1983; 2nd edn., 1993).

Das Natürliche und das Vernünftig:. Aufsätze zur philosophischen Anthropologie (Munich/Zürich: Piper, 1987).

Glück und Wohlwollen: Versuch über Ethik (Stuttgart: Klett-Cotta, 1989; 4th edn., 1998).

Die Zweideutigkeit des Glücks (pub. privately; Stuttgart, 1990).

Personen: Versuche über den Unterschied zwischen 'etwas' und 'jemand' (Stuttgart: Klett-Cotta, 1996; 2nd edn., 1998; 3rd edn., 2006).

Das unsterbliche Gerücht: Die Frage nach Gott und die Täuschung der Moderne (Stuttgart: Klett-Cotta, 2007; 2nd edn., 2007; 3rd edn., 2007).
Der letzte Gottesbeweis, Mit einer Einführung in die großen Gottesbeweise und einem Kommentar zum Gottesbeweis Robert Spaemanns von Rolf Schönberger (Munich: Pattoch, 2007).

Books edited and co-edited by Spaemann

SPAEMANN, ROBERT, *Ethik-Lesebuch: Von Platon bis heute* (Munich/Zürich: Piper, 1987); new edn., ed. Robert Spaemann and Walter Schweidler, *Ethik—Lehr- und Lesebuch: Texte, Fragen, Antworten* (Stuttgart: Klett-Cotta, 2006; 2nd edn., 2007).

SPAEMANN, CORDELIA, *Gedichte und Prosa* (pub. privately; Stuttgart 2005).

SPAEMANN, ROBERT, and BÖCKENFÖRDE, ERNST-WOLFGANG (eds.) *Menschenrechte und Menschenwürde: Historische Voraussetzungen—säkulare Gestalt—christliches Verständnis* (Stuttgart: Klett-Cotta, 1987).

SPAEMANN, ROBERT, and FUCHS, THOMAS (eds.), *Töten oder sterben lassen? Worum es in der Euthanasiedebatte geht* (Freiburg im Breisgau: Herder, 1997; 2nd edn., 1998).

SPAEMANN, ROBERT, and KOSLOWSKI, PETER (eds.), *Evolutionstheorie und menschliches Selbstverständnis: Zur philosophischen Kritik eines Paradigmas moderner Wissenschaften* (Civitas-Resultate, vi) (Weinheim: Acta Humaniora, 1984).

SPAEMANN, ROBERT, and KRIELE, MARTIN (eds.), Anonymus d'Outre tombe, *Die Großen Arcana des Tarot, Meditationen: Einführung von Hans Urs von Balthasar*, 4 vols. (Sammlung Überlieferung und Weisheit) (Basle: Herder, 1983).

SPAEMANN, ROBERT, GEACH, PETER, and INCIARTE, FERNANDO (eds.), *Persönliche Verantwortung* (Lindenthal-Institut Colloquium, Cologne, 1982) (Cologne: Adamas, 1982).

SPAEMANN, ROBERT, KOSLOWSKI, PETER, and LÖW, REINHARD (eds.), *Moderne oder Postmoderne? Zur Signatur des gegenwärtigen Zeitalters* (Civitas-Resultate, x) (Weinheim: Acta Humaniora/VCH, 1986).

SPAEMANN, ROBERT, LÖW, REINHARD, and KOSLOWSKI, PETER (eds.), *Evolutionismus und Christentum* (Civitas-Resultate, ix) (Weinheim: Acta Humaniora/VCH, 1984).

——— ——— ——— (eds.), *Expertenwissen und Politik* (Civitas-Resultate, xii) (Weinheim: VCH, 1990).

SPAEMANN, ROBERT, SCHÖNBORN, CHRISTOPH, and GÖRRES, ALBERT (eds.), *Zur kirchlichen Erbsündenlehre: Stellungnahmen zu einer brennenden Frage* (Kriterien, lxxxvii) (Einsiedeln/Freiburg im Breisgau: Johannes, 1991; 2nd edn., 1994).

SPAEMANN, ROBERT, WELSCH, WOLFGANG, and ZIMMERLI, WALTHER Ch. (eds.) *Zweckmäßigkeit und menschliches Glück: Bamberger Hegelwochen 1993* (Bamberg: Fränkischer Tag, 1994).

SPAEMANN, ROBERT, et al. (eds.), *Disiecta Membra: Studien Karlfried Gründer zum 60. Geburtstag* (Basle: Schwabe 1989; Darmstadt: Wissenschaftliche Buchgesellschaft, 1989).

Important essays and short works by Spaemann (not contained in the collections of essays listed above)

'Der Dichter und das Ganze', in *Die Lücke: Zeitschrift für Kulturpolitik und Kunst*, 1 (1947), 20–3. 'Das Vertrauen als sittlicher Wert', in *Die Kirche in der Welt*, 1 (1947/8).

'Der Dichter und das Ganze', in *Die Lücke: Zeitschrift für Kulturpolitik und Kunst*, 1 (1947), 20–3. 'Das Vertrauen als sittlicher Wert', in *Die Kirche in der Welt*, 1 (1947/8).

'Der Spötter', in *Frankfurter Hefte*, 3 (1948), 640–4.

'Die Benediktiner', in *Kirche und Leben*, 28 (10 July 1949).

'Das Buch "Koheleth"', in *Frankfurter Hefte*, 4 (1949), 413–21.

'Der Christ und die demokratische Autorität', in *Kirche und Leben*, 39 (25 Sept. 1949).

'Der heilige Franz und seine Söhne', in *Kirche und Leben*, 30 (24 July 1949).

'Die Jesuiten', in *Kirche und Leben*, 39 (29 Sept. 1949).

'Der Sonntag christlich verstanden', in *Kirche und Leben*, (11 Sept. 1949).

'Wer es fassen kann . . . Warum es den Ordensstand gibt', in *Kirche und Leben*, 27 (3 July 1949).

'Zur Frage der Notwendigkeit des Schöpfungswillens Gottes', in *Philosophisches Jahrbuch*, 60 (1950), 88–92.

'Die Zäsur des neunzehnten Jahrhunderts', in *Wort und Wahrheit*, 6 (1951), 71–3.

'Das neue Dogma und die Dogmentheorie', in *Münchner Theologische Zeitschrift*, 3 (1952), 151–60.

'Der Irrtum der Traditionalisten: Zur Soziologisierung der Gottesidee im 19. Jahrhundert', in *Wort und Wahrheit*, 8 (1953), 493–8.

' "Politik zuerst"? Das Schicksal der Action Française', in *Wort und Wahrheit*, 8 (1953), 655–62.

'Die Sendung der Jeanne d'Arc', in *Wort und Wahrheit*, 8 (1953), 376–8.

'Die Schwindsucht des Spinoza', in *Wort und Wahrheit*, 8 (1953), 787–90.

'Christliche Antworten auf die soziale Frage: Franz Baader und die Romantiker', in *Die Mitarbeit*, 3/8 (1954/5), 6–9.

'Ein Schlüsselloch für die Ungläubigen? Die Öffentlichkeit des Kultes und die Fernsehübertragung der Messe', in *Wort und Wahrheit*, 9 (1954), 165–8.

'Wenn die Liebe auf Widerspruch stößt', *Caritas: Zeitschrift für Caritasarbeit und Caritaswissenschaft*, 57 (1956), 278–80.

'Wiedereinführung der Todesstrafe?', in *Wort und Wahrheit*, 11 (1956), 49–53.

'Das Zeichen, dem widersprochen wird: Ein Wort über die Kirche beim Kölner Katholikentag', in *Wort und Wahrheit*, 11 (1956), 893–905.

'Weltgeschichte und Heilsglaube', in *Hochland*, 50 (1957/8), 297–311.

'Philosophie zwischen Metaphysik und Geschichte: Philosophische Strömungen im heutigen Deutschland', in *Neue Zeitschrift für systematische Theologie*, 1 (1959), 290–313.

SPAEMANN, ROBERT, and GRÜNDER, KARLFRIED, 'Geschichtsphilosophie', in Josef Höfer and Karl Rahner (eds.), *Lexikon für Theologie und Kirche*, iv, 2nd edn. (Freiburg im Breisgau: Herder, 1960), 783–91.

SPAEMANN, ROBERT, and BÖCKENFÖRDE, ERNST-WOLFGANG, 'Christliche Moral und atomare Kampfmittel', in *Militärseelsorge: Zeitschrift des katholischen Militärbischofsamtes*, 3 (1961), 267–301.

'Dialektik und Pädagogik', in Johannes Zielinski (eds.), *Pädagogische Aspekte in unserer Welt: Festschrift für Ernst Lichtenstein zum 60. Geburtstag 13.12.1960 von seinen
Freunden, Kollegen und Schülern* (Ratingen: Henn, 1961), 21–36.

SPAEMANN, ROBERT, and BÖCKENFÖRDE, ERNST-WOLFGANG, 'Noch einmal: Christliche
Moral und atomare Kampfmittel', in *Militärseelsorge: Zeitschrift des katholischen
Militärbischofsamtes*, 4 (1962), 213–29.

'Fénelon et l'argument du pari', in *Archives de Philosophie*, 29 (1966), 163–74.

'Gesichtspunkte der Philosophie', in Hans Jürgen Schultz (ed.), *Wer ist das eigen-
tlich—Gott?* (Munich: Kösel 1969), 56–65.

'Autonomie, Mündigkeit, Emanzipation: Zur Ideologisierung von Rechtsbegriffen', in
Siegfried Oppolzer (ed.), *Erziehungswissenschaft 1971: Zwischen Herkunft und Zukunft der Gesellschaft. In memoriam Ernst Lichtenstein* (Wuppertal: Henn, 1971),
317–24.

'"Fanatisch" und "Fanatismus"', in *Archiv für Begriffsgeschichte*, 15 (1971), 256–74;
rev. as 'Fanatisch und Fanatismus', in Joachim Ritter and Karlfried Gründer (eds.),
Historisches Wörterbuch der Philosophie, ii (Basle: Schwabe, 1972), 904–8.

'"Fanatisch" und "Fanatismus"', in *Archiv für Begriffsgeschichte*, 15 (1971), 256–74;
rev. as 'Fanatisch und Fanatismus', in Joachim Ritter and Karlfried Gründer (eds.),
Historisches Wörterbuch der Philosophie, ii (Basle: Schwabe, 1972), 904–8.

'Von Einem, der davonkam', in *Wort und Wahrheit*, 26 (1971), 170–3.

'Freiheit IV', in Joachim Ritter and Karlfried Gründer (eds.), *Historisches Wörterbuch
der Philosophie*, ii (Basle: Schwabe, 1972), 1088–98.

'Genius malignus', in Joachim Ritter and Karlfried Gründer (eds.), *Historisches Wörterbuch der Philosophie*, iii (Basle: Schwabe, 1974), 309–10.

'Glück. III. Neuzeit', in Joachim Ritter and Karlfried Gründer (eds.), *Historisches
Wörterbuch der Philosophie*, iii (Basle: Schwabe, 1974), 697–707.

'Gut, höchstes', in Joachim Ritter and Karlfried Gründer (eds.), *Historisches Wörterbuch der Philosophie*, iii (Basle: Schwabe, 1974), 973–6.

'Philosophie als institutionalisierte Naivität', in *Philosophisches Jahrbuch*, 81 (1974),
139–42.

'Der Verzicht auf Teleologie—Diskussionsbemerkungen', in Rolf E. Vente (ed.),
Erfahrung und Erfahrungswissenschaft (Stuttgart: Kohlhammer, 1974), 90–5.

'Religion und Ethos', in Erich Kellner (ed.), *Religionslose Gesellschaft: Sind wir morgen
Nihilisten?* (Gespräche der Paulus-Gesellschaft, vi) (Wien: Europa, 1976), 89–107.

'Bildung zwischen Emanzipationsideologie und Leistungsdruck', in *Lehren und Ler-
nen—Zeitschrift der Landesstelle für Erziehung und Unterricht*, 3/2 (1977), 37–50.

'Staat und Gesellschaft', in Walter Leisner (ed.), *Staatsethik* (Gesellschaft, Kirche,
Wirtschaft, ix) (Cologne: Hanstein, 1977), 40–4.

'Überzeugungen in einer hypothetischen Zivilisation', in Oskar Schatz (ed.),
Abschied von Utopia? Anspruch und Auftrag der Intellektuellen (Graz: Styria,
1977), 311–31.

'Wovon handelt die Moraltheologie? Bemerkungen eines Philosophen', in *Communio*, 6 (1977).

'Christliche Erziehung in der christlichen Schule', in *Marchtaler pädagogische Beiträge*, 1 (1978), 11–22.

'Der Streit der Philosophen', in Hermann Lübbe (ed.), *Wozu Philosophie? Stellungnahmen eines Arbeitskreises* (Berlin: de Gruyter, 1978), 91–106.

'Die christliche Religion und das Ende des modernen Bewusstseins: Über einige Schwierigkeiten des Christentums mit dem sogenannten modernen Menschen', 8 (1979), 251–70.

Gut und böse, relativ? Über die Allgemeingültigkeit sittlicher Normen (Antwort des Glaubens, xii), 2nd edn. (Freiburg im Breisgau: ,1979; 2nd edn., 1982).

'Christentum und Kernkraft: Ethische Aspekte der Energiepolitik—Ein Beitrag zur Diskussion', in *Die politische Meinung*, 25/192 (1980), 39–46.

'Emanzipation', in Martin Greiffenhagen (ed.), *Kampf um Wörter? Politische Begriffe im Meinungsstreit* (Schriftenreihe der Bundeszentrale für politische Bildung, clxiii) (Munich/Vienna: 1980), 149–56.

'Die Existenz des Priesters: Eine Provokation in der modernen Welt', in *Communio*, 9 (1980), 481–500.

'Über nichtrationale Voraussetzungen des Vernunftgebrauchs', in Michael Zöller (ed.), *Aufklärung heute: Bedingungen unserer Freiheit* (Texte und Thesen) (Zürich: 1980), 116–27.

'Humanwissenschaften oder praktische Weisheit? Bemerkungen zur "neuen Moral" des Pater Andre Guindon', in *Studia Moralia*, 19/2 (1981), 259–79.

'Laudatio', in *L'heritage de Kant: Mélanges philosophiques offerts au P. Marcel Régnier* (Paris: Beauchesne, 1981), 17–23.

'Was ist das Neue? Vom Ende des modernen Bewußtseins', in *Die politische Meinung*, 203 (July/Aug. 1982), 11–27.

'Zwei Psalmenmeditationen', in Johannes Bours (ed.), *Das Fischernetz Gottes* (Freiburg im Breisgau: Herder, 1983), 69–85.

'Aus der Laudatio zum 80. Geburtstag von Hans Jonas', in *Scheidewege*, 13 (1983/4), 103–5.

'Christliche Hoffnung und weltliche Hoffnungsideologien', in Zentralkomitee der Deutschen Katholiken (ed.), *Dem Leben trauen, weil Gott es mit uns lebt*, 88: *Deutscher Katholikentag vom 4. bis 8. Juli 1984. Dokumentation* (Paderborn: Bonifatius, 1984), 214–27.

'Die Dialektik des Wohlbefindens', in Karl Otto Apel et al. (eds.), *Funkkolleg Praktische Philosophie/Ethik: Studientexte*, iii (Weinheim/Basle: Beltz, 1984), 935–58.

'Moral, provisorische', in Joachim Ritter and Karlfried Gründer (eds.), *Historisches Wörterbuch der Philosophie*, vi (Basle: Schwabe, 1984), 172–4.

'Die technologische und ökologische Krisenerfahrung als Herausforderung an die praktische Vernunft', in Kurt-Otto Apel et al. (eds.), *Funkkolleg Praktische Philosophie/Ethik: Dialoge*, i (Frankfurt am Main: Fischer, 1984), 402–21 (written with Gunnar Skirbekk).

'Die technologische und ökologische Krisenerfahrung als Herausforderung an die praktische Vernunft', in Kurt Otto Apel et al. (eds.), *Funkkolleg Praktische Philosophie/Ethik: Studientexte*, ii (Weinheim/Basle: Beltz, 1984), 470–92.

'Das Verhältnis des Menschen zu dem, was nicht von ihm abhängt', in Kurt Otto Apel et al. (eds.), *Funkkolleg Praktische Philosophie/Ethik: Studientexte*, iii (Weinheim/Basle: Beltz, 1984), 889–906.

'Rationalität als "Kulturelles Erbe"', in *Scheidewege*, 14 (1984/5), 307–13.

'Der Spiritualismus der wissenschaftlichen Zivilisation und die Leibhaftigkeit des Menschen', in *Schwarz auf Weiß, Informationen und Berichte der Künstler-Union Köln*, 17/2 (1985), 13–22.

'Welche Erfahrungen lehren uns die Welt verstehen? Bemerkungen zum Paradigma von Whiteheads Kosmologie', in Friedrich Rapp and Reiner Wiehl (eds.), *Whiteheads Metaphysik der Kreativität* (Freiburg im Breisgau: Alber, 1986), 169–81.

'Über die Bedeutung des "sum" im "cogito sum"', in *Zeitschrift für philosophische Forschung*, 41/3 (1987), 373–82.

'Kausalität', in Helmut Seiffert and Gerard Radnitzky (eds.), *Handlexikon zur Wissenschaftstheorie* (Munich: Ehrenwirth, 1987), 160–4.

'Kommentar', in *Die Unantastbarkeit des menschlichen Lebens: Zu ethischen Fragen der Biomedizin*, Instruktion der Kongregation für die Glaubenslehre (Freiburg im Breisgau: Herder, 1987), 67–95.

'Laudatio', in Börsenverein des Deutschen Buchhandels (ed.), *Friedenspreis des Deutschen Buchhandels 1987: Hans Jonas. Ansprachen aus Anlaß der Verleihung* (Frankfurt am Main: Buchhändler-Vereinigung, 1987), 19–32.

'Leibniz' Begriff der möglichen Welten', in Venanz Schubert (ed.), *Rationalität und Sentiment: Das Zeitalter Johann Sebastian Bachs und Georg Friedrich Händels. Eine Ringvorlesung der Universität München* (Wissenschaft und Philosophie, v) (St Ottilien: EOS, 1987), 7–35.

'Eine materialistische Erklärung des Gegensatzes von Idealismus und Materialismus? Kritik an der Selektion/Die Leistungsgrenzen der evolutionären Erkenntnistheorie/Literatur', in Rupert Riedel and Franz M. Wuketits (eds.), *Die evolutionäre Erkenntnistheorie: Bedingungen—Lösungen—Kontroversen* (Berlin: Parey, 1987), 178–83.

'Teleologie', in Helmut Seiffert and Gerard Radnitzky (eds.), *Handlexikon zur Wissenschaftstheorie* (Munich: Ehrenwirth, 1987), 366–8.

'Universalismus oder Eurozentrismus', in Krzysztof Michalski (ed.), *Europa und die Folgen* (Castelgandolfo-Gespräche, iii) (Stuttgart: Klett-Cotta, 1988), 313–22.

'Evolution—Wissenschaft oder Weltanschauung?', in *Communio*, 17 (1988), 251–62.

Das Glück des Menschen und seine Verantwortung für die Natur—Aspekte einer angewandten Ethik (Hagen: Fernuniversität, 1988).

'Bemerkungen über das Verhältnis von Zeit und Freiheit bei Boethius und Kant', in Robert Spaemann et al. (eds.), *Disiecta Membra: Studien Karlfried Gründer zum 60. Geburtstag* (Basle: Schwabe 1989; Darmstadt: Wissenschaftliche Buchgesellschaft, 1989), 20–4.

'Zur Einführung: Philosophiegeschichte nach Martin Heidegger', in Thomas Buchheim (ed.), *Destruktion und Übersetzung: Zu den Aufgaben von Philosophiegeschichte nach Martin Heidegger* (Weinheim: Acta Humaniora/VCH, 1989), 1–6.

'Ars longa vita brevis', in Robert Spaemann, Reinhard Löw, and Peter Koslowski (eds.), *Expertenwissen und Politik* (Civitas-Resultate, xii) (Weinheim: VCH, 1990), 15–26.

'Einleitung', in Thomas Aquinas, *Über die Sittlichkeit der Handlung: Summa theologiae I–II q. 18–21. Lateinisch–Deutsch. Übersetzt, kommentiert und hrsg. von Rolf Schönberger* (Acta Humaniora) (Weinheim: Acta Humaniora/VCH, 1990), vii–xvi.

'Geleitwort', in Till Bastian (ed.), *Denken—schreiben—töten: Zur neuen 'Euthanasie'—Diskussion und zur Philosophie Peter Singers* (Stuttgart: Wissenschaftliche Verlagsgesellschaft, 1990).

'Niklas Luhmanns Herausforderung der Philosophie: Laudatio', in Luhmann, *Paradigm Lost: Über die ethische Reflexion der Moral* (Frankfurt am Main: Suhrkamp, 1990), 47–73.

'Sind alle Menschen Personen?', in *Communio*, 19 (1990), 108–114.

'Mensch und Natur: Zur Eröffnung des Museums "Mensch und Natur" in München', in *Scheidewege*, 21 (1991/2), 121–8.

'Transformationen des Sündenfallmythos', in Willi Oelmüller (ed.), *Worüber man nicht schweigen kann: Neue Diskussionen zur Theodizeefrage* (Munich: Fink, 1992), 15–24.

'Die Unvollendbarkeit der Entfinalisierung', in Jacques Follon and James McEvoy (eds.), *Finalité et intentionnalité: Doctrine thomiste et perspectives modernes. Actes du colloque de Louvain-la-Neuve et Louvain, 2–23 mai 1990* (Éditions de l'Institut Supérieur de Philosophie, xxxv) (Paris/Leuven: Édition de l'Institut Supérieur de Philosophie, 1992), 305–24.

'Christliche Meditation über den 45 Psalm', in Benedikt Dissell (ed.), *Esse in verbo: Festschrift für Heinrich Reinhardt zur Priesterweihe und Primiz* (Kisslegg: FE, 1993), 122–9.

'Die kostbare Perle und der banale Nihilismus', in Sekretariat der Deutschen Bischofskonferenz (ed.), *Christentum und Kultur in Europa: Gedächtnis—Bewußtsein—Erinnerung. Akten des präsynodalen Symposiums. Vatikan, 28. bis 31. Oktober 1991* (Stimmen der Weltkirche, xxxiii) (Bonn: Sekretariat der Deutschen Bischofskonferenz, 1993), 39–45.

'Ist der Mensch ein Anthropomorphismus?', in Robert Spaemann, Wolfgang Welsch, and Walther Ch. Zimmerli (eds.) *Zweckmäßigkeit und menschliches Glück: Bamberger Hegelwochen 1993* (Bamberg: Fränkischer Tag, 1994), 35–55.

'Liberalismus und Fundamentalismus: Podiumsgespräch zwischen Robert Spaemann, Wolfgang Welsch und Walter Ch. Zimmerli', in Robert Spaemann, Wolfgang Welsch, and Walther Ch. Zimmerli (eds.), *Zweckmäßigkeit und menschliches Glück: Bamberger Hegelwochen 1993* (Bamberg: Fränkischer Tag, 1994), 57–112.

'Die Zweideutigkeit des Glück', in Robert Spaemann, Wolfgang Welsch, and Walther Ch. Zimmerli (eds.), *Zweckmäßigkeit und menschliches Glück: Bamberger Hegelwochen 1993* (Bamberg: Fränkischer Tag, 1994), 15–34.

'Christentum und Philosophie der Neuzeit', in Herrmann Fechtrup, Friedbert Schulze, and Thomas Sternberg (eds.), *Aufklärung durch Tradition: Symposion der Josef Pieper Stiftung zum 90. Geburtstag von Josef Pieper, Mai 1994 in Münster* (Münster: LIT, 1995).

'Einleitende Bemerkungen zum Opferbegriff', in Richard Schenk (ed.), *Zur Theorie des Opfers: Ein interdisziplinäres Gespräch* (Collegium Philosophicum, i) (Stuttgart/Bad Cannstatt: frommann-holzboog, 1995), 11–24.

'Ähnlichkeit', in *Zeitschrift für Philosophische Forschung*, 50 (1996), 286–90.

'Aufhalter und letztes Gefecht', in Karlheinz Stierle and Rainer Warning (eds.), *Das Ende: Figuren einer Denkform* (Poetik und Hermeneutik, xvi) (Munich: Fink, 1996), 564–77.

'Sittliche Normen und Rechtsordnung', in Heiner Marré, Dieter Schümmelfeder, and Burkhard Kämper (eds.), *Das christliche Freiheitsverständnis in seiner Bedeutung für die staatliche Rechtsordnung* (Essener Gespräche zum Thema Staat und Kirche, xxx) (Münster: Aschendorff, 1996), 5–17.

'Christliche Spiritualität und pluralistische Normalität', in *Communio*, 26 (1997), 163–70.

'Der innere Widerspruch der Aufklärung: Diskussionsbemerkung', in Krzysztof Michalski (ed.), *Aufklärung heute* (Castelgandolfo-Gespräche, vii) (Stuttgart: Klett-Cotta, 1997), 231–5.

'Liturgie als Ausdruck des Glaubens: Bemerkungen eines Laien', in Franz Breid (ed.), *Die heilige Liturgie. Referate der 'Internationalen Theologischen Sommerakademie 1997' des Linzer Priesterkreises in Aigen/M.* (Steyr: Ennsthaler 1997), 36–71.

'Die Philosophenkönige (Platon, Politeia 573b–504a)', in Otfried Höffe (ed.), *Platon, Politeia* (Klassiker auslegen, vii) (Berlin: Akademie, 1997), 161–77.

'Person und Versprechen: Einführung', in Richard Schenk (ed.), *Kontinuität der Person: Zum Versprechen und Vertrauen* (Collegium Philosophicum, ii) (Stuttgart/Bad Cannstatt: frommann-holzboog, 1998), 3–6.

'Die Aufgabe der Philosophie heute', in Vittorio Hösle, Peter Koslowski, and Richard Schenk (eds.), *Die Aufgaben derPhilosophie heute: Akademie anlässlich des zehnjährigen Bestehens des Forschungsinstituts für Philosophie Hannover am 26. November 1998* (Vienna: Passagen, 1999), 71–81.

'Wirklichkeit als Anthropomorphismus', in *Was heißt 'wirklich'? Unsere Erkenntnis zwischen Wahrnehmung und Wissenschaft* (Sonderdruck der Vortragsreihe in der Bayerischen Akademie der Schönen Künste) (Waakirchen-Schaftlach: Oreos, 2000), 13–34.

'Person und Wiedergeburt', in Walter Schweidler (ed.), *Wiedergeburt und kulturelles Erbe: Reincarnation and cultural heritage. Ergebnisse und Beiträge des Internationalen Symposions der Hermann-und-Marianne-Straniak-Stiftung. Weingarten 1999* (West-östliche Denkwege, iii) (Sankt Augustin: Academia, 2001), 243–50.

'Habermas über Bioethik', in *Deutsche Zeitschrift für Philosophie*, 50 (2002), 105–9.

'Ritual und Ethos', in *Sinn und Form*, 54 (2002), 310–24.

'Vorwort', in Eduard Picker, *Menschenwürde und Menschenleben: Das Auseinander-driften zweier fundamentaler Werte als Ausdruck der wachsenden Relativierung des Menschen* (Stuttgart: Klett-Cotta, 2002), xiii–xv.

'Sind alle Menschen Personen?', in Walter Schweidler, Herbert A. Neumann, and Eugen Brysch (eds.), *Menschenleben—Menschenwürd: Interdisziplinäres Symposion zur Bioethik* (Ethik interdisziplinär, iii) (Münster/Hamburg/London: Lit, 2003), 45–50.

'Der Beginn des menschlichen Lebens', in *Zeitschrift für Lebensrecht*, 13 (2004), 62–6.

'Bemerkungen zur Euthanasiedebatte', in *Die Neue Ordnung*, 58 (2004), 324–9.

'Ein Gespräch über die letzten Dinge', in Wladyslaw Bartoszewski (ed.), *Die Kraft des Augenblicks: Begegnungen mit Papst Johannes Paul II* (Freiburg im Breisgau/Basle/Vienna: Herder 2004), 114–18.

'Emanzipation und Substantialität', in Ulrich Dierse (ed.), *Joachim Ritter zum Gedenken* (Akademie der Wissenschaften und der Literatur Mainz, Abhandlungen der Geistes- und Sozialwissenschaftlichen Klasse, 2004/4) (Stuttgart: Steiner, 2004), 163–70.

'Habermas oder Reemtsma: In eigener Sache', in *Merkur*, 60 (2006), 467–8.

'Seelen', in Friedrich Hermanni and Thomas Buchheim (ed.), *Das Leib-Seele-Problem: Antwortversuche aus medizinischnaturwissenschaftlicher, philosophischer und theologischer Sicht* (Munich: Fink, 2006), 71–83.

'Sterben—heutzutage', in *Communio*, 35 (2006), 177–9.

'Wert oder Würde des Menschen', in Konrad-Paul Liessmann (ed.), *Der Wert des Menschen: An den Grenzen des Humanen* (Philosophicum Lech, ix) (Vienna: Zsolnay, 2006), 21–46.

'Das Gezeugte, das Gemachte und das Geschaffene', in *Scheidewege*, 36 (2006/7), 300–16.

'Was heißt: "Die Kunst ahmt die Natur nach"?', in *Philosophisches Jahrbuch*, 114 (2007), 247–64.

'Grenzen der Verantwortung', in Ludger Heidbrink (ed.), *Staat ohne Verantwortung? Zum Wandel der Aufgaben von Staat und Politik* (Frankfurt am Main: Campus, 2007), 37–53.

'Postsäkulare Gesellschaft', in Walter Schweidler (ed.), *Postsäkulare Gesellschaft: Perspektiven interdisziplinärer Forschung* (Freiburg im Breisgau: Alber, 2007), 65–75.

'Perspektive und View from Nowhere', in Walter Schweidler (ed.), *Weltbild—Bildwelt: Ergebnisse und Beiträge des Internationalen Symposiums der Hermann und Marianne Straniak-Stiftung, Weingarten 2005* (West-östliche Denkwege, x) (St Augustin: Academia, 2007), 13–20.

Important interviews

'Fragebogen: Robert Spaemann', in *Magazin der Frankfurter Allgemeine Zeitung* (July 1985).

SPAEMANN, ROBERT, and NISSING, HANNS-GREGOR, 'Die Natur des Lebendigen und das Ende des Denkens: Entwicklungen und Entfaltungen eines philosophischen Werks. Ein Gespräch', in Nissing, (ed.), *Grundvollzüge der Person: Dimensionen des Menschseins bei Robert Spaemann* (Munich: Institut zur Förderung der Glaubenslehre, 2008), 121–36.

SPAEMANN, ROBERT, and ZABOROWSKI, HOLGER, 'An Animal That Can Promise and Forgive', trans. Lesley Rice, in *Communio*, 34 (2007), 511–21.

English translations of Spaemann's works

'Mysticism and Enlightenment', trans. Simon King in Johann Baptist Metz and Jean-Pierre Jossua (eds.), *The Crisis of Religious Language* (Concilium) (New York: Herder and Herder, 1973), 70–83.

'Remarks on the Problem of Equality', in *Ethics*, 87 (1977), 363–9.

'Side-effects as a Moral Problem', trans. Frederick S. Gardiner, in Darrel E. Christensen et al. (eds.), *Contemporary German Philosophy*, ii (University Park and London: The Pennsylvania State University Press, 1983), 138–51.

Basic Moral Concepts, trans. T. J. Armstrong (London: Routledge, 1989).

'On the Concept of Life', trans. Jeremiah Alberg in *Zen-Buddhism Today*, 7 (1989), 77–83.

'Remarks on the Ontology of "Right" and "Left" ', trans. in *Graduate Faculty Philosophy Journal*, 10 (1984), 89–97; repr. in Reiner Schürmann (ed.), *The Public Realm: Essays on Discursive Types in Political Philosophy* (New York: State University of New York Press, 1989), 146–53.

'Which Experiences Teach Us To Understand the World? Observations on the Paradigm of Whitehead's Cosmology', trans. Gordon Treash in Friedrich Rapp and Reiner Wiehl (eds.), *Whitehead's Metaphysics of Creativity* (Albany, NY: State University of New York Press, 1990), 152–64.

'Conscience and Responsibility in Christian Ethics', trans. in John M. Haas (ed.), *Crisis of Conscience* (New York: The Crossroad Publishing Company, 1996), 111–34.

'Is Every Human Being a Person?', trans. Richard Schenk, in *The Thomist*, 60 (1996), 463–74.

'Genetic Manipulation of Human Nature in the Context of Human Personality', in Juan de Dios Vial Correa and Elio Sgreccia (eds.), *Human Genome, Human Person and the Society of the Future: Proceedings of the Fourth Assembly of the Pontifical Academy for Life (Vatican City, February 23–25, 1998)* (Città del Vaticano: Libreria Editrice Vaticana, 1999), 340–50.

'Death—Suicide—Euthanasia', in Juan de Dios Vial Correa and Elio Sgreccia (eds.), *The Dignity of the Dying Person: Proceedings of the Fifth Assembly of the Pontifical Academy for Life (Vatican City, February 24–27, 1999)* (Città del Vaticano: Libreria Editrice Vaticana, 2000), 123–31.

Happiness and Benevolence, trans. Jeremiah Alberg (Notre Dame, Ind.: Notre Dame University Press, 2000).

'Christianity and Modern Philosophy', trans. in Brian J. Shanley, OP (ed.), *One Hundred Years of Philosophy* (Studies in Philosophy and the History of Philosophy, xxxvi) (Washington, DC: The Catholic University of America Press, 2001), 169–80.

'The Dictatorship of Values', in *Project Syndicate: An Association of Newspapers Around the World*, August 2001 (<http://www.project-syndicate.org/commentary/spaemann1>, accessed July 2009).

' "The Reform of the Reform" and the Old Roman Rite', trans. Laurence Lombardi in *Sacred Music*, 129/3 (Fall 2002), 5–10.

'The Death of Death', in *Project Syndicate: An Association of Newspapers Around the World*, Apr. 2003 (<http://www.project-syndicate.org/commentary/spaemann2>, accessed July 2009).
'Rationality and Faith in God', trans. D. C. Schindler in *Communio*, 32 (2005), 618–36.
'Begotten, not Made', trans. Michelle K. Borras, in *Communio*, 33(2006), 290–297.
'When Death Becomes Inhuman', trans. Adrian J. Walker in *Communio*, 33 (2006), 298–300.
Persons: The Difference between 'Someone' and 'Something', trans. Oliver O'Donovan (Oxford: Oxford University Press, 2007).
'The Return of Just Wars?', in *Project Syndicate: An Association of Newspapers Around the World*, December 2008 (<http://www.project-syndicate.org/commentary/spaemann3>, accessed July 2009).

Festschriften in honour of Spaemann

BUCHHEIM, THOMAS, SCHÖNBERGER, ROLF, and SCHWEIDLER, WALTER (eds.), *Die Normativität des Wirklichen: Über die Grenze zwischen Sein und Sollen. Robert Spaemann zum 75. Geburtstag* (Stuttgart: Klett-Cotta, 2002).
LÖW, REINHARD (ed.), *Oikeiosis: Festschrift für Robert Spaemann* (Weinheim: Acta Humaniora/VCH, 1987).

Important secondary sources about Spaemann's philosophy

AMORI, MATTEO, 'Il pensiero di Robert Spaemann tra critica della modernità ed ontologia teleologica', in *Rivista di filosofia neoscolastica*, 97 (2005), 55 ff.
BUTTIGLIONE, ROCCO, 'Robert Spaemann: Una guía para los perplejos', in *Humanitas*, 11 (1998), 406–10.
DÖLLE-OELMÜLLER, RUTH, 'Euthanasie—philosophisch betrachtet: Ein Diskussionsbeitrag zu Argumenten von Spaemann und Singer', in *Zeitschrift für medizinische Ethik*, 39 (1993), 41–54.
GONZÁLEZ, ANA MARTA, *Naturaleza y dignidad: Un estudio desde Robert Spaemann* (Colección filosifica, cv) (Pamplona: Eunsa, 1996).
HAHN, E., review of Hermann Lübbe (ed.), *Wozu Philosophie? Stellungnahmen eines Arbeitskreises* (Berlin/New York: de Gruyter, 1978) in *Contemporary German Philosophy*, iv (1980), 320–6.
HOYE, WILLIAM J., review of ROBERT SPAEMANN, *Glück und Wohlwollen: Versuch über Ethik* (Stuttgart: Klett-Cotta 1989), in *Theologische Revue*, 87/2 (1991), 42–4.
ISAK, RAINER, *Evolution ohne Ziel? Ein interdisziplinärer Forschungsbeitrag* (Freiburg im Breisgau/Basle/Vienna: Herder, 1992) (Freiburger theologische Studien, cli).
JANTSCHEK, THORSTEN, 'Von Personen und Menschen: Bemerkungen zu Robert Spaemann', in *Deutsche Zeitschrift für Philosophie*, 46 (1998), 465–84.
LANGTHALER, RUDOLF, 'Über "Seelen" und "Gewissen": Robert Spaemanns Aktualisierung thomistischer Motive', in *Deutsche Zeitschrift für Philosophie*, 46 (1998), 485–500.
LARMORE, CHARLES, 'Person und Anerkennung', in *Deutsche Zeitschrift für Philosophie*, 46 (1998), 459–64.
LEGGEWIE, CLAUS, 'Kritik an der konservativen Zukunft? R. Spaemann und die Civitas-Gruppe', in Leggewie (ed.), *Der Geist steht rechts* (Berlin: Rotbuch 1987), 145 ff.

MADIGAN, ARTHUR, 'Robert Spaemann's "Philosophische Essays" ', in *Review of Metaphysics*, 51 (1997), 105–32.

MESTRE, ALBERTO,' Robert Spaemann: Ética de la responsabilidad cristiana', in *Ecclesia*, 21 (2007), 371–85.

NISSING, HANNS-GREGOR (ed.), *Grundvollzüge der Person: Dimensionen des Menschseins bei Robert Spaemann* (Munich: Institut zur Förderung der Glaubenslehre, 2008).

OLLIG, HANS-LUDWIG, 'Umstrittene Philosophie: Zur neueren Selbstverständnisdiskussion in der deutschen Gegenwartsphilosophie', in *Theologie und Philosophie*, 56 (1981), 161–203.

—— 'Philosophie und Zeitdiagnose: Aspekte deutscher Gegenwartsphilosophie', in *Theologie und Philosophie*, 57 (1982), 348–88.

—— 'Die Aktualität der Metaphysik: Perspektiven der deutschen Gegenwartsphilosophie', in *Theologie und Philosophie*, 68 (1993), 52–81.

PATZIG, GÜNTHER, 'Gibt es Grenzen der Redefreiheit?', in *Zeitschrift für Philosophische Forschung*, 54 (2000), 581–92.

PLEINES, JÜRGEN-ECKARDT, 'Das Dilemma der Ethik: Positionen und Probleme der Gegenwart', in *Philosophische Rundschau*, 38 (1991), 48–82.

SABUY, PAULIN SABANGU, *Persona, natura e raggione: Robert Spaemann e la dialettica del naturalismo e dello spiritualismo* (Rome: Armando, 2005).

SCHENK, OP, RICHARD, 'The Ethics of Robert Spaemann in the Context of Recent Philosophy', in Brian J. Shanley, OP (ed.), *One Hundred Years of Philosophy* (Studies in Philosophy and the History of Philosophy, xxxvi) (Washington, DC: The Catholic University of America Press, 2001), 156–68.

SCHICK, FRIEDRIKE, 'Philosophie des Geistes und Philosophy of Mind—Bewußtsein und Subjektivität im Spiegel neuerer Theorien', in *Philosophische Rundschau*, 45 (1998), 239–60.

SCHNARRER, JOHANNES M., *Norm und Naturrecht verstehen: Eine Studie zu Herausforderungen der Fundamentalethik* (Frankfurt am Main: Lang, 1999).

SCHÖNBERGER, ROLF, 'Robert Spaemann', in Julian Nida-Rümelin (ed.), *Philosophen der Gegenwart in Einzeldarstellungen: Von Adorno bis Wright* (Stuttgart: Kröner, 1991), 571–5 (2nd edn., 1999), 706–11.

SEUBERT, HARALD, 'Die Aktualität des Guten: Über ein neues Paradigma in der Ethik', *Ethica*, 7 (1999), 69–76.

SUN HSIAO-CHIH, JOHANNES, *Heiligt die gute Absicht ein schlechtes Mittel? Die Kontroverse über Teleologie und Deontologie in der Moralbegündung unter besonderer Berücksichtigung von Josef Fuchs und Robert Spaemann* (Dissertationen: Philosophische Reihe, xii) (St Ottilien: EOS, 1994).

WÄCHTER, JÖRG-DIETER, *Vom Zweck der Erziehung: Das Teleologieproblem in der Erziehungs- und Bildungstheorie* (Hildesheimer Beiträge zu den Erziehungs- und Sozialwissenschaften, xxxv) (Hildesheim/New York: Olms, 1991).

WILS, JEAN-PIERRE, *Verletzte Natur: Ethische Prolegomena* (Forum Interdisziplinäre Ethik, i) (Frankfurt am Main: Lang, 1991).

WOLF, JEAN-CLAUDE, 'Utilitaristische Ethik als Antwort auf die ökologische Krise', in *Zeitschrift für Philosophische Forschung*, 44 (1990), 619–34.

ZABOROWSKI, HOLGER, 'Ethik, Metaphysik und die Frage nach Gott', in *Jahrbuch für Religionsphilosophie*, 1 (2002), 120–37.

ZABOROWSKI, HOLGER, 'Menschen, Personen und die Natur jenseits des Naturalismus: Bemerkungen zu Thorsten Jantscheks Kritik an Robert Spaemann', in *Philosophisches Jahrbuch*, 109 (2002), 185–95.

—— 'Humane Normalität in der Anerkennung von Grenzen: Robert Spaemanns Überlegungen zur ethischen Dimensionen des Handelns', in *Communio*, 31 (2002), 565–9.

ZWIERLEIN, EDUARD, 'Das höchste Paradigma des Seienden: Anliegen und Probleme des Teleologiekonzepts Robert Spaemanns', in *Zeitschrift für Philosophische Forschung*, 41 (1987), 117–29.

Further secondary sources

ABBEY, RUTH, *Charles Taylor* (Princeton, NJ/London: Princeton University Press, 2000).

ADORNO, THEODOR W., and HORKHEIMER, MAX, *Dialektik der Aufklärung*, in Horkheimer, *Gesammelte Schriften*, ed. Alfred Schmidt and Gunzelin Schmid Noerr (Frankfurt am Main: Fischer, 1987).

—— ——*Dialectic of Enlightenment*, trans. John Cumming (London: Verso, 1986).

ALBERG, JEREMIAH, *Die verlorene Einheit: Die Suche nach einer philosophischen Alternative zur Erbsündenlehre von Rousseau bis Schelling* (Frankfurt am Main: Lang, 1996).

ANON. 'Gloire', in *Encyclopédie Philosophique Universelle, ii. Les Notions Philosophiques. Dictionnaire*, i (Vendôme: Press Universitaires de France, 1990), 1073.

ANSCOMBE, G. E. M., review of GARETH B. MATTHEWS's *Philosophy and the Young Child*, in *Philosophy and Phenomenological Research*, 43 (1982), 265–7.

APEL, Karl-Otto, *Towards a Transformation of Philosophy*, trans. Glyn Adey and David Frisby, foreword Pol Vandevelde (Marquette Studies in Philosophy, xx) (Milwaukee, Wis.: Marquette University Press, 1998).

ACKROYD, PETER, *T. S. Eliot* (London: Hamilton, 1984).

Complete Works of Aristotle: The Revised Oxford Translation, ed. Jonathan Barnes, i–ii (Princeton, NJ: Princeton University Press, 1984).

ASMUTH, CHRISTOPH, *Das Begreifen des Unendlichen: Philosophie und Religion bei Johann Gottlieb Fichte 1800–1806* (Spekulation und Erfahrung, xli. II) (Stuttgart/Bad Cannstatt: frommann-holzboog, 1999).

ASSHEUER, THOMAS, 'Das Zarathustra-Projekt: Der Philosoph Peter Sloterdijk fordert eine gentechnische Revision der Menschheit', in *Die Zeit*, 36 (1999).

AUGUSTINE, *City of God*, trans. Henry Bettenson (London: Penguin, 1984).

BACON, FRANCIS, *De Dignitate et augm entis scientiarum*, in *Works of Lord Bacon*, ii (London 1841).

BALDUCCI, E., 'Gloria', in *Enciclopedia Filosofica*, iii (Firenze: Sansoni, 1967), 264–5.

BALTHASAR, HANS URS VON, *Herrlichkeit: Eine theologische Aesthetik*, i–iii (Einsiedeln: Johannes, 1961–9).

—— *The Glory of the Lord: A Theological Aesthetics*, trans. Erasmo Leiva-Merikakis, ed. Joseph Fessio and John Riches (San Francisco, Calif.: Ignatius, 1983–91).

BARION, HANS, 'Kirche oder Partei?', in *Der Staat*, 4 (1965), 131–76.

BERTENS, HANS, *The Idea of the Postmodern: A History* (London/New York.: Routledge, 1995).

BLACK, MAX, *A Companion to Wittgenstein's Tractatus* (Cambridge: Cambridge University Press, 1964).

BLUMENBERG, HANS, *The Legitimacy of the Modern Age* (Cambridge, Mass.: MIT Press, 1983).

BLUMER, KARIN, 'Sind Tiere Personen? Eine Analyse terminologischer Kontroversen in der gegenwärtigen bioethischen Diskussion dargestellt am Beispiel der Position von Peter Singer', in *Theologie und Philosophie*, 73 (1998), 524–37.

BÖCKENFÖRDE, ERNST-WOLFGANG (ed.), *Collegium Philosophicum: Studien. Joachim Ritter zum 60. Geburtstag* (Basle/Stuttgart, 1965).

BONALD, L. G. A. de, *Théorie du pouvoir politique et religieux dans la société civile démontrée par le raisonnement et par l'histoire* (Constance, 1796).

BOWIE, ANDREW, *Schelling and Modern European Philosophy: An Introduction* (London/New York: Routledge, 1993).

BOWLER, PETER J., *Charles Darwin: The Man and His Influence* (Oxford: Blackwell, 1990).

BRAGUE, RÉMI, 'Zur Vorgeschichte der Unterscheidung von "Sein" und "Sollen" ', in Thomas Buchheim, Rolf Schönberger, and Walter Schweidler (eds.), *Die Normativität des Wirklichen: Über die Grenze zwischen Sein und Sollen* (Stuttgart: Klett-Cotta, 2002), 21–34.

BRESCH, CARSTEN, *Zwischenstufe Leben: Evolution ohne Ziel?* (Frankfurt am Main: Fischer, 1979).

BUCHHEIM, THOMAS, *Eins von allem: Die Selbstbescheidung des Idealismus in Schellings Spätphilosophie* (Hamburg: Meiner, 1992).

CASPER, BERNHARD, *Das dialogische Denken: Eine Untersuchung der religionsphilosophischen Bedeutung Franz Rosenzweigs, Ferdinand Ebners und Martin Bubers* (Freiburg im Breisgau: Herder, 1967).

CHERRY, CHRISTOPHER, 'The Possibility of Computers Becoming Persons: A Response to Dolby', in *Social Epistemology*, 3 (1989), 337–48.

—— 'Machines as Persons?', in David Cockburn (ed.), *Human Beings* (Cambridge: Cambridge University Press, 1991), 11–24.

CHESTERTON, G. K., *The Everlasting Man*, in *Collected Works II* (San Francisco, Calif.: Ignatius, 1986).

COLLINI, STEFAN, 'The European Modernist as Anglican Moralist: The Later Social Criticism of T. S. Eliot', in Mark S. Micale and Robert L. Dietle (eds.), *Enlightenment, Passion, Modernity: Historical Essays in European Thought and Culture* (Stanford, Calif.: Stanford University Press, 2000), 207–29.

CONNOR, STEVEN (ed.), *The Cambridge Companion to Postmodernism* (Cambridge: Cambridge University Press, 2004).

CHRETIEN, JEAN-LOUIS, *La voix nue: phénoménologie de la promesse* (Paris: Minuit, 1990).

CROSBY, JOHN F., *The Selfhood of the Human Person* (Washington, DC: The Catholic University of America Press, 1996).

CROSBY, JOHN F., 'The Individuality of Human Persons: A Study in the Ethical Personalism of Max Scheler', in *The Review of Metaphysics*, 52 (1998), 21–50.

CURRAN, MARY BERNARD, 'What Is Pure, What Is Good? Disinterestedness in Fénelon and Kant', in *Heythrop Journal*, 50 (2009), 195–205.

DAMROSCH, LEO, *Jean-Jacques Rousseau: Restless Genius* (Boston, Mass./New York: Houghton Mifflin, 2005).

DANCY, JONATHAN (ed.), *Reading Parfit* (Oxford: Blackwell, 1997).

DAWKINS, RICHARD, *The Selfish Gene* (Oxford: Oxford University Press, 1989).

—— *River Out of Eden: A Darwinian View of Life* (London: Weidenfeld & Nicolson, 1995).

—— 'Universal Darwinism', in David L. Hull and Michael Ruse (eds.), *The Philosophy of Biology* (Oxford: Oxford University Press, 1998), 15–37.

The God Delusion (Boston, Mass.: Houghton Mifflin, 2006).

DENKER, ALFRED, et al. (eds.), *Heidegger und Aristoteles* (Heidegger-Jahrbuch, iii) (Freiburg im Breisgau/Munich: Alber, 2006).

DESCARTES, RENÉ, *Meditations on First Philosophy*, in *The Philosophical Writings of Descartes*, trans. John Cottingham, Robert Stoothoff, and Dugald Murdoch, ii (Cambridge: Cambridge University Press, 1984).

DEW, PETER (ed.), *Habermas: A Critical Reader* (Oxford: Blackwell, 1999).

DIERSE, ULRICH, 'Joachim Ritter und seine Schüler', in Anton Hügli and Poul Lübcke (eds.), *Philosophie im 20. Jahrhundert, i. Phänomenologie, Hermeneutik, Existenzphilosophie und Kritische Theorie*, 3rd edn. (Hamburg: Rororo, 1998), 237–78.

DREYER, MECHTHILD, and FLEISCHHAUER, KURT (eds.), *Natur und Person im ethischen Disput* (Freiburg im Breisgau/Munich: Alber, 1998).

DUPRÉ, LOUIS, *Passage to Modernity: An Essay in the Hermeneutics of Nature and Culture* (New Haven, Conn./London: Yale University Press, 1993).

EBELING, HANS (ed.), *Subjektivität und Selbsterhaltung: Beiträge zur Diagnose der Moderne* (Frankfurt am Main: Suhrkamp, 1976).

ELIOT, T. S., 'The Idea of a Christian Society', in *Christianity and Culture* (New York: Harcourt, Brace, 1949), 1–77.

EMRICH, HINDERK M., 'Das Gefühlshafte der Wirklichkeitserfahrung', in Thomas Buchheim, Rolf Schönberger, and Walter Schweidler (eds.), *Die Normativität des Wirklichen: Über die Grenze zwischen Sein und Sollen* (Stuttgart: Klett-Cotta, 2002), 173–189.

FICHTE, JOHANN GOTTLIEB, *Versuch einer neuen Darstellung der Wissenschaftslehre*, in *Johann Gottlieb Fichte—Gesamtausgabe der Bayerischen Akademie der Wissenschaften*, ed. Reinhard Lauth, Hans Jacobs, and Hans Gliwitzky (Stuttgart/Bad Cannstatt: frommann-holzboog, 1970), i. IV.

—— *Wissenschaftslehre 1804*, 2nd edn., in *Johann Gottlieb Fichte—Gesamtausgabe der Bayerischen Akademie der Wissenschaften*, ed. Reinhard Lauth and Hans Gliwitzky (Stuttgart/Bad Cannstatt: frommann-holzboog, 1985), ii. VIII.

FINNIS, JOHN, *Natural Law and Natural Rights* (Oxford: Oxford University Press, 1980).

FLAY, J. C., 'The History of Philosophy and the Phenomenology of Spirit', in *Hegel and the History of Philosophy*, ed. Joseph J. O'Malley, Keith W. Algozin, and Frederick G. Weiss (The Hague: Nijhoff, 1974).

FRANK, MANFRED, 'Geschweife und Geschwefel: Die düster-prophetische Rede über den "Menschenpark" beunruhigt, und die Art, wie Sloterdijk mit Kritikern umspringt, ist empörend. Auch sein Angriff auf die Kritische Theorie geht fehl. Ein offener Brief', in *Die Zeit*, 39 (1999).

FUHRMANN, M., et al. 'Person', in Joachim Ritter and Karlfried Gründer (eds.), *Historisches Wörterbuch der Philosophie* (Basle: , 1989), vii. 269–338.

FUKUYAMA, FRANCIS, *The End of History and the Last Man* (New York: Maxwell Macmillan, 1992).

GADAMER, HANS-GEORG, 'Dialogues in Capri', in *Religion*, ed. Jacques Derrida and Gianni Vattimo (Stanford, Calif.: Stanford University Press, 1998).

Truth and Method, 2nd, rev., edn., trans.and rev. Joel Weinsheimer and Donald G. Marshall (London: Continuum, 2006).

GARRARD, GRAEME, *Rousseau's Counter-Enlightenment: A Republican Critique of the Philosophes* (Albany: State University of New York, 2003).

GEACH, PETER, *The Virtues: The Stanton Lectures 1973–74* (Cambridge: Cambridge University Press, 1977).

Gedenkschrift Joachim Ritter zur Gedenkfeier zu Ehren des am 3 August 1974 verstorbenen em. ordentlichen Professors der Philosophie Dr. phil. Joachim Ritter (Münster: Aschendorff, 1978).

GEORGE, ROBERT P., *Natural Law Theory: Contemporary Essays* (Oxford: Clarendon, 1992).

—— *In Defense of Natural Law* (Oxford: Oxford University Press, 2004).

GILLESPIE, MICHAEL ALLEN, *The Theological Origins of Modernity* (Chicago, Ill./London: University of Chicago Press, 2008).

GILSON, ETIENNE, 'French and Italian Philosophy,' in Etienne Gilson, Thomas Langhan, and Armand A. Maurer, *Recent Philosophy: Hegel to the Present* (New York: Random House, 1966), 169–408.

GRANT, GEORGE, *Time as History* (Toronto: Canadian Broadcasting Corporation, 1969).

GUARDINI, ROMANO, *The End of the Modern World: A Search for Orientation* (Wilmington, Del.: ISI, 1998).

HABERMAS, JÜRGEN, *The Theory of Communicative Action*, trans. Thomas McCarthy, 2 vols. (Boston, Mass.: Beacon, 1984/1987).

—— *The Philosophical Discourse of Modernity*, trans. Frederick Lawrence (Cambridge, Mass.: MIT Press, 1987).

—— *Moderne—ein unvollendetes Projekt: Philosophisch-politische Aufsätze* (Leipzig: Reclam, 1994).

—— 'Modernity. An Unfinished Project', in Maurizio Passerin d'Entrèves and Seyla Benhabib (eds.), *Habermas and the Unfinished Project of Modernity: Critical Essays on* The Philosophical Discourse of Modernity (Cambridge, Mass.: MIT Press, 1997), 38–55.

—— *Glauben und Wissen* (Frankfurt am Main: Suhrkamp, 2001).

HADOT, PIERRE, *Exercices spirituels et philosophie antique* (Paris: Etudes Augustiniennes, 1981).

HAKSAR, VINIT, *Equality, Liberty, and Perfectionism* (Oxford: Clarendon, 1979).

HARE, R. M., *Essays on Bioethics* (Oxford: Clarendon, 1993).

HARRISON, Paul R., 'Niklas Luhmann and the Theory of Social Systems', in David Roberts (ed.), *Reconstruction Theory: Gadamer, Habermas, Luhmann* (Melbourne: Melbourne University Press, 1995), 65–90.

HARVEY, DAVID, *The Condition of Postmodernity: An Enquiry into the Origins of Cultural Change* (Oxford: Blackwell, 1990).

Hassing, Richard (ed.), *Final Causality in Nature and Human Affairs* (Studies in Philosophy and the History of Philosophy, xxx) (Washington, DC: The Catholic University of America Press, 1997).

Hegel, G. W. F., *Hegel's Philosophy of Right*, trans. T. M. Knox (Oxford: Oxford University Press, 1967).

—— *Phenomenology of Spirit*, trans. A. V. Miller (Oxford: Oxford University Press, 1979).

HEIDEGGER, MARTIN, *Unterwegs zur Sprache* (Pfullingen: Neske, 1959).

—— *Discourse on Thinking*, Eng. trans. of *Gelassenheit*, introd. John M. Anderson (New York: Harper, 1969).

—— *Holzwege*, ed. Friedrich-Wilhelm von Herrmann (*Gesamtausgabe*, v) (Frankfurt am Main: Klostermann, 1977).

—— *Nietzsche*, trans. with notes and analysis David Farrell Krell, 4 vols. (San Francisco, Calif.: Harper & Row, 1979–87).

—— *Being and Time*, trans. John MacQuarrie and Edward Robinson (Oxford: Blackwell, 1983).

—— *Basic Writings from* Being and Time (*1927*) *to* The Task of Thinking (1964)*, rev. and expanded edn., ed. David Farrell Krell (San Francisco, Calif.: HarperCollins, 1993).*

—— *Ontologie (Hermeneutik der Faktizität)*, ed. Käte Oltmans-Bröker (*Gesamtausgabe*, lxiii), 2nd edn. (Frankfurt am Main: Klostermann, 1995).

—— 'Gelassenheit', in his *Reden und andere Zeugnisse eines Lebensweges 1910–1976* (*Gesammelte Werke*, xvi) (Frankfurt am Main: Klostermann, 2000), 517–29.

HEMMERLE, KLAUS, *Franz von Baaders philosophischer Gedanke der Schöpfung* (Freiburg im Breisgau/Munich: Alber, 1961).

—— *Gott und das Denken nach Schellings Spätphilosophie* (Freiburg im Breisgau/Basle/Vienna: Herder, 1968).

HENRICH, DIETER, 'Trinität Gottes und der Begriff der Person', in Odo Marquard and Karlheinz Stierle (eds.), *Identität* (Munich: Fink, 1979), 612–20.

—— 'Was ist Metaphysik, was Moderne? Thesen gegen Habermas', in *Merkur*, 40 (1986), 495–508.

—— *Selbstverhältnisse: Gedanken und Auslegungen zu den Grundlagen der klassischen deutschen Philosophie* (Stuttgart: Reclam, 1993).

—— *Bewußtes Leben: Untersuchungen zum Verhältnis von Subjektivität und Metaphysik* (Stuttgart: Reclam, 1999).

HERRMANN, FRIEDRICH-WILHELM VON, *Hermeneutik und Reflexion: Der Begriff der Phänomenologie bei Heidegger und Husserl* (Frankfurt am Main: Klostermann, 2000).

HILDEBRAND, DIETRICH VON, *Das Wesen der Liebe* (*Gesammelte Werke*, ed. the Dietrich von Hildebrand Legacy Project, iii) (Regensburg: Habbel, 1971).

HILDEBRAND, DIETRICH VON, *Metaphysik der Gemeinschaft: Untersuchungen über Wesen und Wert der Gemeinschaft* (=*Gesammelte Werke*, ed. the Dietrich von Hildebrand Legacy Project, iv) (Regensburg: Habbel, 1975).

HOBBES, THOMAS, *Leviathan*, ed. Richard Tuck (Cambridge: Cambridge University Press, 1999).

HOLMES, STEPHAN, *The Anatomy of Antiliberalism* (Cambridge, Mass.: Harvard University Press, 1993).

HOPING, HELMUT, 'Göttliche und menschliche Personen: Die Diskussion um den Menschen als Herausforderung für die Dogmatik', in *Theologie der Gegenwart*, 41 (1998), 162–74.

HÜGLI, ANTON, 'Selbstsein', in Joachim Ritter and Karlfried Gründer (eds.), *Historisches Wörterbuch der Philosophie* (Basle: Schwabe, 1995), ix. 520–8.

HULLIUNG, MARK, *The Autocritique of Enlightenment: Rousseau and the Philosophes* (Cambridge, Mass.: Harvard University Press, 1994).

HUME, DAVID, *An Enquiry Concerning Human Understanding*, ed. Tom L. Beauchamp (Oxford: Oxford University Press, 1999).

—— *A Treatise of Human Nature*, ed. L. A. Selby-Bigge, 2nd edn., with rev. text and variant readings by P. H. Nidditch (Oxford: Clarendon, 1985).

—— *A Treatise of Human Nature*, ed. David Fate Norton and Mary J. Norton (Oxford: Oxford University Press, 2000).

HUSSERL, EDMUND, *The Crisis of European Sciences and Transcendental Phenomenology: An Introduction to Phenomenological Philosophy*, trans. with an introd. David Carr (Evanston, Ill.: Northwestern University Press, 1970).

—— *Shorter Works*, ed. Peter McCormick and Frederick A. Elliston (Notre Dame, Ind.: University of Notre Dame Press, 1981).

—— *Logical Investigations*, trans. J. N. Findlay (New York: Humanity, 2000).

JASPERS, KARL, *Philosophie* (Berlin: Springer, 1948).

JOHN PAUL II, *On the Relationship between Faith and Reason* (*Fides et Ratio*) (Washington, DC: United States Catholic Conference, 1998).

JONAS, HANS, *The Imperative of Responsibility: In Search of an Ethics for the Technological Age*, trans. Jonas with David Ferr (Chicago, Ill.: University of Chicago Press, 1985).

KASPER, WALTER, *Das Absolute in der Geschichte: Philosophie und Theologie der Geschichte in der Spätphilosophie Schellings* (Mainz: Grünewald, 1965).

—— (ed.), *Im Dialog—Die Logik der Liebe Gottes* (Mainz: Grünewald, 2006).

KAUBE, JÜRGEN, 'Was ist Bonaldismus? Originelles Völkchen, diese Konterrevolutionäre: Robert Spaemann zeigt, dass die ursprüngliche Einsicht in die Wirklichkeit den großen Zerstörern gefehlt hat', in *Frankfurter Allgemeine Zeitung*, 27 Sept. 1999.

KISIEL, THEODORE, *The Genesis of Martin Heidegger's 'Being and Time'* (Berkeley, Calif.: University of California Press, 1993).

KLINCK, DAVID, 'Louis de Bonald: The Foreshadowing of the Integral Nationalism of Charles Maurras and the Action Française', in *History of European Ideas*, 15 (1992), 327–32.

KLINCK, DAVID, 'The French Counterrevolution and the Rise of Sociology: The Question of the Modernity of Louis de Bonald's Science of Society', in *Selected Papers: Proceedings of the Consortium on Revolutionary Europe 1750–1850*, 24 (1994), 705–13.

—— *The French Counterrevolutionary Theorist Louis de Bonald (1754–1840)* (Studies in Modern European History, xviii) (New York: Lang, 1996).

KOBUSCH, THEO, *Die Entdeckung der Person: Metaphysik der Freiheit und modernes Menschenbild* (Darmstadt: Wissenschaftliche Buchgesellschaft, 1997).

KOHLMANN, U., 'Überwindung des Anthropozentrismus durch Gleichheit alles Lebendigen?', in *Zeitschrift für philosophische Forschung*, 49 (1995), 15–35.

KÖRNIG, STEPHAN, *Perspektivität und Unbestimmtheit in Nietzsches Lehre vom Willen zur Macht: Eine vergleichende Studie zu Hegel, Nietzsche und Luhmann* (Basler Studien zur Philosophie, ix) (Bern: francke, 1999).

KOSLOWSKI, PETER, *Gesellschaft und Staat: Ein unvermeidlicher Dualismus* (Stuttgart: Klett-Cotta, 1982).

—— *Evolution und Gesellschaft: Eine Auseinandersetzung mit der Soziobiologie*, 2nd edn. (Tübingen: Mohr, 1989).

—— *Die Prüfungen der Neuzeit: Über Postmodernität, Philosophie der Geschichte, Metaphysik, Gnosis* (Vienna: Passagen, 1989).

—— *Der Mythos der Moderne: Die dichterische Philosophie Ernst Jüngers* (Munich: Fink, 1991).

—— (ed.), *Sociobiology and Bioeconomics: The Theory of Evolution in Biological and Economic Theory* (Berlin: Springer, 1999).

—— *Philosophien der Offenbarung: Antiker Gnostizismus, Franz von Baader, Schelling* (Paderborn: Schöningh, 2001).

—— and Friedrich Hermanni (eds.), *Die Wirklichkeit des Bösen: Systematisch-theologische und philosophische Annäherungen* (Munich: Fink, 1998).

KÖTT, ANDREAS, *Systemtheorie und Religion: Mit einer Religionstypologie im Anschluss an Niklas Luhmann* (Würzburg: Königshausen & Neumann, 2003).

KRANZ, WALTER (ed.), *Die Fragmente der Vorsokratiker* (Dublin/Zürich: Weidmann, 1972).

KRAUSS, WERNER, *Gesammelte Aufsätze zur Literatur- und Sprachwissenschaft* (Frankfurt am Main: Klostermann, 1949).

KRAYNOK, ROBERT P., and TINDER, GLENN (eds.), *In Defense of Human Dignity: Essays for our Times* (Notre Dame, Ind.: University of Notre Dame Press, 2003).

KUHN, THOMAS S., *The Structure of Scientific Revolutions* (Chicago, Ill.: University of Chicago Press, 1970).

KÜNG, HANS, *Global Responsibility: In Search of a New World Ethic* (New York: Crossroad, 1991).

—— *A Global Ethic for Global Politics and Economics* (New York: Oxford University Press, 1998).

—— and Schmid, Helmut, *A Global Ethic and Global Responsibilities: Two Declarations* (London: SCM, 1998).

LARMORE, CHARLES, *The Morals of Modernity* (Cambridge: Cambridge Univesity Press, 1997).

LEVINAS, EMMANUEL, *Autrement qu'être ou au-delà de l'essence* (Paris: Librairie Générale Française, 1990).

LEWIS, C. S., *Miracles: A Preliminary Study* (New York: Macmillan, 1947).

—— *The Abolition of Man, or Reflections on Education with Special Reference to the Teaching of English in the Upper Forms of Schools* (Glasgow: Collins, 1982).

LOCKE, JOHN, *An Essay Concerning Human Understanding*, ed. and foreword Peter H. Nidditch (Oxford: Clarendon, 1979).

LORENZ, GABRIELE, *De Bonald als Repräsentant der gegenrevolutionären Theoriebildung: Eine Untersuchung zur Systematik und Wirkungsgeschichte* (Französische Sprache und Literatur, ccxvi) Frankfurt am Main: Lang, 1997).

LÖW, REINHARD, *Philosophie des Lebendigen: Der Begriff des Organischen bei Kant, sein Grund und seine Aktualität* (Frankfurt am Main: Suhrkamp, 1980).

—— *Nietzsche. Sophist und Erzieher: Philosophische Untersuchungen zum systematischen Ort von Friedrich Nietzsches Denken* (Weinheim: Acta Humaniora/VCH, 1984).

—— 'Natur und Zweck: Einige neuere Aspekte zum Problem der Naturteleologie', in *Scheidewege: Jahresschrift für skeptisches Denken*, 14 (1984/5), 342–58.

—— (ed.), *Islam und Christentum in Europa* (Hildesheim: Morus, 1994).

—— *Die neuen Gottesbeweise* (Augsburg: Pattloch, 1994).

—— *Über das Schöne: Warum das Schöne schön ist* (Stuttgart/Vienna: Weitbrecht, 1994).

LÖWITH, KARL, *Meaning in History: The Theological Implications of the Philosophy of History* (Chicago, Ill.: University of Chicago Press, 1957).

—— *Mein Leben in Deutschland vor und nach 1933: Ein Bericht* (Stuttgart: Metzlersche, 1986).

LÜBBE, HERMANN, *Religion nach der Aufklärung*, 3rd edn. (Munich: Fink, 2004).

LUHMANN, NIKLAS, *Soziologische Aufklärung: Aufsätze zur Theorie sozialer Systeme* (Cologne/Opladen: Westdeutscher, 1970).

—— *Funktion der Religion* (Frankfurt am Main: Suhrkamp, 1977).

—— *The Differentiation of Society*, trans. Stephen Holmes and Charles Larmore (New York: Columbia University Press, 1982).

—— *Religious Dogmatics and the Evolution of Societies*, trans. and introd. Peter Beyer (Studies in Religion and Society, ix) (New York/Toronto: Mellen, 1984).

—— *Die Religion der Gesellschaft*, ed. André Kieserling (Frankfurt am Main: Suhrkamp, 2000).

—— *Theories of Distinction: Redescribing the Descriptions of Modernity*, ed. and introd. William Rasch (Stanford, Calif.: Stanford University Press, 2002).

LYOTARD, JEAN-FRANÇOIS, *La Condition Postmoderne: Rapport sur le Savoir* (Paris: Editions de Minuit, 1983).

MACDONALD, PAUL S., *Descartes and Husserl: The Philosophical Project of Radical Beginnings* (New York: State University of New York Press, 2000).

McGRATH, ALISTER E., and McGRATH, JOANNE COLLICUTT, *The Dawkins Delusion? Atheist Fundamentalism and the Denial of the Divine* (Downers Grove, Ill.: IVP, 2007).

McInerny, Ralph, *Ethica Thomistica: The Moral Philosophy of Thomas Aquinas* (Washington, DC: The Catholic University of America Press, 1982).

MacIntyre, Alasdair, *Marcuse* (London: Fontana/Collins, 1970).

—— *After Virtue: A Study in Moral Theory* (London: Duckworth, 1985).

McMahon, Darrin M., *Enemies of the Enlightenment: The French Counter-Enlightenment and the Making of Modernity* (New York: Oxford University Press, 2001).

Madell, Geoffrey, *The Identity of the Self* (Edinburgh: Edinburgh University Press, 1981).

Manent, Pierre, *The City of Man*, trans. Marc A. LePain, foreword Jean Bethke Elshtain (Princeton, NJ: Princeton University Press, 1998).

Marion, Jean-Luc, *God Without Being*, trans. Thomas A. Carlson (Chicago, Ill.: University of Chicago Press, 1991).

Maritain, Jacques, *The Peasant of the Garonne: An Old Layman Questions Himself about the Present Time* (London/Dublin: Chapman, 1968).

Marquard, Odo, *Philosophie des Stattdessen: Studien* (Stuttgart: Reclam, 2000).

Marsden, George, 'Matteo Ricci and the Prodigal Culture', in James L. Heft (ed.), *A Catholic Modernity? Charles Taylor's Marianist Award Lectures* (New York/Oxford: Oxford University Press, 1999).

Marx, Karl, 'On Feuerbach', in *Early Political Writings*, trans. and ed. Joseph O'Malley and Richard A. Davis (Cambridge: Cambridge University Press, 2006).

Matthews, Gareth B., *Philosophy and the Young Child* (Cambridge, Mass./London: Harvard University Press, 1980).

Mauthner, Fritz, *Beiträge zu einer Kritik der Sprache, i. Zur Sprache und zur Psychologie*, in Fritz Mauthner, *Das philosophische Werk: Nach den Ausgaben letzter Hand herausgegeben von Ludger Lütkehaus* (Vienna/Cologne/Weimar: Böhlau, 1999), ii. I.

Meier, Heinrich, *Carl Schmitt, Leo Strauss und 'Der Begriff des Politischen': Zu einem Dialog unter Abwesenden* (Stuttgart: Metzler, 1998).

Meilaender, Gilbert, *The Taste for the Other: The Social and Ethical Thought of C. S. Lewis* (Grand Rapids, Mich.: Eerdmans, 1998).

—— 'Sweet Necessities: Food, Sex, and Saint Augustine', in *Journal of Religious Ethics*, 29 (2001), 3–18.

Mercer, Christia, *Leibniz's Metaphysics: Its Origins and Development* (Cambridge: Cambridge University Press, 2001).

Metz, Johann-Baptist, and Moltmann, Jürgen, *Faith and the Future: Essays on Theology, Solidarity, and Modernity*, introd. Francis Schüssler Fiorenza (Maryknoll, NY: Orbis, 1995).

Milbank, John, *Theology and Social Theory: Beyond Secular Reason* (Oxford: Blackwell, 1997).

—— Pickstock, Catherine, and Ward, Graham (eds.), *Radical Orthodoxy: A New Theology* (London: Routledge, 1999).

Moeller, Hans-Georg, *Luhmann Explained: From Souls to Systems* (Chicago/La Salle, Ill.: Open Court, 2006).

Moore, George Edward, *Principia Ethica* (Cambridge: Cambridge University Press, 1954).

NEHAMAS, ALEXANDER, *Nietzsche: Life as Literature* (Cambridge, Mass.: Harvard University Press, 1985).

NIDA-RÜMELIN, JULIAN (ed.), *Philosophen der Gegenwart in Einzeldarstellungen: Von Adorno bis Wright* (Stuttgart: Kröner, 1991).

NIETZSCHE, FRIEDRICH, *Human, All-Too-Human: A Book for Free Spirits*, pt. II, trans. Paul V. Cohn (London Foulis, 1911).

—— *Zur Genealogie der Moral*, in *Kritische Gesamtausgabe*, ed. Giorgio Colli and Mazzino Montinari (Berlin: de Gruyter, 1968), vi. II.

—— *Human, All Too Human*, trans. R. J. Hollingdale, introd. Richard Schacht (Cambridge: Cambridge University Press, 1996).

—— *Beyond Good and Evil: Prelude to a Philosophy of the Future*, ed. Rolf-Peter Horstmann and Judith Norman, trans. Judith Normann (Cambridge: Cambridge University Press, 2000).

NOZICK, ROBERT, *Anarchy, State, and Utopia* (New York: Basic, 1974).

OAKES, EDWARD T., and MOSS, DAVID (eds.), *The Cambridge Companion to Hans Urs von Balthasar* (Cambridge: Cambridge University Press, 2004).

O'DONOVAN, JOAN LOCKWOOD, 'The Concept of Right in Christian Moral Discourse', in Michael Cromartie (ed.), *A Preserving Grace: Protestants, Catholics, and Natural Law* (Washington, DC: Ethics and Public Policy Center, 1997).

O'DONOVAN, OLIVER, *The Problem of Self-Love in St Augustine* (New Haven/London: Yale University Press, 1980).

—— *Resurrection and Moral Order: An Outline for Evangelical Ethics* (Grand Rapids, Mich.: Eerdmans, 1986).

—— *The Desire of the Nations: Rediscovering the Roots of Political Theology* (Cambridge: Cambridge University Press, 1996).

—— *Begotten or Made?*, 2nd edn. (Oxford: Clarendon, 1998).

OUTKA, GENE, *Agape: An Ethical Analysis* (New Haven/London: Yale University Press, 1972).

PAIGE, NICHOLAS D., *Being Interior: Autobiography and the Contradictions of Modernity in Seventeenth-century France* (Philadelphia, Pa.: University of Pennsylvania Press, 2001).

PARFIT, DEREK, *Reasons and Persons*, 2nd edn. (Oxford: Clarendon, 1987).

PARFIT, DEREK, 'Persons, Bodies, and Human Beings', in Theodore Sider, John Hawthorne, and Dean W. Zimmerman (eds.), *Contemporary Debates in Metaphysics* (Oxford: Blackwell, 2008), 177–208.

PERCY, WALKER, *The Message in the Bottle: How Queer Man Is, How Queer Language Is, and What One Has to Do with the Other* (New York, NY: Farrar, Strauss and Giroux, 1986).

PLATO, *The Platonic Epistles*, trans. J. Harward (Cambridge: Cambridge University Press, 1932).

—— *The Collected Dialogues of Plato*, ed. Edith Hamilton and Huntington Cairns (Princeton, NJ: Princeton University Press, 1987).

POLLOCK, JOHN L., *How to Build a Person? A Prolegomenon* (Cambridge, Mass.: MIT Press, 1989).

PRANCHÈRE, JEAN-YVES, 'The Social Bond According to the Catholic Counter-Revolution: Maistre and Bonald', in Richard A. Lebrun (ed.), *Joseph de Maistre's Life, Thought, and Influence: Selected Studies* (Montreal/Kingston: McGill-Queen's University Press, 2001), 190–219.

PRUFER, THOMAS, *Recapitulations: Essays in Philosophy* (Studies in Philosophy and the History of Philosophy, xxvi) (Washington, DC: The Catholic University of America Press, 1993).

QUINE, W. V., review of MILTON K. MUNITZ (ed.), *Identity and Individuation*, in *Journal of Philosophy*, 69 (1972), 488–97.

QUINLAN, MARY HALL, *The Historical Thought of the Vicomte de Bonald* (Washington, DC: The Catholic University of America Press, 1953).

RAHNER, KARL, 'Christology within an Evolutionary View of the World', in Rahner, *Theological Investigations*, v, trans. K.-H. Kruger (Baltimore, Md.: Helicon, 1966), 157–92.

—— *Foundations of Christian Faith: An Introduction to the Idea of Christianity*, trans. William V. Dych (New York: Crossroad, 1982).

RASCH, WILLIAM, *Niklas Luhmann's Modernity: The Paradoxes of Differentiation* (Stanford, Calif.: Stanford University Press, 2000).

REEDY, W. JAY, 'Maistre's Twin? Louis de Bonald and the ENLIGHTENMENT', in RICHARD A. LEBRUN (ed.), *Joseph de Maistre's Life, Thought, and Influence: Selected Studies* (Montreal/Kingston: McGill-Queen's University Press, 2001), 173–89.

RITTER, JOACHIM, *Docta ignorantia: Die Theorie des Nichtwissens bei Nikolaus Cusanus* (Leipzig: Teubner, 1927).

—— *Mundus intelligibilis: Eine Untersuchung zur Aufnahme und Umwandlung der neuplatonischen Ontologie bei Augustinus* (Frankfurt am Main: Klostermann, 1937).

—— 'Wesen der Philosophie', in *Aufgaben deutscher Forschung*, i, ed. Leo Brandt (Cologne/Opladen: Westdeutscher, 1956), 65–71.

—— 'Die Universität vor den Ansprüchen der Zeit: Zur gesellschaftlichen Funktion freier Forschung und Lehre', in *Strukturprobleme unserer wissenschaftlichen Hochschulen*, ed. the Friedrich Naumann Foundation (Bonn/Cologne/Opladen: Westdeutscher, 1965), 49–61.

—— *Metaphysik und Politik* (Frankfurt am Main: Suhrkamp, 1969).

—— *Subjektivität: Sechs Aufsätze* (Frankfurt am Main: Suhrkamp, 1974).

—— *Hegel and the French Revolution: Essays on the 'Philosophy of Right'*, trans. and introd. Richard Dien Winfield (Cambridge, Mass.: MIT Press, 1982).

ROUSSEAU, JEAN-JACQUES, *Discourse on the Sciences and Arts (First Discourse)*, ed. ROGER D. MASTERS and CHRISTOPHER KELLY, trans. JUDITH R. BUSH, ROGER D. MASTERS, and CHRISTOPHER KELLY (Hanover: University Press of New England, 1992).

—— *Social Contract*, in *The Collected Writings of Rousseau*, iv, ed. Roger D. Masters and Christopher Kelly (Hanover, NH/London: University Press of New England, 1994), 221.

—— *The Social Contract*, trans. G. D. H.Cole, introd. Alissa Ardito (New York: Barnes & Noble, 2005).

RUDMAN, STANLEY, *Concepts of Person and Christian Ethics* (New Studies in Christian Ethics, xi) (Cambridge: Cambridge University Press, 1997).

VOLKER RÜHLE, 'Dieter Henrich', in Julian Nida-Rümelin (ed.), *Philosophie der Gegenwart in Einzeldarstellungen: Von Adorno bis Wright* (Stuttgart: Kröner, 1991), 571–5.

SANDEL, MICHAEL J., *The Case against Perfection: Ethics in the Age of Genetic Engineering* (Cambridge, Mass.: Harvard University Press, 2007).

SARTRE, JEAN-PAUL, *Existentialism Is A Humanism*, trans. Carol Macomber, introd. Annie Cohen-Solal, notes and preface Arlette Elkaim-Sartre, ed. John Kulka (New Haven, Conn.: Yale University Press, 2007).

SCHEFFLER, SAMUEL (ed.), *Consequentialism and its Critics* (Oxford: Oxford University Press, 1988).

SCHELER, MAX, *Die Wissensformen und die Gesellschaft* (Leipzig: Neue-Geist, 1926).

—— *Schriften aus dem Nachlass, i.. Zur Ethik und Erkenntnislehre* (Bern: francke, 1957).

SCHELLING, FRIEDRICH WILHELM JOSEPH, *System der Weltalter: Münchener Vorlesung 1827/ 28 in einer Nachschrift von Ernst von Lasaulx*, ed. and introd. Siegbert Peetz, 2nd edn. (Frankfurt am Main: Klostermann, 1998).

SCHELSKY, HELMUTH, *Einsamkeit und Freiheit: Zur sozialen Idee der deutschen Universität* (Schriften der Gesellschaft zur Förderung der Westfälischen Wilhelms-Universität zu Münster, xlv) (Münster: Aschendorff, 1960).

—— *Die skeptische Generation: Eine Soziologie der deutschen Jugend* (Düsseldorf: Diederichs, 1963).

SCHENK, OP, RICHARD (ed.), *Kontinuität der Person: Zum Versprechen und Vertrauen* (Stuttgart/Bad Cannstatt: frommann-holzboog, 1998).

SCHMIDT-WELLENBURG, CHRISTIAN, *Evolution und sozialer Wandel: Neodarwinistische Mechanismen bei W. G. Runciman und N. Luhmann* (Opladen: Budrich, 2005).

SCHMITT, CARL, *Politische Romantik*, 3rd edn. (Berlin: Duncker & Humblot, 1968).

—— *Political Theology: Four Chapters on the Concept of Sovereignty*, trans. George Schwab (Cambridge, Mass.: MIT Press, 1985).

—— *Political Romanticism*, trans. Guy Oakes (Cambridge, Mass: MIT Press, 1986).

—— *Politische Theologie, ii. Die Legende von der Erledigung jeder Politischen Theologie*, 4th edn. (Berlin: Duncker & Humblot, 1994).

—— *The Concept of the Political*, trans. George Schwab (Chicago, Ill./London: University of Chicago Press, 1996).

—— *Politische Theologie: Vier Kapitel zur Lehre von der Souveränität* (Berlin: Duncker & Humblot, 1996).

SCHOPENHAUER, ARTHUR, *The World as Will and Representation*, ii, trans. E. F. J. Payne (New York: Dover, 1958).

SCHULTE, CHRISTOPH, *Radikal böse: Die Karriere des Bösen von Kant bis Nietzsche* (Munich: Fink, 1991).

SEXTUS EMPIRICUS, *Against the Logicians*, in *Works*, trans. R. G. Bury (Cambridge, Mass.: Harvard University Press, 1933).

SINGER, PETER, *Animal Liberation*, 2nd edn. (London: Thorsons, 1990).

SINGER, PETER, *Practical Ethics* (Cambridge: Cambridge University Press, 1993).

—— *How Are We to Live? Ethics in an Age of Self-interest* (Oxford: Oxford University Press, 1997).

FRANCIS SLADE, 'Ends and Purposes', in Richard Hassing (ed.), *Final Causality in Nature and Human Affairs* (Studies in Philosophy and the History of Philosophy, xxx) (Washington, DC: The Catholic University of America Press, 2000), 83–5.

—— 'On the Ontological Priority of Ends and its Relevance to the Narrative Arts', in Alice Ramos (ed.), *Beauty, Art, and the Polis* (Washington, DC: American Maritain Association, 2000), 58–69.

SLOTERDIJK, PETER, *Regeln für den Menschenpark: Ein Antwortschreiben zu Heideggers Brief über den Humanismus* (Frankfurt am Main: Suhrkamp, 1999).

—— 'Die Kritische Theorie ist tot: Peter Sloterdijk schreibt an Assheuer und Habermas', in *Die Zeit*, 37 (1999).

SMITH, BARRY, and Woodruff-Smith, David (eds.), *The Cambridge Companion to Husserl* (Cambridge: Cambridge University Press, 1995).

SMITH, JAMES K. A.,*Introducing Radical Orthodoxy: Mapping a Post-secular Theology* (Grand Rapids, Mich.: Baker, 2004).

SNOW, DALE, *Schelling and the End of Idealism* (New York: SUNY, 1996).

SOKOLOWSKI, ROBERT, *Introduction to Phenomenology* (Cambridge: Cambridge University Press, 2000).

—— *Christian Faith and Understanding: Studies on the Eucharist, Trinity, and the Human Person* (Washington, DC: The Catholic University of America Press, 2006).

—— *Phenomenology of the Human Person* (Cambridge: Cambridge University Press, 2008).

SPAEMANN, HEINRICH, *Das Prinzip Liebe* (Freiburg im Breisgau: Herder, 1986).

—— *Stärker als Not, Krankheit und Tod: Besinnung und Zuspruch* (Freiburg im Breisgau: Herder, 1991).

—— *Er ist dein Licht: Meditationen für jeden Tag. Jahreslesebuch*, ed. Ulrich Schütz (Freiburg im Breisgau/Basle/Vienna: Herder, 1992).

—— *Was macht die Kirche mit der Macht? Denkanstöße* (Freiburg im Breisgau: Herder, 1993).

SPINOZA, BENEDICT DE, *Ethics*, trans. W. Hale White, rev. trans. Amelia Hutchison Stirling (Oxford: Oxford University Press, 1937).

STEINER, GEORGE, *Real Presences* (Chicago, Ill.: University of Chicago Press, 1991).

STRIET, MAGNUS, *Der neue Mensch? Unzeitgemäße Betrachtungen zu Sloterdijk und Nietzsche* (Frankfurt am Main: Knecht, 2000).

—— and Tück, Jan-Heiner(eds.), *Hans Urs von Balthasar—Vermächtnis und Anstoß für die Theologie* (Freiburg im Breisgau: Herder, 2005).

TAYLOR, CHARLES, *Philosophical Papers 1 and 2* (Cambridge: Cambridge University Press, 1985).

—— *The Ethics of Authenticity* (Cambridge, Mass./London: Harvard University Press, 1991).

—— *Sources of the Self: The Making of the Modern Identity* (Cambridge: Cambridge University Press, 1998).

THEISSMANN, U., and NIEWÖHNER, F., 'Herrlichkeit,' in Joachim Ritter and Karlfried Gründer (eds.), *Historisches Wörterbuch der Philosophie*, iii (Basle/Stuttgart: Schwabe, 1974), 1079–84.

THEUNISSEN, MICHAEL, *The Other: Studies in the Social Ontology of Husserl, Heidegger, Sartre, and Buber* (Cambridge, Mass.: MIT Press, 1984).

THOMAS, GÜNTHER, and SCHÜLE, ANDREAS (eds.), *Luhmann und die Theologie* (Darmstadt: Wissenschaftliche Buchgesellschaft, 2006).

TODA, MICHEL, *Louis de Bonald: Théoricien de la contre-révolution* (Étampes Cedex: Clovis, 1996).

TOULMIN, STEPHEN, *Cosmopolis: The Hidden Agenda of Modernity* (New York: Free Press, 1990).

TUGENDHAT, ERNST, 'Es gibt keine Gene für die Moral: Sloterdijk stellt das Verhältnis von Ethik und Gentechnik schlicht auf den Kopf', in *Die Zeit*, 39 (1999).

VELKLEY, RICHARD, *Freedom and the End of Reason: On the Moral Foundation of Kant's Critical Philosophy* (Chicago, Ill.: University of Chicago Press, 1989).

WALSH, DAVID, *The Modern Philosophical Revolution: The Luminosity of Existence* (Cambridge: Cambridge University Press, 2008).

WEBSTER, JOHN, *Theological Theology: An Inaugural Lecture Delivered Before the University of Oxford on 27 October 1997* (Oxford: Clarendon, 1998).

WEBSTER, JOHN, and SCHNER, GEORGE P., *Theology after Liberalism: A Reader* (Oxford: Blackwell, 2000).

WELKER, MICHAEL (ed.), *Theologie und funktionale Systemtheorie: Luhmanns Religionssoziologie in theologischer Diskussion* (Frankfurt am Main: Suhrkamp, 1985).

WIGGINS, DAVID, *Sameness and Substance* (Oxford: Blackwell, 1980).

WILLIAMS, BERNARD, *Morality: An Introduction to Ethics* (Cambridge: Cambridge University Press, 1993).

WILLIAMS, DAVID LAY, *Rousseau's Platonic Enlightenment*, foreword Patrick Riley (University Park, Penn.: Pennsylvania State University Press, 2007).

WILSON, E. O., *Sociobiology: The New Synthesis* (Cambridge, Mass.: Harvard University Press, 1977).

WITTGENSTEIN, LUDWIG, *Philosophical Investigations*, trans. G. E. M. Anscombe (New York: Macmillan, 1958).

—— *Tractatus Logico-Philosophicus: The German Text of Ludwig Wittgenstein's Logisch-Philosophische Abhandlung*, trans. D. F. Pears and B. F. McGuiness, introd. Bertrand Russell (London: Routledge & Kegan Paul, 1961).

—— ed. G. E. M. Anscombe and G. H. von Wright, trans. Anscombe (Oxford: Blackwell, 1967).

—— *Culture and Value: A Selection from the Posthumous Remains*, ed. Georg Henrik von Wright with Heikki Nyman, rev. edn. of the text Alois Pichler, trans. Peter Winch (Oxford: Blackwell, 1998).

Select bibliography

WOIWODE, MATTHIAS, *Heillose Religion? Eine fundamentaltheologische Untersuchung zur funktionalen Religionstheorie Niklas Luhmanns* (Münster: LIT, 1997) (Studien zur systematischen Theologie und Ethik, x).

ZABOROWSKI, HOLGER, 'Reason, Truth, and History: The Early Hegel's Philosophy of History', in Alfred Denker and Michael Vater (eds.), *Hegel's Phenomenology of Spirit: New Critical Essays* (Amherst, NY: Prometheus, 2003), 21–58.

—— 'Tragik und Erlösung des Menschen: Hans Urs von Balthasars "Theodramatik" im Kontext', *Communio*, 34 (2005), 128–35.

—— 'Mythos und Geschichte: Hans Urs von Balthasar und die griechische Tragödie', in Walter Kasper (ed.), *Im Dialog—Die Logik der Liebe Gottes* (Mainz: Grünewald , 2006), 45–63.

—— ' "Der verwüstenden Sandstürme nicht vergessen . . ."—Zur Diskussion über das Verhältnis Martin Heideggers zum Nationalsozialismus', in Bernd Martin (ed.), *'Die Wahrheit wird Euch frei machen': Historische Festschrift zur 550. Jahrfeier der Alber-Ludwigs-Universität Freiburg im Breisgau*, ii (Freiburg im Breisgau/Munich: Alber, 2007), 355–73.

—— 'Fall and Freedom: A Comparison of Fichte's and Saint Paul's Understandings of Original Sin', in Daniel Breazeale and Tom Rockmore (eds.), *After Jena: New Essays on Fichte's Later Philosophy* (Evanston, Ill.: Northwestern University Press, 2008), 162–82.

—— *Spielräume der Freiheit: Zur Hermeneutik des Menschseins* (Freiburg im Breisgau/ Munich: Alber, 2009).

—— 'Kontingenzbewältigung in der Moderne: Zu Hermann Lübbes Verständnis von Aufklärung und Religion', in Hanns-Gregor Nissing (ed.), *Zur Philosophie Hermann Lübbes* (Darmstadt: Wissenschaftliche Buchgesellschaft), 101–116.

—— 'Why There Is Something Rather Than Nothing: F. W. J. Schelling and the Metaphysics of Freedom', in John Wippel (ed.), *The Ultimate Why Question* (Studies in Philosophy and the History of Philosophy) (Washington, DC: The Catholic University of America Press, forthcoming).

—— (ed.), *Natural Law in Contemporary Society* (Studies in Philosophy and the History of Philosophy) (Washington: Catholic University of America Press, 2010).

ZABOROWSKI, HOLGER, and STUMPF, CHRISTOPH, 'Menschenwürde versus Würde der Kreatur: Philosophische und juristische Überlegungen zur Personalität und Würde des menschlichen und des nicht-menschlichen Lebens', in *Rechtstheorie: Zeitschrift für Logik und Juristische Methodenlehre, Rechtsinformatik, Kommunikationsforschung, Normen- und Handlungstheorie, Soziologie und Philosophie des Rechts*, 36 (2005), 91–115.

ZIMMERLI, WALTHER Ch. 'Die Evolution in eigener Regie. In einem Punkt hat Sloterdijk Recht: Über die Normen für gentechnische Eingriffe muss öffentlich debattiert werden', in *Die Zeit*, 40 (1999).

Index